Aging and Rehabilitation II

Stanley J. Brody, J.D., M.S.W., is Professor Emeritus of Physical Medicine and Rehabilitation in Psychiatry, School of Medicine; Professor Emeritus of Health Care Systems, Wharton School of Finance and Commerce; Professor, School of Social Work; and Director of the Research and Training Center for Rehabilitation of Elderly Disabled Individuals at the University of Pennsylvania. He has served as visiting lecturer at more than 30 institutions of higher education and is the author of more than 100 articles, monographs, and book reviews, and editor/coeditor of several books.

He is a Fellow of the Gerontological Society of America and the 1985 recipient of the GSA Donald P. Kent Award; and past member of the Governing Council, Special Constituency Section for Aging and Long-Term Care, American Hospital Association. He has also chaired the Gerontological Health Section of the American Public Health Association and was the recipient of the 1987 Key Award for that section. He was formerly a member of the Assessment of Disorders Causing Dementia Advisory Panel, Congressional Office of Technology Assessment, and was also a member of the National Academy of Sciences, Institute of Medicine Committee on the study of Aging and Medical Education. In 1985, he was recognized by the American Occupational Therapy Association with their Health Advocacy Award, and in 1986, he was recognized by the Haak-Lilliefors Lecture on Aging at Michigan State University.

L. Gregory Pawlson, M.D., M.P.H., is presently the Chairman of the Department of Health Care Sciences at the George Washington University Medical Center, and holds the academic title of Professor of Health Care Sciences, Medicine, and Health Services Administration. In his work in Geriatric Medicine at GWU, he is Director of the Center for Aging Studies and Services. He has also served as Medical Director of the Thomas House Retirement Center and Associate Director of The Washington Home.

Dr. Pawlson, received his Medical degree from the University of Pittsburgh in 1969, and did his internship and residency at Stanford University in Palo Alto, California. In 1976, he completed his Master of Public Health from the University of Washington where he also was a Robert Wood Johnson Clinical Scholar and a Fellow of the National Fund for Medical Education. In 1979, Dr. Pawlson was a visiting Fellow in Geriatric Medicine at the Universities of Glasgow and Edinburgh in Scotland. In 1986–87, as a Robert Wood Johnson Health Policy Fellow, he worked as a health policy aide on the staff of Senator George Mitchell (D-Maine). Dr. Pawlson is board certified in internal medicine and specializes in geriatric medicine.

Dr. Pawlson's areas of interest and research include medical education, health policy, health services, and health care financing, especially as they relate to the elderly and Geriatric Medicine. Dr. Pawlson is the section editor of law and public policy for the *Journal of the American Geriatrics Society*. He has served on the board of directors of the Society for General Internal Medicine and of the American Geriatrics Society. He was chairman of the AGS Public Policy Committee and is currently (1989–90) president of the AGS.

AGING AND REHABILITATION II
THE STATE OF THE PRACTICE

Stanley J. Brody, J.D., M.S.W.
L. Gregory Pawlson, M.D., M.P.H.
Editors

Springer Publishing Company
New York

Springer Publishing Company, Inc.
536 Broadway
New York, NY 10012

90 91 92 93 94 / 5 4 3 2 1

Library of Congress Cataloging-in-Publication Data

Aging and rehabilitation : the state of the practice / Stanley J.
   Brody, L. Gregory Pawlson, editors.
       p.   cm.
   This volume is based on a conference held in Arlington, Va., Dec.
1988.
   Includes bibliographical references.
   Includes index.
   ISBN 0-8261-7080-3
   1. Aged—Rehabilitation—Congresses.   I. Brody, Stanley J.
II. Pawlson, L. Gregory.
   [DNLM: 1. Aging—congresses.   2. Geriatrics—congresses.
3. Rehabilitation—in old age—congresses.   WB 320 A2675]
RC953.5.A35   1990
618.97'06—dc20
DNLM/DLC
for Library of Congress   90-9921
                                                              CIP
Printed in the United States of America

Contents

III THE PRACTICE MODEL: MOBILITY

IV THE PRACTICE MODEL: ENVIRONMENT

V THE PRACTICE MODEL: CONTINENCE

Contributors

F. M. Baker, M.D., M.P.H., Associate Professor and Director, Geriatric Psychiatry Program, The University of Texas Health Science Center at San Antonio.

Henry R. Betts, M.D., Chief Executive Officer, Rehabilitation Institute of Chicago.

Robert H. Binstock, Ph.D., Henry R. Luce Professor of Aging, Health, and Society, Case Western Reserve University, Cleveland, OH.

Barbara Blackney, M.S., R.N., Lifeline Program, Boston City Hospital.

Jennifer Bottomley, M.S., P.T., Clinical Supervisor, Department of Physical Therapy, Cushing Hospital, Framingham, MA.

Elaine M. Brody, M.S.W., Associate Director of Research, Philadelphia Geriatric Center, and Adjunct Professor of Psychiatry, University of Pennsylvania Medical Center, Philadelphia.

James F. Budde, Ed.D., Director, Research and Training Center on Independent Living, The University of Kansas, Lawrence, KS.

Barry Corbet, Filmmaker, Golden, CO.

David S. Espino, M.D., Assistant Professor and Director, Geriatric Program, Department of Family Practice, The University of Texas Health Science Center at San Antonio.

Gerald Felsenthal, M.D., Medical Director, Sinai Rehabilitation Center, and Chief, Department of Rehabilitation Medicine, Sinai Hospital of Baltimore, Maryland.

Gary Gottlieb, M.D., M.B.A., Associate Professor of Psychiatry, University of Pennsylvania Medical Center, Philadelphia.

Arthur E. Helfand, D.P.M., F.A.C.F.O., Professor and Chairman, Department of Community Health and Aging, Pennsylvania College of Podiatric Medicine, Philadelphia.

Lorraine G. Hiatt, Ph.D., Consultant in Environmental Design and Aging, New York.

Margot C. Howe, Ed.D., O.T.R., Tufts University.

Masayoshi Itoh, M.D., M.P.H., Deputy Associate Director, Department of Rehabilitation Medicine, Goldwater Memorial Hospital, and Associate Professor of Clinical Rehabilitation Medicine, New York University School of Medicine, New York.

Louise M. Kamikawa, B.A., Director, National Pacific/Asian Resource Center on Aging, Seattle.

Robert L. Kane, M.D., Dean, School of Public Health, University of Minnesota, Minneapolis.

M. Powell Lawton, Ph.D., Director, Behavioral Research, Philadelphia Geriatric Center, Pennsylvania.

Barry D. Lebowitz, Ph.D., Chief, Center for Studies of the Mental Health of the Aging, National Institute on Mental Health, Rockville, MD.

Mathew H. M. Lee, M.D., M.P.H., F.A.C.P., Acting Director, Howard A. Rusk Institute of Rehabilitation Medicine, New York University Medical Center, and Professor of Clinical Rehabilitation Medicine, School of Medicine, New York University, New York.

Spero Manson, Ph.D., Associate Professor and Director of the National Center for American Indians and Alaska Natives Mental Health Research, University of Colorado Health Science Center, Department of Psychiatry, Denver.

Lorraine C. Mion, R.N., M.S.W., Gerontological Clinical Nurse Specialist, Cleveland Metropolitan General Hospital, and Clinical Instructor,

Frances Payne Bolton School of Nursing, Case Western Reserve University, Cleveland, OH.

Terrence O'Malley, M.D., Chelsea Medical Center, Massachusetts General Hospital.

Neil M.Resnick, M.D., Chief of Geriatrics, Brigham and Women's Hospital Continence Clinic, Beth Israel Hospital, Boston.

Avalie R. Saperstein, A.C.S.W., Director, Social Services/Therapeutic Activities, and Director, Community Services, Philadelphia Geriatric Center, Pennsylvania.

David G. Satin, M.D., Newton-Wellesley Hospital.

Helen Smith, O.T.R., Tufts University.

Barry D. Stein, M.D., Department of Rehabilitation Medicine, Sinai Hospital of Baltimore, Maryland.

Ruth L. Weg, Ph.D., Professor of Gerontology (biology), Andrus Gerontology Center, University of Southern California, Los Angeles.

Thelma J. Wells, R.N., Ph.D., F.A.A.N., F.R.C.N., Professor of Nursing, University of Rochester School of Nursing, Rochester, NY.

T. Franklin Williams, M.D., Director, National Institute on Aging, U.S. Department of Health and Human Services, Bethesda, MD.

May Wykle, R.N., Ph.D., F.A.A.N., Florence Cellar Professor and Chairperson of Psychiatric/Mental Health and Gerontological Nursing, Frances Payne Bolton School of Nursing, Case Western Reserve University, Cleveland, OH.

Preface

An aging society engenders new perceptions of health and changing expectations. It is within this context that the extension of therapeutic optimism to disabled elderly began, marked by a convening of a first national conference on aging and rehabilitation in December 1984.

The role of rehabilitation in the care of older people had been largely overlooked by health care providers before that time. Both rehabilitation and gerontology had shared the same time in history for their development, and to some extent both had been stimulated by two different aspects of the same demographic phenomenon—the aging of the American society. One was motivated by the growth in the number of disabled persons who are living longer; the other, by the increase in the number of old-old, who tend to be more disabled.

The first conference was on the "state of the art," an effort to correlate existing multidisciplinary knowledge about rehabilitating disabled elderly. The conference summarizers captured the climate of excitement the meeting generated and agreed that what emerged was the recognition that we were already into an aging society, and within such a society there must be a different set of priorities for health care. Continuity of care is paramount, and rehabilitation and geriatrics are the key services in assuring such continuity.

The proceedings of that conference, *Aging and Rehabilitation: Advances in the State of the Art,* edited by S. J. Brody and G. E. Ruff, were published by Springer Publishing Company in 1986.

Out of these efforts grew a request from the attendees for a follow-up meeting on the "state of the practice." This excitement also initiated a series of national and regional meetings by such organizations as the American Public Health Association, the American Congress of Rehabilitation Medicine, and other professional groups such as those of the physical and occupational therapists, all focusing on therapeutic optimism in rehabilitating the elderly disabled. Journals such as *Topics in Geriatric Rehabilitation* and multiple research initiatives were undertaken, reinforcing this new perception of the aged. Congressional hearings, led by the late Claude Pepper, to whom this volume is dedicated, endorsed a positive approach to aging. Activities of daily living (ADL), the marker for rehabilitation efforts, became the buzzword in congressional discussions of long-term care and was incorporated in the Medicare Catastrophic Coverage Medicare Act of 1988 as part of the eligibility criteria for respite services. In addition, the National Center for Health Statistics began a cross-sectional as well as a longitudinal collection of data on the functional status of the nation's elderly. States followed, allocating Older Americans Act funds, with formulas based in part on the prevalence of disabilities among the elderly as described in functional terms. This virtual revolution in multiperception of the elderly disabled called for a new national response.

The Research and Training Center for Rehabilitation of Elderly Disabled Individuals (RTCED) at the University of Pennsylvania Medical Center, which had organized the first conference, undertook to respond to an increasing interest and demand for a practice-oriented meeting through a grant under the Innovation Program of the National Institute on Disability and Rehabilitation Research (NIDRR). They were joined in this support by the National Institute on Aging (NIA), the National Institute of Mental Health (NIMH), and the Administration on Aging (AoA).

At a meeting independently convened by the Bureau of Health Professions in December 1987, it became evident that they too, in cooperation with NIA, had a parallel conference in mind, one focusing on multidisciplinary education for rehabilitation of the aged disabled. It was decided to join forces and conduct one conference on both education and the state of the practice in geriatric rehabilitation in December 1988 in Arlington, Virginia. Dr. L. Gregory Pawlson of George Washington University and Dr. Stanley J. Brody from RTCED served as co-chairpersons.

The Bureau of Health Professions was assigned the responsibility of publishing abstracts for all of the presentations, emphasizing the educational content, and it produced them in the fall of 1989. RTCED undertook to edit the plenary session papers and selected other presentations to explore the state of practice, with Dr. Pawlson actively sharing the editing task.

We are appreciative of the support from the Schimper Foundation, which has made this volume possible, in addition to the interest expressed through grants from AoA, the Bureau of Health Professions, NIDRR, and NIMH. Beyond these organizations, we particularly would like to acknowledge the help we received from Ms. Emily Cromar, the

Department of Education project officer who has shepherded the RTCED for almost 10 years, and Mrs. Delores C. Foster-Kennedy, the administrator of RTCED, whose continuous editorial reviews and cooperation have made this volume possible.

Introduction

This volume is based on the second national conference on aging and rehabilitation. Its goal is to provide opportunities to improve educational experience for health professionals in rehabilitative care of older persons. The two related objectives are to (1) provide a state-of-the-art overview of the interrelationships between rehabilitation and geriatrics and (2) assist faculty leaders and others to acquire the knowledge and skills with which to design and implement courses and other educational activities demonstrating their interactions. As the multidisciplinary team is the cornerstone of both rehabilitative and geriatric care, this approach is emphasized throughout the volume.

The first two chapters provide, in Dr. Williams's introduction, the conceptual base for the book and, in Dr. Brody's chapter, the basic data emerging from the expanding information on the disabled elderly. Another introductory chapter, by Dr. Henry Betts, emphasizes the role of the medical specialty of physical medicine over time, particularly in giving leadership to and developing the multidiscipline team approach.

The second part of the book begins with a chapter by filmmaker Barry Corbet. His film *Survivors*,[1] reviewed the lives of more than a dozen aging disabled, many of whom had decades of experience in coping with severe disability. Mr. Corbet, a long-time spinal cord injury survivor himself, challenges health providers to deliver coordinated, comprehensive, multidisciplinary services to the disabled while preserving the autonomy of those they assist. The development of the independent living movement, a response to the demand for autonomy by the disabled, is described historically and in terms of concept and practice by Dr. James Budde of the NIDRR-supported Research and Training Center on Independent Living at the University of Kansas.

In Part III, by focusing on one of the ADLs—mobility—the contributors attempt to discover multidisciplinary practice approaches to particular functional problems. Their goal is to prevent, modify, and maintain those elderly who have limitations of mobility. Different points

of view were sought. The editors have not attempted to reconcile con-
flicting or duplicative content, in an effort to fully explore the multidisciplinary state of rehabilitation practice. Jennifer Bottomley and her
colleagues focus on the general medical and rehabilitative therapists'
contribution. The importance of the physical condition of the feet to
the elderly is recognized through the contribution of the podiatrist as
represented by Dr. Arthur Helfand. The role of the physiatrist in assessing, prescribing, and marshaling the multidisciplinary team is described by Dr. Gerald Felsenthal and Dr. Barry Stein.

In Part IV, the multidisciplinary practice and research group from the
Philadelphia Geriatric Center (PGC), Dr. M. Powell Lawton, Dr. Elaine
Brody, and Avalie Saperstein, describe the total environment in which
rehabilitation of the elderly disabled occurs. The family's key supportive
role with the disabled has long been recognized by the rehabilitation
field but was totally focused on developmentally disabled children. The
work of the PGC group has, through gerontological research largely
supported by NIMH, made major gains in understanding the contribution of the family in support of disabled elderly. They have also been
instrumental in giving leadership to understanding the significance of
the physical environment through Dr. Lawton's efforts. The importance
of the environment is further expanded on by Dr. Lorraine Hiatt, who
has been a major influence in the application and practice of environmental modification to enhance the mobility of the elderly, particularly
in institutional settings.

Nutrition is a major overlooked item in the rehabilitation of the disabled elderly. It has a role, both in preventing disabling conditions and
in supporting the rehabilitation process. Dr. Ruth Weg reviews these
two aspects of nutrition, highlighting not only the significance of the
issue but the serious lack of research on the subject.

The social environment that affects the practice of rehabilitation therapy includes the multiple ethnic backgrounds of the disabled elderly.
Dr. F. M. Baker and her colleagues examined those of the Afro-American, the American Indian, the Asian-American and Pacific Islander, and
the Hispanic groups who make up almost one third of the pluralistic
U.S. population.

Some ADL deficits have been seen as not elemental but rather as
cutting across the five basic ADL: mobility, dressing, grooming, transferring, and eating. Continence is such a deficit; it involves mobility,
transferring, and dressing and is contingent on cognitive capacity. In
Part V, Drs. Neil Resnick and Thelma Wells discuss continence from
medical and nursing perspectives, with a view to prevention and modification of this functional limitation.

Part VI presents four chapters from different professions—nursing,
psychiatry, physiatry, and social work—which examine the mental

health problems associated with the disabled elderly. Dr. May Wykle and Lorraine Mion lead off with a review of the emotional problems presented by the disabled who are elderly and how the various professions may adjust their practice to accommodate these concerns. Increasingly, cognitive deficits, represented in large part by Alzheimer's disease patients, is of concern to rehabilitation teams. In the past, inevitable decline in physical function and impending death from chronic disease such as amyotropic lateral sclerosis has not deterred the rehabilitation team from focusing on residual strengths to maximize function and quality of life in the remaining time. A similar approach is being undertaken in work done by Dr. Gary Gottlieb, particularly within the orbit of RTCED and focused on applying rehabilitation concepts to Alzheimer's disease patients and their families. Pain is a concomitant of disability and often the cause of some loss of function. Drs. Mathew Lee and Masayoshi Itoh discuss positive rehabilitative approaches to the control of pain with a goal of improving the level of function. The environment for the rehabilitation of the mentally ill is often hostile and nonsupportive. Dr. Barry Lebowitz discusses the climate of public support for treatment modalities and the barriers to effective care for those elderly incapacitated by mental health problems.

In Part VII, Dr Robert Kane's review of assessment as it affects the disabled elderly raises major questions about the interface of cognitive deficits with an ADL approach for evaluating need for services.

Finally, in Part VIII, Dr. Robert Binstock reinforces therapeutic optimism through rehabilitation of the disabled elderly, calling attention to the ongoing ethical dispute that challenges affirmative efforts to improve the quality of life for the aged regardless of their age, life expectation, or condition. This debate is reflected in the political resolution of a public commitment of resources for the rehabilitation of the aged. Dr. Binstock emphasizes the importance of framing the question through conferences such as this so that issues are clarified and political decision making is facilitated.

As in the first volume of this series, the editors recognize that there is an unevenness in the depth of some of the presentations. Moreover, it is also acknowledged that the editors are not in agreement with all of the positions taken. Any volume purporting to reflect the state of the practice must respect the differences of individuals and among disciplinary perceptions of rehabilitative practice.

NOTE

1. *Survivors* (1988) is available from B. Corbet, Access/Inc., Golden, CO.

Part I

Basic Issues in Rehabilitation of the Elderly

1

Introduction to Rehabilitation and Aging

T. Franklin Williams

The real goal of geriatrics is fundamentally rehabilitative: to restore and/or maintain the maximum degree of independence possible for each older person. This is what every person, older or not, wants: to be able to choose and do what he or she prefers to do, to be autonomous in daily living and in short- and long-range life choices.

Not only is this the preferred goal, it has become more and more apparent that it is a *reasonable* goal for most older persons. We now know, from much recent research as well as everyday observations, that the majority of older persons, even those with some partially disabling conditions, can maintain good overall vigor in very late years—the nineties at least and possibly longer. The results of the Baltimore Longitudinal Study of Aging, as well as other studies, clearly show that most of the organs of the human body do not wear out (Lindeman, Tobin, & Shock, 1985; Rodeheffer et al., 1984; Schaie, 1983) and also that through use, such as physical exercise and mental activity much of previously lost function due to inactivity can be regained, with measurable benefits to muscle, bone, heart, and mind (Dalsky et al., 1988; Seals, Hagberg, Hurley, Ehsani, & Holloszy, 1984a, 1984b).

We also know in considerable detail the rapid and serious losses that occur with immobility, including bed rest. The evidence has recently been well summarized (Harper & Lyles, 1988): the negative effects on cardiovascular and pulmonary function; on bone and muscle mass and strength; on joints, skin, and bowel and bladder function; on sensory deprivation and attitude. I return later to the implications of this evidence for acute hospital care for older persons.

In addition, there are both well-established and exciting new approaches and technologies in the fields of rehabilitation and geriatrics that can unquestionably benefit many older persons who have disabling conditions. The basic multidisciplinary approach to rehabilitation is virtually universally accepted, and the parallel necessity for multidisciplinary assessment and planning for care in geriatrics is also now the standard of practice, endorsed by the National Institutes of Health Consensus Development Conference (NIH Consensus Statement, 1988; Solomon, 1988) and many other sources.

This volume presents a wide range of specific approaches and technologies in rehabilitation therapy. In addition, I have been impressed by the annual report of the Veterans Administration Rehabilitation Research and Development Center in Palo Alto, California, describing new approaches to fracture healing and implant design and studies on improving coordination of movement, on neuromuscular stimulation, and on use of robotics for both mobility and communication; and the new approaches to low-vision aids of the Atlanta Veterans Administration Medical Center. At the most fundamental levels we are, I believe, on the threshold of being able to use various growth factors to encourage and speed up regeneration of nerves, bones, cartilage, and possibly muscle, to help mammals (including humans) to achieve some of the remarkable regeneration of tissues that we can observe in amphibians, for example.

Furthermore, at a more immediately usable level, we have clear examples of what can be accomplished through a marriage of geriatric and rehabilitative efforts. One of my favorite examples is that of the geriatric rehabilitative program at Edinburgh, Scotland, developed by Professor James Williamson and his colleagues. In one aspect of that program the geriatric-rehabilitation team, by prior agreement, reviews all older patients on the orthopedic service of the Edinburgh Royal Infirmary for potential for benefit from transfer to the geriatric-rehabilitation service. They have found that 25% to 50% of those patients, in particular those with hip fractures, are potential candidates. In a randomized clinical trial they demonstrated that, through transferring such patients to their service for more comprehensive, active rehabilitation targeted to the needs of older patients, they could achieve a considerably higher rate of recovery of function and discharge to home than occurred for the control group, who remained on the orthopedic wards with usual rehabilitation (Burley, Scorgie, Currie, Smith, & Williamson, 1984).

Even more recently, Kennie, Reid, Richardson, Kiamari, and Kelt

(1988) of the Royal Infirmary in Stirling, Scotland, reported the results of a randomized clinical trial of geriatric rehabilitation with patients aged 65 and older with fracture of the proximal femur; they showed a median stay in hospital of 24 days in their experimental group, compared with 41 days for the control group, and more independence in activities of daily living, fewer discharges to institutional care, and more discharges to their own homes.

Therefore, if there is general agreement about the common goals of geriatrics and rehabilitation, about the dangers of immobility and loss of function, about the contributions rehabilitation can make to geriatric medicine, and about the clear value of combined geriatric-rehabilitation approaches, what are the challenges, what are the problems? Let me cite briefly what I think are our major challenges in achieving the full benefits from our potential combined efforts.

First, there continues to be the widespread problem of ageist attitudes. As Phyllis Rubenfeld (1986), president of the American Coalition of Citizens with Disabilities, pointed out at the 1984 conference on aging and rehabilitation, older persons are actually under the double jeopardy of the prejudices of "ageism" and "disabilityism" (the negative view of oneself that comes with having a disability). Furthermore, we professionals are at least as guilty of this as older persons, dismissing problems as "just old age"; and when we do prescribe or provide care, we all too often provide dependent care, perpetuating the dependency status rather than trying to encourage and restore independence.

There are many documented examples of this counterproductive approach by professionals. In a recent study on risk factors for immobility, Selikson, Damus, and Hamerman (1988) at the Montefiore Medical Center, Bronx, New York, found among other things that immobility was not identified on the problem lists of 85% of the immobile patients in a presumably better than average nursing home. Kvitek, Shaver, Blood, and Shepard (1986) demonstrated that physical therapists assessing hypothetical patient descriptions indicated that they would be much less aggressive in their treatment goals for an older, compared to a younger, patient with the same condition. Studies of medical advice on preventive measures also indicate less vigorous efforts by physicians with older, compared to younger, patients.

A second challenge, which this book will address directly, is to share much more specific knowledge about rehabilitation capabilities, approaches, resources, and skills with those specializing in geriatrics, and conversely, to share the growing knowledge about aging and geriatrics, much of it vastly different from past views and myths, with those in the rehabilitation professions.

A third challenge for those in both fields is to study and develop more capabilities to serve the growing numbers of persons who are "aging in" with long-standing disabilities. We have increasing numbers of persons with developmental disabilities and with disabling conditions like strokes, spinal cord injuries, and postpolio syndrome who are living into late years and are now facing the medical, psychological, and social challenges of older persons in general superimposed on their chronic disabilities. Many of these people, having benefited from the strong emphasis on independent living in their earlier years, including use of whatever prostheses were necessary to achieve independence, are bringing very desirable perspectives and demands into the arena of geriatrics.

Fourth, there is the challenge to achieve a true, full marriage of these two fields, to develop more, and more truly combined, geriatric-rehabilitation services (Williams, 1987). We have seen this model work well in the United Kingdom and other places, such as Australia, but there are few examples of it here in the United States. My dream is to see in every general hospital (or in another setting in easy reach) a comprehensive geriatric-rehabilitation service at both the acute- and extended-care levels. I would like every older patient who is admitted to an acute-care hospital service to have an automatic geriatric-rehabilitation team consultation. There would be clear arrangements for arriving at agreement about the prompt transfer of appropriate patients to the acute geriatric-rehabilitation service as soon as the acute problem that led to the admission is stabilized—that is, within the first 1 to 3 days. The aim would be to begin immediately to mobilize the patient, physically and psychosocially: out of bed, in regular clothes, in as close to normal daily routine as possible, using every rehabilitative skill to avoid functional losses and restore independence—even while the necessary treatment of the acute condition is continuing.

Finally, we all have the challenge, as an integral part of our geriatric-rehabilitation philosophy and approach, to respect fully the individuality and autonomy of all older persons, wherever they are—in hospital, nursing home, day program, office, or home. Our language betrays our problems in this area: we talk of "institutionalizing" patients, in nursing homes in particular—that is, adapting them to institutional routines rather than adapting the services of the institution to achieve the individual goals of the patient and family. What *they* want should be the primary guide.

Perhaps the most egregious violation of respect for the individual is the widespread use of restraints, physical and chemical, in nursing homes and hospitals, with virtually no established justification. There *are* settings, in countries such as Sweden, the Netherlands, and Scotland, and a few in this country and Canada as well, where restraints are simply not used. The patients' need are met through imaginative, practical, individualized care; and all—patients, families, and staff—are far happier. The often-expressed fear for the safety of some patients if restraints are not used is simply not borne out by studies of restraint-free care; in fact, there is formidable evidence of injury and death secondary to use of restraints. An excellent review of this problem has recently been published (Evans & Strumpf, 1989).

Those of us committed to geriatrics and rehabilitation should certainly be in the forefront of efforts to achieve truly individualized care for all of our older patients, wherever they may be.

REFERENCES

Burley, L. E., Scorgie, R. E., Currie, C. T., Smith, R. G., & Williamson, J. (1984). The joint geriatric orthopaedic service in South Edinburgh: November 1979–October 1980. *Health Bulletin* (Edinburgh), *42*(3), 133–140.

Dalsky, G. P., Stocke, K. S., Ehsani, A. A., Slatopolsky, E., Lee, W. C., & Birge, S. J. (1988). Weight-bearing exercise training and lumbar bone mineral content in postmenopausal women. *Annals of Internal Medicine, 108,* 824–828.

Evans, L. K., & Strumpf, N. E. (1989). Tying down the elderly: A review of the literature on physical restraint. *Journal of the American Geriatrics Society, 37,* 65–74.

Harper, C. M., & Lyles, Y. M. (1988). Physiology and complications of bed rest. *Journal of the American Geriatrics Society, 36,* 1047–1054.

Kennie, D. C., Reid, J., Richardson, I. R., Kiamari, A. A., & Kelt, C. (1988). Effectiveness of geriatric rehabilitative care after fractures of the proximal femur in elderly women: A randomized clinical trial. *British Medical Journal, 297,* 1083–1085.

Kvitek, S. D. B., Shaver, B. J., Blood, H., & Shepard, K. F. (1986). Age bias: Physical therapists and older patients. *Journal of Gerontology, 41,* 706–709.

Lindeman, R. D., Tobin, J., & Shock, N. (1985). Longitudinal studies on the rate of decline in renal function with age. *Journal of the American Geriatrics Society, 33,* 278–285.

National Institutes of Health. (1988). Consensus Development Conference statement: Geriatric assessment methods for clinical decision-making. *Journal of the American Geriatrics Society, 36,* 342–347.

Rodeheffer, R. J., Gerstenblith, G., Becker, L. C., Fleg, J. L., Weisfeldt, M. L., & Lakatta, E. G. (1984). Exercise cardiac output is maintained with advancing age in healthy human subjects: Cardiac dilatation and increased stroke volume compensate for diminished heart rate. *Circulation, 69,* 203–213.

Rubenfeld, P. (1986). Ageism and disabilityism: Double jeopardy. In S. J. Brody & G. E. Ruff (Eds.), *Aging and rehabilitation: Advances in the state of the art* (pp. 323–328). New York: Springer Publishing Co.

Schaie, K. W. (1983). The Seattle Longitudinal Study: A 21-year exploration of psychometric intelligence in adulthood. In K. W. Schaie (Ed.), *Longitudinal studies of adult psychological development* (pp. 54–135). New York: Guilford.

Seals, D. R., Hagberg, J. M., Burley, B. F., Ehsani, A. A., & Holloszy, J. O. (1984a). Effects of endurance training on glucose tolerance and plasma lipid levels in older men and women. *Journal of the American Medical Association, 252,* 645–649.

Seals, D. R., Hagberg, J. M., Hurley, B. F., Ehsani, A. A., & Holloszy, J. O. (1984b). Endurance training in older men and women: I. Cardiovascular responses to exercise. *Journal of Applied Physiology, 57,* 1024–1029.

Selikson, S., Damus, K., & Hamerman, D. (1988). Risk factors associated with immobility. *Journal of the American Geriatrics Society, 36,* 707–712.

Solomon, D. H. (1988). Geriatric assessment: Methods for clinical decision making. *Journal of the American Medical Association, 259,* 2450–2452.

Williams, T. F. (1987). The future of aging. *Archives of Physical Medicine & Rehabilitation, 68,* 335–338.

2

Geriatrics and Rehabilitation: Common Ground and Conflicts

Stanley J. Brody

For 250 years modern medical science has followed the René Descartes dictum that reduced complex problems to their smallest and simplest elements. This approach, which has enjoyed some remarkably successful results, has permeated teaching and practice as well as research in medicine. The 19th-century development by clinicians of the doctrine of specific etiology—cause and effect—particularly in infectious disease, led to the work of Pasteur and Koch and the germ theory. Dubos (1968) points out that "there is no more spectacular phenomenon in the history of medicine than the rapidity with which the germ theory of disease became accepted by the medical profession" (p. 324).

So pervasive has the Cartesian model been that even the so-called soft sciences have followed the lead of the self-described hard sciences. In the world of social problems, I have called this the "holy grail" syndrome—the reduction of complex problems to simplistic solutions (Brody, 1970). An example is the recent focus on "alternatives to institutionalization," a successor to the deinstitutionalization of the mentally ill.

H. L. Menken observed that complex questions seek simple answers that are usually in error. Nevertheless, the acceptance of reductionist thinking led Engel (1977) to describe the biomedical model as a cultural imperative, a dogma equivalent to "the witchcraft of Western civilization." Not unusual, then, is the clinician who focuses through reductionist reasoning on the disease and not on the host.

During this development of modern scientific medicine, the popula-

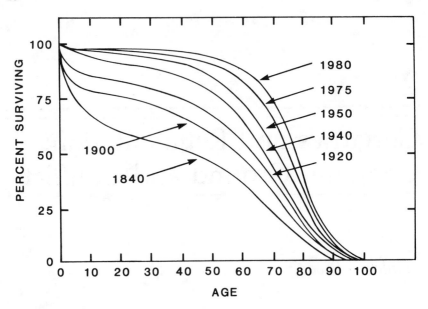

Figure 2-1 The increasingly rectangular survival curve. Reprinted from *Aging America: Trends Projections 1984.*

tion at risk has changed radically, at least in demographic terms (Figure 2-1). For example, at the beginning of this century life expectancy had doubled over a 2,400-year history; an individual born in 1900 could expect to live 43 years. Today, less than 100 years later, we have lengthened life expectancy by 33 years, 1 1/2 times the extension that occurred during the previous 24 centuries. Even more dramatic, there were 13,000 centenarians in 1980; by the year 2000 there will be 100,000, and predictions are that by the mid-21st century there will be 1 million Americans 100 years of age and over.

The older person today presents a different picture from even 20 years ago. The problems that the elderly endure are chronic conditions, some of which are the results of what Gruenberg (1977) has called the "failures of success"; that is, people survive as the result of medical intervention but often with reduced function. Thomas (1974) speaks of halfway technology that neither cures nor cares.

We have pointed out that the 1910 Flexner (1960) report on medical education was 30 years in advance of the development of a firm scientific base for modern medicine—an extension of the reductionist approach (Brody, 1987). This was compared with the effect of the 1956 report of the Commission on Chronic Illness, which established "chronic care as a major health problem of this generation" (Brody, 1973). As Strauss and Corbin (1988) note, chronic illness is now "the equivalent of the plagues and scourges of yesteryear" (p. 10).

The net result of many of the public health and welfare interventions is an older generation that, for the most part, is healthy but contains a significant proportion who experience what has been described as the trajectories of disability (Strauss and Corbin, 1988).

Three subgroups are identifiable within the disabled aged population. For the first time many developmentally disabled people are now surviving past middle age. The introduction of antibiotics and the control of respiratory infection have enabled large cohorts of the mentally retarded to face the problems of aging. Second, because of improved medical care, adults who suffered trauma earlier in their lives are also aging in large numbers. The third and largest group are those aged who have become disabled because of traumata (such as falls and other accidents) or late-onset diseases. These diseases are more intense in the eighth stage of life because of the reduced physical, social, and psychological reserves of the elderly. Many of the aged have had medical/surgical interventions that were effective but left them with residual impairments that often result in disability. The major target population of impaired and disabled elders is made up of those suffering the residual consequences of disease or trauma, as represented in Figure 2-2.

The distinctions among the terms *impairment, disability,* and *handicap* have been clarified by the World Health Organization (1982):

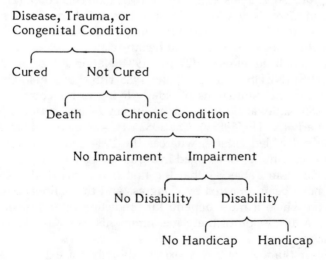

Figure 2-2 Decision tree.

Impairment: Any loss or abnormality of psychological, physiological, or anatomical structure or function.

Disability: Any restriction or lack (resuling from an impairment) of ability to perform an activity in the manner or within the range considered normal for a human being.

Handicap: A disadvantage for a given individual, resulting from an impairment or disability, that limits or prevents the fulfilment of a role that is normal, depending on age, sex, social, and cultural factors, for that individual.

The National Center for Health Statistics and the Census Bureau, reflecting the shift from an exclusively acute-care orientation that was measured by mortality and morbidity, are now providing data on the prevalence of chronic illness and disability. The pioneering work by Katz, Ford, Moskowitz, Jackson, and Jaffee (1963) and Lawton and E. Brody (1969) has provided the framework from which to measure disability through calibration of the levels of functioning in two major categories: the activities of daily living (ADL) and the instrumental activities of daily living (IADL). The ADL used by the federal national data-gathering agencies are bathing; dressing; toileting, or using the toilet; eating; transferring, or getting in and out of bed or chairs; continence; and mobility. The IADL are ability to use the telephone, shopping, food preparation, housekeeping, laundry, using public transportation, taking medications, and managing finances.

In the last 4 years, four major national samplings of the elderly have used the Katz ADL items as a core for their data collection: (1) the 1982 Long Term Care Survey (LTC) by the Bureau of the Census for the Department of Health and Human Services, designed to estimate the personal characteristics and use of health-related services by disabled, noninstitutionalized elderly; (2) the 1984 National Health Interview Survey (HIS) (NCHS, 1987a); (3) the 1986 HIS, household-based surveys of functional limitations of elderly living in the community; and (4) the 1985 National Nursing Home Survey of use of nursing homes by the elderly (NCHS, 1987b). The 1982 LTC survey was a limited sample of only disabled elderly, whereas the 1984 and 1986 HIS surveys were broader samples of all aged living in the community.

It is clear from Table 2-1 that the first five items of the Katz ADL formula have been repeated by Congress and the national data collections upon which it must depend for prediction of an at-risk population. (For a discussion of these measurements, see Kane, Chapter 18, this volume).

For the first time reliable data exist to describe the extent of disability among the elderly. As we have noted, most elderly are "healthy" in

Table 2-1 Governmental Use of Katz ADL Scales

Katz et al. (1963)	Catastrophic Act, Sec. 205(b)	LTC 1982	HIS 1984	Nursing Home Survey 1985
Bathing	Bathing	Bathing	Bathing	Bathing
Dressing	Dressing	Dressing	Dressing	Dressing
Going to the toilet	Toileting	Toileting	Using the toilet	Using the toilet
Feeding	Eating	Eating	Eating	Eating
Transfer	Transferring in and out of bed or in and out of a chair	Getting out of bed	Getting in and out of bed and chairs	Transferring from a bed or chair
Continence		Continence		Continence
		Getting around indoors	Walking	
			Getting outside	

the Dubos (1968) sense: they are independent—an independence that reflects the ability to cope with their environment. A series of tables summarizing these new data were prepared by William Scanlon (1988) and have been modified for this volume (see Figures 2-3 through 2-8).

For the last 15 years the degree of disability among the aged seems to be decreasing. Whether that reflects a real improvement or the availability of better national data is not clear. The burden of proof using indirect information, such as the reduction of hospital admissions and the stability of physician visits for the aged, indicates that indeed the elderly are functioning better as a group. Their per capita use of the health care system is prima facie evidence of such a conclusion. For the last decade the rates of admissions to hospitals and lengths of stays of elderly patients have been steadily decreasing. Although those over 65 years of age are growing older as a group, the per capita number of physician visits has remained stable. Nevertheless, although the elderly as a group are healthier, the gross number of disabled are greater because there are so many more elderly (Brody, 1987).

Whereas 76% of the elderly are functionally independent, almost 5%—those with five or six ADL deficits—are severely disabled (Figure 2-3). These data include both those living in the community and those

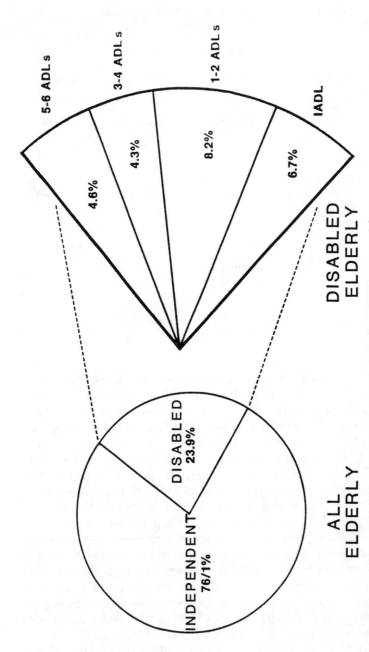

5-6 ADLs

3-4 ADLs

1-2 ADLs

IADL

4.6%

4.3%

8.2%

6.7%

DISABLED
ELDERLY

DISABLED
23.9%

INDEPENDENT
76/1%

ALL
ELDERLY

Figure 2-3 Distribution of elderly by degree of disability, 1985. Estimated from Candace Macken, "A Profile of Functionally Impaired Aged Persons in the Community," *HFCA Review*, and Esther Hing, "Use of Nursing Homes by the Elderly: Preliminary Data from the 1985 National Nursing Home Survey," NCHS.

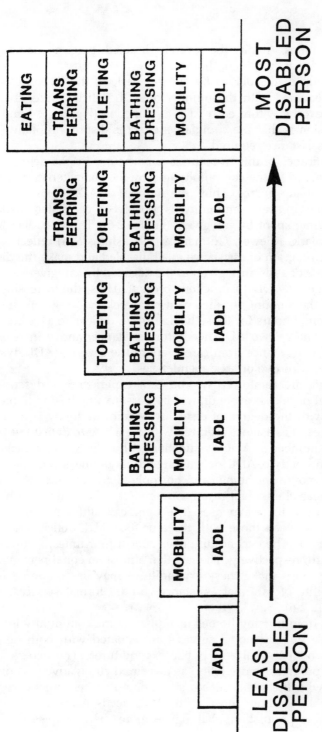

Figure 2-4 Disabilities can be ranked by severity. Persons with a more severe disability usually have all lesser disabilities.

15

in nursing homes. Among the severely disabled, twice as many live in the community as in nursing homes.

The ranking of disabilities by severity reflects the hypothesis that severity is equated with the number of ADL deficits rather than the degree of severity within each ADL dysfunction (Figures 2-4 and 2-5). The conclusion is that the cumulative effect is disproportionate to the amount of assistance required.

The significance of this hypothesis is borne out by the degree of assistance required in the community and by the characteristics of those elderly in nursing homes. Thus, the number of ADL deficits of those elderly living in the community is positively correlated with the amount of time spent by caregivers (Figure 2-5). The Canadian Manitoba data (Stark, Kliewer, Gutman, & McCashin, 1984) reflect a complete public program of assistance to all disabled and make the distinction in degree of assistance given to the disabled by caregivers in terms of the number of ADL dysfunctions present. Thus, the increasing progression of the amount of time spent per week by caregivers virtually doubles, from 9 hours for those having IADL deficits to 14.1 hours for those with one or two ADL needs for assistance, and it increases to 27.2 hours of assistance from caregivers to the severely ADL dysfunctional, those with five or six dependencies.

These data are reinforced by the U.S. experience as described in terms of out-of-pocket expenditures by persons purchasing home care correlated with the degree of disability. Again, disability is measured not by degree of assistance required within each ADL deficit but by the cumulative number of ADL dysfunctions. Thus, both individuals with IADL or one or two ADL deficits spend about the same amount of money per month for home care, but only 18.9% of those with IADL do so whereas almost half again as many (25.1%) of those with minimum ADL incur these expenses. The significant difference in expenditure occurs between those with three or four ADL deficits and those with five or six. The expenditure rises almost four times, from $117 to $439 a month, respectively. The fact that almost an equal percentage of these two groups make these expenditures may be accounted for by the availability of informal assistance, funds, formal services, or all three (Figure 2-6).

The data from nursing homes reemphasize the community information because nursing home services are equated with both need for assistance and personal and public expenditures. The experience of those with progressive disability, as measured cumulatively, is directly correlated with the receipt of nursing home services. Again we see a doubling phenomenon: those with IADL needs make up 5% of the nursing home population; that figure more than doubles (12%) for

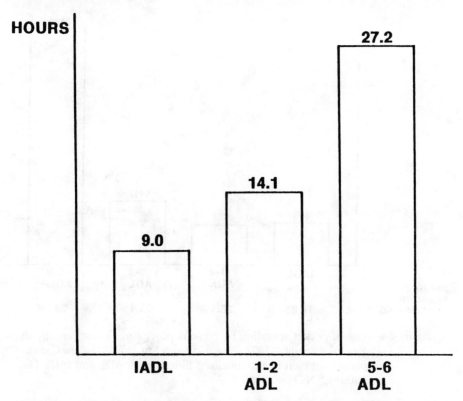

Figure 2-5 Average time spent per week by caregivers for persons with different levels of dependency. Adapted from Manitoba Longitudinal Study of the Aging.

those with one or two ADL needs and almost redoubles (23%) for those with three or four ADL deficits. Half of the nursing home population (50.9%) is severely disabled, with five or six ADL deficits (see Figure 2-7).

Yet another correlation is worth noting. The demographic revolution of the aging society has been described as occurring in two stages. The first extension of longevity occurred primarily as the result of public health and welfare measures, which helped many who otherwise would have not survived childhood diseases to reach age 65. This occurred in the second quarter of this century despite the severe depression of the 1930s. The second change in life expectancy occurred during the last 20 years, with an increase of 20% in life expectancy at age 65. This second extension has been credited to the contributions of high-technology medical and surgical interventions and to their univer-

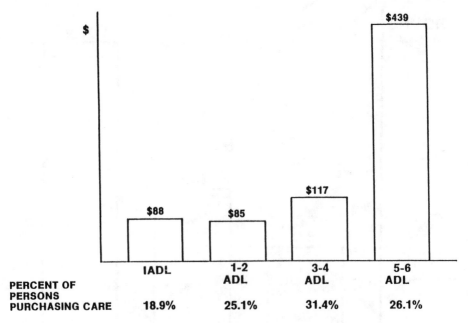

Figure 2-6   Out-of-pocket spending by persons purchasing home care, by degree of disability, 1982. Adapted from Liu et al., "Home Care Expenses for Non Institutionalized Elderly with ADL and IADL Limitations," NCHSR, 1985.

sal availability through Medicare. In this context the effects of age on
the probability of having an ADL or an IADL disability are marked: a
small proportion of those in the 65–74-year-old group are disabled, but
slightly more than half of the very old, those over 85 years of age, have
one or more disabilities (Figure 2-8).

The danger of extrapolation from such data is that it encourages the
expectation, with the aging of those over age 65, of a more disabled
population in the future. However, the recent increase in those over 85
years old has not resulted in a corresponding increase in the percentage of the elderly needing assistance by reason of disability or of the
per capita use of health facilities, although the gross number is greater.
(For a full discussion, see Brody, 1985a, 1987.)

The significance of disability is reinforced, however, by Katz's finding that prior to death many people experience an average of 4 1/2 years
of disability (Katz et al., 1983) and by the fact that movement of the
aged out of hospitals is negatively affected by the presence of severe
disability (Meiners & Coffey, 1985).

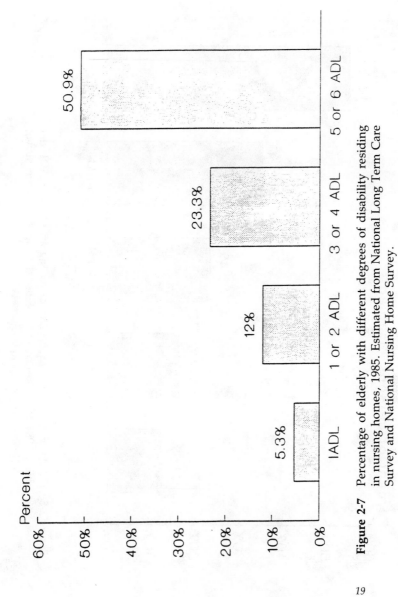

Figure 2-7 Percentage of elderly with different degrees of disability residing in nursing homes, 1985. Estimated from National Long Term Care Survey and National Nursing Home Survey.

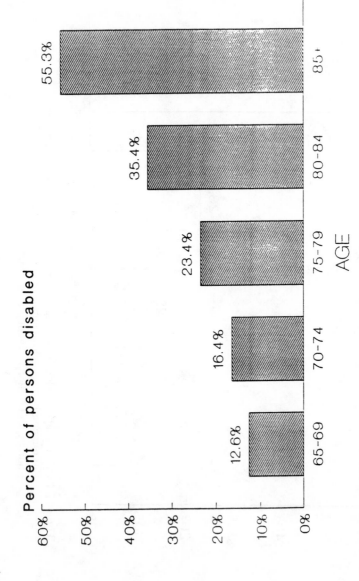

Figure 2-8 Effects of age on the probability of having an IADL or ADL disability 1984–85. Adapted from National Long Term Care Survey and National Nursing Home Survey.

Chronic disabilities tend to involve multiple impairments resulting from multiple diseases, appear to follow an uncertain course, and may be constant or intermittent over a long period. Very little is known of their trajectory over time other than that they disturb the homeostasis of individuals and their informal support systems. The complexities of chronic conditions and their interactions require a broad spectrum of allied health professionals and services with an intricate set of fiscal, individual, and family arrangements.

Eight guidelines enumerated by Strauss and Corbin (1988, pp. 143–145) for chronic illness can be paraphrased and expanded to provide the framework for understanding the trajectory of chronic disability:

1. Chronic disability management must be seen through the eyes of those who are experiencing it. Barry Corbet's presentation (see Chapter 4), which initiated the main frame of this conference, emphasizes the importance of maximizing the autonomy of the disabled and understanding their requirements as they age by listening to their perceptions of their situations.

2. Chronic disability must be seen as a long-term experience passing through many phases and requiring continuity of care through a synergism of the acute, transitory, and long-term care systems.

The acute-care medical approach is ill-suited to continuity of care because the need for assistance is calibrated, both clinically and in the health system, by the severity of disease. In this approach the disease is often the single focus of treatment and fiscal support, and the complexity of the hosts' conditions and of the environment is ignored clinically and almost totally unsupported by the formal health system.

Nevertheless, the chronically disabled continuously move within the formal health system, albeit haphazardly, between the hospital, the physician's office, home care, and the nursing home. The relationships among these formal services are seen in Figure 2-9, with the DRG acting as an incentive to accelerate the movement from acute care to subacute, transitory, or short-term long-term care. Kane has characterized this often rapid movement from the acute care discharge to nursing homes and vice versa as Ping-Ponging.

We have attempted to quantify this movement by adapting a chart of the annual movement of persons 65 years of age and over through the health care system. The data recorded here reflect the state of the art in available information, with some of the figures, such as acute-care and nursing home admissions and discharges, being relatively firm. Other movement data is based on small samples and, we hope, informed speculation (Figure 2-9).

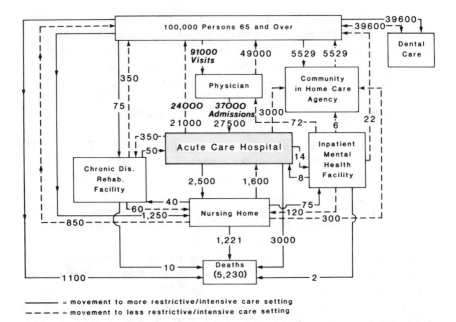

                    = movement to more restrictive/intensive care setting
        ― ― ― ― = movement to less restrictive/intensive care setting

Figure 2-9   Annual movement of persons 65 and over through the health care
                system. Adapted from Paul Denson, The elderly and the health
                care system. *Milbank Quarterly*, 65 (4), 1987, 616.

3. The health care system and providers must consider, in addition
to medical needs, the life history and personality development, the
structural and life-style needs of the chronically disabled and their families. The family or informal support system provides more than 80% of
health care for the elderly disabled. In rehabilitation, the family is seen
as an active participant with the patient in the recovery or maintenance
process. (See Lawton, Brody & Saperstein, Chapter 9, this volume, for
the Philadelphia Geriatric Center staff exposition).

The environment too is a key consideration in assessing the need for
support of the chronically disabled. The availability of toilet facilities on
the same floor on which the individual with limited mobility spends
his or her waking or sleeping time plays a critical role in life-style and
quality of life. (See chapters 9 and 10, this volume, for Lawton's and
Hyatt's discussions of environment.) In good rehabilitation practice, a
home visit evaluating the environment to which the patient is to return
is a key element of treatment.

4. Management of chronic disability requires providers to develop
collaborative partnerships among themselves and with the disabled
and their informal support system. Such collaboration requires that the

disabled and their informal support systems be informed about the nature and course of the underlying condition; about the treatment and
the plan of management of the ensuing disabilities; and about the opportunities, services, and helps that are available. Inherent in this
guideline is respect for the autonomy of the disabled and their families
and for their right to choose from whatever options may be available to
them. Practice advises of the need to repeat the same information
many times because at moments of crisis and stress the patients or
their support groups are often unable to focus or understand the information the provider is making available (cf. Bottomley et al., Chapter
6, this volume).

5. The health care system must recognize continued lifelong support
as essential for the management of chronic conditions, even though the
type, amount, and intensity can vary with the illness phase. The essence of the needs of the chronically disabled population is continuity
of care. On the one hand, the risk of mortality over a 2-year period is
strongly associated with disability level. Thus, a person living in the
community with five or six ADL deficits has a 37.2% probability of
death in 2 years, compared to 8.1% for elders who did not report disability. On the other hand,

> of persons who had been chronically disabled in 1982, a large proportion
> manifested significantly improved functional status two years later. For
> example, 22.2% of persons with five or six ADL impairments showed
> some improvement in functional status two years later. It is also interest-
> ing to note that persons with three or four ADL impairments were the
> most "unstable" group, with only 22.8% remaining at that level of impair-
> ment two years later (compared with 30.9% of persons with five or six
> ADL impairments in 1982). Thus this appears to be a transition group,
> with highest risks of any of the groups for a change in status. (Manton,
> 1988, p. 223)

If decedents during this 2-year period were excluded, 35% of those
with five or six ADL deficits who survived 2 years and 31% of those
with 3 or 4 ADL deficits showed some significant long-term improvement in functional status (Manton, 1988, p. 225). Manton concludes
that "inadequate attention has been paid to processes of home care and
to the effects of short-and medium-term illness and rehabilitative conditions" (p. 224).

As we have pointed out, even in the acute-care hospital the level of
functioning is a major determinant of the length of stay. A health care
system that avoids focusing on functional capacities does so at its own
peril, as do the providers who participate in what may be irrelevant
practices.

6. Providers of quality care of the chronically disabled must accept them where they are and work in tandem with them from that point on. Acceptance implies providers' listening to and understanding the perceptions and expectations of the elderly disabled. At the same time "where they are" means not only working with their sense of self but also appreciating the realities of the physical and social environments in which they find themselves.

7. Where severe disability is present, as defined by three or more ADL deficits, an "arrangements coordinator" or "articulator of care" (case manager) is needed. Choosing three or more ADL deficits is based on the data in Figures 2-5 and 2-6 as well as Manton's (1988) analysis comparing the 1982 and 1984 Long-Term Care Surveys. The arrangements coordinator does not necessarily have to be a professional because informed families often perform this function adequately. In all situations the coordinator or case manager must be prepared not only to assess needs and resources but also to suggest treatments that are acceptable to the patient and family. In this process, counseling becomes a major contribution the coordinator can perform so that both the nature of and need for services are understood and utilized. Where counseling is indicated, professional help in the form of a referral is required if the coordinator is not qualified (cf. sections by E. Brody and Saperstein in Chapter 9, this volume).

8. Quality of care for the chronically disabled must be based on therapeutic optimism—a statement of the Williams (1984) dictum that rehabilitation of the aged "is an approach, a philosophy, and a point of view" (p. xiii). The emerging data from the 1982 and 1984 national Long-Term Care Surveys have confirmed earlier conclusions for the exercise by providers of "therapeutic optimism" for the disabled elderly (for discussions of ethical implications of therapeutic optimism see Binstock, Chapter 19, this volume; Brody, 1986, 1987).

The medical response has not been consonant with these guidelines. The Cartesian reductionist approach does not allow for complex care for complex problems. This is reflected in service, research, and teaching, not only in medicine but in many of the allied health professions as well. Public policy too has followed the medical response to the new health needs of the elderly by funding acute care primarily (Brody, 1979).

Within the medical specializations, two stand out as exceptions in that they focus on the host rather than the disease: geriatrics and physiatry. Both heed the Williams (1984) admonition that at the "heart of all care of aging persons" is the goal "to restore an individual to his/her former functional and environmental status, or alternately to maintain or maximize remaining function . . . in order to help them continue to live as full a life as possible" (p. xiii).

"Medicine and the behavioral sciences have mirrored societal attitudes," Butler has asserted (Butler & Lewis, 1973). We have suggested that it may well be the reverse, that societal values may be conditioned by perceptions of science. Whatever the cause or effect, negative attitudes toward the aged are exacerbated by generations of societal rejection of the disabled. I have suggested that the issue is not so much "ageism" as "age disabilityism." Indeed, the elderly themselves identify becoming old as becoming disabled.

There has been little training or preparation of health professionals for rehabilitation of the disabled aged patient or the concept of continuity of care it represents. Even within the two medical specialties that have been identified as embracing functional goals for the aged there are problems. Geriatrics leaders are often uncomfortable in acknowledging the need to use resources beyond acute medical care. The geriatric "team" is almost always limited to the geriatrician, nurse, and social worker and *does not* include occupational, physical, speech, and other therapists. The research issues are presented in terms of "human biology."

Six years ago, Steinberg (1984), then chairman of the Geriatric Rehabilitation Committee of the American Academy of Physical Medicine and Rehabilitation, reported on a survey of physiatrists' attitudes toward geriatric rehabilitation: "Many of the responses mirrored the ambivalence of physicians towards geriatric rehabilitation. One respondent stated bluntly: 'Rehabilitation of the aged is a contradictory statement'" (p. 10).

The difficulty in changing educational programs for health professionals to include geriatrics has been well documented (Institute of Medicine, 1978). It has been equally difficult to introduce rehabilitation content into the curricula of medicine, nursing, social work, the therapies, and health care administration (Fowler, 1982). Until these tasks are accomplished, health professionals will continue to be resistive to rehabilitation of the aged. Moreover, until the educational establishment moves rehabilitation into the mainstream of curricula, recognizing the multiple peer-professional inputs of physicians, nurses, social workers, and the therapies (audiologic, occupational, physical, and speech), the disabled elderly will be subject to interruptions in the continuity of care they require.

Despite the contemporaneous emergence 40 years ago of physical medicine and rehabilitation and of geriatrics as medical specialties, they have followed separate and isolated but parallel paths. Consistently, the knowledge base of each field has been ignored by the other and by their respective service activities. Neither field accesses the other's literature in working with a common problem. For more than 20 years, both specialties have recognized functional assessment as a critical tool (Brody, 1985a). Nevertheless, at a conference on assessment a few years ago, under the auspices of NIA, virtually no use was made of the extensive relevant rehabilitation literature.

There has been a lack of mutual acknowledgment in the clinical field as well. Physical medicine is not given departmental status in many medical schools, and it is not unusual to find a medical student being graduated without any opportunity to know of the existence of the field of rehabilitation, much less experience it through a clinical rotation. At the same time, geriatric medicine is being given begrudging academic recognition but rarely at a departmental level. The same medical student may emerge from that experience without any familiarity with geriatric content and very little understanding of chronic illness. Just as in rehabilitation, clinical rotation through a geriatric service or a nursing home is a rarity. Even more striking is the lack of integration of the two areas in the few schools that have both rotations.

There is minimum use of the physiatrist in many inpatient or outpatient geriatric hospital services. Similarly, there is little call for the geriatrician in rehabilitation inpatient and outpatient situations. The sensitivity to turf is extreme. The DRG regulations that exempt inpatient rehabilitation units have already been challenged as discriminating against geriatric inpatient units, which allegedly give the same service (Department of Health and Human Services, Health Care Financing Administration, 1984).

Within the various allied health services, the recognition of geriatrics or rehabilitation is similarly uneven. Opportunities for education or training in geriatric rehabilitation are limited, and such training usually appears only sporadically on the continuing education agenda. There is also little interface between the public service systems of health education, aging, mental health, and rehabilitation. The two national Aging and Rehabilitation Conferences in 1984 and 1988 are isolated examples of systems interface.

But there has been some progress. The two specialty boards of internal medicine and of physical medicine and rehabilitation are actively considering authorizing a joint 5-year residency program leading to certification in both programs, although geriatrics may not be included as a major focus of the discussion. At least three of the national health and professional organizations (the American Congress of Rehabilitation Medicine, the American Physical Therapy Association, and the American Public Health Association) focused their recent annual meetings on aging and geriatric rehabilitation. Although it is still rare for physiatrists, geriatricians, and allied health professionals to give presentations at each other's scientific meetings, it is beginning to occur.

More important is the societal attitude that finally is expressed in publicly supported programs through legislation. For the first time, proposals for the provision of chronic care that recognize the need for continuity of care for the disabled are being seriously discussed in Congress. There are at least four bills that were sponsored individually by leaders in the 100th Congress but share a common concern with providing continuity of care. In the House of Representatives, Henry Waxman, chairman of the Subcommittee on Health in the Energy and Commerce Committee, has introduced the Elder-Care Bill, and Fourtney (Pete) Stark, chairman of the Ways and Means Subcommittee on Health, has sponsored the Chronic Care Bill. In the Senate, Edward Kennedy, chairman of the Labor and Human Resources Committee, has introduced the Life-care proposal, and George Mitchell, who is now majority leader of the Senate, and chairman of the Subcommittee on Health of the Finance Committee, has introduced the Long-Term Care Assistance Act of 1988.

All of these bills address the chronic care needs of the aged and disabled and establish eligibility criteria based on ADL. They all offer some form of nursing home coverage as well as homemaker and adult day-care benefits. All are concerned with continuity of care and assessment, using case management as the administrative mechanism, rather than physician certification, to authorize services.

As the legislators move beyond medically oriented perceptions of need, they are becoming concerned about the number and quality of providers who will be available to deliver the programs they propose to authorize. They are probing for the availability of adequately trained service personnel of all levels of care. Congress is now prepared to respond to the needs of the new elderly disabled populations as subject not only to acute illness but also to multiple chronic disabilities, and that at a time when the elderly are also having to contend with personal losses and social, psychological, and economic constraints.

Complex problems require well-orchestrated, complex solutions involving varied disciplinary supports in assessment, treatment, and care. The second conference on Aging and Rehabilitation focused on chronic problems requiring hands-on interdisciplinary efforts. We must augment the reductionist approach with a new focus on synergism. Not only does this require each of us to learn and research our craft in its broadest dimensions; it also requires each of us to join in a solution that is greater than the sum of its parts.

REFERENCES

Brody, S. J. (1970). Maximum participation of the poor: Another Holy Grail? *Social Work*, 15(1), 68–75.

Brody, S. J. (1973). Comprehensive health care for the elderly: An analysis (the continuum of medical, health, and social services for aging). *Gerontologist*, 13(4), 412–418.

Brody, S. J. (1979). The thirty-to-one-paradox: Health needs of the aged and medical solutions. *National Journal*, 11(44), 1869–1873.

Brody, S. J. (1985a). The future of nursing homes. *Rehabilitation Psychology*, 30(2), 109–120.

Brody, S. J. (1985b). Rehabilitation and nursing homes. In E. L. Schneider, C. J. Wendland, A. W. List, & M. Ory (Eds.), *The teaching nursing home: A new approach to geriatric research, education, and clinical care* (pp. 147–156). New York: Raven Press.

Brody, S. J. (1986). Impact of the formal support system on rehabilitation of the elderly. In S. J. Brody & G. E. Ruff (Eds.), *Aging and rehabilitation: Advances in the state of the art* (pp. 62–86). New York: Springer Publishing Co.

Brody, S. J. (1987). Strategic planning: The catastrophic approach. *The Gerontologist*, 27(2), 131–138.

Butler, R. N., & Lewis, M. I. (1973). *Aging and mental health: Positive psychosocial approaches*. St. Louis: C. V. Mosby.

Department of Health and Human Services, Health Care Financing Administration. (1984). Medicare program: Prospective payment for Medicare inpatient hospital services. [42 CFR Parts 405, 409, and 489. Final Ruling.] *Federal Register*, 49(1), 240.

Dubos, R. (1968). *Man, medicine, and environment*. New York: Frederick A. Praeger.

Engel, G. L. (1977). The need for a new medical model: A challenge for biomedicine. *Science*, 196(4286), 129–136.

Flexner, A. (1960). *Medical education in the United States and Canada*. (Commissioned in 1910 by the Carnegie Foundation for the Advancement of Teaching.) Washington, DC: Science and Health Publications.

Fowler, W. M. (1982). Viability of physical medicine and rehabilitation in the 1980's. *Archives of Physical Medicine and Rehabilitation*, 63(1), 1–5.

Gruenberg, E. M. (1977). The failures of success. *Milbank Memorial Fund Quarterly*, 55(7), 3–24.

Institute of Medicine. (1978). *Aging and medical education*. Washington, DC: National Academy of Sciences.

Katz, S., Branck, L. G., Branson, M. H., Papsidero, J. A., Beck, J. C., & Greer, D. S. (1983). Active life expectancy. *New England Journal of Medicine*, 309(20), 1218–1224.

Katz, S., Ford, A. B., Moskowitz, R. W., Jackson, B. A., & Jaffee, M. W. (1963). Studies of illness in the aged: The index of ADL: A standardized measure of biological and psychosocial function. *Journal of the American Medical Association*, 185, 914–919.

Lawton, M. P., & Brody, E. M. (1969). Assessment of older people: Self-maintaining and instrumental activities of daily living. *The Gerontologist, 9,* 179–186.

Manton, K. G. (1988). Planning long-term care for hetergeneous older populations. In G. L. Maddox & M. P. Lawton (Eds.), *Annual review of gerontology and geriatrics* (Vol. 8, pp. 217–255). New York: Springer Publishing Co.

Meiners, M. R., & Coffey, R. M. (1985). Hospital DRGs and the need for long-term care services: An empirical analysis. *Health Services Research, 20*(3), 359–384.

National Center for Health Statistics. (1987a). *National Health Interview Survey: Advancedata 133.* Hyattsville, MD: U.S. Department of Health and Human Services, Public Health Service.

National Center for Health Statistics. (1987b). *The 1985 National Nursing Home Survey: Advancedata 135.* Hyattsville, MD: U.S. Department of Health and Human Services, Public Health Service.

Scanlon, W. J. (1988). A perspective on long-term care for the elderly. *Health Care Financing Review/1988 Annual Supplement,* 7–15.

Stark, A. J., Kliewer, E., Gutman, G. M., & McCashin, B. (1984). Placement changes in long-term care: Three years' experience. *American Journal of Public Health, 74*(5), 459–463.

Steinberg, F. U. (1984). Education in geriatrics and physical medicine residency training programs. *Archives of Physical Medicine and Rehabilitation, 65*(1), 8–10.

Strauss, A., & Corbin, J. M. (1988). *Shaping a new health care system.* San Francisco: Jossey-Bass.

Thomas, L. (1974). *The living cell.* New York: Bantam Books.

Williams, T. F. (Ed.). (1984). *Rehabilitation and the aging.* New York: Raven Press.

World Health Organization. (1982). *World programme of action concerning disabled persons.* Geneva: Author.

3

Rehabilitation and the Elderly: A Physiatrist's View

Henry B. Betts

In the faces of the elderly most of us see the eyes of our mothers and fathers, our grandparents, those who shaped our world and nurtured us, who prepared us for the experiences we encounter in our lives. We may also see the eyes of fear and uncertainty, eyes often tortured by the prospect of death.

The elderly fear not just death but death perhaps preceded by a long and painful period of physical and mental decline that may strip individuals of their dignity, drain their resources, and impose burdens on their loved ones. They may fear that such burdens will, over time, transform love and respect into attitudes of obligation and sacrifice and at their demise will evoke feelings more of relief than of sorrow from their loved ones.

With respect to the elderly, we stand today at the threshhold of perhaps the greatest challenge and the greatest opportunity for positive contribution in the history of our health care delivery system. Of us all, our elderly are most profoundly in need of health care delivered by all provider disciplines.

For them, the need for health care draws most heavily on their individual resources. And for society, providing their care represents the greatest potential drain on all resources devoted to health care. How will we approach the health care needs of this growing segment of our population? What will be the primary modality of treatment for the aging? What can we do, within available social resources, to impart a better quality to their lives as the natural decline in function imposes itself on them?

It is my basic thesis that physiatry offers the most profound and beneficial responses to the health concerns of the elderly in this nation. We in the health care system must move more vigorously toward the collaborative team approach that is physiatry's invention and basic tool of providing care. This approach to rehabilitation must be inculcated early in medical education; information about it and an appreciation of its benefits must be communicated through society in general.

To a great extent, it is up to our public policymakers to pave the way, to be an indirect part of the team, and to adjust the role of public health structures in ways that foster geriatric rehabilitation. But it is our responsibility to facilitate this adjustment by demonstrating that the future of health care for the elderly lies most properly in the area of physical medicine and rehabilitation.

GOALS OF REHABILITATION

In considering the applicability of rehabilitation, particularly to an elderly patient population, we need to bear in mind that the primary goal of rehabilitation is generally not to cure a disease or to eliminate a disabling condition. The disabilities of our patients are sometimes permanent; they become part of the definition of the individual who is afflicted by them.

What we have in rehabilitation is a very pragmatic program of function-oriented goal setting and therapy. We are engaged in a process of restoring patients to maximum efficiency, bringing them to a level of maximum function and then teaching them and influencing their surrounding circumstances so that they can adjust to whatever residual disability remains.

In this context, we in rehabilitation see patients with disabling conditions that can occur in any age group: brain or spinal cord injuries, cerebrovascular accidents, neuromuscular impairments, amputations, arthritis, and a variety of other primary impairments. And of course, many patients come to us with disabilities that are somewhat secondary to the primary causes of impairment, such as chronic pain or ambulatory disability, communicative disorders, and a host of psychological deficits.

In our country, 10% to 15% of the population is to some extent disabled, and 70% will experience disability at some time in their lives. More than 20% of our elderly are disabled by one or more specific conditions; about 80% of our citizens over 65 suffer from at least one chronic illness. When diminution of function is considered in relation to the reduction in muscle fiber that accompanies the aging process, the rehabilitation needs of the elderly can be seen to be universal. Each of us will at some time in our lives benefit from rehabilitative intervention.

PHYSIATRY'S EXPERIENCE

For most of this century, physiatry alone among the medical specialties has automatically taken a comprehensive approach, dealing with the whole patient—his other primary disabling condition, attendant physical and mental and psychological deficits, life-style, and environment—in rehabilitating the patient to maximum function. Physiatry invented the collaborative team concept, which is critical to success but very difficult to achieve. Although others are now seeing that this is a necessary approach to care for the elderly and are "reinventing" it under other names, it is our product.

To return the patient to a high level of function, every circumstance that can influence the effectiveness of this process must be considered. Patients do not come to us with specific conditions in isolation of all other elements of their physical or psychological makeup, nor do they emerge without a sociological context of their own. Each has his or her own history, habits, set of preferred activities, and aspirations for the future. For elderly patients, particularly, what may be seen as a simple disability must be viewed in the light of a more complex physical, psychological, and sociological situation.

Consider, for example, the case of an elderly man for whom the priority need appears to be repair of a hernia. A physician admits him to an acute-care hospital, a surgeon repairs the hernia, and the patient is discharged. But that patient may also be depressed because of the death of his spouse or of a poker-playing friend. He may have anxiety about finances. He may be weak or short of breath. In fact, the hernia may have been a minor factor in a more comprehensive set of conditions that decrease his ability to function in life.

Of course, it is possible for him to receive treatment for all of those conditions at any modern hospital. But it is also possible—perhaps even probable in most circumstances—for him to go in for treatment of the hernia and have nothing else addressed. The system does not deal fully with his needs automatically; in most situations, the collaborative instinct is not there.

CONTINUUM OF CARE

Nor is it typical for a continuum of response to the patient's needs to be fully considered and treated. Just as the complete diagnosis accounts for a multiplicity of conditions, the therapy must account for the patient's situations over a time continuum. In this regard, social factors are a key. Will the patient be discharged to an independent living arrangement, to a spouse or family, to a specific vocation, to a nursing home? For elderly patients, these issues are of prime importance in goal setting, in devising the plan of rehabilitation.

It might be an ambitious objective for a certain elderly man to gain the ability to dress and feed himself; but if that is the difference between being able to go home to a busy family rather than to a nursing home, the effort toward that goal of rehabilitation might be very worthwhile. However, if discharge will be to a nursing home, where slow behavior is generally not allowed and where staff will find it easier to dress and feed the patient than to wait for him to meet those needs for himself, then there would be no point in pursuing the goal of enabling him to do so.

Similarly, imparting homemaking skills and assessing what might be done to make a home or an apartment more accessible would be proper steps in the rehabilitation of a patient who will be discharged to an independent living arrangement. But such therapy might be less useful if the patient is to be sent to a nursing home or to a daughter who really would prefer not to have her parent cluttering up the kitchen.

These examples may seem trivial, but they illustrate a vital element of any reasonable rehabilitation effort. And in the context of the comprehensive and collaborative methods of physiatry, these factors are automatically taken into account.

SOCIAL HISTORY

Another way of expressing our mission would be to say that we work to prevent the disabled patient from becoming handicapped. These are two different conditions. I have a patient, for example, who at 60 is totally quadriplegic. He is a former legislator, with a family, substantial means, and primarily intellectual interests. In relationship to his lifestyle and goals, he is not very handicapped. But another patient of mine has only one disability, the slight loss of function of one finger; but because he is a concert pianist, he is severely handicapped.

The point of this is to underscore the importance of the patient's social history. This key element in rehabilitation is likely to be under-emphasized or may even be ignored by physicians generally. First, it is considered boring. And patients have ways of making it even more boring; they are well known for diverting facts, evading questions, taking undue time to respond. There is a tendency on the part of physicians to delegate this issue entirely to social workers. In my view, it would be impossible to overstate the value of the contributions made by social workers in rehabilitation; but to be successful, the individual physician must somehow get involved in this process. He or she must convey to patients an interest in their social history.

PSYCHOLOGICAL FACTORS

There are certain parallels between the psychological problems of the elderly and those of disabled patients in general. When an elderly person becomes disabled, therefore, therapy challenges of considerable magnitude occur as one type of problem is superimposed on another.

One such parallel is fear of rejection. In our society it is no secret that youth and beauty are highly prized. Elderly people know they are not going to be asked to model bathing suits or pose for shampoo ads. Historically, there have been societies that have treated their elderly more kindly than ours does, some even with reverence. But brutality was often the rule in antiquity, as with the Greeks, who threw their elderly from mountaintops; the Japanese, who put them out in the snow on mountains; and the Eskimos, who put them adrift on ice floes.

For historical and contemporary reasons, fear of rejection is normal to the elderly, whether there are disabilities or not. When disabilities are added, the fear becomes more acute and complicates rehabilitation efforts significantly.

Depression is another parallel. Simply being elderly can lead to unremitting depression. The fact of losing physical stamina and abilities can lead to dysphoria. Organic changes leading to memory loss and impaired intelligence can be depressing. The failure of friends, families, and colleagues to extend needed affection and help can be comparable to the trauma that the young feel when they are disabled.

And then there is guilt. Most people with physical disabilities suffer from some degree of guilt. In the elderly, guilt is especially pronounced and frequently precedes physical disability in the abstract; there is an absurd underlying feeling in society that we are not supposed to get old—or at least we are not supposed to seem old. With all of the plastic surgery tucks available, all of the potions and dyes and cures at hand, if we are really clever we should be able to hide our age and infirmity from all beholders. In a sense the old seem to feel that they have failed to fool the world, have not protected themselves and their families from this dreadful embarassment.

Also, with age one tends to review the past and especially to consider one's relationships. We wonder if we have handled every situation as well as possible. When an elderly person feels rejected by his or her children, for example, guilt is very frequent, in respect to wondering "Where did I go wrong?" All parents feel that they should have raised their children well enough that they will be good to *their* parents.

Anger is another inevitable consequence of disability. Because anger is an emotion that springs from feelings of despair and self-pity, the elderly often get angry whether they are disabled or not. Anger can, in fact, become a facilitator of rehabilitation if it leads to constructive action. But if it creates irrational, nondirective behavior, it can contribute to the presentation of an unpleasant and disruptive person whom others can come to genuinely dislike and therefore reject even more than before. And in the elderly, all too often anger is diffuse and not directed at problem solving.

This is a critical time in the rehabilitative process, and the physician must play a role. Unchecked, this manifestation of anger can lead to hostility and bitterness and overwhelming self-pity, which will paralyze the positive forces and doom the rehabilitation process to failure.

It is clear that rehabilitation is indicated under circumstances in which the patient suffers from one or more disabilities that evoke or are superimposed on a significant pattern of other physical, psychological, or functional deficits. For the elderly, this may be the case with respect to almost any episode of serious illness or incident of trauma.

It is even worthy of consideration that some elderly individuals would benefit from rehabilitative processes at some time during their lives without regard to whether they have experienced such unfortunate occurrences. The emotional response to aging itself, in combination with the accumulation of physical and psychological deficits, might simply bring about a condition that calls for a general rehabilitative program.

METHODS OF PHYSIATRY

Physiatry is best positioned among the health care disciplines to take the lead in rehabilitation of the elderly. Over the last four decades we have developed and refined the fundamental strategy—the collaborative approach—that is most applicable to the complex circumstances under which the elderly find themselves in need of care. The drawing together of an interactive team of specialists to define the situation for each individual patient and to respond to all of that patient's needs under a plan developed by consensus—this is the strategy of proven effectiveness.

This is far different from the increasingly standard practice of housing specialists from the various health care disciplines "all under one roof," like a department store, so that the physician can simply make the appropriate referrals if he or she feels the patient needs physical therapy and counseling and speech and language intervention. As logical as it might seem, the simple referral system does not fit the patient who needs a comprehensive rehabilitation program.

What we see here is a patient and a whole environment, plus a special need for all elements of a complex network to interact in a fluid and mutually reinforcing way. This does not happen when each element is considered in isolation but only when all parts of the whole are in tune, when all work as a team in the interest of the individual patient. The physician, the nurse, the various therapists, the orthotist or prosthetist, the social worker, the psychologist, the spouse, the community support system—and the patient—all must interact as members of the team and work toward identified and achievable goals.

ALLIANCE FOR THE PATIENT

So physiatry is more than just a tactic. It is the establishment of an alliance for the patient. It is no denegration of the solo practitioner to observe that it would be a rare professional who possessed the skills and the insights, or even the time and the inclination, to approach in his or her own way the benefits that the alliance described here can bring to the patient. Similarly, even if referrals are made to each specialist acting more or less in isolation of the others, it is clear that true collaboration will achieve more for the patient.

This seems simple, even trite. On the surface, it might be perceived as an easy alliance to create. In fact, many writers have begun recently to "discover" the collaborative approach, in effect to reinvent the wheel of physiatry, which has been rolling to a prominent position in the health care delivery system for the better part of this century. But our experience tells us that collaborative treatment does not come about simply because a physician decides it would be a good idea and encourages the other professionals involved in a particular case to "work together" as much as possible.

There are individual egos involved, biases toward one's own professional discipline, gaps in understanding of others' areas of expertise, even the need to understand certain overlaps that in fact exist among some disciplinary practices. When collaboration is formalized and draws on the accumulation of experience that has been developed in the refinement of this tool of health care, then you have the optimum chance of success. And then you have, of course, physiatry. The bottom line is that, in physiatry, collaboration is the only approach we have ever used.

Similarly, physiatry has a long track record in meeting the needs of the elderly population. The techniques of physiatry have been evolving throughout the century in dealing with the rehabilitation challenges presented by victims of such diseases as polio and later in meeting the needs of wounded veterans of World War II and subsequent conflicts. The same techniques have been successfully applied to the needs of the elderly for the past 40 years.

In caring for elderly patients, for example, practitioners require unusual communication skills, particularly with regard to listening. To know the patient and, just as important, to help patients know themselves, it is necessary to tune in on the subtleties of communication. Knowing what patients mean by what they say and how they say it, and even by what they do not say, can be the key to gaining their confidence and therefore their compliance.

The communication element has been a major emphasis in the growth of physiatry over the years. Our team members are particularly well trained in this regard. We have had to be; without compliance and motivation, there is no rehabilitation.

Historically, of course, medical practitioners have not specialized on the basis of patient age groupings, except in the case of pediatrics, but rather along the lines of categories of illnesses or injuries. For the last decade or so, the question of geriatric medicine has been passed around. The interest in dealing with elderly populations has been appropriated to some extent by geriatricians and gerontologists.

This area of medical specialty remains today in the process of evolving and maturing. Most medical schools still lack a core curriculum in geriatric medicine. Most practitioners gain their expertise from exposure to patients, and most of that is in an acute-care setting. This is unlike geriatric medical specialists in England, for example, and in other countries, who feel they are specialists in geriatric rehabilitation.

But in physiatry, because of our concern with the whole patient and a whole environment—and because this approach is particularly important to the elderly patient—we have been meeting the needs of this population all along. At the Rehabilitation Institute of Chicago, about one in four of our patients has been elderly. And the percentage has been much higher at other similar institutions around the nation. Without placing a formal label on our programs that deal specifically and primarily with the aging population, we have nonetheless had them in place for many years.

Again, this is not to discount the experiences of thousands of practitioners who, because of the nature of their practices, have had high percentages of elderly in their caseloads. But generally these experiences have not been with total, comprehensive rehabilitation. It is one thing to know, for example, when a recovering stroke victim needs a brace but another to have the experience to know when in the recovery process the brace should be applied, what kind of brace to obtain, how to train the patient to apply the brace and to whom the patient should be referred for such a training, what the limitations of the brace will be, and how to train the patient to avoid falls.

THE TEAM

When a patient enters a place like the Rehabilitation Institute of Chicago, he or she is responded to by a team from a variety of professional areas—rehabilitation nursing, physical therapy, occupational therapy, psychology, social work, chaplaincy, vocational counseling, and therapeutic recreation. Obviously, each of these groups cannot be left to function autonomously, so there is a physician who manages each team.

The rehabilitation nurses carry out the duties that all nurses do in any health care setting, but in addition they are vital to the process of determining what activities the patients can carry over in their lives and to encourage them in those activities. The physical therapists increase the patients' abilities in activities of daily life; they prescribe the devices patients may require to get around, such as wheelchairs and braces; they are instrumental in pain prevention and reduction. Occupational therapists deal with strength-building exercises and coordination.

Therapeutic recreation plays a more important role in rehabilitation than might appear on the surface. Sometimes, and particularly with regard to the elderly, recreation is the main interest of a patient. Providing them with experiences such as a baseball game, a movie, or a trip to a museum plays a strong role in gaining the compliance and imparting the motivation that are critical to success in rehabilitation. Similarly, vocational rehabilitation is an important part of the process. Just because a patient is elderly does not mean that he or she does not aspire to work at a job. Often the prospect of employment is a strongly motivating factor.

Also among the key members of the rehabilitation team are the psychologists and social workers, for their contributions to the determination of whether rehabilitation is even indicated for a particular patient and for determining the psychosocial factors that will guide the process to success. In many cases speech pathologists and specialists in alternative communications systems are instrumental, as are orthotists, prosthetists, and specialists in pulmonary rehabilitation and electromyography, depending on the needs of the patient.

It should be observed as well that in any rehabilitation setting everyone must be aware of the necessity of considering the psyche of the patient. This includes the staff at the front desk, who deal with the family and see the patients for the first time; the housekeepers; and other support staff. In a rehabilitation process, the whole environment must be considered (cf. Hiatt, Chapter 10, this volume).

THE FAMILY

The importance of the family as a member of the rehabilitative team cannot be overstated. The family is the line between the patient and the rest of society. The willingness of the family to provide support, to become a part of the process of bringing about maximum function of the patient, and to help structure the environment in which the patient will find himself or herself after discharge will largely determine the shape of the particular plan of rehabilitation to be pursued (cf. section by E. Brody in Chapter 9, this volume).

In this regard, it should be noted that "family" is a term that may not conform to traditional definitions. For many elderly patients, there is no spouse. There may be no children. There may be children who are either unable or unwilling, given their own situations, to become part of the process.

Often, friends of the patient become the family participants in rehabilitation, or perhaps a concerned landlord or neighbor. Patients from rural areas seem to be more likely to have the support of traditional family members, even to the extent of grandchildren, nephews, or nieces. In urban areas it is not uncommon for there to be no kinship between patients and the individuals on whom they depend for support.

Once the team is assembled on the basis of the patient's full set of circumstances—the specific disability, assessment of deficits, prognosis, level of function, potential for increased function, the patient's interests, and the nature of the environment in which he or she is to be discharged—the plan for rehabilitation is addressed. The alliance for the patient has been formed. It remains as a unit throughout the process of rehabilitation, contributes to the patient's achievements, shares in successes, and draws the patient back over an often long and difficult road to a level of function, to a perception of having value, to a perspective from which the patient can view his or her life as more than just tolerable, an experience to be savored.

PUBLIC POLICY

Today we need greater understanding on the part of public policy-makers of the importance of what can be achieved through rehabilitation of the elderly. We must look for more than just a humane and compassionate public policy. We are in fact talking about a level of understanding from which policy can evolve and that is also in keeping with the cost-containment goal—the idol at whose feet so many of our elected officials have come to worship. What we see is the potential for a life that is not only prolonged but is also, from the patient's perspective, worthy of being prolonged.

We must reexamine health care for the elderly, in keeping with the realization that rehabilitation of the elderly conforms with the public policy objective of conserving resources. This is not to say that rehabilitation processes are inexpensive. Certainly they are not. To always have trained professionals responding not only to the illness of the day but also to the superimposed deficits of the patient might impose a short-term drain on public funds. But these short-term costs must be measured in comparison with long-term gains, many of which are also financial.

It would also be less expensive, for example, for patients to be able to live with a measure of independence than to be warehoused in an environment in which medication must be administered to them, in which they must be moved from bed to wheelchair and rolled into the dayroom to drift in and out of consciousness in front of a television set, in which they must be fed, turned over in bed periodically to avoid the onset of pressure sores, and treated for pressure sores when workers in the nursing home forget or simply neglect that duty, and in which they must be prepared by an overworked and undertrained staff person for a visit from relatives. In the long run, these "services" are as expensive as they are repugnant.

PROSPECTIVE PAYMENT

In the mid-1960s, health care–related costs amounted to about 6% of the total gross national product (GNP) in America. By 1987 health care had risen to 11.1% of the GNP, with the federal government paying nearly one third of a total societal outlay of more than $500 billion. Concern over this growth in health care costs led to a variety of responses. In the Medicare program, which accounts for more than one third of all hospital payments in the nation and is the principal sponsor of services to the elderly, the federal government's response has been simply to tell providers "prospectively" what it will pay for care for an individual patient, depending on the illness (classified by diagnostically related groups, or DRGs) precipitating hospitalization.

Leaving aside the question of whether the DRG payment rates were appropriately established when the Medicare Prospective Payment System (PPS) was initiated in 1983, those rates have not been adjusted to account for inflation in the costs of goods and services required in the provision of health care. In fact, the rates have risen only about half as much as inflation of true health care costs, as measured under federally approved methodologies.

This has caused a gap between the promise of 1983 PPS legislation and the realities of payments, resulting in a cost-shifting burden that must be spread among the provider institutions. What has been the response of the institutions? For some, PPS underfunding has contributed to the closing of their doors. And although there is no significant body of statistical evidence to prove it, distressingly numerous and growing anecdotal reports indicate that, with costs forced into the process as a consideration in prescribed programs of therapy, the patients are simply getting less service per episode of illness.

This is a particularly serious situation for elderly patients. It must be remembered that the primary diagnosis for which they are hospitalized is likely to be only one of a number of true illnesses that afflict them and that they are also likely to be suffering from one or more chronic ailments and functional deficits. In moving a patient from the acute-care setting directly back to an independent living arrangement, or even to a nursing home, these circumstances should be taken into account. If they are not, the consequences can be serious or even fatal.

Consider again the 80-year-old hernia patient. The operation is a relatively simple one, but for him it requires forced bed rest for a few days. The debilitating effects of bed rest are fully documented and will be more damaging for him than they would be for a younger, stronger patient.

He goes home weak and dizzy and cannot stand up for long periods of time. His family believes he needs to rest more until he is stronger. This intensifies his need for physical therapy, which he is not getting. There is more deterioration. Eventually, he is unable to function at home; he is admitted to a local nursing facility, where he is likely to get even more bed rest. He becomes one more case that we so often hear of in which "Grandpa never really recovered from his hernia operation." The operation was fine; the system let him down.

In rehabilitation, we know that enlightened public policy—and this is directly related to the concern we so often hear expressed as the "staggering" or "soaring" costs of health care—includes rehabilitative social policy. Seatbelt and airbag legislation, handgun control legislation, environmental issues, and public health and safety issues in general bear directly on both quality of life and federal fiscal concerns. It has been estimated that the fiscal impact of hip fractures suffered by elderly patients when they fall approaches $2 billion annually; it is also known that fall-prevention programs dramatically reduce the incidence of falls. Funding fall-prevention programs would be both sound fiscal policy and compassionate health care policy.

CHALLENGE: COMMUNICATION

Our challenge now is to send a message to the makers of policy in this nation. At the state level and the federal level, we must make lawmakers and bureaucrats see their responsibility as not just to respond to the demand for health care in ways that are politically expedient, not merely to be able to say they have "done something" for the elderly; they must accomplish in fact what the rhetoric of a compassionate society expresses.

In recent decades we in health care have learned a great deal about influencing public policy. Indeed, we have had to. In times past, our role was perceived by those who make policy as so benign and so warm and so vital that we were largely immune to adverse policy. We went about our business of making the medical arts evolve, keeping pace at least with our colleagues in other developed nations, and meeting the health care needs of all whom we could draw under the umbrellas of our charitable missions.

But the tide of support for what we do started to turn when public funding began to take the place of charity for the elderly and the poor, when we began to push back the average age of mortality, when our technological and procedural advances allowed us to achieve more in medicine than many believed we could afford to achieve. We began to see mounting opposition to many of our public policy interests. There are those in legislatures across our nation and in the halls of Congress who have made "reforming a rampaging and uncontrolled health care system" part of their ongoing social and political—especially political—agendas.

We have had to respond, to engage in the practices of influencing public policy that are as sophisticated in their design as have been our practices of delivering health care. We have developed state- and federal-level lobbying arms that are heavily supported through contributions to our professional associations. Our data bases have become as vital to our advocacy efforts as they are to our ability to monitor and refine the effectiveness of health care delivery itself. We have turned to public relations programs, as much to shed the light of public understanding on our status among social priorities as for any objectives of interdisciplinary or institutional competition.

These are resources we must draw on and refine with regard to establishing the benefits of rehabilitation in an expanded way for the benefit of the growing elderly population in our country. We need not reinvent the modality of most effectiveness; it is there, fully developed and refined and tested in the decades of physiatric experience. But it is not automatically drawn on in the treatment of millions of aging Americans.

The establishment of health care as a basic right of citizenship, as implied by the enactment of Medicare and Medicaid in the 1960s and in refinements and expansions of coverage under those programs since that time, has been a positive expression of what our society is and wants to be. It is now our responsibility to move beyond that, to move toward an enlightened program that considers the full environment, to become, in the words of our newly elected president, "a kinder and gentler America."

Part II

Autonomy of the Elderly Disabled

4

A Disabled Person Looks at Aging

Barry Corbet

It is common in our society to view approaching age an as implacable enemy, as something to be postponed, denied, and devalued. We often isolate and patronize those who are experiencing their old age, and when the reality is truly upon us, we hide it in hospitals, back rooms, and nursing homes. We are embarrassed by the finality of aging because it reminds us of our mortality.

Curiously, this response is not reserved for the aged alone. It is a daily phenomenon in the lives of people with disabilities. We too remind people of their worst fears, and society has visited upon us the same indignities it affords the aged. As a result of decades of this kind of experience, we have developed a point of view about aging that is slightly skewed. It is based not only on social response to our apparent differences but also on our long-term expectations.

Disability has long bestowed an excuse to live fast, love hard, and die young, and most of us expected to do just that. Fifty years ago, we died of our injuries. If we didn't die from our injuries, we died of complications soon thereafter. Our survival rate improved over time, but it was always assumed that our lives would be significantly abbreviated. So if we suppose for a moment that there is a single common view about aging from the disabled, which is only a little cavalier, we would see that it springs out of surprise—surprise that we're still here, and the delightful new surprise that suddenly we've got lots of company.

*Non*disabled Americans are getting older; they're living longer, there are vastly more of them, and they're getting old nonfatally. In short, they're becoming more disabled, more like us. All at once, it seems, there are a lot of formerly nondisabled people around.

We've had unlikely survivors before. Back in the late 1940s, when penicillin first became available to soldiers with spinal cord injuries, the nation's attention was galvanized when suddenly it realized that these people who used to die predictably were now going to live full life terms. Those early survivors taught us a lot, and survivors of polio have done similarly: they taught us that preservation of life is one thing, and quality of life is another.

It was not easy back in the 1940s and 1950s for society to decide that our lives were worth investing in, not at all obvious that our lives could be "meaningful," to use the term of the day. But somehow the affirmative decisions were made. When we made the switch from survival to quality of life, then rehabilitation was born.

People with disabilities, the early pioneers, have lived through the entire history of rehabilitation. Rehabilitation is what has allowed us to *be*, but the reverse is also true. We were the product, the assessed outcome, and we shaped rehabilitation as it shaped us.

And now we have this much larger population of people aging into their disabilities. Rehabilitation will change them and once again be changed *by* them.

This new group will need services, education, equipment, home support, environmental adaptation, and affordable help, just as we did decades ago. They too will live at risk of complications, live progressively closer to their physical limits. They will overstrain finite resources, outlive support groups, and face the sticky choices between custodial and home care. They will confront attitudinal barriers and limited opportunity. How will we respond? Will we once again agonize over whether rehabilitation is worthwhile or feasible or "legitimate"? Will the hard decisions about quality of life and justice need to be made all over again?

I would like to say that presumably they will not. I would like to say that these days we automatically feel that all life is worthy of investment, intrinsically worth caring for. But the truth is that, in the guise of economics, the same questions are being asked, the same barriers thrown up. We try to prove the cost-effectiveness of rehabilitation by multiplying a projected (and therefore highly suspect) quality of life assessment by life expectancy, and we come up short with those who become disabled in old age. The elderly often don't work, but we define meaningful and productive life only in limited terms of people generating income and paying back the system. We conclude that rehabilitation dollars make sense for a 20-year-old but that rehabilitation for the elderly somehow adds up to an inequitable raid on the resources of young America.

Most providers see late-blooming disabilities as acts of God, not as postsurgical events that could have been foreseen and financed as part and parcel of many common procedures. Acute care utilizes and reimburses a broader spectrum of institutional resources than does chronic care, so administrators tend toward selective admission policies. Federal medical spending cutbacks seem destined to continue; and as Medicaid cases become financially unattractive, hospitals drop them. If other providers pick up the slack, they often come to feel abused by the system and become less generous in providing care for the indigent. Alleged misuse of Medicare dollars by physicians, hospitals, and nursing homes taints care for the elderly with hints of unsavory practices. Employers and insurers shrink from underwriting any form of long-term care; they substitute restrictive "managed care" plans for traditional open-ended coverage. Prospective payment systems encourage early discharge, saving money in the short term but costing dearly in terms of long-term complications. It's nice that rehabilitation is exempt from DRG reimbursement, but the fact remains that many iatrogenic ailments are not. The national health care bill continues to drain the bank.

We want the best of everything for everyone, but we cannot seem to pay for it. It is easily foreseeable that assessing our willingness and ability to pay for geriatric rehabilitative care is going to be excruciating. The hard decisions will not only have to be made again, but they will have to be made in the face of stiffer opposition.

The question may not be whether we the society will care enough but whether those disabled in aging will care enough. If it was hard for those of us who acquired our disabilities at a very young age to realize that rehabilitation was a good idea, and it *was* hard, then how hard must it be for people who are in their 70s and 80s and 90s? After all, we'd have preferred a cure, and so will they. Rehabilitation may represent mere mitigation, a failure to heal.

Newly disabled older people will think that life is all over, just as we once did. They too will say they can't—won't—live with less function, less independence, less opportunity. They will wonder if they are really worth rehabilitating. Perhaps they will welcome some advice from those who have faced these considerations before.

THE OPTIONS GROUP

We who have lived our lives with the need for ongoing long-term health management have somthing to say to those who are just now beginning to need those services, as well as to those delivering them. Loss of mobility and physical impairment are old hat to most of us. We know about limitations, and we know about overcoming them. We understand human diversity, perhaps more than people who have never experienced being different. Some of us have learned to depend on others without losing our own identities. And some of us have learned how to grow old with a disability.

So I'd like to present the Options Group.

In a quarter century of work as a filmmaker, I've had the good fortune to meet a lot of people who acquired their disabilities long before I came on the scene. Many of these people were profiled in the book *Options* (Corbet, 1980), hence the name Options Group.

We are not a cohesive cohort but a peer group of strangers unified only by our disabilities and a common appearance in print. We have no organized structure or credo, no academic or clinical credentials. We do have a lot of experience in living with disabilities—22 years apiece, on average—and that experience tends to emerge anecdotally. From that information it is possible to draw some generalizations about life satisfaction, and perhaps some indications of how it might be for people who have become disabled in their later years.

Our quality of life, in our own estimation, is pretty good. That's not a very astounding remark because people tend to value what they perceive as being their own. "It's my life. I'd *better* like it." Even so, this group makes a statement about the quality of lives lived differently than anyone could have planned. The sum and substance of the message from the Options Group to the newly disabled and to health professionals is that life circumstances do not dictate life quality. They never did, and they don't now.

Even though science confirms that life satisfaction can remain high in the face of seemingly overwhelming obstacles and impairments, we seem to have trouble believing this when faced with a disability. There is a human tendency to believe that even if other people are content, *we* would perish or fail given the same circumstances. We think that people who cope well with disabilities are somehow faking it, distorting the reality, jollying themselves along. It is time for health care providers to overcome their own preconceptions—and concurrently those of their patients—about what are and are not acceptable circumstances. We need to celebrate the fact that the human spirit can and routinely *does* rise above what we perceive as impossibly cruel fate. This is not to say that living with a disability is easy, but it is to say that things can be hard and good at the same time. This is the rule, not the exception, and if providers can pass that message on to newly disabled consumers with conviction and high expectation, they will help to refute the pervasive postinjury fiction that life is over.

SHORTCOMINGS OF THE HEALTH CARE SYSTEM

People with disabilities have much more contact with the health care system than most consumers do, so it is not surprising that the Options Group has generated some critiques of the system. When I ask people if health care is getting better or worse, most tell me it is getting worse. They say that except for a few dazzling examples of continuing enlightened outlook, it is not as good as it was 10 or 15 years ago. They remember the ringing declarations of rehabilitation philosophy once heard so often about the interdisciplinary approach, the efficacy of prevention, the benefits of reevaluations—and find the real thing harder to find, not easier. Some feel that the Golden Years of Rehabilitation are long gone.

For this we blame absolutely everybody. Out of one side of our mouths we blame current cost-containment measures, and from the other we blame costs to the consumer that are beyond comprehension. We blame increasing specialization in medicine; we blame the emphasis on acute care over preventive care; we blame patronizing attitudes that dismiss our own accumulated expertise and autonomy.

We blame rehabilitation centers—Model Spinal Cord Injury (SCI) Systems included—for lax follow-up care and for atrocious long-term documentation. We can't predict where we're going because we don't know where we've been. We lament the fact that often we can't find state-of-the-art care locally but must look to distant locations. We particularly hate this cruel irony: that we must compete with newly disabled patients for services, and we must do so at a disadvantage. Providers are more interested in the early stages of disability than in the long term. And we'd really like to find more good old-fashioned spinal cord injury doctors who can orchestrate the activities of the specialists and the entire rehabilitation team. It is not an extinct species, it seems, but it is endangered.

Thirty, forty, and fifty years after our injuries, most of us do not receive health care through a rehabilitation center, do not schedule preventive reevaluations, and do not have a primary care physician to help us run the show. We would like to have these things, but we do not. Instead, we get our health care from specialists recruited one by one whenever and wherever we need crisis intervention. The specialists treat the symptoms or the dysfunction but not the entire person. They don't know each other, let alone talk to each other. For the great majority of us, there's nobody taking the broad long-term view.

So we manage our own health care. This may say something good about the concept of patient responsibility, but it also says something about the general unavailability of coordinated multidisciplinary health care in this country. It has implications for the newly disabled elderly, more perhaps than for anybody else, because coordinated health care is what they most urgently need. They need broad-spectrum interventions that make it possible for them to live as they are, in the world as it is, not brushfire suppression of organic disruptions. When that care is not delivered, we pay a terrible price in dollars and lost potential.

The Options Group has more specific complaints. Thirty-eight years after his injury, a man with C-7, C-8 quadriplegia says, "I feel that after all these years, I know a little bit about my body and how it functions. Some doctors respect this." He means that most do not. From a C-5, C-6 quadriplegic man, 30 years postinjury: "They know their specialty, but often they just can't relate it to what goes on in the rest of the body. That's wrong. It all works together." A woman with C-3, C-4 quadriplegia: "I've got to sit here and talk to them about an interdisciplinary approach as if I were the expert on this stuff. They're the ones who are supposed to understand that."

Uniformly, we feel that health providers would do well to temper what they know with what we know, to take advantage of what we have learned in many years of living with our disabilities. We are not dismayed so much because professionals have not learned what makes our bodies work but more because they often *think* they have. We are dismayed by specialists who cannot see beyond their reductionist expertise. We have come to love providers who have the grace to admit they don't know all things and who will join us in quest for workable answers.

WORKING WITH THE SYSTEM

People who acquire their disabilities in old age will face the same paternalism. Health providers will tell them what is good for them in terms of prevailing wisdom, but prevailing wisdom may not serve their specific situations or overall needs. So newly disabled consumers will have to reverse a lifetime of passivity with the health care system to become active participants. How can we help them do that?

How can one become a better-informed and more assertive consumer? Here is some advice from a woman with high quadriplegia on what she calls physician management: "I think physicians need to understand how disabled people see themselves in the world, and what place physicians occupy in that world of disabled people. You know, my mother and my ablebodied peers consult doctors once a year or so and take what is handed down to them with a great deal of awe and gratitude. That's fine for them, but I think of a good relationship with a physician as an amenity, like a good relationship with a clerk in a grocery store." She especially values a doctor who will respect her own knowledge of her condition and at least consider implementing whatever she thinks is appropriate treatment. "A quad of my level lives on the edge all the time, and I know I may lose the battle any day. What I don't need is a doctor who pussyfoots around with defensive medicine. What I do need is someone who will cooperate and try to figure out the best way to keep the train rolling."

Physician management is a contentious term, particularly to doctors, but we do need partnerships with our medical providers. People aging into their disabilities, along with their families, will need to learn how to forge these cooperative relationships.

From a T11 paraplegic man, 28 years postinjury: "I've always used doctors as a resource. I insist that they explain everything they're thinking, and anything that applies to me I think I have a right to know. Most doctors won't do that because if every patient asked them to do that they'd have no time left. So you have to convince them that you have a need for the information. A good doctor will generally go along with it, and maybe doctors dealing with SCI should encourage that more. People with disabilities need to be very good at knowing how things work or don't work."

When rehabilitation began as a specialty, it was characterized by flexibility and openness to whatever was practical for the individual. It didn't matter if something was done the right way; any way that worked was the right way. This was so because we were going bravely into the unknown. But now we have learned so much that rehabilitation is in danger of becoming ossified by its own aggrandized data base. The field needs to regain its freedom from the known and return to functional basics.

We—the aging disabled and the disabled aging—don't need something new; we need something old. What we need is a better and broader application of classical rehabilitation philosophy and practice. That is the challenge and the opportunity we see for geriatric rehabilitation.

Health professionals are not the only objects of our ire, and some issues keep reappearing. We'd like to see solutions to the high cost of durable equipment, aggravated by low third-party reimbursement; to the lack of affordable and accessible housing; to marriage penalties and work disincentives (still!); to reluctant mass transit authorities and airlines; to the "insurance crisis"; to the unremitting dissimulation of dealing with bureaucracies. People who acquire their disabilities in old age may express sudden amazement that these things have not already been resolved by a progessive society, and they will certainly need help confronting the truth that they have not.

It is not a terrible thing to have a disability, but some things about living with a disability are nevertheless truly terrible. If we ignore those realities, by way of being hopeful, then we miss much of the total situation. We are wantonly misinformed.

The Harris poll on disabled American's self-perceptions, taken in 1985, tells us that to have a disability is tantamount to having less of virtually all things. We have in our lives less education, less employment, less opportunity, less mobility, less social contact, less recreation, less entertainment, and less self-esteem. We work shorter days at lower wages. Many of us spend tens of thousands of dollars a year on our disabilities, money we might well have spent on food and shelter. According to the poll, we're the lowest-income minority in America. This will not be true for all people who become disabled with age, but disability will do little to enhance anyone's economic and social position.

Most people with disabilities foresee high medical costs at the end of a lifetime of economic forfeit, and we wonder how we'll pay for them. If we're retired early, unemployed, or self-employed, chances are we're uninsured and uninsurable. In this country, for a person with a disability, financing lifetime care is a very tall order. It will be similarly scary for people aging into their disabilities. The time frames are shorter, but sudden exposure to astronomical costs is devasting to anyone. How many of us are prepared to finance the consequences of a stroke?

There are other ongoing problems. Some of us need help with chronic pain and have for decades, but our treatment still consists of ignoring it, effectively repudiating it. That may be the best treatment we have, but it's nowhere near the best we can imagine. We feel that we've been showing the right stuff for years, but now it's old stuff. Newly disabled geriatric patients may feel equally insulted when they learn that it is considered appropriate to medicate terminal or acute pain but not chronic pain. They may feel overprotected from the bugaboo of addiction.

The issue of independence has always been, and remains, a burning issue for people with disabilities, and it becomes so with all aging people. But we're seeing a shift among the disabled. The concept of *relative independence* is coming into play—some kind of psychological independence that is not so desperately held as was our physical and economic independence during the early years. We're not such compulsive overachievers anymore, and we're better for it. I think we're more mellow about accepting help, feeling less alienated from our society as we all get older. That's gratifying. Aging is a great equalizer, and we're reaping some unexpected benefits from the graying of America. There's a vague sense of coming home, of being less Martian.

We're seeing an encouraging housing trend, instigated not by us but by all aging Americans. There is now a smorgasbord of living options for us—rental apartments, cooperatives, congregate housing, and continuing care facilities. Developers are focusing on the needs and desires of older people, which now include accessibility and functional independence.

Because some of us started off our disabled lives warehoused in nursing homes, sometimes for years, we're terrified of going back to one. But that old specter is now more diffuse. The need for help is no longer labeled as the problem, but rather the loss of control. If personal control can be maintained, we're thinking, quality of life may follow. And the fact that most of us are not in nursing homes after all these years should be encouraging to those who have recently become disabled. Disability, even when lifelong, is not a signal that choiceless dependence will follow.

The Options Group hopes that rehabilitation will apply its greatest lesson—that disability does not exist in a social vacuum—to the elderly disabled. We know that lack of family support, housing, opportunity, respite, social services, and financial incentives all have unhealthy consequences that are directly observable in the lives of people aging with disabilities, just as they will be for people aging *into* disabilities. What the first group has needed for decades is now required by the second. We hope that geriatrics and rehabilitation, the two *caring* specialties, can rise to meet the challenge of treating people and lives, not just bodies.

And we hope that we have finally put to rest the notion that adjustment has an end point. It does not—no more than the idea of "Justice for All" has an end point.

REFERENCE

Corbet, B. (1980). *Options: Spinal cord injury and the future.* Denver: A. B.
    Hirschfeld Press.

5

Independent Living Rehabilitation: Concepts and Practices

James Budde

Independent living is a popular concept that has broad implications for the fields of rehabilitation and aging. However, the overall concept varies in meaning and application across various disciplines, fields, and services. Independent living developed from a consumer-oriented movement that began about 1960, involving a number of new and novel concepts and practices. Many of those ideas and methods have merit for the field of aging, and some transfer is beginning to occur. Independent living concepts and practices have also occurred in various disciplines concerned with the field of aging. Continued development and refinement will occur in the future because the concept of independence has broad implications for this country's economic base and for citizens of all ages.

The overall concept of independent living rehabilitation includes three integral components: facilitating attainment of valued life outcomes, facilitating valued levels of independence, and consumer control. Facilitating attainment of valued life outcomes is achieved through *environmental support*. Facilitating valued levels of independence is achieved through *non-dependency-creating services*. Facilitating consumer control is an approach in itself, but it is included in both environmental support and non-dependency-creating services. Each of these concepts is interrelated; the combined use of all three produces a synergistic effect.

CONCEPTS

Independent Living and Independent Living Rehabilitation

The idea of independent living was formulated by persons with disabilities and by early leaders who were concerned about the repression of the disabled and the consequent diminished quality of life. They felt that people with severe disabilities should take responsibility for their lives and live in and contribute to their community like any other citizens. In the late 1950s and early 1960s, persons with severe disabilities had limited options. They typically had to be satisfied with life outcomes (Budde & Bachelder, 1986) such as living with their families or in constant-care facilities. This situation is paralleled by that of persons who are considered fragile elderly. Both groups are living longer because of medical advances and increasing life spans, but both often lack options and the autonomy needed to attain life outcomes that they value (cf. Corbet, Chapter 4, this volume).

Being unable to attain valued life outcomes has detrimental effects. For example, being forced to live with one's family can cause family hardship or erosion of self-dignity. Being forced to live in a constant-care facility is often costly and limits opportunities for independence. This is not to say that living with one's family or in a constant-care facility is an inappropriate life outcome for everyone. Living with one's family in a constant-care facility, or independently in one's home are all life outcome options on a continuum. However, a critical problem occurs when individuals cannot attain valued life outcomes because there are no options or because they are forced to select life outcomes they *do not* value.

Another dimension interrelated with independent living is the degree to which individuals choose to depend on others or want others to depend on them. It involves selecting levels of interdependence (Goldenson, 1978; Thibaut & Kelly, 1961; Wright, 1983), or what is generally called independence.

If individuals cannot choose life outcomes that they value or the level of independence that they elect, it is not possible to live independently. Consequently, the process and outcome of making choices autonomously, pursuing and attaining various life outcomes and levels of independence, is described as independent living (Budde & Bachelder, 1986).

Independent living rehabilitation (ILR) can be defined as the process of assisting individuals to attain independent living; it involves (1) developing new options that individuals can use to attain their valued life outcomes, (2) assisting individuals to attain valued levels of independence, and (3) facilitating autonomy of individuals to choose and pursue both.

Environmental Support

Any individual who has ever thought about being trapped between floors in an elevator realizes that without control of one's environment one cannot reach a desired destination. Such an individual might even speculate on various levels of helpless emotions or stress that would be experienced during the time spent trapped in the elevator. The same can be true for persons who are elderly and have disabilities. If our society does not provide options and allow them to seek their desired options and autonomy, their ability to attain their independent-living life outcomes will be limited. If our society is not accessible or if it does not provide functional options, it impedes community participation and independent living. Attainment of independence and life outcomes can be restricted socially and physically (Budde & Bachelder, 1986). Conversely, independent living can be enhanced or facilitated socially or physically, resulting in environmental support. Without this environmental support it is difficult (if not impossible) to provide successful ILR.

Social mores dictate the level of freedom and opportunity allowed to the elderly or persons with disabilities. If society believes that all persons over age 65 who have disabilities cannot make decisions rationally or care for themselves then those people will be treated as inept individuals who require continuous supervised care. There would be a proliferation of continuous-care facilities.

On the other hand, if society believes that individuals who are elderly and have disabilities should be treated with dignity and accorded the rights of other citizens, they will be treated like other citizens. There would be a expansion of accommodations and options that facilitate independent living and the least restrictive environment.

If society believes that all individuals who are elderly and have disabilities should be given the opportunity to live independently, that belief or perception will facilitate physical environmental support. Physical barriers would be removed through alterations of the physical environment, including handicapped parking, ramps, accessible bathrooms, and curb cuts. Removing physical communication barriers is achieved through accommodations such as brailled menus and floor numbers in elevators and use of telephone typewriters or telephone devices for individuals with hearing impairments. Options would be developed through low-cost, accessible housing, personal attendant care, accessible public transportation, and disability benefits that are necessary for independent living.

In ILR, staff, administrators, board members, volunteers, and consumers work together to improve both the social and physical environment. Independent living centers (ILCs) devote 20% to 80% of their time to improving the community environment (Berkeley Planning Associates et al., 1986). Environmental support is not only recognized in the independent living field but is facilitated through various activities that are included in the 1978 Amendments to the Rehabilitation Act of 1973.

Non-Dependency-Creating Services

Individuals who hear about ILR for the first time may think it is an accessible housing project where individuals with disabilities live and receive services that meet all of their needs. That is contrary to the concept of ILR. Rather, services are designed to enable individuals with disabilities to live independently in a setting and with individuals of their choosing. For example, an ILC would help an individual with a disability to locate an accessible, affordable residence in the community. It might help the individual to obtain personal care assistance, financial benefits, peer support, or the skills training needed to live in the residence. The ILC would not establish and operate a housing service such as a group home.

The intent of the non-dependency-creating service is to assist individuals to live independently but not to do the things for their consumers that consumers must do themselves to live independently. For example, an ILC would not train and manage attendants to perform personal care services for their consumers. The non-dependency-creating approach would be to help consumers train and manage their own attendants.

Emphasis is placed on getting agencies or organizations that are responsible for other community services to provide services using non-dependency-creating approaches. For example, rather than providing accessible transportation, an ILC would help a private business to establish the service. They would help the business obtain funds, set up a transportation board, and train drivers.

Without consumer control, it can be difficult to ensure non-dependency-creating services. The example of working with a private business to develop and provide accessible transportation seems like a good idea. However, in a real situation the owner dismissed the transportation board (containing some consumers), would not train new drivers, provided poor service to individuals with disabilities, and used the buses for other services a large portion of the time. As a last resort, the ILC developed its own transportation service, but it assumed responsibility to operate transportation service only until it could get the city or another agency to provide accessible transportation.

Consumer control is an essential factor in ILR. Individuals cannot become independent unless they make their own decisions and take responsibility for their own lives. If this does not occur, the individual gives up responsibility, and society takes on a costly and often nonproductive role. Even when individuals make decisions and take responsibility, they must have an environment that supports their independent-living goals. Even with consumer control and a supportive environment, some individuals need assistance. Non-dependency-creating services are used to assist individuals to attain their independent-living goals. Consumer control, a supportive environment, and non-dependency-creating services are all essential links in ILR. Alone, each can facilitate some independent living, but together they produce a synergistic approach that can facilitate total independent living.

Consumer Control

Consumer control is the vanguard of independent living. The concept is so prevalent that it is found in all popular, contemporary independent-living definitions (Budde & Bachelder, 1986; DeJong, 1979; Frieden, 1978; Stoddard, 1978). The concept is also operationalized throughout ILR practices.

In ILR, consumer control denotes that individuals are not mere recipients of service or treatment (DeJong, 1979). Individuals with disabilities who use independent-living services are called consumers. They use services as any citizen would use the services of a private business. Control is gained as consumers select options and services or participate significantly in decisions about services that will enable them to live independently according to their needs and goals.

In ILR, it is recognized that consumers best know their needs and goals and must take responsibility for acquiring and using options and services that enable them to attain their valued level of independence or life outcomes. Individuals are never viewed as too disabled or too old to make their own decisions or to take responsibility for their own lives. They are treated with dignity and attended to as though they were customers in a store who were about to make a substantial purchase.

The concept of controlling one's own life is highly valued by our society. Individuals who do not take control are viewed as weak or inept. Because persons with disabilities are stigmatized as being too weak or inept to make decisions, forced choice is a characteristic of our society for that group (Hamilton, 1976). Similar stigmata are often associated with older persons. Thus, service providers, parents, spouses, and administrators often use their personal values or needs or their perception of what is appropriate as the basis for making decisions for others or to force decisions. In some situations, where there are clear competency deficits, it may be necessary to make decisions for an individual. Certainly, this is true for individuals with advanced Alzheimer's disease.

If one forces another to make a decision, both parties will likely experience excess problems as the result of the process. When others make decisions for an individual or force an individual to make a decision, it can lead to attempts to regain freedom of choice (Brehm, 1966; Wicklund, 1974), increased unattractiveness or devaluation of the option being forced on the individual (Hammock & Brehm, 1966), or antagonism (Apsler, 1972) and hostility (Worchel, 1971). Although forced choice can cause individuals to comply with the decisions of others (Frank, 1961; Milgram, 1974), it impedes independent living and can eventually create learned helplessness (Seligman, 1975).

A variety of reasons have been given to justify making decisions for others. Some include opposing values, feeling that the decision-making process takes too long or is too expensive, or they lack the knowledge or skills to help others to make decisions. Another reason is lack of courage to say no when dependent clients or family members ask that decisions be made for them. Although these reasons explain why decisions are made for others, they do not justify making those decisions.

When individuals cannot make decisions autonomously and thereby give up responsibility for their lives, society must take on that responsibility. This often results in costly dependency-creating services, with others making decisions or performing tasks that the disabled individual could make or perform. There is a high cost for services society must bear and also high personal costs to the individuals.

A comparison of an expert decision maker and an ordinary citizen demonstrates little difference in the way they think. The variation is in the information the expert possesses (Fischoff, 1983). Professionals from various disciplines are becoming more facilitative of autonomous decision making. They use their years of training and experience to help those they serve to make informed decisions. Many interdisciplinary teams assist those they serve to use their combined team knowledge to make informed decisions. They use jargon-free information, explain alternatives, and provide prognoses for various alternatives.

There are instances when others should be involved in the decision-making process. For example, a family might get to point in life where a member's disability requires considerable personal care from other family members. In this instance, all of the family might be involved in a decision-making process designed to decide if a personal care attendant is to be employed. If it becomes difficult for family members to express their views, obtain needed information, or use a rational decision-making process, a trained counselor could become a major resource in helping the family resolve its problems.

Although decision making is critical for consumer control, it is only one variable. Consumer control involves having the knowledge and the will to take responsibility and develop or use options that facilitate independent living. At the highest level it involves improving society so that all persons who are included in elderly and disability populations have the opportunity to live independently.

PRACTICE

Short History of ILR

Historically, potential consumers of independent living services led the effort to establish a new approach. Many had lived independently prior to disability caused by a war, an accident, or disease. Others who had disabilities from birth or from an early age had lived in a rich environment that enabled them to develop values or practices that facilitated independence. As self-perceived consumers, many of these citizens sought and facilitated development of services and options that would enable them to attain valued life outcomes or levels of independence. Life outcomes typically included (but were not limited to) living in one's own home with an attendant, roommate, spouse, or family and participation in community life.

One of the earliest examples of developing new ILR approaches came in 1962, when four students with severe disabilities were transferred from an isolated constant-care facility to an accessible residence closer to their campus at the University of Illinois at Champaign-Urbana. This development provided the students with access to an education and an opportunity for higher levels of independent living. The students also helped to make the campus accessible and developed some of the first self-help and ILR policies that promoted ILR. In the 1970s the idea of an ILC (as an expansion of the Illinois program) was put into practice at the University of California at Berkeley. Again, it involved a sizable number of persons with disabilities. The expansion included refinement of consumer control, development of new options through environmental support, and non-dependency-creating services. The Berkeley demonstration project led to the development of two other ILCs in Boston and Houston. By 1980 the demonstration ILCs had become so popular that Congress decided to expand the centers so that people with disabilities throughout the United States could be assisted to live independently. This was accomplished through Title VII, Part B, of the Rehabilitation Act of 1978. Today 180 ILCs are funded through Title VII, Part B, and approximately 150 other ILCs are funded through state and other sources.[1] Each year these ILCs serve more than 104,000 persons with disabilities (Berkeley Planning Associates et al., 1986).

Persons over the age of 60 participated in the services of ILCs. In the sample population used by Berkeley Planning Associates to evaluate the ILC program, 10.8% were found to be between 61 and 70 years of age, and 10.8% were over the age of 71. Thus, about 22% of all ILC consumers are over the age of 61. Although persons in the aging population who have disabilities use a good portion of the services, they also benefit from community development activities such as making communities accessible or monitoring misuse of handicapped parking.

One way to serve individuals who are elderly and have disabilities is to refer them to ILCs. Another is to use some successful ILR approaches in other services to the aged. The ILC approach can be used within a variety of disciplines and settings, including those that use interdisciplinary practices.

ILC Methods and Techniques

In ILR, a variety of nontraditional activities are used to remove social and physical barriers and develop independent living options. Standards have been developed for the activities (Budde, Lachat, Lattimore, Jones, & Stolzman, 1987) in order to facilitate quality and uniformity.

Community and systems advocacy is the practice of improving the social and physical environment through negotiation, demonstration, confrontation, collaboration, and other methods. Leaders and coalitions identify, track, and influence action that could facilitate or impede independent living. Effective action results in improved agreements, contracts, policies, and laws, or their enforcement. Community and systems advocacy is commonly used to remove physical barriers and develop options. For example, an ILC might advocate for higher fines for handicapped parking violations or for economical accessible public transportation. A variety of advocacy approaches have been used by various groups and organizations across the nation to achieve these ends.

Public awareness is the dissemination of information designed to promote positive portrayals of individuals with disabilities or to develop understanding of their needs. For example, an ILC might make a number of presentations about how individuals with disabilities serve as leaders in community organizations. A variety of techniques are used for public awareness. They include television and radio spots, public speaking, billboards, newspaper articles, and newsletters.

Technical assistance is a process in which expertise is used to help others improve the social and physical accessibility of a business or public facility on request. Upon completion of the assessment, they make recommendations or provide information to make and finance accessibility improvements.

Outreach is a marketing process used to inform consumers and service providers about ILC services and resources. For example, an ILC developed and implemented a marketing plan to ensure that potential consumers were aware of available services.

Community involvement is a process of establishing and putting into action community roles for individuals with disabilities. The goals are to provide opportunities for individuals with disabilities and to enable them to become role models for their peers and society. For example, an ILC advocated for and obtained a mayor's committee on disability issues. Individuals with disabilities were appointed to membership and leadership positions on the committee. The experience was designed to stimulate interest, develop skills, and lead to participation in other community activities.

Concepts of Methods

Non-dependency-creating services are designed to enable consumers to become independent. There are traditional services, such as transportation, equipment repair, and skills training, but there are additional services, such as peer counseling, individual advocacy, personal care attendant management, and housing assistance, that focus on developing autonomy. Regardless of whether services are classified as traditional or novel, they are designed to meet specific needs of persons with severe disabilities, many of whom live below or near the poverty level.

Independent living needs fall into two categories (Budde, Petty, Nelson, & Couch, 1986): (1) survival and (2) higher levels of independent living. During a pilot study, investigators at the Research and

Training Center on Independent Living at the University of Kansas asked nondisabled subjects what they needed to live independently. Most said, "Enough money." However, when the same question was asked of subjects with disabilities, they said they needed accessible housing and transportation. They also said they needed personal care assistance and enough income. Housing, transportation, personal care assistance, and adequate income are all needed in our society for survival (Budde et al., 1986; Fawcett et al., 1989; Suarez de Balcazar, Bradford, & Fawcett, 1988). Thus, ILR has evolved to the point where services have been developed on a priority basis to address the survival needs of individuals with severe disabilities. If survival needs can be met, attention is then given to higher-level needs, such as employment, education, or recreation.

Individual advocacy involves the application of an array of procedures by persons with disabilities to represent their interests and achieve their independent living goals, legal rights, or benefits. ILCs assist consumers to advocate through training, information, encouragement, and interventions.

Housing assistance is a process of aiding consumers to acquire subsidized, affordable, or accessible housing or to modify housing so that it meets consumers' needs. Housing information, matching, and referral services are used to assist consumers to achieve housing goals.

Transportation services involve various accessible modes that enable consumers to get to their destinations on time. Although some ILCs provide transportation, they generally advocate for communities to provide this costly but vital service. ILC transportation is often reserved for emergencies, access to the center, or destinations not included in other community services. Some ILCs pool their services with area offices on aging.

Personal care services are typically used to enable consumers to obtain, employ, and manage their personal care attendants. Some centers provide lists of personal care aides and assist with abuse problems.

Peer counseling is a helping process that uses persons with disabilities as counselors, advisors, mentors, and role models. It provides information and social support that enable consumers to clarify and achieve their independent living goals.

Skills training involves individual and group instruction designed to help consumers acquire skills needed to live independently. Training involves areas such as daily living tasks, nutrition, budgeting, social skills, and so on.

Employment service is designed to enable consumers to become employed. It often involves assisting consumers with training and placement services, such as state vocational rehabilitation services. Prevocational and job-readiness training are also used.

Other services found at some ILCs include family counseling, equipment repair and tryout, recreation, education, and communication.

Consumer Control

In ILR, the terms of *self-help*, *autonomy*, and *empowerment* are associated with consumer control. These terms and others, such as *individual strength, courage, vigor*, and *authority*, define the essence of consumer control. Consumer control is the desire, ability, and right to govern one's life. It is the process of pursuing and attaining independent-living goals of one's choosing. It also involves making society a better place for others. Although consumer control might seem like an unquestionably correct pursuit, it can be difficult to achieve.

Today's parents, children, and professionals place a high value on consumer control. However, it is still necessary to be alert and sensitive. Families who are sorry for or choose to protect members who are elderly or have disabilities can impede consumer control, even though they feel that they are doing the right thing. For example, an elderly mother made decisions for her son who had had a disability all of his life. When she died, the middle-aged son did not know what to do. The stress of identifying and choosing a new residential outcome was so high that it led to medical problems and hospitalization. In another instance, a daughter felt she must bathe her disabled father herself, even though he protested, rather than help him to acquire and manage an attendant who could perform the bathing task. Professionals can also use their authority to impede consumer control. For example, a physician informed the spouse of an elderly person with a disability that the individual should be put in a continuous-care facility for the benefit of the family, without consulting the individual *or* the family. For some, use of the continuous-care option may be viable, but for others it may not be. In either instance, a single recommendation by an authority figure can put a family or individual in a forced-choice situation.

Numerous examples have demonstrated that the individuals who are elderly and severely disabled can control their lives and contribute in many ways to their families and society. Although some individuals might not appear to be able to control their lives and live independently, decisions should be left to them. It might even be necessary to provide information, support, or skill training to enable a consumer to make decisions about independent living. Individuals who are elderly and have disabilities should be afforded the rights of any other citizen. These include the dignity or the risk of making decisions—even if the decisions prove to be wrong.

There is an unwritten code of ethics in ILR that affirms that the consumer being served makes the decisions. During initial orientation to services, consumers are informed that they will be presented with information and options but that they will make the final decision. After selection of goals or a course of action, the staff is limited to providing assistance reinforcing the individual assumption of responsibility and the learning of skills and strategies needed to live independently. Only in a crisis situation should an intervention be provided that facilitates independent living. For example, a consumer might be experiencing immediate eviction from an apartment because of his or her disability and might be totally unprepared to advocate on his or her own behalf. The staff might intervene by providing individual advocacy. After the crisis has passed or during the process, ILR services providers would assist the consumer in learning the skills necessary to become an effective advocate.

Skill building plays a major role in consumer control. Individuals with disabilities can be assisted to develop a variety of skills that are tailored to each individual. Training can involve traditional independent-living skills such as budgeting, activities of daily living (ADL), personal medical care, and so on. But skill training often involves nontraditional skills, such as advocacy or decision making.

Role modeling is another approach. Directors, staff, volunteers, and consumers at ILCs serve as role models. Consumers experience social learning such as that described by Bandura (1977). They observe action and the effects of that action by their role models. Then consumers are more likely to adopt higher-level values and goals. They will be more willing to try new and bolder strategies.

One approach to enhancing consumer control that is not used in any formal way in ILR is to increase an individual's internal locus of control. Individuals who believe that they can control their environment, rather than that the environment controls them, have an internal locus of control (Stricklund, 1978). It has been demonstrated that an individual's locus of control can be changed from external to internal. Although there are no research studies to validate changes from external to internal or increases in levels of internal locus of control at ILC's, field observations have led the author to believe that internal locus of control may be enhanced. No single variable appears to increase internal locus of control.

ILR employs several practices to promote consumer control beyond the individual level. One method involves integrating individuals with disabilities into management. Strong affirmative action is used to recruit, employ, and promote individuals with disabilities within ILCs. Consumers are also involved on boards of directors. The 1984 amendments to the Rehabilitation Act of 1973 require that 51% of the ILC board of directors be individuals with disabilities. Including consumers in a number of community and national activities (usually advocacy efforts) is another means designed to improve the overall service system while enhancing the image of persons with disabilities.

ILR In One's Home Environment

ILCs provide one needed alternative in the ILR continuum; other disciplines and services also provide needed alternatives. Home service is a critical alternative that is used for individuals who have serious limitations and wish to remain in their homes as long as they choose.

There are many in the aging population who might like to attain the independent-living goal of full community participation but cannot because of serious limitations. Chronic conditions, such as hip fractures, strokes, and sensory impairments, create serious functional limitations that often restrict individuals to activities that occur in or near their homes. Psychological limitations can accompany functional loss or further restrict independent living. Younger individuals with progressive disabilities, such as advanced muscular dystrophy, multiple sclerosis, or other severe disabilities, experience similar functional and psychological limitations. For this population, the concept of independent living must be expanded. It is necessary to perceive independent living as the maximum level of care, dignity, and autonomy that one chooses to achieve in one's immediate environment.

With progressive and chronic illness an individual's environment becomes more restrictive. Both the degree and number of functional limitations in ADL increase with age. The progression seems to move from an inability to perform heavy work or activities outside one's home to the inability to carry out activities inside the home. Ultimately, ability in self-care activities decreases, and assistance from other individuals is required for personal care.

Interventions

Individuals with loss of ADL or functional status can attain and maintain chosen levels of independence through interventions that involve use of equipment, therapy, and help from other individuals. Functional status is becoming more readily accepted than health status for planning interventions because individuals with disabilities define health status in terms of their ADL independence levels. The intervention goal is to restore functional or environmental status or to maximize remaining functional status in areas that the individual views as having priority. This can be done with the assistance of others or with equipment. Assessment needed to develop interventions involves direct participation of the individual, who determines the relationship of his or her functional loss to his or her priority goals.

As new needs appear or as old needs become more complex, personal assistance is combined with health, nutritional, communication, social, and other interventions. Some of the service interventions might be provided by ILCs. For example, home services might be coordinated with housing or a benefit service provided by an ILC. Service collaboration could also involve other organizations, such as Meals-on-Wheels, visiting nurses, or rehabilitation hospitals.

An organized interdisciplinary or multidisciplinary approach is required to manage intervention involving multiple needs. The individual benefiting from the intervention should be a key participant and decision maker in the process. Team member sensitivity to individual need and autonomy promotes trust, confidence, and independent living.

Financing

For the most part, rehabilitation in one's home is possible only if funds are available to provide needed services and equipment. Title XVIII of the Social Security Act provides for Medicare funding used by various agencies for home rehabilitation. In some states, Medicaid may also provide support. The only other significant existing source is personal or family finances.

Personal care assistance is a critical variable in independent living. Of the approximately 6 million individuals who receive personal care, less than one sixth receive some financial help from home-based, publicly funded programs. However, efforts are being undertaken to extend personal care assistance to the elderly.

In the 100th Congress, 1986 to 1988, several proposals were advanced by House and Senate leadership to provide the disabled elderly with funding for home care services (see Brody, Chapter 2, this volume).

Personal care will need to be expanded to personal assistance. Efforts are currently underway to improve legislation so that assistive tasks such as shopping can be included. In addition, payment for assistance could be made to family members who perform the tasks.

A recently passed law, the Technology-Related Assistance for Individuals with Disabilities Act of 1988 (PL 100-407), is designed to improve the use and availability of technology. Individuals with disabilities are required to be involved in a state's effort to identify assistive technology needs of individuals, identify resources to improve service delivery, provide assistive technology devices and assistance, and provide training and technical assistance to use assistive devices.

Even with the level of available and proposed support, neighbors, spouses, friends, and family will continue to play a critical role in personal care. Most provide the care on an informal basis without pay. Expanded personal care assistance services are undoubtedly needed, but so are recognition of and assistance to those who provide and will continue to provide personal care without remuneration.

CONCLUSION

ILR is in its formative years, a time that has seen many barriers and some significant successes. The momentum gained in this field will likely persist, and new approaches and technology will continue to be developed to meet the changing needs of increasing numbers of disabled elderly. If society's understanding of the value of autonomy for the disabled elderly and for their potential continues to mature, greater opportunities will be afforded. ILR can be a strong force in enabling this country to pass the test of a great nation: integration, equality, and freedom for the aged and persons with disabilities.

NOTE

1. *Director of Independent Living Programs*, ILRU Research and Training Center on Independent Living, aTIRR: 3400 Bissonnet, Suite 101, Houston, TX, 77005; $8.50 including updates.

REFERENCES

Apsler, R. (1972). Effects of the draft lottery and a laboratory analogue on attitudes. *Journal of Personality and Social Psychology, 24*, 262–272.

Bandura, A. (1977). *Social learning theory*. Englewood Cliffs, NJ: Prentice-Hall.

Berkeley Planning Associates, Research and Training Center on Independent Living, and Center for Resource Management . (1986). *Comprehensive evaluation of Title VII, Part B: Centers for independent living programs* (Final Contract No. 300–84–0209). Washington, DC: Rehabilitation Services Administration, Office of Special Education and Rehabilitation.

Brehm, J. W. (1966). *A theory of psychological reactance.* New York: Academic Press.

Budde, J. F., & Bachelder, J. L. (1986). Independent living: The concept, model, and methodology. *Journal of the Association for Persons with Severe Handicaps, 2*(1), 240–245.

Budde, J. F., Lachat, M. A., Lattimore, J. L., Jones, M. L., & Stolzman, L. (1987). *Standards for independent living centers.* Lawrence, KS: University of Kansas, Research and Training Center on Independent Living.

Budde, J. F., Petty, C. R., Nelson, C., & Couch, R. (1986). Evaluating the impact of independent living centers on consumers and the community. *Journal of Rehabilitation, 52*(3), 39–43.

DeJong, G. (1979). *The movement for independence: Origins, ideology, and implications for disability research* (monograph). East Lansing, MI: Michigan State University, University Center for International Rehabilitation.

Fawcett, S. B., Suarez de Balcazar, Y., Whang-Ramos, P. L., Seekins, T., Bradford, B., & Mathews, R. M. (1989). The concerns report: Involving consumers in planning for rehabilitation and independent living services. *American Rehabilitation, 14*(3), 17–19.

Fischhoff, B. (1983). Predicting frames. *Journal of Experimental Psychology, 9,* 103–116.

Frank, J. (1961). *Persuasion and healing.* Baltimore: Johns Hopkins Press.

Frieden, L. (1978). Independent living: Movement and programs. *American Rehabilitation, 3*(6), 6 –9.

Goldenson, R. M. (1978). Independent living: Ways and means. In J. R. Bunhan (Ed.), *Disability and rehabilitation handbook.* New York: McGraw-Hill.

Hamilton, D. (1976). Cognitive biases in the perceptions of social groups. In J. S. Carroll & J. W. Payne (Eds.), *Cognitive and social behavior.* New York: Lawrence Erlbaum Associates.

Hammock, T., & Brehm, J. W. (1966). The attractiveness of choice alternatives when freedom of choice is eliminated by social agents. *Journal of Personality, 34,* 546–555.

Milgram, S. (1974). *Obedience to authority.* New York: Harper & Row.

Seligman, R. M. (1975). *Helplessness.* San Francisco: W. H. Freeman.

Stoddard, S. (1978). Independent living: Concepts and programs. *American Rehabilitation, 3,* 2–5.

Stricklund, B. R. (1978). Internal/external expectancies and health related behavior. *Journal of Consulting and Clinical Psychology, 46,* 1192–1211.

Suarez de Balcazar, Y., Bradford, B., & Fawcett, S. B. (1988). *Common concerns of disabled Americans: Issues and options.* Lawrence, KS: University of Kansas, Research and Training Center on Independent Living.

Technology-Related Assistance for Individuals with Disabilities Act of 1988. 102, Statute 1044. Public Law 100–407, 100th Congress, p. 2201.

Thibaut, J. W., & Kelly, H. H. (1961). *The social psychology of groups.* New York: Wiley.

Wicklund, R. A. (1974). *Freedom and reactance.* Potomac, MD: Lawrence Erlbaum Associates.

Worchel, S. (1971). *The effects of simple frustration, violated expectancy, and reactance and the instigation to aggressions.* Unpublished doctoral dissertation, Duke University, Durham, NC.

Wright, B. (1983). *Physical disability: A psychosocial approach* (2d ed.). New York: Harper & Row.

Part III

The Practice Model: Mobility

6

Rehabilitation and Mobility of Older Persons: An Interdisciplinary Perspective

Jennifer M. Bottomley, Barbara Blakeney,
Terrence O'Malley, David G. Satin,
Helen Smith, and Margot C. Howe

Mobility problems in the elderly introduce multifactorial considerations involving psychosocial, medical, physical, and environmental components. The needs arising from mobility problems in the aged often require an interdisciplinary perspective to address all possible avenues for improving an individual functional status and enhancing quality of life.

This chapter addresses how goals of intervention are derived, the medical and disease issues relating to impaired mobility, rehabilitation and mobility issues that need to be addressed when caring for the elderly patient in light of the "normal aging process," and environmental and functional considerations that enhance mobility. The concept of an interdisciplinary team providing health care for an aging population is important when considering the multisystem changes in aging. An interdisciplinary team provides assessment and intervention from varying points of view. When all components of mobility problems are examined, the potential for enhancing maximal functional capabilities in the elderly is substantially increased.

GOAL DEVELOPMENT

There are two broad topics to be addressed in this section: the importance and derivation of the goals of intervention and the medical issues relating to impaired mobility.

The single most important determinant of intervention is a clear statement of the specific goals toward which the intervention is targeted. The goals are established primarily by the patient but are also influenced by members of the interdisciplinary team based on specific knowledge concerning cause, prognosis, and availability and effectiveness of interventions.

The establishment of these goals begins with a discussion with the patient concerning specific individual goals. For any particular impairment—an amputation, for example—the goals might range from reestablishing full function with complete mobility to developing the ability to turn in bed independently, without plans to transfer or ambulate. Where patients choose to set their goals within this range will depend on other associated impairments, motivation, and information regarding therapeutic options. The goals must be individualized.

Each member of the interdisciplinary team brings useful skills and information to the process of educating the patient to set appropriate goals. It is important that we view the process of establishing goals as negotiation rather than prescription. The patient brings the final prism through which the views of the team are refracted, rather than being the passive recipient of the projected views of the team.

Teaching this patient-oriented view of team functioning is best accomplished through actual case management sessions in which this approach is displayed. In this way, other less obvious benefits of the team approach become apparent. For example, each team member, at times, serves to remind the team to focus on the goals of the patient rather than on each member's individual goals. This principle of mutual support extends to interventions as well, when the collective energy of the team is directed toward achieving the patient's goals.

THE AGING PROCESS: EFFECTS ON MOBILITY

The "normal" process of aging accompanies and often complicates the functional capabilities of elderly individuals with other chronic mobility problems. There are changes in sight and hearing and changes in the physical areas of coordination, muscular strength, flexibility, and endurance. All of these factors alter the stimulus elderly individuals receive from their environment. They result in the inability to maintain safe functioning within their environment.

Vision

Vision is a noticeable area of change in the older person. Several changes occur within the aging eye. The lens begins to thicken and become yellow, and the muscles that control dilation of the pupil weaken. The thickening of the lens and delayed pupil dilation mean that the glare and reflections often encountered in the environment cannot be tolerated (Andreasen, 1985). The older person has difficulty with depth perception and color differentiation, which can interfere with activities of daily living (ADL), ambulation, and driving an automobile.

Hearing

Many elderly people have decreased ability to separate one sound or voice from the din of background noise as a result of normal aging changes of the ear. Specific effects of aging on the auditory system include a decrease in auditory acuity and poorer speech discrimination skills based on pure tonal losses (Marshall, 1981). In other words, as the ear ages there is a greater distortion of auditory signals.

Neuromuscular Changes

The nervous system is the communication system of the body. It relays information and initiates motor activity. A breakdown in the system can lead to less efficient communication and a slowing of the body's responses. It is important to consider the degenerative effects of the body of an aging nervous system. Neuromuscular changes with aging include deficits in coordination, strength, and speed of motion. With aging there is a loss of neurons, postmitotic cells that do not duplicate themselves (Gutman, 1972). Cell loss results in narrowing of the convolutions and widening of the sulci in the aging brain. Brain mass decreases by 10% to 20% by 90 years of age (Payton & Poland, 1983). The areas of the brain that show the greatest loss of neurons with normal aging are the frontal lobe (the area of cognition), the superior area of the temporal lobe (the main auditory area), the occipital area (the visual area), and the prefrontal gyrus (the major sensorimotor area of the brain) (Brody, 1979). A significant loss of neurons in any one area of the brain results in a decrease in function. The rehabilitation of an elderly individual is directly affected by these changes.

Compensation for cognitive, hearing, and visual decrements needs to be incorporated in the design of treatment programs. Diminished tactile sense often accompanies aging. Although sight and sound are the predominant means of communication, touch is an important physical sensory communicator and should be considered when designing a program for elderly patients. Information from receptors in muscles, joints, and the inner ear aid in movement and positioning. Decreased kinesthetic sensitivity owing to a general slowing and loss of receptor sensitivity in the elderly results in postural instability and difficulty in reacting to bodily position changes.

Muscle strength relative to neurological function is defined by the rate of motor unit firing, the number and frequency of motor unit recruitment, and the cross-sectional diameter of the muscle (Lewis, 1985). The effects of the aging process on the neuromuscular system are seen clinically in the areas of strength, speed, motor coordination skills, and gait. Muscular atrophy may be attributed to decreases in the quantities of both white and red fibers of the muscle (McCarter, 1978), as well as in the clear differentiation of fiber types: red fibers have an increased speed of contraction followed, as aging continues, by a decrease in the speed of concentration of white fibers (Gutman & Hanzlikova, 1976; Moritini, 1981). It has also been suggested that muscle weakness in aging is the result of an increasing proportion of skeletal muscle being replaced by fibrous tissue rather than free fat (MacLennan, Hall, & Timothy, 1980). There is a great variability in the amount of strength that is lost. Despite the obvious relationship between neuromuscular changes and loss of strength, disuse appears to play a very important role in determining the extent of strength decline in the elderly (Lewis, 1985). The loss of strength appears to result from changes in life-style and decreased use of the neuromuscular system (Ragen & Mitchell, 1980).

Speed of motion slows with aging and with disuse. Older individuals are slower on reaction-time tasks. Nerve conduction velocity decreases at a rate of approximately 0.4% per year starting at 20 years (Payton & Poland, 1983). It is important to remember that reaction-time tasks measure a very complex response pattern. Pathways involved in reaction-time responses include central processing, afferent pathways, and the effector organ (muscles). Sensory stimuli and cognitive functioning are intimately involved in reaction time.

There are significant differences between the young and the old on tests measuring coordination and fine motor skills (Murray, 1975). There is an increase in the "sway" noted for normal balance correction, diminishing the ability to maintain balance as effectively. As a result of this sway, gait changes are observed. A wide base of support is naturally employed to ward off balance loss. Declines in sensory input resulting from inactivity lead to sensorimotor deficits, which further alter gait patterns. The changes seen in the aging nervous system would compound disabilities that develop as a result of cognitive declines or superimposed chronic disabilities.

Musculoskeletal Changes

Musculoskeletal changes that occur with aging influence flexibility, strength, posture, and gait. Functional changes in life-style and inactivity impact on these age-related changes.

Collagen, the supportive protein in skin, tendon, bone, cartilage, and connective tissue, changes as one ages (Smith & Serfass, 1981). The collagen fibers become irregular in shape as a result of increased cross-linking with age (Smith & Serfass, 1981). This closer meshing and decreased linear relationship reduces the elasticity of the collagen fibers.

Inactivity also has been shown to decrease muscle and tendon flexibility. Full immobilization in bed results in loss of strength of approximately 3% per day (Payton & Poland, 1983). Increased time spent in sitting clearly affects the body's flexor muscles. Adhesions are more likely to develop if the flexors of the body are maintained in a shortened position for extended periods of time. This has been demonstrated in studies on astronauts, drawing many parallels between "aging" and "disuse" (Shepard & Sidney, 1987).

A decrease in lean muscle mass and changes in muscular function result from a variety of factors, including a decrease in efficiency of the cardiovascular system to deliver nutrients and oxygen to the working muscles and changes in the chemical composition of the muscle. Glycoproteins, which produce an osmotic force important in maintaining the fluid content of muscle tissues, are reduced in aging (Carlson, Alston, & Feldman, 1964). The inability of the muscle tissues to retain fluid results in hypotrophic changes observed in aging muscles. There is a decrease in the efficiency permeability of the muscle cell membrane. At rest there are high concentrations of potassium, magnesium, and phosphate ions in the sarcoplasm, while sodium, chloride, and bicarbonate ions are prevented from entering the cell. In the senescent muscle there is a shift in this resting balance, with a decrease in potassium. Lack of potassium in the aging muscle reduces the maximum force of contraction generated by the muscle (Gutman, 1972).

Decrease in total bone mass, or osteoporosis, is a characteristic change with age. Four times more women than men and 30% women over the age of 65 are osteoporotic (Payton & Poland, 1983). The older person with a poor nutritional history is at greater risk for this condition. Hormonal changes (seen with menopause in women) and circulatory changes (seen with decreased activity) also play a role in the development of osteoporosis. Though often asymptomatic, osteoporosis can be a major cause of pain, fractures, and postural changes in the musculoskeletal system (Lewis, 1985). Bone growth is enhanced by weight-bearing activities. The pull of muscle on bone enhances trabecular formation and increased bone strength at the site of muscle insertion. Exercise and ambulation are needed by all aging individuals to prevent the demineralization of bone that results from inactivity. Increased calcium intake and hormonal therapy in women also needs to be explored.

Balance, flexibility, and strength provide the posture necessary to ensure efficient ambulation. Poor posture in aging results from declines in flexibility and strength and bone changes, resulting in less safe gait patterns. Gait is the functional application of motion. Changes in the gait cycle seen in the elderly include the following (Lewis, 1985):

1. Mild rigidity (greater proximally than distally, producing less body movement).
2. Fewer automatic movements and a decreased amplitude and speed (such as arm swing).
3. Less accuracy of foot placement and speed of cadence.
4. Shorter steps as a result of changes in kinesthetic sense and slower rate of motor unit firing.
5. Wider stride width to enhance safety.
6. Decrease in swing-to-stance ratio (improving safety by allowing more time in the double-support phase).
7. Decrease in vertical displacement (usually secondary to stiffness).
8. Decrease in toe-to-floor clearance.
9. Decrease in excursion of the leg during swing phase.
10. Decrease in heel-to-floor angle (usually caused by lack of flexibility of the plantar flexor muscles and weakness of dorsiflexors).
11. Slower cadence (another safety mechanism).
12. Decrease in velocity of limb motions during gait.

Cardiovascular Changes

Exercise is a physical stimulus that produces a metabolic increase above the resting levels. In a healthy young individual the cardiovascular system responds quickly to increase the metabolic rate by increasing heart rate, stroke volume, and peripheral blood flow to deliver oxygen to the working muscles. The elderly show variation in these responses and demonstrate a delayed response time of the cardiovascular system in restoring homeostasis when the level of physical activity has been increased (Shepard, 1987). Elderly individuals have a lower resting cardiac output and basal metabolic rate, primarily caused by age-related loss of lean body mass (Smith & Serfass, 1981) and inactivity (Shepard, 1987). As exercise levels increase, the age-related reduction in heart rate and stroke volume (0.7% decrease per year after 30 years of age, from approximately 5L/min at 30 years to 3.5L/min at 75 years) manifest as reduced oxygen uptake (Ragen & Mitchell, 1980). In respiration there is a 50% decrease in the maximum volume of ventilation and 40% decrease in the vital capacity by the age of 85 (Payton & Poland, 1983). These limitations in oxygen transport capability translate directly into a reduced physical work capacity in the elderly person.

Falls

Falls, which are one extreme of impaired mobility, are most often a manifestation of the patient's general condition rather than the result of a specific illness. There are, however, specific neurological and cardiac causes that should be considered. Arrhythmias, seizures, cerebrovascular disease, and valvular heart disease represent the majority of potentially remediable causes. However, intervention usually is directed at removing extrinsic conditions that compromise the patient's limited postural competence and nonspecifically improving the patient's overall condition.

Falls are not part of the normal aging process. They are the result of an interaction of underlying physical dysfunction, medications, and environmental hazards (Christiansen & Juhl, 1987). Poor health status, impaired mobility from inactivity or chronic illness, postural instability, and a history of previous falls are observable risk factors in falling. The ultimate goals of rehabilitating elderly individuals are to combat inactivity and loss of mobility that predispose them to falls.

Some of the ad hoc measures currently used to prevent falls, such as physical restraints and medications to reduce activity, are now suspected of increasing the risk of falling (Christiansen & Juhl, 1987). With precautions of good basic patient and family education and modification of the environment to reduce hazards, it is often possible to prevent falls through methods that do not undermine mobility or autonomy. It is important to identify and treat reversible medical conditions and to identify and treat physical impairments in gait and balance. Many falls can be prevented through proper exercise to maintain strength, sensory integration techniques to promote all functional activities, good shoes and orthotics to provide a proper base of support, and gait training activities.

DISEASE AND MEDICAL ISSUES

The role of the medical consultant to the interdisciplinary rehabilitation team is to provide accurate diagnosis and to instruct the team and the patient concerning prognosis and potential impact of treatment. This includes the nature and cause(s) of the impairment(s) leading to altered mobility as well as associated conditions affecting survival, strength, and endurance.

It is important to remember that altered mobility and altered functional status in the elderly are often the nonspecific result of an illness or generalized condition such as pneumonia, urinary tract infection, dehydration, impaired nutrition, or cancer. If any condition results in decreased activity, then the effects of deconditioning are rapidly superimposed on the primary problem and cause further functional decline. As a result, there can be a cascading of an initial impairment of mobility from even minor illness.

There are two important clinical implications that result from these observations. The first is that early intervention and mobilization are essential if prolonged impairments are to be avoided. The second is that even brief illnesses unrelated to the musculoskeletal system can present with impaired mobility. Impaired mobility should be viewed as a marker for illness in the same way that changes in mental status and nutrition are nonspecific markers for illness.

There are several conditions that profoundly and directly affect mobility, are easily diagnosed without invasive testing, and respond to specific treatment. These are the potentially "reversible causes" of impaired mobility, and they are analogous to the reversible causes of dementia. These conditions can usually be diagnosed or excluded by bedside testing and confirmed with noninvasive testing (Table 6-1).

Drug Side Effects

Because mobility requires the coordinated interaction of the senses, brain, nerves, muscles, and joints, it is not surprising that many drugs can impair mobility by upsetting the delicate balance among these components by directly affecting one or more of them. A complete review of drug side effects on mobility is beyond the scope of this chapter, but some of the more significant and commonly encountered problems are listed in Table 6-2.

Table 6-1 Reversible Causes of Impaired Mobility

Drug side effects
Arthritis
Myopathy
Polymyalgia rheumatica
Neuropathy
Parkinson's syndrome
Cervical myelopathy
Normal pressure hydrocephalus

Drug side effects are probably the most common reversible cause of impaired mobility. Before an extensive workup for gait disorder is undertaken, all medications, prescription and over-the-counter, should be reviewed. Drug holidays are often effective ways to establish the diagnosis of drug side effects.

Table 6-2 Adverse Effects on Mobility from Commonly Used Drugs

Effect on mobility	Drugs
Impaired alertness	Sedatives (Valium®, Serax®, etc.)
	Antihistamines (Benadryl®, etc.)
	Narcotics (codeine, oxycodone)
	Alcohol (cough suppressants)
	Anticonvulsants (Dilantin®, Tegretol®, phenobarbital)
Impaired balance	Sedatives
	Antihypertensives (by orthostatic hypotension)
	Anticonvulsants
Impaired strength	Diuretics (by hypokalemia)
	Steroids (myopathy)
	Thyroid hormone (myopathy)
Impaired coordination	Sedatives
	Narcotics
	Anticonvulsants
Altered muscle tone	Neuroleptics (Haldol®, Mellaril®)
	Metochlopramide (Reglan®)
Impaired sensation	Nitrofurantoin (by peripheral neuropathy)
	Angiotensin-converting enzyme inhibitors (captopril, etc.) (by peripheral neuropathy)
	Disulfiram (by peripheral neuropathy)
	Diphenylhydantoin

Substances that are often misused or abused by elderly include prescription drugs; over-the-counter medications such as sleeping pills, pain medications, laxatives, and cough/cold medicines; alcohol; and caffeine. Often these misuses result in sleep disorders, behavioral changes, balance and coordination changes, and an altered nutritional status, all of which affect mobility.

Arthritis

Pain, weakness, and loss of joint movement secondary to arthritic changes in weight-bearing joints are the chief mechanisms by which arthritis affects mobility. Bedside diagnosis is usually not difficult because findings of joint deformity, crepitus, and limited ranges of motion are typical. Although the anatomical changes of degenerative joint disease can be altered only with surgery, joint functioning can often be enhanced with strengthening exercises, anti-inflammatory medications, analgesics, and adaptive devices. The presence of associated bursitis (hip and knee especially) should be sought because medically steroid injection is both safe and frequently effective in relieving the associated pain and, consequently, enhancing mobility. Physical therapy offers modalities such as heat, paraffin, interferential electrical stimulation, and oscillatory manual therapy techniques that decrease joint discomfort and enhance mobility of the joints in a less invasive way.

Myopathy

Muscle weakness and stiffness are the most frequent symptoms associated with myopathy. Disuse atrophy due to associated joint disease is probably the most common cause of weakness. This is not technically a myopathy, however, because there is no associated intrinsic muscle disease. Hypokinetics accelerate the loss of Type II fibers normally associated with the "aging process." Intrinsic muscle disease, such as muscular dystrophies, are not common in the elderly. Myositis, or an inflammation of the muscles, makes up most of the cases of myopathy in the elderly. Myositis most often presents with shoulder and hip girdle weakness. Individuals often have difficulty rising from a chair, ascending or descending stairs, lifting objects above shoulder level, or combing their hair. Mobility is affected by muscle imbalances. Typically, elders develop hypotonicity of the extensor muscles resulting from osteoporotic changes in the spine. The position of the thoracic spine in kyphosis, the cervical spine in hyperextension with a forward head, and the decrease of the lumbar spine in lordosis, all place a stretch on the extensor muscles of the back and hips, making them biomechanically less efficient.

On examination, myopathy can be suspected when there is a loss of proximal muscle strength greater than distal strength while peripheral nerve function remains intact. Diagnosis can be established by demonstrating elevated levels of muscle enzymes in the blood, characteristic changes on electromyography (EMG) and muscle biopsy. An accurate assessment of muscle imbalances, with emphasis on strengthening the weak, overstretched muscles and stretching opposing muscle groups, has been effective in preventing myopathic changes.

An unrelated condition that may mimic myopathy, polymyalgia rheumatica (PMR), is exclusively a disease of the elderly; it is characterized by hip and shoulder girdle stiffness and weakness. Although an arteritis, not a myositis, it presents with similar symptoms, is steroid-responsive, and often causes significant mobility impairments: muscle weakness, stiffness in the neck, and pain down both arms are common complaints. An elevated sedimentation rate is always present. PMR is sometimes associated with an inflammation of large to medium-size arteries, called temporal arteritis or giant cell arteritis. The presence of headache, temporal tenderness, or visual changes in a patient with symptoms of PMR suggests the need for further evaluation with temporal artery biopsy. Arteritis, if left untreated, results in irreversible blindness and consequent loss of mobility.

Neuropathy

Paresthesias, burning, or diffuse pain, usually involving the feet, lower legs, and then the fingers, is typically characteristic of neuropathy. The symptoms are most often associated with loss of deep tendon reflexes and vibration sense. Neuropathies affect mobility through pain and through the loss of proprioception, which makes walking and maintaining balance difficult. The most common neuropathies in the elderly are the result of diabetes, nutritional deficiencies (cf., Weg, Chapter 11, this volume), and pressure neuropathies. Diabetes can cause symmetrical polyneuropathies, autonomic neuropathies (associated with orthostatic hypotension and syncope), and mononeuritis multiplex, which results in asymmetrical nerve palsy, such as peroneal nerve injury, causing foot drop. Diagnosis of neuropathy can usually be made on clinical grounds alone and can be confirmed with nerve conduction studies. Appropriate laboratory studies can establish a reversible cause in a small percentage of cases.

Parkinson's Syndrome

When Parkinson's syndrome is fully developed, there is characteristic increased muscle tone, rigidity, difficulty initiating movement, and tremor that is abolished with intentional movement. The initial presentation, however, can be quite subtle: slightly stooped posture that gradually progresses, asymmetrical tremor, gradual loss of facial movement, and reduction of all spontaneous movements. Mobility is affected by ataxia, which limits gait safety; bradykinesia, which makes ADL cumbersome and slow; and tremors, which affect the individual's ability to rest. Gait disturbances such as shuffling, forward leaning, scissoring, balance and coordination deficits, and ataxia lead to falls in the elderly. When Parkinson's syndrome is superimposed on the aging process, mobility can become severely limited.

Neuroleptic drugs such as Haldol® frequently cause reversible Parkinson's syndrome. Other causative agents include metochlopramide (Reglan®) and reserpine. Parkinson's disease is a progressive degenerative disease of the central nervous system. Treatment includes removal or reduction of offending drugs, initiating physical and occupational therapy, and using drugs that either increase the amount of dopamine in the brain (i.e., L-dopa), mimic the actions of dopamine (bromocriptine), or block the competing cholinergic neurons (amantadine).

Cervical Spondylosis

Impingement on the cervical spinal cord by bony spurs or ruptured disks results in a progressive disorder characterized by a clumsy, spastic, and stiff gait. It may progress, resulting in incontinence and diminished sensation in the legs. Characteristically, the deep tendon reflexes in the legs are markedly increased, whereas sensation is normal or slightly decreased. The clinical suspicion can be confirmed by cervical CT, myelogram, or MRI. Treatment requires surgical decompression of the cord. Preventive physical therapy can enhance muscle tone and head posturing, and a cervical collar may be employed to maintain proper head positioning during functional ADL.

The other common spinal cord compression syndrome, spinal stenosis, frequently occurs in the lumbar spine and results in claudication-like pain and weakness in the lower legs, which worsens with hyperextension of the spine and is often relieved by flexing the spine. Lumbar CT scan or myelogram confirms the diagnosis. Decompression is the treatment of choice. Strengthening exercises for the weakened muscles and stretching of the opposing shortened muscles are important components in preventing functional losses by progressive deformity.

Normal Pressure Hydrocephalus

Normal pressure hydrocephalus (NPH) presents with the clinical triad of dementia, slow shuffling gait, and urinary incontinence. Dilation of the ventricles with hydrocephalus is thought to affect the function of the surrounding brain tissue, which controls leg motion and bladder function. CT scan of the head can establish the presence of ventricular enlargement but cannot determine whether it is caused by atrophy of brain tissue. However, in selected patients who have shown clinical improvement after repeated removal of cerebrospinal fluid, placement of a surgical shunt occasionally results in resolution of the dementia and gait disorder.[1]

REHABILITATION OF MOBILITY PROBLEMS

The goal of rehabilitation for the elderly patient is to maintain or restore independent function in both basic ADL (such as bathing, toileting, dressing, eating, mobility, self-maintenance of medication, and communication) and instrumental activities of daily living (IADL, e.g., meal preparation, shopping, money management, homemaking, and driving). It is the goal of the interdisciplinary rehabilitation team to maximize the assets of the aged and assist them in maintaining purposeful, meaningful, and active lives. Physical and occupational therapists traditionally contribute expertise in problem solving, activity analysis, and activity adaptation, to assist the aged in performing more effectively and thereby enhancing quality of life. It is important that the patient be involved in the rehabilitation process. He or she should be encouraged to offer suggestions and be given as much control as possible in goal setting, decision making, and treatment.

Treatment may be preventive (an orthotic in a properly fitting shoe to improve stability and comfort of ambulation or a positioning splint to prevent loss of range), restorative (increasing muscle strength, range of motion, and endurance), or to maintain function, including physical, cognitive, and social skills. In treatment the individual will learn adaptive techniques in order to carry out ADL and maintain the highest possible functional capabilities. Examples include one-hand dressing, use of adaptive equipment such as built-up utensil handles to compensate for decreased grasp, and walking or wheelchair aids to improve mobility. These techniques and devices improve safety during performance, reduce the energy expenditure, and increase the performance speed, making activity less frustrating for the impaired elderly. Adaptive devices should, however, be used only when needed. Energy-saving and work-simplification techniques should also be included in the treatment plan because older persons have decreased vitality during mobility activities. It is important that patients as well as families learn problem-solving skills and be given the opportunity to use those skills. In addition, they should be informed of and instructed in the utilization of community resources. Throughout the entire treatment process, safety must be emphasized.

Mobility represents freedom to move in the environment as one chooses and gives a sense of control to the individual. It often means independence. The factors affecting mobility from a rehabilitation perspective include respiratory and cardiac status, posture, muscle strength and imbalances, joint mobility, sensory loss, presence or absence of pain, nutrition, cognition, physical environment, adequate footwear, and adequate aids. In addition, factors such as self-image, breadth of interests, and life satisfaction may influence the desire for mobility (Dwyer, 1988).

The majority of older persons continue to be independent and are active members of the community. Normal age changes occur gradually, allowing the person to adapt to them. Many musculoskeletal changes associated with aging are attributable to disuse rather than to normal physiological change (Lewis, 1985).

Vision changes associated with aging may necessitate modification of the physical environment to achieve safe as well as independent ambulation (Bottomley, 1989). Both the ability to see objects clearly and adaptation to darkness become problems. The older person requires nine times more light than a younger person does. Going from a brightly lighted area into a dark area requires time for the eyes to adapt to the change in the intensity of light. To increase the intensity of light in an area, increase the amount of illumination. Sheer curtains or window blinds help to reduce glare from bright sunshine. Avoid unevenness in lighting by illuminating dark areas with table lamps. Night lights that turn on automatically at dusk and wall light switches that glow in the dark are helpful. To compensate for losses, environmental adaptations can be suggested for the safe performance of ADL and IADL. Technology has provided devices such as "the clapper," which turns a light on or off in response to a hand clap, and remote control modules that control lights and appliances from any room.

Another visual problem is the decreased ability to discriminate colors in the blue, green, and violet range (Andreasen, 1985). Red, orange, and yellow can be more easily seen. Contrasting colors assist individuals in seeing objects in the environment. The edges of the top and bottom step may be painted or outlined with tape of a contrasting color to alert the individual of the change in level (Cristarella, 1977). Several authors suggest the need for large-pattern designs or solid colors in upholstery and textiles to enhance visibility, interest, and appeal (reducing the likelihood of bumping into or falling over furniture). Small patterns can produce blurring of vision and eye fatigue (Sharpe, 1974).

Bright and sharply contrasting colors can facilitate independence.

Color-coding of walls and corridors using bright and attractive colors can facilitate the finding of the patient's room, bathroom, or other area by color matching. Contrast is all-important. Contrasting colors can eliminate the difficulty of independently managing a stairwell or a poorly lit hall, where shadows can be hazards. Also, different colors have differing effects on individuals' emotional states (Sharpe, 1974). The colors red, yellow, and orange have been associated with excitement, stimulation, and aggression (Sharpe, 1974). Red is reported to increase muscular tension and increase blood pressure. It could be used as a visual stimulant with the elderly to alert them of environmental changes or hazards such as stairs or level changes. (For a full discussion of the effect of environment, see Hiatt, Chapter 10, and section by Lawton in Chapter 9, this volume.)

Other sensory losses, such as decreased hearing, decreased sensitivity to touch, and decreased ability to smell and taste, must also be considered. Reducing background noise, facing the person, or lowering the voice while talking are sometimes helpful for the person with a hearing problem. For decreased sensitivity of touch, compensate by using slight and coarse textures on objects.

Decreased sensory input on weight bearing can produce balance loss and resulting falls. In addition, structural foot changes from ill-fitting shoes or arthritic changes can produce instability resulting from pain.

A common mobility problem is that of an elderly woman recovering from surgery following a hip fracture. She has progressed to an ambulatory level, aided by a walker and with minimal assistance and verbal cues. The goal of rehabilitation is to have this woman perform ADL and IADL safely and independently prior to discharge. In preparing this individual and her family for discharge, certain environmental and supportive technology should be considered. To prevent falling, scatter rugs should be removed, and rugs with torn or frayed edges should be tacked down. A number of devices might be provided by physical and occupational therapy. If she has difficulty rising from a chair, the chair could be elevated with blocks or furniture extenders. If hip muscles are weak, a leg lifter (a long piece of webbing with a loop in the end) will make it easier to lift the legs onto a bed, cognizant that daily exercises should be undertaken to improve muscle strength and eliminate muscle imbalances. To compensate for an inability to flex her hip past 90 degrees, elastic shoelaces, a long-handled shoehorn, and a stocking device would allow her to independently don her stockings and shoes. Properly fitting shoes, with an orthotic to stabilize the heel in the neutral position, are also recommended to enhance safety on weight bearing. In addition, there is often a shortening of the lower extremity on the involved side, necessitating a lift on that shoe to prevent kinetic chain dysfunction from the imposed imbalances. Safety is a priority in the bathroom. Needed equipment may include a raised toilet seat with one side cut down to accommodate the involved hip, a safety bench in the shower stall or tub, grab bars, a hand-held showerhead, and a non-skid surface or safety strips on the shower or tub floors (Davis & Kirkland, 1986).

SUMMARY

The reversible causes of impaired mobility need to be reviewed and ruled out by the medical consultant as part of the program to restore mobility. Particular attention must be paid to drug side effects. This area is best addressed by the pharmacist and physician. Programs to enhance mobility require the input of physical therapy, occupational therapy, and nursing so that the patient's goals for mobility can be attained. Social service can be consulted to determine financial and community resources available to the elderly person. As with other problems seen in frail older persons, social work, mental health, nutrition, and legal services may be useful in some instances.

Prevention is the key to maintaining functional independence within an elder's environment. Patient and family education relative to exercise, nutrition, and healthful habits could prevent the loss of mobility by potentially avoidable or reversible causes.

The challenge is to consider that scopes of practice are not, nor need they be, as rigidly defined as proposed by the various professional groups. There is much to discover about what other disciplines can offer. The shared knowledge base within the various health care disciplines serves to strengthen care of the elderly. If there was ever a clinical field in which the interdisciplinary model was needed, it is the field of geriatrics. The aged are more likely than any other age group to have multiple health problems requiring the best thinking and skills of several disciplines, either concurrently or serially. In no other age group are we likely to experience such an interrelatedness among health systems—physical, interpersonal, emotional, and cognitive—in the aged.

As our society continues to age and the cost of health care continues to rise, and as we discover more ways to extend and maintain life, we must also begin to recognize our responsibility to provide models of care that work for the aged and the clinicians involved in the care of the aged.

NOTE

1. For a fuller discussion of medical issues, see Dwyer (1988), Rowe and Besdine (1988), and Williams (1984).

REFERENCES

Andreasen, M. K. (1985). Making a safe environment by design. *Journal of Gerontological Nursing, 11*(6), 18–22.

Bottomley, J. M. (1989). Rehabilitation of the Alzheimer's patient. In J. L. Cummings & B. L. Miller (Eds.), *Alzheimer's disease: Treatment and long-term management* (pp. 245–252). New York: Marcel Dekker.

Brody, H. (1979, November). The aging brain: A multidisciplinary consideration. Paper presented at the Thirty-third Annual Scientific Meeting of the Gerontological Society, Washington, DC.

Carslon, K. E., Alston, W., & Feldman, D. J. (1964). Electromyographic study of the aging skeletal muscle. *American Journal of Physical Medicine, 43*, 141–152.

Christiansen, J., & Juhl, E. (Eds.). (1987). The prevention of falls in later life. *Danish Medical Bulletin, 34*(Suppl. 4), 1–24.

Cristarella, M. C. (1977). Visual functions of the elderly. *American Journal of Occupational Therapy, 31*(7), 432.

Davis, L. J., & Kirkland, M. (Eds.). (1986). The role of occupational therapy with the elderly. Rockville, MD: American Occupational Therapy Association.

Dwyer, B. (Ed.). (1988). *Focus on geriatric care and rehabilitation 2*(3). Rockville, MD: Aspen Publishers, Inc.

Gutman, E. (1972). *Age changes in the neuromuscular system.* London: Bristol.

Gutman, E., & Hanzlikova, V. (1976). Fast and slow motor units in aging. *Gerontology, 22*, 280–300.

Lewis, C. B. (1985). *Aging: The health care challenge.* Philadelphia: F. A. Davis.

MacLennan, W. J., Hall, M. R. P., & Timothy, J. I. (1980). Postural hypotension in old age: Is it a disorder of the nervous system or of blood vessels? *Age and Ageing, 9*, 25–32.

Marshall, L. (1981). Auditory processing in aging listeners. *Speech and Hearing Disorder, 46*, 226–238.

McCarter, R. (1978). Effects on age on contraction of mammalian skeletal muscle. In Kalkor and DiBattista (Eds.), *Aging in muscle.* New York: Raven Press.

Moritini, T. (1981). Training adaptations in the muscles of older men. In E. L. Smith & R. C. Serfass (Eds.), *Exercise and aging: The scientific basis.* Hillside, NJ: Enslow.

Murray, M. P. (1975). Normal postural stability and steadiness: Quantitative assessment. *Journal of Bone and Joint Surgery, 57*(A), 510.

Nystrom, E. P., & Evans, L. S. (1966). The interdisciplinary team approach in the role of occupational therapy with the elderly. Rockville, MD: American Occupational Therapy Association.

Payton, O. D., & Poland, J. L. (1983). Aging process: Implications for clinical practice. *Physical Therapy, 63*(1), 41–48.

Ragen, P. B., & Mitchell, J. (1980). The effects of aging on the cardiovascular response to dynamic and static exercise. In M. L. Weisfelt (Ed.), *The aging heart*. New York: Raven Press.

Rowe, J. W., & Besdine, R. W. (Eds.). (1988). *Geriatric medicine*. Boston: Little, Brown.

Sharpe, D. T. (1974). *The psychology of color and design*. Chicago: Nelson-Hall.

Shepard, R. J. (1987). *Physical activity and aging*. (2d ed.). Baltimore: Aspen.

Shepard, R. J., & Sidney, K. H. (1987). Exercise and aging. *Exercise and Sport Reviews, 6*, 1.

Smith, E., & Serfass, R. (1981). *Exercise and aging: The scientific basis*. Hillside, NJ: Enslow.

Williams, T. F. (Ed.). (1984). *Rehabilitation in the aged*. New York: Raven Press.

7

Limiting Mobility Loss from Foot Problems

Arthur E. Helfand

Foot problems in the elderly are common and are major factors in limiting mobility, causing functional disability, impairment, ambulatory dysfunction, pain, and discomfort. Some foot problems also are risk factors that may lead to significant complications of multiple systemic diseases and the potential for lower extremity amputation. Through the course of one's lifetime, the foot undergoes a great deal of trauma, misuse, and neglect. The stress of normal mobility, the changes associated with the aging process, systemic diseases, focal impairment, and environmental factors associated with ambulation, create discomfort that can change the patient's ability to function as an independent member of society and generate additional psychological correlates.

If one recognizes that goals in the care of the elderly include cure and comfort, the need for primary and preventive foot care becomes an essential element in management and rehabilitation. The ability to move about, render self-care, and remain an active and productive member of society can be limited when foot problems exist. The loss of mobility translates to social segregation, a loss of efficiency, declining health, and personality and emotional changes. Thus, foot problems may not only produce immobility, they may contribute to loss of self-respect and increase the likelihood of social isolation.

There are many factors that contribute to the etiology of foot problems in the elderly, including, but not limited to, the following:

1. The degree of walking and ambulatory function.
2. The duration of immobility during hospitalization or institutionalization.
3. Presence or absence of previous professional foot care.
4. The environment, such as walking surfaces, and environmental factors, such as footwear compatibility as to fit and function.
5. Emotional adjustment to functional changes.
6. Current medications and therapeutic programs.
7. Localized foot disease processes.
8. Past foot conditions and/or manifestations of diseases.
9. The presence of systemic diseases with risk of pedal complications.
10. Limitations of coverage by Medicare and Medicaid of some forms of primary and preventive foot care services.

There is a greater risk of local infection related to disease and of avascularity and decreased sensitivity related to age. Older persons also have a higher prevalence of cognitive dysfunction and suffer more personal and societal losses leading to physical and emotional stress. Loss of physical function, changes in living style, and social isolation also add to limitations in mobility. The elderly also tend to be more prone to injuries of the feet and lower extremities.

Any degree of hospitalization that reduces mobility magnifies minor foot problems and increases limitation of activity. Foot infections are more common, and, with tissues that are slower in healing, the risk for even minor procedures becomes greater.

PODIATRIC ASSESSMENT

The assessment, evaluation, and examination of the elderly patient in relation to podiatric or foot health involves more than the clinical knowledge of the foot and its demonstrated symptoms and signs. There should be a recognition of the patient's concerns and needs and a special focus on comfort. An interdisciplinary approach, using the precepts of rehabilitation (i.e., to restore the patient to a maximum level of function and maintain that function once achieved) is appropriate. The clinician must anticipate projected changes that relate to ambulation and foot care needs and provide an assurance of individual dignity.

Foot complaints and/or conditions need to be related to both activities of daily living (ADL) (ambulation, dressing, grooming, bathing, etc.) and to instrumental activities of daily living (IADL) (shopping, housekeeping, transportation, etc.).

The initial element of the assessment should include demographic data on the patient and the patient's living conditions. The chief complaint of the patient should be explored in the patient's own terms. There should be a review of the patient's own perception of how foot problems effect his or her daily life and activities. Footwear should be assessed in relation to fit, function, use, and compatibility with foot types and ambulatory use. The present condition should be noted as to duration, location, severity, prior treatment and results, and relation to other general medical conditions.

A systems review should be completed along with notation of other practitioners of record. Current medications and responses should be identified in relation to existing and past therapeutic programs. The past medical history should include infections, operations, fractures, injuries, drug sensitivities, and allergies. In addition, problems and

Table 7-1 Problems and Diseases That May Affect Mobility

Alcohol abuse	Malabsorption
Ambulatory dysfunction	Malnutrition
Anemia	Mental illness
Arteriosclerosis	Mental retardation
Atopic dermatitis	Milroy's disease
Burger's disease	Multiple sclerosis
Cancer	Neurosyphilis
Cerebral vascular accidents/stroke	Obesity
Chemical/substance abuse	Osteoarthritis
Chronic renal disease	Parkinson's disease
Chronic obstructive pulmonary disease	Patients on anticoagulants
Chronic thrombophlebitis	Peripheral neuropathies
Congestive heart failure	Pernicious anemia
Coronary artery disease	Post-trauma
Diabetes mellitus	Pruritus
Drug interactions	Psoriasis
Edema	Psychogenic tremors
Functional disability	Raynaud's disease/syndrome
Gout	Rheumatoid arthritis
Hemiparesis or quadriparesis	Thyroid disease
Hemophilia	Toxic states
Hereditary disorders/disease	Transient ischemic attacks
Hyperhidrosis	Uremia
Hypertension	Urticaria
Hysterical paralysis	Venous stasis
Ischemia	Ventilator dependence
Leprosy	Vitamin deficiencies
Localized neurodermatitis	

diseases that have pedal complications and/or affect care and ambulation should be noted. Examples are delineated in Table 7-1.

A review of the patient's past podiatric history and foot care history should be noted, as well as elements of self-care and the use of commercial foot care products. The past occupational history should be explored, and foot/work-related activities, military service, residence outside temperate zones, percentage of weight bearing, flooring, and footwear should be noted.

The social history should include sleeping habits; the use of tea, alcohol, coffee, tobacco, sedatives/hypnotics, narcotics, and other drugs; and the reaction of the patient to his or her illness or condition.

The subjective symptoms should be clearly noted, as described by the patient, and an attempt should be made to focus on, but not be limited to, the clinical notations listed in Table 7-2.

Clinical findings of hyperkeratosis, onychia, and dermatologic lesions should be recorded as signs of disease, deformity, and/or a disor-

Table 7-2   Clinical Notations (Subjective Symptoms)

Dermatology
  Exquisitely painful or painless lesions
  Slow-healing or nonhealing wounds or necrosis
  Skin color changes such as cyanosis or redness
  Chronic itching, scaling, or dry feet
  Recurrent infections such as paronychia, athlete's foot, fungal toenails, etc.
Peripheral vascular
  Cold feet
  Intermittent claudication involving the calf or foot
  Pain at rest, especially nocturnal, relieved by dependency
Musculoskeletal
  Gradual change in foot shape
  Change in shoe size
  Painless change in foot shape
  Ambulatory dysfunction
  Joint changes and deformity
Neurologic
  Sensory change
  Burning
  Tingling
  Clawing sensation
  Motor changes
  Weakness
  Foot drop
  Autonomic, such as diminished sweating

---

der. The pedal vasculature and related structures should be evaluated. See Table 7-3 for examples of common foot conditions.

Absent popliteal or femoral pulses, bruits, dependent rubor with plantar pallor on elevation and prolonged capillary filling time (3–4 seconds), altered skin temperature, and blood pressure should be noted. Doppler studies, pulse volume recordings, and oscillometric readings also may be useful. Radiographic studies should be obtained as indicated and may include weight- and non-weight-bearing comparisons.

Table 7-3   Clinical Findings

Abscess
Angulation
Arthropathy
Chronic tinea pedis
Diminished or absent hair growth
Dryness of the skin
Foot type
Frank deformities
   Cavus feet
   Drop foot
   Hallux valgus
   Digiti flexus (hammer toes)
Gait
Hypertrophic deformity
Incurvated or involuted toenails
Keratotic lesions
Onychauxis (hypertrophic and thickened nails)
Onychia (inflammation)
Onychocryptosis (ingrown toenail)
Onychogryphosis (ram's-horn nail)
Onychomycosis (fungal nails)
Onychopathy (trophic nail changes)
Onychophosis (calloused nail grooves)
Palpation of pain
Paronychia (infection and inflammation)
Postural deformities
Pressure ulcerations
Range of motion
Subkeratotic hemorrhage (plantar and digital)
Subungual hemorrhage
Trophic ulcerations
Ulceration (disease complication)
Xerosis

The neurologic elements should include gait review, reflexes (patellar, achilles, and superficial plantar), ankle clonus, vibratory sense, weakness, sensory deficits (proprioception, pain, and temperature perception), hyperesthesia, and autonomic dysfunction.

The drug history should focus on, but not be limited to, antihypertensives, antidiabetics, cortisone, sedatives, topicals, antibiotics, antiarthritics, and other related medications utilized for and by the elderly. The use of over-the-counter foot care remedies, including caustic keratotic applications, should be explored.

Finally, because of narrow limits of Medicare reimbursement for foot care, those findings and/or conditions that might allow Medicare reimbursement should also be identified (Table 7-4).

RECOGNIZING COMMON FOOT PROBLEMS IN THE ELDERLY

Skin

The skin is one of the first structures to demonstrate age- and disease-related change. There is a loss of hair due to vascular insufficiency and atrophy. There is a gradual appearance of brownish pigmentations, anhidrosis, and xerosis. Early fissure lines occur with prolonged periods of repeated microtrauma, diminished nutrition, and excessive dryness. Pruritis often accompanies these changes, giving rise to excoriations

Table 7-4 Medicare-Covered Foot Conditions

Class A
  Nontraumatic amputation of the foot or an integral skeletal portion thereof
Class B
  Absent posterior tibial pulse
  Absent dorsalis pedis pulse
  Advanced trophic changes
    Hair growth—decreased or absent
    Nail changes—thickening
    Pigmentary changes—discoloration
    Skin texture—thin and shiny
    Skin color—rubor or cyanosis
Class C
  Claudication
  Temperature changes, e.g., cold feet
  Paresthesias, e.g., abnormal spontaneous sensations in the feet
  Burning
  Edema

and other skin irritations. Initial consideration should be given to the use of hydration and lubrication.

Other considerations include contact dermatitis, tinea pedis, and pyoderma. Depending on the etiology, the use of topical steroids, antifungals, and antibiotics may be appropriate, with continued monitoring of the patient. Given the coexistence of foot deformity and related systemic diseases, such as arteriosclerosis and diabetes mellitus in many cases, initial abrasions can result in the development of ulceration, deeper infection, necrosis, and the loss of a part of the total lower extremity. Early evaluation and intervention are keys to the reduction of complications of foot problems in the elderly.

Hyperkeratotic lesions, such as tyloma and the clinical varieties of heloma, are of concern to the elderly patient. These lesions represent both primary pathology and symptoms of other, related foot deformities. Their treatment in the elderly is often management of the residual deformities and related systemic diseases, such as diabetes mellitus, arterial insufficiency, and degenerative joint disease.

Hyperkeratosis represents, to some degree, a protective mechanism to stress and may act as space replacements due to atrophy of soft tissue. Fixed deformities, a loss of muscle mass, contractures, atrophy, decreased function, and shoe-to-foot incompatabilities tend to decrease ambulation and result in pain and discomfort. It is important to recognize that these lesions are not normal and require treatment and ongoing care if the patient is to remain pain-free, comfortable, and ambulatory.

Nails

Multiple onychial dystrophies can be demonstrated in the elderly population. Thickened toenails may be present as onychauxis or, if care is neglected, onychogryphosis. They are the residual of a decrease in the vascular supply to the nail bed, poor nutrition, and repeated microtrauma. One needs to remember that the foot is often housed in a shoe with significant continuing abrasion between the underside of the toe box and the dorsal surface of the toenails. Associated onychomycosis (fungal infection of the nail) increases the prevalence of the deformity, hypertrophy, and hyperplasia.

Diabetic onychopathy also produces changes in the configuration of the nail plate. These include onychorrhexis, atrophy of the eponychium, involution, subungual hemorrhage, and a degree of hypertrophy. The normal curvature of the nail is lost and subungual keratosis may become pronounced, with onycholysis. Onychophosis gives rise to pain and, with incurvation, may cause pain and marked limitation of ambulation. Continuing pressure can initiate ulceration.

Management includes periodic debridement of the nail plate. Partial avulsion may be required initially, depending on the stage of involvement. The use of emollients to lubricate the xerotic areas and to provide for mild keratolytic effects are also appropriate. If the deformity continues to cause excessive pain, avulsion and excision of the nail may be indicated.

There should be appropriate review of the vascular and metabolic status of the patient prior to any surgical consideration. One should also consider the use of shoes with a high toe box and protective materials, such as lamb's wool and polyfoam caps, to reduce pressure to the nail plate. The pain and discomfort that can result from these conditions and their inappropriate management limits ambulation and can produce significant complications for the elderly patient.

Onychomycosis (fungal infection) of the toenails is a common problem in the elderly, related not only to the presence of the organism but also to the associated environmental factors. Some of these factors include repeated microtrauma, shoe friction, and the dark, moist, warm environment within the shoe. The superficial infection remains, the organisms invade the nail plate dorsally and distally and destroy the nail plate itself. Onycholysis is common, with subungual mycosis and debris noted. Hypertrophy follows, and an associated brownish-yellow color and musty odor can be demonstrated. Onychia and paronychia can develop, with continuing irritation and infection. Pain and discomfort usually result from hypertrophy and pressure. Subungual keratosis develops with prolonged onycholysis and pressure. Traumatic and autoavulsion are also common in the elderly and are complicating factors if early management is not provided.

Management of this chronic infection should consist of periodic debridement, the use of mild keratolytics, and initial topical antifungal solutions to provide some stability for treatment. One must view the continuing management of onychomycosis like that of other chronic infections, to prevent complications and provide for comfort and ambulation.

Musculoskeletal Problems

The biomechanical and pathomechanical changes that occur in the musculoskeletal system serve as the prime etiologic factors for the development of hyperkeratotic lesions. It should be noted that, with time, these lesions are both hypertrophic and hyperplastic and related to both atrophy and xerosis.

Each of the conditions noted in Table 7-5 produces some degree of limitation of motion, with discomfort and pain. There is often a rela-

Table 7-5 Musculoskeletal Problems

Bursitis
Calcaneal spurs
Digital and phalangeal rotational deformities
Digiti flexus
Enthesopathy
Exostosis
Fasciitis
Fibrositis
Hallux abducto valgus
Hallux limitus
Hallux rigidus
Hallux valgus
Hyperostosis
Morton's syndrome
Myofasciitis
Myositis
Neuritis
Neuroma
Pes planus
Pes valgo planus
Plantar imbalance
Prolapsed metatarsal heads
Soft tissue atrophy
Spur formation
Tendonitis
Varus and valgus deformities

tionship of these problems to inadequate, inappropriate, or incompatible footwear.

Proper shoe selection, fit, and modification may be indicated; they can be augmented by the use of orthotics, special lasts, or the fabrication of molds from some of the newer materials available, which reduce shock, minimize stress, reduce shearing, and redistribute weight.

Systemic Diseases

Many systemic diseases produce serious foot complications. Osteoarthritis or degenerative joint disease can be a major factor in limiting walking. Fixed deformities and inflammatory reactions to repeated microtrauma produce swelling, stiffness, and pain. In most cases, fasciitis, calcaneal erosions, spur formation, enthesopathy, periostitis, and tendonitis are the primary demonstrable clinical entities in the elderly. Management includes medication for pain, foot orthotics for increased stability, and physical medicine and rehabilitation to provide pain relief, restoration of function, and maintenance of mobility in the future.

The primary form of traumatic arthritis in the elderly is hallux limitus. As deformity and spur formation increase, the condition becomes one of hallux rigidus with associated bunion deformity. Orthotics and shoe modifications to bridge the joint and eliminate motion at the first metatarsophalangeal joint usually eliminates pain and retains ambulation. The addition of physical modalities to assist in the management of the acute symptoms increases foot function.

Other forms of arthritis (i.e., neurotrophic, infectious, gouty, and rheumatoid) frequently lead to degenerative changes present in older individuals. Osteolysis and osteoporosis should be considered, particularly with associated pain. Neurotrophic changes are most often associated with long-standing diabetes mellitus. Acute gout gives rise to severe pain and swelling. The chronic changes include urate deposits and ulceration, as well as pronounced deformity and degeneration. The continuing use of diuretics for hypertension and cardiac disease may produce a pseudo-goutlike syndrome in the elderly, with marked discomfort, pain, and limitation of ambulation. The end result of rheumatoid arthritis in the elderly includes residual deformity, atrophy, contractures, rigidity, and gait changes, which add to ambulatory disability and increase the potential for falls, with all of their residual complications.

Diabetes mellitus presents a significant morbidity state in the elderly patient. Occasionally, a foot complaint or problem will be the initial symptom for which the patient seeks medical care for diabetes, thus making the foot condition the portal of entry into the health care system. Early supportive measures can help limit future disability and reduce the possibility of severe ambulatory dysfunction in persons with degenerative changes. The pedal manifestations involve multiple structures in the foot and multiple problems, many which are listed in Table 7-6.

Lower Extremity Loss

The pathways that precipitate the potential for lower extremity amputation include—as associated with diabetes mellitus—obesity, hypertension, smoking, hyperlipidemia, hyperglycemia, peripheral vascular disease, neuropathy, minor trauma with decreased or lack of perception, infection, inadequate health education, lack of preventive measures, and poor foot care. Additional risk factors include a loss of protective sensation, existing foot deformity, and a prior history of pedal ulceration.

Table 7-6 Degenerative Changes in the Foot

Absent pedal pulses
Angiopathy
Dermopathy
Infection
Ischemia
Motor weakness
Muscle atrophy
Necrosis and gangrene
Neuropathy
Neurotrophic arthropathy
Neurotrophic ulceration
Onychopathy
Paresthesia
Reflex loss
Sensory impairment
Trophic changes

The developmental characteristics of diabetic ulceration in the elderly generally include a poor knowledge of foot care, a period of continuous pressure and local arterial ischemia related to deformity and improper gait, counterpressure from hyperkeratotic lesions; continued and repeated microtrauma, and friction with thrusting and shearing. Subcallosal or subhyperkeratotic hemorrhage is usually the earliest sign of impending or potential ulceration. Coexistent pathomechanical and fixed deformities additionally contribute to the development of foot ulcers. When one considers the cost of a lower extremity amputation and the residuals for the patient, the family, and society, foot health education becomes a cost-effective intervention as an initial step in prevention of foot loss.

Peripheral arterial insufficiency is present to some degree in many older persons. Overt indications of decreased arterial supply are summarized in Table 7-7.

Pedal ulcerations resulting from arterial insufficiency are usually painful and extremely slow to heal. Dry gangrene is a characteristic compared to the infection more characteristic of diabetic ulceration. Loss of collateral circulation and vasospasm add to the problems experienced by the patient.

Management usually consists of treatment of infection, if present, reduction of pressure, efforts to provide revascularization and local measures (see Table 7-8).

Disease of the neurologic system may also affect the foot and thus ambulation. Cerebrovascular accidents, Parkinson's disease, and pe-

Table 7-7   Indications of Decreased Arterial Supply in the Foot

Absent pedal pulses
Atrophy of soft tissue
Burning
Calcification noted radiographically
Claudication
Coldness
Cramps
Dryness
Edema
Hair loss
Muscle fatigue
Muscle wasting
Pain
Pallor
Paresthesia
Tropic skin changes

ripheral neuropathies are examples of conditions that may limit ambulation by producing deformities and keratotic lesions. The key again is early and continuing management and careful follow-up.

PSYCHOSOCIAL CORRELATES

Patients may present with foot problems as a manifestation of emotional illness. Psychological problems can manifest in the foot as hysterical paralysis, psychogenic tremors, localized neurodermatitis, hy-

Table 7-8   Local Measures in Foot Treatment

Materials and procedures to absorb shock and accommodate existing deformities and modifications to provide for joint stability
Surgical shoes, such as the DARCO shoe, with modification during initial local care programs
Full contact orthosis, such as Plastazote
Extra-depth inlay shoes
Reinforced shoe counters
Thermold shoes
Custom-molded shoes
Special considerations, including blucher lasts, Velcro closures, sole wedges for stabilization, heel flares, heel elevations, metatarsal rocker bars, high and wide toe boxes, soft uppers, cushion soles (such as Spenco, PPT, etc.), and metatarsal bars

perhidrosis, and pruritis. Clearly, many diseases affecting the foot may be complicated by secondary emotional concerns. Some examples include gout, diabetes mellitus, obesity, vascular insufficiency, psoriasis, urticaria, and atopic dermatitis.

In some instances, when the symptoms do not match the clinical findings, a foot problem may present as a cry for help. The foot, foot pain, and limitation of ambulation can be expressions of deeper problems, particularly in the elderly mentally ill and retarded. Thus, neglect of common foot problems in the elderly in mental health programs usually results in decreased ambulation, which encourages institutionalization.

LONG-TERM CARE

The 1988 Standards for Long-Term Care, as developed by the Joint Commission on Accreditation of Healthcare Organizations, include foot health and care as a quality assurance issue. A similar component is being instituted for the current revision of the Medicare and Medicaid Conditions of Participation for Long-Term Care. These documents suggest, as a basic consideration, administrative guidelines to assure foot health and care for patients as follows:

Foot care and/or podiatric services are organized and staffed in a manner designed to meet the foot health needs of patient/residents.

The facility's foot health services should be provided by a podiatrist or other appropriate licensed practitioner with a consultant podiatric practitioner.

A foot health program should be an integral part of the facility's total health care program.

Written policies and procedures should be developed to serve as a guide to the provision of podiatric/foot care services.

The consulting or supervising podiatrist participates in patient/resident care management as appropriate.

The quality and appropriateness of podiatric services are monitored as an integral part of the overall quality assurance program, consistent with other practitioner/professional services.

CONTINUING PROFESSIONAL EDUCATION

A program of professional, in-service, and patient education should form a part of a total geriatric and rehabilitation program. See Table 7-9 for a suggested program outline.

Table 7-9   Podiatric Continuing Education

Relationship of foot problems to the total geriatric patient
  Needs
  Ambulation and independence
  Risk diseases
  Factors that modify foot care in the society and health care
      Medicare and Medicaid
  Mental health considerations
  Long-term care
  Rehabilitation
Primary foot care
  Assessment and examination
  Nail disorders
  Skin disorders
  Hyperkeratotic disorders
  Foot orthopedic and biomechanical (pathomechanical) changes
  Foot deformities associated with aging
  Risk diseases
      Diabetes mellitus
      Arthritis
      Gout
      Vascular insufficiency
      Other
  Management
  Interdisciplinary considerations
Foot health education
  Professional and interdisciplinary
  Patient
Care delivery
  Ambulatory care
  Acute hospital considerations
  Rehabilitation
  Long-term care
  Home care
  Mental health and retardation
Interdisciplinary education
Footwear and related considerations

SUMMARY

The Final Report of the 1981 White House Conference on Aging stated:
"Recommendation Number 148: Comprehensive foot care be provided
for the elderly in a manner equal to care provided for other parts of the
human body, to permit patients to remain ambulatory. . . . Implemen-

tation: Remove current Medicare exclusions which preclude comprehensive foot care."

The ability to ambulate requires appropriate foot health. Keeping patients walking is a goal that needs to be met if the older person is to maintain a high degree of quality of life.

Given the high prevalence of foot problems in the elderly, especially in those patients with chronic diseases and mental health problems, foot care needs are essential. Foot care should be part of the comprehensive health care for older Americans. The ability to remain active and ambulatory is one means of assuring dignity and self-esteem for the elderly.

REFERENCES

Bild, D. E., Selby, J. V., Sinnock, P., Browner, W. S., Braverman, P., & Chowstack, J. (1981). Lower extremity amputation in people with diabetes: Epidemiology and prevention. *Journal of Diabetes Care, 12*(1), 24–31.

Chalkins, E., Davis, P. J., & Ford, A. B. (1986). *The practice of geriatrics.* Philadelphia: W. B. Saunders.

Eng. W. W. (Ed.). (1986–87). Geriatric podiatry. In *Geriatric curriculum resource guides for health professionals.* Richmond, VA: Virginia Commonwealth University, Geriatric Education Center.

Helfand, A. E. (Ed.). (1981). *Clinical podogeriatrics.* Baltimore: Williams and Wilkins.

Helfand, A. E. (1987). *Public health and podiatric medicine.* Baltimore: Williams and Wilkins.

Helfand, A. E., & Bruno, J. (Eds.). (1984). Rehabilitation of the foot. In *Clinics in podiatry.* Philadelphia: W. B. Saunders.

Libow, L. S., & Sherman, F. T. (Eds.). (1981). *The core of geriatric medicine.* St. Louis: C. V. Mosby.

Neale, D., & Adams, I. (1985). *Common foot disorders* (2nd ed.). Edinburgh: Churchill Livingston.

Reichel, W. (Ed.). (1988). *Clinical aspects of aging* (3rd ed.). Baltimore: Williams and Wilkins.

Scardinia, R. J. (1983). Diabetic foot problems: Assessment and prevention. *Clinical Diabetes, 1,* 1–7.

Steinberg, U. (ed.). (1983). *Care of the geriatric patient* (6th ed.). St. Louis: C. V. Mosby.

Williams, T. F. (ed.). (1984). *Rehabilitation in the aging.* New York: Raven Press.

Yale, J. A. (1987). *Yale's podiatric medicine* (3rd ed.). Baltimore: Williams and Wilkins.

U.S. Department of Health, Education and Welfare. (1970). *Feet first.* Washington, DC: National Institutes of Health, Public Health Service.

8

Rehabilitation of Dysmobility in the Elderly: A Case Study of the Patient with a Hip Fracture

Gerald Felsenthal and Barry D. Stein

Dysmobility may be defined as the inability to go from where one is to where one wishes to be with enough energy remaining to do the task that one had in mind. Inherent in this definition is the ability to transfer safely from the supine or sitting position into a wheelchair or onto one's feet, with or without assistive devices. Dysmobility may be inherent in the patient as a result of physical impairment (Sabin, 1982) or may be secondary to extraneous factors (Rubenstein et al., 1988). Extraneous factors may be environmental, architectural (Mace, 1976; Mace & Laslett, 1977), or host-related (Table 8-1). Understanding the interaction between the patient and the extraneous factors is crucial to the understanding of the dysmobility and to planning any mode of action to correct the dysmobility.

Occasionally, dysmobility may be caused solely by extraneous factors rather than inherent in any impairment, such as with the following three examples. All three are elderly female patients who were seen for the complaint of difficulty in walking.

The first patient presented as an emergency. She was having difficulty in balance and was falling backward. Upon evaluation, the most notable factor was heel cord tightness bilaterally. History then revealed that she was accustomed to wearing 1½-inch heels on her shoes. She became convinced that she was too old for high heels and should wear flat-soled shoes. When she began using flat-soled shoes, she also be-

Table 8-1   Etiology of Dysmobility

Organ system impairment
  Acute insult, i.e., hip fracture
  Deconditioning/inactivity
  Physiologic effect of aging
  Multiple system impairment/interaction
Iatrogenic causes
  Medications
  Immobility orders, i.e., bed rest
Architectural factors
  Stairs/steps
  Lighting
  Accessibility of bathroom, kitchen, bedroom
Environmental factors
  Weather
  Accessibility of stores
  Slip mats/furniture/extension cords
  Cracked pavement/uneven ground
Host factors
  Shoe style
  Unfamiliar living arrangement
  Nutrition

gan to have balance difficulty with falling. This patient was unable to bring her feet flat on the ground without leaning backward because of the heel cord contractures. Her balance difficulty and ambulation problem resolved when she was given a 1½-inch heel on her shoes.

A second patient was hospitalized in a rehabilitation unit. Over a weekend she developed a sudden complaint of pain in walking. Investigation revealed that she had received a gift of new slippers. Her pain onset coincided with the use of these slippers. When the slippers were examined, packing was found in the toes of both shoes. The packing had not been removed by the patient; she had jammed her feet into the shoes. Removal of the packing alleviated the pain and facilitated ambulation.

A third patient was seen as an outpatient because of increasing difficulty in walking. In observing her gait pattern it was noticed that she was wearing shoes with 1½-inch heels and straps. As she walked away from the examiner, it was noted that her heels were slipping off the shoes. When the straps were tightened, this problem was alleviated and the dysmobility resolved.

Another concept basic to the rehabilitation of the patient with dysmobility is to determine whether the cause of the dysmobility is rapidly progressive, static, or reversible. With a rapid progressive disorder, mobility such as ambulation may be an impractical goal, and wheelchair mobility should be emphasized. An example of this would be a rapidly progressive degenerative disorder such as motor neuron disease. Accommodation to the functional deterioration might be the indicated rehabilitation goal—that is, wheelchair mobility rather than ambulation. A static or slowly progressive neurological disorder, such as Parkinson's syndrome, may be approached more aggressively, especially if the patient has been recently diagnosed and restoration/maintenance of function emphasized. Examples of reversible disorders causing dysmobility are medication toxicity, which may be treated by stopping the medication or lowering the dosage (i.e., Dilantin® toxicity), and hip fracture. Any impairment that is felt to be the cause of dysmobility should be considered in these terms to help determine appropriate rehabilitation goals and the subsequent rehabilitation program.

Data based on household interviews of the civilian, noninstitutionalized population of the United States in 1979 (Feller, 1983) revealed that 3.9% of adults of both sexes, from 65 to 74 years of age, had difficulty in walking; 8.4% of adults 75 to 84 years of age and 26% of adults 85 years and older had difficulty in walking. When this is broken down by gender, 3.7% of males aged 65 to 74, 7.4% of males aged 75 to 84, and 20.5% of males over age 85 had difficulty in walking. Corresponding numbers for female respondents were 4% between ages 65 and 74, 9% between ages 75 and 84, and 29% age 85 and over. A study of functional disability in the hospitalized elderly (Warshaw et al., 1982) indicated that the percentage of patients confined to chair or bed increased from under 20% in the 70-to-74 age group to 40% in the 80-to-84 age group and to approximately 55% in the 85-plus age group. During fiscal year 1987 at Sinai Hospital in Baltimore, 1,333 inpatients with the complaint of dysmobility were seen. Table 8-2 indicates the impairments noted as the primary diagnosis in these patients. The three most common impairments were cardiovascular, cerebrovascular, and fracture. All of these patients were 65 years or older, and all were started on progressive ambulation training programs.

Thirty-eight percent of the patients referred with the complaint of dysmobility were seen in consultation by the physiatrist. The remainder were directly referred for physical therapy. In contrast to the usual medical consultation, the physiatrist is not only concerned with the identification of the impairment causing the dysmobility but is equally concerned with prescribing a rehabilitation program with the goal of lessening the patient's disability. These diagnostic and treatment aspects of patient care are approached concurrently. In fact, even if a

Table 8-2 Impairments Associated with Dysmobility in the Hospitalized Elderly

Impairment	No.	%
Cardiovascular	262	19.6
Cerebrovascular	186	14.0
Fractures	169	12.7
Arthropathies	93	7.0
Carcinoma	80	6.0
Symptoms, no specific etiology	74	5.6
Central nervous system	60	4.5
Dorsopathies	49	3.7
Gastrointestinal	48	3.6
Peripheral vascular disease	47	3.5
Pulmonary	42	3.2
Infections	41	3.1
Amputation	35	2.6
Postsurgical	33	2.5
Psychological	28	2.1
Endocrine/metabolic	22	1.6
Peripheral nervous system	18	1.4
Toxic	2	0.2
Other	44	3.3
	1,333	100.2%

specific diagnosis is not made, the patient may still benefit from a rehabilitation program.

The physiatric evaluation of a patient adds two aspects to the usual
medical consultation. First, the physiatrist is concerned with establishing a prognosis in regard to prospects for independence of function.
Second, in addition to establishing a medical problem list, a functional
problem list must be formulated that will serve as the basis for the
rehabilitation team approach. The physiatric approach to the patient
with the chief complaint of dysmobility is exemplified by the case of a
patient who has sustained a hip fracture (Zuckerman & Newport,
1988).

Table 8-3 comprises a list of predictors of function in patients who
have sustained a hip fracture. These predictors are gleaned from medical literature as well as from personal experience. Overall, it should be
noted that function after a hip fracture is usually not better than the
premorbid level of function. Thus, if the patient was poorly mobile
prior to sustaining a fracture, he or she is unlikely to become more
functional after sustaining the insult of a hip fracture. This is particularly true if the dysmobility resulted from impairment rather than ar-

Table 8-3   Predictors of Function in Patients with Hip Fracture

History
  Age
  Sex
  Current illness predictors
    Time from onset of fracture and/or surgery until initiation of rehabilitation
    Ambulation status prior to fracture
    Ambulation ability 2 wks postfracture
    Pain in affected extremity
    Type of surgical repair
    Weight-bearing status
  Immediate postoperative complications
    Failure of components
    Failure of fixation
    Decubitus ulcer
    Infection: surgical site, pulmonary
    Deep venous thrombosis/pulmonary embolism
    Delirium
  Other illness predictors
    Continence of bowel/bladder
    Cancer
    Cardiac disease
    Neurologic disorders
    Osteoporosis
    Pulmonary disorder
    Renal disorder
    Arthropathies/dorsopathies
    Carpal tunnel syndrome
  Social predictors
    Ability to leave home prior to fracture
    Family support
    Living with significant other
    Initial ADL score
    Not institutionalized prior to fracture
    Architectural barriers

Physical examination
  Signs of organ system impairment compatible with current illness and other
    illness predictors
  Psychological predictors
    Mental status: delirium, dementia, orientation
    Motivation
  Physical predictors
    Communication skills
    Physiological changes of aging
      Balance: proprioception, vestibular function, vision
      Strength

Range of motion: contractures
Posture
Gait
Leg length discrepancy
Obesity

chitectural, environmental, or host factors. However, as with all general rules or predictors, there are exceptions. For example, if the immobility is caused by fear of urinary incontinence and this factor can be reversed, then the patient may actually be more functional subsequent to the hip fracture and treatment of incontinence than previously.

The critical importance of the time from onset of fracture and/or surgery until initiation of rehabilitation should be emphasized. It is during this period that the patient is prone to development of many immobility complications, mostly as a result of deconditioning. They include the loss of strength with bed rest and the development of contractures, skin lesions, pulmonary infections, and the like. One extremely important but poorly recognized complication is the development of dependency. Elderly patients at bed rest may become accustomed to nurses taking care of their needs and often express resentment when the rehabilitation team, including the rehabilitation nurse, tries to force them to perform those activities of daily living that they are capable of performing safely.

In patients with hip fractures, as with other conditions, limitations for the rehabilitation program may be set by the primary physician. In the case of a patient with a hip fracture, the orthopedic surgeon will place limitations on the stress to which the involved joint may be subjected. Thus, weight bearing and/or range of motion (ROM) of the involved extremity may be limited. We know that one of the physiological changes of aging is decreased ability to balance on one extremity. Thus, a patient may be severely impaired in function while the extremity is not bearing weight and rapidly progress in function once the involved extremity begins limited weight bearing. This also may affect the method of mobility selected: wheelchair mobility may be more practical during a certain phase of mobility training, and the patient may be advanced to ambulation as permitted weight bearing increases.

Another important realization/predictor is that the patient with a hip fracture is not bearing weight bilaterally to the same degree as prior to the fracture. Thus, joints that have previously been asymptomatic may become painful secondary to unaccustomed weight bearing. This is true not only for joints of the lower extremities but for joints of the upper extremities, which are now weight-bearing when assistive devices such as crutches or walkers are used. In addition, compressive neuropathies may become symptomatic because of changes in use and positioning of joints. An example of this is carpal tunnel syndrome, which is brought out by extension at the wrist. We have seen this syndrome become clinically evident in patients using assistive devices such as a walker or crutches because of positioning of the wrist. Symptoms are sometimes alleviated when patients are provided with platform devices attached to walker or crutch that switch weight-bearing stress from the wrist to the forearm.

Architectural factors become a key factor if a patient lives in a multistory dwelling or in a home with outside steps. The patient may be able to function only on one floor. The presence of another person to assist the patient in certain activities of daily living and, more important in maintaining the household and performing out-of-home instrumental activities of daily living (IADL), such as shopping may be crucial in allowing a patient to avoid institutionalization. A patient might live temporarily on one floor of a multistory dwelling, using a daybed or commode if bedroom or toilet is on a different level, until he or she is able to negotiate stairs.

Motivation is a key predictor. Unless the goal (i.e., ambulation) is functionally significant to the patient, the patient will not cooperate with a rehabilitation program. A goal of exercising or ambulation training may be too nonspecific for an elderly patient, but being able to walk to the toilet or dining room meets an obvious functional need. Sometimes creative motivational goal setting is needed, as when an uncooperative immobile patient became interested in attending a family function and then rapidly achieved independence in ambulation.

Some factors related to the physiological changes of aging may be partly reversible. For instance, the elderly frequently develop weakness in proximal muscles, particularly about the hip girdle. This causes difficulty in rising from a seated position. Strengthening the proximal muscles and making an environmental adaptation—a firm chair with armrests—can help to alleviate or remediate this risk factor. Similarly, leg length discrepancies may be adjusted by modifying shoes. With all risk factors, a decision has to be made as to whether they can be overcome by reversing the impairment or by substituting for the impairment. For example, if one is unable to flex enough at the hip to place one's foot in a shoe and tie the shoelaces, then one may substitute pretied elastic shoelaces and simply slip one's foot into the shoe.

For a substitutive methodology to work, the patient must be able to learn and remember new techniques. If recent memory is impaired, then the patient may be rehabilitated to do things in his or her usual manner (i.e., full-weight-bearing ambulation). If the patient is unable to learn substitutive techniques, such as partial weight bearing using assistive devices, his or her ability to benefit from rehabilitation would be limited unless there was someone who could be trained to supervise ambulation for the patient.

After the patient has been examined, medical and functional problem lists are composed. In fiscal year 1987, 121 patients were evaluated by our consultation service with the diagnosis of hip fracture. Table 8-4 indicates the functional problems seen in these patients. The primary problem, as anticipated, was the ambulation difficulty noted in 92.6% of these patients. Inability to get onto the feet in order to ambulate was noted: 64.5% had problems with transfers; 33.1%, with bed mobility. ROM problems were noted in 31.4%, translating into difficulties in washing and dressing of lower extremities. Similarly, balance impairment in 8.3% translated into other self-care deficits. Additional self-care problems were noted in 7.4% of these patients. In summary, all inpatients admitted to our rehabilitation units during the year had self-care/homemaking deficits.

Once the patient consultation has been completed, specific rehabilitation orders have to be written. The primary rehabilitation diag-

Table 8-4 Hip Fracture Problem List, Inpatient Consult Service (121 Patients)

Problem	No.	%
Ambulation	112	92.6
Transfers	78	64.5
Strength	56	46.3
Bed mobility	40	33.1
Range of motion	38	31.4
Pain acute extremity	19	15.7
Balance	10	8.3
Self-care	9	7.4
Joint deformity	7	5.8
Equipment needs	6	5.0
Hearing	6	5.0
Endurance	5	4.1
Architectural barriers	4	3.3
Skin	4	3.3
Tone	3	2.5
Pulmonary function	3	2.5
Intellectual-cognitive	3	2.5

nosis is identified as well as other functionally significant secondary diagnoses. Precautions concerning the patient's ability to participate in the rehabilitation program are also indicated. For example, mentation impairment impacts on the ability to learn and retain new information and techniques. Cardiac impairments may require monitoring. Other precautions could be limited weight bearing on the involved extremity, balance impairment, visual impairment, and so on. The rehabilitation sections to be involved are listed, and each is given initial orders. The rehabilitation orders are a form of communication between physician and therapist. They allow safe, accurate initiation of a rehabilitation program. They also perform an educational function, particularly in institutions with training programs. Special requirements for an accredited training program in physical medicine and rehabilitation include the necessity for specific treatment orders. Initial orders are modified according to patient progress and after interaction between the physician/resident and the treating section.

When the evaluation indicates that the patient would benefit from a more intensive therapy program than can be provided in an acute-care hospital, then he or she becomes a candidate for transfer to a rehabilitation unit. Such patients must meet the Medicare guidelines for admission to a comprehensive inpatient rehabilitation unit (Health Care Financing Administration, 1986). These guidelines include the need for medical supervision 24 hours a day, 7 days a week. Nursing, including rehabilitation nursing, must be available and needed 24 hours a day, 7 days a week. The patient should be able to benefit from therapy and have significant functional goals that can be achieved in a generally predictable period of time. He or she must be able to participate in and benefit from 3 hours of therapy a day, this could include physical therapy, occupational therapy, and speech-language pathology if there is a communicative or swallowing disorder. In special circumstances, orthotic/prosthetic services or other rehabilitation services may be a component of the 3 hours. All of these components must be appropriately documented.

Once the patient has been transferred to the rehabilitation unit, the physiatrist's role changes. Although still the consultant for the rehabilitation medicine portion of the patient's program, the physiatrist may also serve as the primary physician (Felsenthal et al., 1984), unless, as on some units, this role is fulfilled by a second physician. The rehabilitation team (Table 8-5) is now of paramount importance in evaluating and treating the patient. The physiatrist serves as a team manager and as program director for the patient. Each section evaluates the patient and establishes appropriate goals, and bi-weekly team meetings are needed, according to Medicare guidelines, to coordinate manage-

Table 8-5 The Rehabilitation Team

Patient and family[a]
Physician and specialist in rehabilitation (physiatrist)[a]
Medical physician/geriatrician[a]
Other medical specialists[a]
Rehabilitation nurse[a]
Physical therapist[a]
Occupational therapist[a]
Social service worker[a]
Psychologist[a]
Speech-language pathologist
Registered dietitian
Recreational therapist
Audiologist
Driver training teacher
Chaplain
Orthotist/prosthetist
Vocational counselor
Other

[a]Core team members, others according to patient need.

ment of the patient's functional problems. The patient serves as a key member of the team because the goals cannot be significant unless they meet the needs of the patient. The initial referring physician is an important part of the team, in that he or she provides the past medical history and may provide ongoing supervision after the patient is discharged from the unit. Communication with the patient's personal physician and other family members continues throughout the course of the rehabilitation program.

CASE HISTORY

E. M. B. is an 84-year-old woman who sustained a left transcervical, displace femoral neck fracture from a fall in her apartment. She had been walking in the kitchen when her left leg "gave out," and she fell. Her son and daughter carried her to bed. The next day she awoke with continued left hip and knee pain and was brought to the local community hospital's emergency room.

In the emergency room the patient was noted to be in discomfort, with an ecchymotic left hip and knee. The left lower extremity was shortened and externally rotated. Pelvic and left hip films revealed a transcervical left femoral fracture with displacement and impaction of the fracture site. Bilateral knee films showed severe osteoarthritic changes.

Social history revealed that the patient lived in a second-floor walk-up apartment. She lived with her son and daughter but was alone during the day. Prior to her fracture she was completely independent in all aspects of self-care. However, she did not venture out of her apartment except to visit other members of the family or her doctor.

The patient's past medical history was significant for mild systolic hypertension, congestive heart failure, osteoarthritis, and osteopenia. Past surgeries included cholecystectomy and appendectomy. Her medications were digoxin and piroxicam (Feldene®). Preoperative hemoglobin was 10.8 g/dl; hematocrit was 31.8%, with a mean corpuscular volume of 81.5 fL. The other preoperative laboratory results were unremarkable. Two units of packed red blood cells were given preoperatively. Medical clearance was given for the operation.

The following day the patient was taken to the operating room, where insertion of a cemented Thompson endoprosthesis was performed. Operative time was 55 min under spinal anesthesia. Roentgenograms of the left hip showed good anatomical positioning of the endoprothesis in relation to the acetabulum and femoral shaft. In the recovery room bilateral antiembolism stockings were applied. The postoperative medical course was unremarkable.

On the second postoperative day physical therapy was begun for gait training. The orthopedic surgeon prescribed weight bearing as tolerated for the patient's involved extremity. The physical therapist taught the patient precautions regarding hip motions and assessed ROM, sensation, and strength. Transfer to a chair with moderate assistance was performed. During the succeeding days the patient improved to requiring minimum assistance from bed to a standing position. She was able to ambulate 20 feet in the hallway with a walker with contact guard. Her dynamic balance was rated as good but not normal. It was also noted that the patient was dependent in dressing, toileting, and bathing skills. Her mental status was describe as alert and oriented. Because she would be alone during the day at home and was not yet independent in mobility, self-care, and homemaking skills (i.e., meal preparations), arrangements were made to transfer her to our rehabilitation hospital on the 8th postoperative day.

On admission to the rehabilitation hospital the patient was noted on physical examination to be a pleasant, alert woman in no acute distress. She was cooperative throughout the exam. Blood pressure was $160/80$. A thigh abduction pillow was in place. The left hip incision was notable for mild erythema at staple sites, but no discharge was noted. The surgical drain site was draining a minimal amount of serosanguineous fluid, with no signs of erythema or purulence.

Hypertrophic changes were noted in the upper extremity distal inter-phalangeal joints, as well as at the knees. Bilateral pitting edema at the ankles was noted; otherwise cardiorespiratory findings were within normal limits. The right lower extremity calf was 30 cm in diameter; the left calf measured 31 cm in diameter; both measurements were made at the same distance (20 cm) from the medial malleolus. There was no calf pain, tenderness, or Homan's sign. Leg lengths were equal at 89 cm from the anterior superior iliac spine to the medial malleolus. Grade I decubitus ulcers were noted at both heels and at the sacrum.

The neurologic exam was significant for a mild deficit in short-term memory, absent vibratory sensation at the toes, ankles, and knees, end-point dysmetria on finger-to-nose testing, and slowed but sym-metrically equal rapid finger movements. The remainder of neurologic examination was within normal limits.

The medical problem list for this patient included the noted or poten-tial problems listed in Table 8-6. Other medical problems frequently occurring in patients following hip fracture but not noted in this pa-tient are urinary incontinence, deep venous thrombosis–pulmonary embolism, myocardial infarction, pneumonia (Steinberg, 1983), post-operative delirium, medication reaction/complication.

The most common medical complication necessitating unplanned discharge from our rehabilitation unit and readmission to an acute-care hospital is deep venous thrombosis–pulmonary embolism. The next most frequent cause of unplanned discharge is myocardial infarction confirmed or suspected. The deep venous thrombosis is most fre-quently diagnosed within 72 hours of admission to the rehabilitation hospital but may occur later in the rehabilitation length of stay. Signs and symptoms of possible myocardial infarction may occur unpredicta-bly during the rehabilitation admission. Other medical problems are usually treated without necessitating readmission to the acute-care hos-pital (Felsenthal et al., 1984). The basic rule is that the medical problem

Table 8-6 Medical Problem List for Case Study Patient

Left transcervical femoral neck fracture treated with Thompson endoprosthesis
Osteopenia
Degenerative joint disease of knees
Hypertensive arterosclerotic cardiovascular disease with peripheral edema
Anemia
Deep venous thrombosis (potential)
Recent memory impairment
Peripheral neuropathy
Grade I decubiti of both heels and sacrum

should not interrupt the rehabilitation program for more than 3 treatment days; otherwise, discharge to an acute-care hospital is indicated.

In addition to the medical problem list, a functional problem list is also generated from the patient's history and physical examination (Table 8-7) and serves as the basis for the initial therapy orders. Initial short-term goals and long-term goals are determined based on the admission assessment and are modified at the bi-weekly rehabilitation team conference as indicated by the subsequent hospital course and response to therapy. The long-term goals for this patient would be restoration of the patient to her premorbid level of function—independence in mobility and self-care with homemaking skills as needed during the day when alone, such as simple meal preparation, making her bed, and so on. These goals are then broken down into segments capable of being accomplished within the 2 weeks between team conferences—short-term goals. In this patient, short-term goals might include ambulation advancing to independence from standby supervision; improving transfers from minimal assistance to contact guard; decreasing dependence in activities of daily living (ADL) (bathing, feeding, dressing, etc.) to minimal assistance, including setting up food tray, bringing grooming devices to the patient, dressing lower extremities.

From the patient's history and physical examination and consequent problem lists (Tables 8-6 and 8-7), a list of precautions is generated (Table 8-8). Other precautions appropriate for patients who have sustained a hip fracture but not pertinent to this patient might include anticoagulation and decreased vision. Precautions must be communicated as part of the orders to the treating therapists to facilitate the patient's ability to benefit from rehabilitation treatment and to prevent complications of that treatment (Currie & Marburger, 1988).

A fracture of the trochanteric region is generally repaired with a compression screw and side plate. Fractures involving the cervical region are repaired with nails (if undisplaced) or prosthetic devices (if dis-

---

Table 8-7   Functional Problem List for Case Study Patient

Minimal assistance required for transfers
Limited weight bearing on left leg secondary to pain
Dependent in dressing
Dependent in toileting
Dependent in grooming
Dependent in bathing
Dependent in meal preparation and other homemaking skills
Skin care—heels and sacrum

Table 8-8   Therapy Precautions for Case Study Patient

Avoid left thigh abduction
Avoid left hip flexion past 90°
Avoid left thigh internal rotation
Cardiac precautions
Recent memory impairment
Monitor for increased pain in left leg
Peripheral neuropathy

played), for example, a Thompson endoprosthesis. Each type of repair involves different rehabilitative concerns. Weight bearing is initially limited with nails, compression screws, and (according to many surgeons) the cementless prosthesis. ROM at the hip is initially limited with cemented or cementless prostheses. Surgical placement of a prosthesis involves opening the capsule of the hip. If one moves one's hip into certain positions (internal rotation, flexion greater than 90°, and adduction across the midline), there is an increased chance of dislocation until the capsular strength improves. The patient with organic brain disease presents a particular compliance challenge with weight-bearing and ROM restrictions.

Our patient had been experiencing pain with weight bearing secondary to osteoarthritis of the knee before her fracture. Although her orthopedic surgeon allowed "weight bearing as tolerated," unloading of the left lower extremity still occurred because of initial discomfort on standing. This temporarily increased the weight on her upper extremities and right lower extremity. Increased pain complaints might be addressed by medication as well as the use of techniques such as transcutaneous electrical neural stimulation (TENS), ice, heat, and judicious use of rest periods during gait and ADL retraining, as needed. Assistive devices such as crutches, canes, and walkers decrease weight-bearing stresses on joints of the lower extremities but increase stress on the upper extremity joints. Also, it must be emphasized that pain, particularly increased or different pain (quality of pain or site of pain), may be a warning of a fracture site complications. When this happens, the patient must be carefully reevaluated before resuming therapy.

Initial orders for the rehabilitation team (Table 8-9) derive from the functional problems identified (Table 8-7). They are goal-specific and should be related to the primary rehabilitation diagnosis or diagnoses (Table 8-6, Medical Problem List), functional problems (Table 8-7), and precautions (Table 8-8).

Patients who have sustained a fracture of a lower limb need to be cautious regarding the resumption of weight bearing during transfers

Table 8-9 Therapy Orders for Case Study Patient

Physical therapy
  Transfer training
  Progressive ambulation training with weight bearing as tolerated on left leg
    and with assistive devices as needed on level and steps/stairs
  Hot packs to reduce ecchymosis, left thigh
  Active assisted ROM, left thigh—within precautions—and instruct patient
    on precautions
  Graded ROM, other joints, involved extremity and major joints uninvolved
    extremities
  Progressive resistive exercises (PRE) weight-stressed muscles, upper
    extremities
  Isometric strengthening exercises, left hip and knee extensors
  PRE, right leg, hip, and knee flexors, extensors, abductors (if knee pain
    increases, use isometric exercises)
Occupational therapy
  Activity of daily living evaluation and treatment
  Homemaking training, i.e., meal preparation
  Functional activities, upper extremities
Psychology
  Evaluation of recent memory loss and advise treatment team re compensation
    techniques/impact on retention of newly learned techniques
Social services
  Evaluate home situation especially in regard to degree of independence
    needed for return home
Dietitian
  Advise re diet, i.e., anemia
Rehabilitation nursing
  Incorporate accomplished short-term goals into patient's nursing unit routine
  Medication education
  Skin care

---

and ambulation. Typically, weight bearing progresses in stages, from non-weight bearing to toe touch, or 10% weight bearing, and then to partial, or 50% weight bearing. Later, weight bearing as tolerated or perhaps full weight bearing will be ordered. The orthopedic surgeon typically manages this aspect of care. When a cemented prosthesis is in place, weight bearing as tolerated is often the initial order. If a screw and side plate have been inserted, non-weight bearing or toe-touch weight bearing may be ordered. Non-weight bearing means the affected leg will swing, pendulum-like, and the person has to hop, initially in the parallel bars and then with a walker or other assistive device. Toe-touch weight bearing is the very light placement of only the forefoot on the ground, with nearly all of the weight supported by the other three limbs. The ability to toe-touch improves the balance (and decreases energy expenditures) during ambulation. However, the ability to walk up stairs with higher restriction would take a very high level of upper limb strength and excellent balance, which is frequently not present in the geriatric population. Thus, an older person is usually restricted to single-floor living until the weight-bearing status improves to partial or beyond. Some orthopedic surgeons are conservative as to when they allow partial or 50% weight bearing. It is a difficult level to determine with any precision. If there is concomitant neuropathy, Parkinson's disease, a prior stroke, dementia, or similar problem, to guarantee 50% weight bearing with each step would be impossible. Thus, full weight bearing might be delayed for 6 weeks to 6 months, until the bony fragments have united.

Restriction of weight bearing on the involved leg during ambulation means that the other three limbs must bear more weight. The arms bear weight in the parallel bars and with use of a walker, crutches, or canes. To do this well requires strong muscles that will not fatigue easily. In the upper extremity, weight-stressed muscles such as the deltoid, triceps, biceps, wrist extensors, and long finger flexors are strengthened. In the uninvolved lower extremity, weight-bearing muscles are strengthened. For the involved extremity the program is different, as the therapist must avoid too much strain initially yet maintain flexibility and increase strength. Isometric quadriceps strengthening and active-assisted ROM exercises within prescribed hip motion limitations are begun. Exercises progress as tolerated, with the patient eventually doing independent joint ROM of the affected limb against gravity. Progressive resistance exercises can be added when indicated clinically.

Pain, weakness, and hip precautions need to be overcome as much as possible for a person to be able to move independently in bed. Inability to do this will rapidly result in skin ulceration, complicate bowel and bladder continence, and increase the risk of deep venous thrombosis; in general, it reflects a weak physical state. Physical and occupational therapists and rehabilitation nurses instruct and motivate patients in various techniques to maximize bed mobility.

Techniques for correcting any impaired sitting or standing balance are instituted as needed. Mirrors, soft and hard surfaces, very large balls for sitting, and other devices may be utilized.

Hip ROM restrictions/precautions impede a large variety of daily activities: moving about in bed, dressing below the waist, washing the legs, bending down to reach low objects, not to mention ingrained habits such as crossing the legs. For this last reason an "abduction pil-

low" (a wedge-shaped piece of foam with Velcro straps) or—less preferred—a regular pillow is placed between the thighs when in bed or a
chair. Much of occupational and physical therapy is concerned with
helping the individual through this period of restriction of hip ROM.

Transfers refer to the ability to shift the body between sitting and
standing, bed and chair, standing and toilet, and getting in and out of
a bathtub, shower, and car. Different transfer techniques, such as a
sliding board, sit-pivot, or stand-pivot, may be appropriate for different persons. In addition, a raised toilet seat with grab bars on either
side and tub seats with wall or seat bars help with bathroom transfer
safety. Seats should be high enough so that the patient does not exceed
90° of hip flexon. Patients are not truly independent in ambulation unless they are independent in bed mobility, balance, and transfers—able
to get onto their feet independently and safely.

ADL include dressing, grooming, the use of toilet (including self-
cleaning), bathing in the bed, at sinkside, or in a shower or bath. To
overcome the initial prescribed limitations of motion, a variety of devices may be utilized such as a dressing stick, sock donner, long-handled sponge, long-handled shoehorn, long-handled reacher, and the
previously mentioned elevated toilet seat (Seeger & Fisher, 1982). Aspects of cognition, coordination, balance, and transfer abilities are all
integrated in the teaching and reinforcement of these ADL. Occupational therapy teaches and rehabilitation nursing reinforces the acquisition of these skills. Home architectural barriers may also be identified
and plans made as needed.

Independent activities of daily living (IADL) are added as patients
progress in their rehabilitation program (Lawton & Brody, 1969). Thus,
kitchen activities, laundry work, simulated shopping, keeping checking accounts, and the like are part of the extended occupational therapy program.

Situational depression and anxiety is commonly noted during the rehabilitation period. Evaluation and support is provided by the psychologist, with family and staff members helping. Also, evaluation of
learning ability and recent memory impairment is crucial in guiding the
rehabilitation team's approach to the patient and in guidance of the
patient's family.

Any patient will have varying amounts of assistance from family and
friends. The social worker identifies any caregivers who can help during the time of disability and mobilizes them to participate in the rehabilitation process, both in hospital and after discharge. In addition,
supportive counseling to patient and family, with identification of community resources, is done.

A valuable service to the patient is the introduction by the recreational therapist of hobbies or other social and personal interests into the hospital stay. This will improve the patient's mood and desire to resume a normal life-style. Recreational therapy can also help the patient translate learned mobility, ADL, and IADL skills into the community living skills required for independent living.

In addition to incorporating achieved ambulatory and self-care skills into the patient's daily nursing unit routine, rehabilitation nursing includes dispensing medications to the patient. It is recognized that appropriate self-medication is crucial to patients' management of their medical problems. Inappropriate medication management leads to medical and functional deterioration, which may preclude the patient's return to community living or staying in the community. Thus, patient/family medication education is a key rehabilitation goal, and independence in medication management parallels functional independence and the ability to stay in or return to community living (Felsenthal, Glomski & Jones, 1986).

The patient (E. M. B.) progressed in the rehabilitation hospital; by the time of discharge she had improved from moderate assistance to distant supervision for transfers. Ambulation with a walker on level surfaces progressed from 20 feet with contact guard to 150 feet independently. By discharge she was able to negotiate a full flight of stairs with contact guard, using one rail and a walker. By that time she had progressed from moderate assistance in lower extremity dressing and dependence for lower extremity washing to independence in both. Occasional verbal cues for hip precautions were needed during self-care activities. Supervision was required during light homemaking activities because of her slightly impaired balance. A family conference, with the patient and rehabilitation team attending, was held prior to discharge to review the patient's functional status and formulate discharge follow-up plans.

At the end of this patient's 15-day stay she was discharged to home with walker, elevated bedside commode, sock donner, long-handled shoehorn and sponge, and dressing stick. On follow-up, the patient was doing well in the home setting.

The goal of returning to the home setting is achieved in approximately 70% of patients treated on a rehabilitation unit (Felsenthal et al., 1984). Length of stay on a rehabilitation unit for a patient who sustains a hip fracture is usually 3 weeks. The goal of restoring the patient as closely as possible to premorbid level of function may be attainable during the inpatient rehabilitation stay, but further home care or outpatient treatment is commonly needed to reach that goal. A case study of dysmobility in a patient who sustained a cerebrovascular accident complicated by an amputation is discussed by Redford (1989).

Rehabilitation of the geriatric patient, including those with fractures and dysmobility, have recently been discussed by Clark and Murray (1988) and Lee and Itoh (1988). Assessment and evaluation of functional outcome is discussed by Frey (1988).

SUMMARY

Dysmobility is a common functional problem of the elderly that increases in prevalence with aging. Its etiology may be organ system impairment, iatrogenic causes, or architectural, environmental, or host factors impacting singly on the patient or, more likely, interacting to cause the dysmobility. Initial physiatric evaluation attempts to identify the etiology of the dysmobility and determine whether the underlying cause is progressive, static, or reversible. Predictors of future function are searched for, and medical and functional problems identified. A specific rehabilitation program with appropriate precautions and both short- and long-term goals is prescribed, and the rehabilitation team initiates evaluation and treatment. Patient progress is carefully monitored, medically and functionally, with periodic modification of program and goals. Patient, family, and primary physician involvement and concurrence with goals is crucial for successful achievement of significant functional goals and maintenance of these goals after discharge from the rehabilitation unit.

REFERENCES

Clark, G. S., & Murray, P. K. (1988). Rehabilitation of the geriatric patient. In J. A. DeLisa (Ed.), *Rehabilitation medicine principles and practices* (pp. 410–429). Philadelphia: J. B. Lippincott.

Currie, D. M., & Marburger, R. A. (1988). Writing therapy referrals and treatment plans and the interdisciplinary team. In J. A. DeLisa (Ed.), *Rehabilitation medicine principles and practices* (pp. 145–157). Philadelphia: J. B. Lippincott.

Feller, B. A. (1983, Sept. 14). Americans needing help to function at home. *Advancedata 92.*

Felsenthal, G., Cohen, B. S., Hilton, E. B., Panagos, A. V., & Aiken, B. M. (1984). The physiatrist as primary physician for patients on an inpatient rehabilitation unit. *Archives of Physical and Medical Rehabilitation, 65,* 375–378.

Felsenthal, G., Glomski, N., & Jones, D. (1986). Medication education program in an inpatient geriatric rehabilitation unit. *Archives of Physical and Medical Rehabilitation, 67,* 27–29.

Frey, W. D. (1988). Functional outcome: Assessment and evaluation. In J. A. DeLisa (Ed.), *Rehabilitation medicine principles and practices* (pp. 158–172). Philadelphia: J. B. Lippincott.

Health Care Financing Administration. (1986). Inpatient rehabilitation hospital care: Section 3101.11(D). Medicare Intermediary Manual: Part 3. Claims process. Transmittal No. 1293, 3–38.8–3–38.9.

Lawton, M. P., & Brody, E. M. (1969). Assessment of older people: Self-maintaining and instrumental activities of daily living. *Gerontologist, 9,* 179–186.

Lee, M., & Itoh, M. (1988). Geriatric rehabilitation management. In J. Goodgold (Ed.), *Rehabilitation medicine* (pp. 393–406). St. Louis: C. V. Mosby.

Mace, R. I. (1976). *Accessibility modifications: Guidelines for modifications to existing buildings for accessibility to the handicapped.* Raleigh, NC: North Carolina Department of Insurance, Special Office for the Handicapped.

Mace, R. I., & Laslett, B. (1977). *An illustrated handbook of the handicapped section of the North Carolina State Building Code.* Raleigh, NC: North Carolina Department of Insurance, Special Office for the Handicapped.

Redford, J. (1989). Rehabilitation and the aged. In W. Reichel (Ed.), *Clinical aspects of aging* (3rd ed.) (pp. 1177–1187). Baltimore: Williams and Wilkins.

Rubenstein, L. Z., Robbins, A. S., Schulman, B. L., Rosado, J., Osterweil, D., & Josephson, K. R. (1988). Falls and instability of the elderly. *Journal of the American Geriatrics Society, 36,* 266–278.

Sabin, T. D. (1982). Biologic aspects of falls and mobility limitations in the elderly. *Journal of the American Geriatrics Society, 30,* 51–58.

Seeger, M. S., & Fisher, L. A. (1982). Adaptive equipment used in the rehabilitation of hip arthroplasty patients. *American Journal of Occupational Therapy, 36,* 503–508.

Steinberg, F. (1983). Complications of hip fracture in a 79-year-old widow. In R. D. T. Cape, R. M. Coe, & I. Rossman (Eds.), *Fundamentals of geriatric medicine* (pp. 377–403). New York: Raven Press.

Warshaw, G. A., Moore, J. T., Friedman, S. W., Currie, C. T., Kennie, D. C., Kane, W. J., & Mears, P. A. (1982). Functional disability in the hospitalized elderly. *Journal of the American Medical Association, 248,* 847–850.

Zuckerman, J. D., & Newport, M. L. (1988). Rehabilitation of fractures in adults. In J. Goodgold (Ed.), *Rehabilitation medicine* (pp. 441–456). St. Louis: C. V. Mosby.

Part IV

The Practice Model: Environment

9

Social, Behavioral, and Environmental Issues

M. Powell Lawton, Elaine M. Brody, and
Avalie R. Saperstein

The larger rubric under which the topics of this particular chapter could be grouped is *the context of rehabilitation*. A great deal of the content of *Aging and Rehabilitation* necessarily focuses on the person who receives rehabilitative services and the professional who delivers the treatment. Whatever the function to be featured, there is a specialist trained in the intricacies of that system and in techniques to elevate that function.

All rehabilitation must occur in a context that includes more than the individual. Indeed, we are sophisticated enough to recognize and to implement the required behavior that takes account of the system nature of the patient in context.

Nonetheless, this chapter will attempt to specify, differentiate, and reintegrate several features of the rehabilitation context that can be critical determinants of how well some of the focused rehabilitative therapies work.

As a beginning, however, it seems desirable to specify what we mean by the context of rehabilitation. Read literally, this phrase portrays the stage, the background, the borders of a scenario in which rehabilitation, one-to-one treatment, occurs. Let us revise that unfortunate connotation. The person receiving the treatment and the professional performing a rehabilitative act are two components of the rehabilitation context. This chapter will treat three other components: the family, the formal treatment system, and the physical environment of rehabilitation. Other contextual elements could include the reimbursement system, the political ideology of the day, social attitudes toward aging or disability, and many other similar influences. The point at which we must begin is that each contextual element represents a possible point for intervention. The following three sections will even more directly advance the points of view that the family, the formal service system, and the physical environment all have underutilized potential for being active sources of intervention. Further, this type of thinking can be incorporated into rehabilitation training in ways that will broaden the perspective of every professional.

A FAMILY-FOCUSED REHABILITATION APPROACH[1]

The family is our full partner and indispensable ally in rehabilitation of the disabled aged. Achievement of professional goals for rehabilitation of the aged patient depends on viewing family members from another perspective as well. The family is our "patient" in a real sense because family members are at risk of mental and physical problems if their caring roles become unduly stressful. Attempts to overutilize the family as an active source of intervention, therefore, may result in losing the caregivers who are critical to the rehabilitation effort. The current situation is such that the risk of undue stress is high. At times, then, a major goal is to help the family to *reduce* the amount of care it provides for its disabled elderly.

It has become customary to characterize the social environment of the disabled aged as being composed of the informal system of care (a bloodless euphemism for the family) and the formal system: government, agency, and professionals. For some years a major social policy issue has concerned the respective roles of the two systems. The climate has been to encourage the family to "shape up" to fulfill obligations it is accused of neglecting. Proponents of increasing family care and reducing the involvement of the formal system have based their stance on the proposition that families nowadays need urging to do what they should. This often is a rationale for saving public policy dollars by failing to expand (or even by shrinking) the formal system. However, as one gerontologist put it a quarter of a century ago, the needs of the elderly have gone beyond the self-solution and the kinship solution to require societal solutions (Blenkner, 1965). A rebalancing of the contributions of the formal and informal systems is even more necessary now.

The dramatic increase of disabled older people has been described, as has the replacement of acute diseases by chronic ailments as the major health problems of the elderly (cf., Chapters 1 and 2). During the same time span that witnessed the increase in the need for rehabilitation and chronic care, another demographic trend occurred. The birth rate fell rapidly, reducing the pool of adult children available to provide that care. Nevertheless, the family met the challenge by continuing to provide the bulk of helping services. Data from the National 1982 Long Term Care survey confirmed the findings of a long series of studies that the vast majority of all health services to disabled older people are provided by family members (cf., Brody, Chapter 2, Table 2-5). Only 15% of all "helper days of care" in the community are provided by all formal (government and agency) services together (Doty, Liu, & Wiener, 1985).

Among the questions asked about the role of the family have been the following: Does provision of formal services result in the withdrawal of family care? And (again prompted by concern for the public dollar) do formal services result in the prevention of costly nursing home care? As the vast amount of research on that question has been reviewed many times, only the consensus conclusions are stated here: Formal services do not encourage families to reduce the amount of care they provide; they complement and supplement family care. Moreover, families are extremely modest in their requests for help, even when offered services freely and encouraged to use them. When older people are severely disabled, community care does not prevent institutionalization. Moreover, for that population, community care is not cheaper in dollars than institutional care.

The Strains of Family Caregiving

Of central importance to professional approaches to rehabilitation of the elderly is the body of knowledge about the effects of caregiving on the caring family members. The rehabilitation literature concerning younger disabled populations emphasizes the effects on the entire family when a family member is disabled. This is no less true with older families. A consistent body of research reports that one half to three quarters of family caregivers experience moderate to severe stress effects in the form of symptoms such as depression, guilt, anxiety, lowered morale, sleeplessness, and emotional exhaustion. Smaller but significant minorities experience financial strain or detrimental effects on the physical health.

Elderly spouses provide most of the care to their disabled husbands or wives, helped by adult children when need be. Such spouses are a high-risk group because they also are in old age and often have health problems themselves. Most of the disabled elderly are very old and widowed, however. They rely primarily on adult daughters. Daughters provide almost one third of all care, but their role increases proportionately to providing more than half of the help received by the most severely disabled aged (Stone, Cafferata, & Sangl, 1987). The changes occurring in the characteristics and lives of adult daughters therefore exemplify the reasons that the formal system requires expansion.

Because the birth rate continues to fall and the number of very old vulnerable people continues to increase, there will be fewer daughters (the traditional caregivers) available to the old. Fewer daughters means that daughters more often have sole responsibility for the care of their own elderly parents, and they more often care for parents-in-law as well in their role as daughters-in-law. Many such women have caregiving careers, in that more and more of them are providing care for two and sometimes more than two older people simultaneously or sequentially. Those careers are often long and arduous. About 45% of daughters helping one elderly parent have been doing so for 1 to 4 years and 19% for 5 or more years (Stone, Cafferata, & Sangl, 1987).

The role of adult children, and of daughters in particular, is highlighted by data concerning their role in delaying nursing home admissions. The lack or loss of social supports in the form of family is a strong predictor of nursing home admission. In fact, it is estimated that 10% to 15% of recent increases in nursing home use related to the fact that today's elderly have fewer children than did their parents (Crystal, 1982). Moreover, the absence of at least one daughter indicates a greater risk of institutionalization at a lower level of disability (Soldo, 1982).

The lives of parent-caring women have been taking increasingly diverse paths, and this too affects their caregiving capacities. Only a quarter of a century ago, almost three fourths of those (other than a spouse) to whom older people turned in a health crisis were married women in their middle years (Shanas, 1961). But several trends have combined to change that picture. The divorce rate has soared, almost tripling between 1962 and 1981 (NCHS, 1985). There has been an increase in the number of never-married women; the marriage rate for all unmarried women is the lowest it has been since data were first recorded in 1940 (NCHS, 1986). It is likely that widowed daughters constitute an increased proportion of caregivers because the disabled elderly come primarily from the ranks of the very old, people whose children are older and therefore more likely to be widowed. At ages 45 to 54 about 7.6% of women are widowed, a proportion that rises steadily to 41.2% at ages 65 to 74 (Brotman, 1980). The net result of these changing patterns in marital status is that 44% of daughter caregivers now are women who do not have husbands (Stone, Cafferata, & Sangl, 1987).

Each group of caregivers experiences special kinds of strains depending on their marital status, and the stress of parent care is superimposed on these problems (E. Brody, 1990). Among the factors associated with depression among women, for example, are being separated or divorced, experiencing stressful life events, and lack of an intimate confiding relationship (U.S. DHHS, 1985), factors that characterize many unmarried daughter caregivers. Moreover, social supports such as that of a spouse serve to buffer caregiver stress (Horowitz, 1985), and that form of support is not available to mitigate the strains of women without husbands. Accompanying the rising divorce rate has been a rise in rates of remarriage, with the divorce rate even higher for remarriages than for first marriages (Weed, 1981). There is virtually no information about special strains of parent care that may occur when caregivers are remarried, nor about patterns of filial loyalty and care provision when the disabled parents are remarried.

There also is increasing diversity in the life stages at which parent care becomes part of women's lives. Not only are more women becoming caregivers when they are older, but more young women are having a first child at later ages and therefore have young children when parent care is needed. At present about one fourth of daughter caregivers are under the age of 45 (Stone, Cafferata, & Sangl, 1987). Another rising form of "double dependency" is caused by the longer lives of developmentally disabled people. Middle-generation women more often care for their disabled adult children as well as for their disabled parents.

The most visible and dramatic trend of all, of course, has been the rapid entry of women into the labor force. Between 1930 and 1985 the proportion of working-age women in the labor force rose from 24% to 70%. It is projected that by 1995 8 of 10 women will work, and they will be nearly 60 million strong (U.S. Department of Labor, 1986). The major increase has been among those between the ages of 45 and 64 (Lingg, 1975), ages that are the peak parent-care years.

Most women work because they and their families need the money they earn. But work and care of parents and parents-in-law are not always compatible. Though the women struggle to meet their responsibilities to husbands, children, homes, jobs, and the disabled elderly, giving up only their own free time in the process, some of them find it necessary to quit their jobs or to reduce their working hours (E. Brody, Kleban, Johnson, Hoffman, & Schoonover, 1987; Stone, Cafferata, & Sangl, 1987). Those who continue to work have other strains: work interruptions and worry about what's going on at home, for example. The social costs are high in terms of the mental and physical health of such women. The opportunity costs have not been fully calculated, but available data suggest that the income losses are incurred primarily by those who can least afford it (E. Brody et al., 1987).

What all this adds up to is that nowadays more women who are daughters and daughters-in-law provide much more care to many more old people who are more disabled, and they do so for much longer periods of time. Prolonged care of more of the older people in their lives, in addition to their work force participation, has added to the multiple roles women have always played. These women, who have been characterized as women-in-the-middle (E. Brody, 1990) are subjected to more strains—some are the old familiar strains, and some are new.

Helping Caregivers Cope

The suffering of many caregivers has been well documented: many of them go far beyond what seem to be the limits of human endurance. Too often, that suffering is not perceived by professionals, who, with tunnel vision, focus on the elderly patient and regard the caregivers simply as people who are available to implement prescribed rehabilitation procedures.

Alleviation of some of that suffering—though we cannot do it all—requires efforts on several levels.

First, publicly financed long-term care insurance must be available to relieve some of the pressures on family members who provide the day-to-day care for the disabled elderly. The highly touted Medicare Catastrophic Coverage Act notwithstanding, we still do not have such a system. Creating that system is a question of values, a political problem (S. Brody, 1987) that demands all of our efforts. The major report of the Brookings Institution states that private insurance should be encouraged but that most people could not afford it.

Second, even when services do exist, they are not always accessible to caregivers.

Third, even when services exist and are accessible, many caregivers do not use them. Among such nonusers are those who are most in need (Lawton, Brody, & Saperstein, 1989).

Fourth, even when services are available, even when they are accessible, and even when caregivers want to use them, the physical environments may present barriers.

If rehabilitation of the elderly is to be an effective reality, all of these interrelated problems require attention. In addition to policy mandates that would put community services in place and make quality institutional care available when needed, the various service elements must be organized into a coherent and accessible system. Caregivers who do not use available services even when their need is great require help to do so (see following section, "Increasing Families' Use of Formal Services"; E. Brody, 1990). The agenda for all of us is to move forward in a positive direction toward those goals.

INCREASING FAMILIES' USE OF FORMAL SERVICES[2]

People are reluctant to use formal services for a myriad of reasons. Attitudes held by caregivers, the psychological dilemmas inherent in caregiving, and problems in the service systems are the primary reasons for this reluctance.

Just as our society places the responsibility of elder care on families, caregivers themselves have internalized this attitude. They frequently refuse services because of the feeling that it is their responsibility alone to provide the care. They may believe that no one can care for their disabled elderly as well as they can or that persons of their ethnic, racial, or religious group "take care of their own." Caregivers' adherence to another social norm, that of family independence, also plays a role. "Good" families are able to take care of each other, and for many people acceptance of outside help implies a loss of social status or power (Fulton & Katz, 1986).

Many caregivers experience difficulty in maintaining an identity separate from that of the caregiver. Caregiving tasks can be totally consuming both in time and in emotional investment. As a result, some caregivers become so involved in meeting the disabled person's needs that their own needs for work, socialization, and leisure time become secondary or are ignored. Furthermore, caregivers struggle to protect what they think the impaired relatives would want done on their behalf, even when it conflicts with their own self-interest. This struggle is vividly illustrated in the use of services. Some of the caregivers in the Philadelphia Geriatric Center's Family Respite Care Program,[3] for example, initially refused respite they needed because, in their perceptions, the impaired persons would not like strangers caring for them.

The guilt that caregivers experience despite the reality of their heroic caregiving efforts also inhibits formal service use. Guilt is experienced by caregivers in many forms: not doing enough or not doing it well enough, unacceptable negative feelings such as wishing the person were dead, getting angry at a helpless person, or wanting some relief from the situation. Caregivers whose guilt is pervasive and severe often reject help because it intensifies their negative feelings or creates anxiety that something will happen to their loved one if left in the care of others.

Families are often overwhelmed by the complexity, difficulty, and time requirements of the caregiving tasks and the rehabilitation regimens they are called upon to perform. Although the use of services may ultimately relieve some of their burden, the initial time and emotional investment in obtaining and trying services requires more energy than some overwhelmed caregivers can expend.

Inherent in using a new service is the concept of change. Change is difficult for people of every age, but it is even more difficult for caregivers of older people whose behavioral patterns and attitudes in regard to health care may have prevailed for 50 or more years. Caregivers of postrehabilitation patients experience multiple changes: the patient's entry into a hospital or into a rehabilitation facility, change in the patient's functional status, and change in living arrangements. Being thrust into another new situation—that of using unfamiliar services—may be resisted.

Rehabilitation efforts seldom return a disabled older person to prior functional status, so caregivers often grieve and mourn the loss of capacity of their loved one or the prior relationship it had supported. Although each caregiver has a unique response to this situation, some may be too depressed to undertake anything new. For others, accepting help may emphasize the change in the patient's status that they are trying to deny.

Families' attitudes toward money can also inhibit use of vitally needed services. As documented in the Family Respite Care Program, as well as in other respite initiatives (i.e., Duke University Aging Center), many families are reluctant to use their financial resources for services until "they really need it"—that is, until they are physically and emotionally depleted. They may fear exhausting their resources for community care so that funds will not be available for nursing home care if that time should come. When services are offered without cost or for modest fees, some caregivers are reluctant to accept "charity." They may feel that someone else's situation warrants it more than theirs does, and some do not wish to subject themselves to public disclosure of income and demeaning means testing.

The formal system of services presents many barriers to its utilization. It is a discontinuous and fragmented system (Brody, Poulshock, & Maschiocchi, 1978), the various service components unrelated to or uncoordinated with each other. Each service has its unique eligibility criteria, for example, age, income, medical status, residency, length of service criteria, costs, and access patterns. To secure most services, families must first identify their specific needs and must know about and seek out the appropriate service(s). There is no universal case management service that identifies needy individuals and assists their access to and utilization of services. As disabled persons move from one level of care to another, services are simply discontinued for each level and not automatically given at the next. It is a baffling system for professionals and families alike, requiring sophistication, motivation, and perseverance.

Families often cite poor-quality services as the reasons to refuse them. Complaints about homemaker service may relate to homemakers' unreliability, lack of motivation, and lack of knowledge about caring for impaired persons adequately. Despite the complex tasks such personnel are called on to perform, they are often untrained and inadequately compensated.

Many services are inaccessible to families. Some require families to leave their homes in order to secure them (e.g., application for entitlements) when the impaired person cannot be left alone or taken along, or the caregiver herself may be too impaired to make the trip. Obtaining appropriate medical care can also present problems. Some families simply cannot manage the logistics of getting their disabled family member to multiple medical appointments, each located in a different place. Long waits in medical clinics present additional barriers.

When community services do exist—day care, homemaker, and respite, for example—they may not be affordable to those who are poor or whose incomes are low and may severely strain the finances of those with middle incomes. Publicly funded services may not exist or may be extremely scarce. The demands for service far exceed the resources available, so people languish on waiting lists or receive only part of what they require.

The criteria eligibility for many publicly funded services pose still additional obstacles for caregivers. Many services funded through the Older Americans Act and Title XX of the Social Security Act (major social funding sources) are targeted for disabled persons who live alone, disregarding the needs of patients and caregivers who live together.

Clinical experience indicates that when families' attitudes and psychological conflicts and the deficits in the service system are addressed, families can be assisted to use formal services effectively. The rehabilitation setting provides a powerful opportunity to deal with such issues and thus to help families use resources, both following discharge from rehabilitation units and as needs arise throughout the course of caregiving. An essential precondition, however, is that the rehabilitation team's framework for working with families includes more than simply helping the family implement rehabilitation goals that have been set for the disabled patient. The framework must focus on families' short-term and long-term needs in providing caregiving as well as rehabilitation because these are interlocked. Such a framework more accurately reflects the reality of caring for a disabled older adult (i.e., trajectory of chronic illness, cf., Chapter 2). From it emerges the context in which to explore families' continuing needs for support over time.

Assessment of the caregiver, that is, an examination of the caregiver's capabilities and needs, can set a positive tone for the use of resources. In focusing on the caregiver it conveys the message that her own needs are important. It can help to communicate that caregivers have needs, roles, and responsibilities separate from that of caregiving and that at times their needs and the needs of the disabled person may compete. This differentiation is essential; frequent reinforcement and reemphasis of this perspective is imperative. Although ultimately a delicate balance must be achieved between the requirements of the caregiver and those of the impaired person, the differentiation must be made before a reconciliation can occur and resources can be utilized.

The caregiver assessment process identifies for family members what they can and cannot do, providing an excellent opportunity for a positive approach to the subject of resources. The rehabilitation team can convey to families that no family can do it all, that it is normal and expected that families need help, and that formal services can assist them to do what they can do more effectively. This approach challenges families' perceptions that they must do it all in order to be "good" families. In short, it normalizes the use of resources.

Because the caregiver assessment process focuses on long-term as well as short-term needs, it can be particularly helpful to those families able to marshal their energies not only for the immediate and demanding situation but for long-term problems as well. The team can help these families to define and prepare for situations in the future that may include the use of formal services.

Another task of the rehabilitation team is to educate families about the community's system of resources. Special emphasis may be placed on homemaker, day care, and respite options. Although details can be overwhelming, caregivers need general information about the types of service available for possible future use. However, very specific information needs to be conveyed about services required at discharge or shortly thereafter. Possible problems about resources should be discussed, not to frighten caregivers but to prepare them for situations they are likely to encounter. Caregivers should not merely be given a list of resources to call after discharge but should be encouraged to connect with at least one resource prior to leaving the rehabilitation setting. In that way, potential problems can be discussed and problem-solving methods adapted. Whenever possible, the family, rather than the rehabilitation team, should make the arrangements in order to gain experience in working with the formal system.

Short-term counseling is a key and often a needed intervention to help families use resources. Although the whole rehabilitation team can be sensitive to the barriers families face in using resources and can be helpful by setting a positive tone, certain issues (such as caregiver guilt or difficulty in differentiating the caregiver's needs from those of the disabled person) can be ameliorated only by means of a therapeutic process. As team members identify each family's unique issues, these can be conveyed to the team social worker. The latter may engage the caregiver in individual counseling or, as often occurs in families of older people, may include the entire family in the counseling process. The importance of such counseling should not be overlooked. Positive professional attitudes and family education are simply not enough to change many of the attitudes and conflicts that impede caregivers' use of resources.

There are, of course, limits to what the rehabilitation team can accomplish. It can offer only a very short-term intervention for a long-term problem and cannot follow the family over time to be on hand when other problems emerge. Team members may only begin to touch on the issues that need long-term resolution. Families may require an ongoing professional relationship, not to cheer them on to perform even more arduous caregiving but to help resolve long-term or newly arising issues and problems. For some caregivers, connection to family counseling agencies or to in-home service programs funded by Area Agencies on Aging can be vitally important. Whenever possible, this type of assistance should be arranged prior to discharge to avoid discontinuity of service.

In conclusion, caregivers of disabled older people have special concerns that need to be addressed before they are willing and able to use resources. When the rehabilitation team addresses these concerns—notably, caregiver attitudes about services and psychological dilemmas about caregiving—caregivers can be helped to use the resources that can benefit their situations, and families can be supported in their efforts to care for and rehabilitate their disabled family members.

PHYSICAL ENVIRONMENT OF REHABILITATION[4]

It has been almost 25 years since the psychologist Ogden Lindsley (1964) coined the term "geriatric behavioral prosthetics." This was the title of a speculative chapter about ways in which some of the presumed deficits associated with aging might be counteracted by interventions in the environment. Therapy was conceived as intervention directed toward the person, with the expectation that the person would change permanently and the treatment eventually would be discontinued. Prosthetics accepts some amount of permanence of impairment and seeks a rearrangement of the physical or social environment that could facilitate an alternative mode of attainment of goals blocked by the impairment, even if the environmental intervention is permanent.

It is convenient to conceive of transactions between the person and the environment in terms of personal competence and environmental press, or demand. The quality of the outcome of a transaction may be seen either in the quality of the resulting behavior or the subjectively perceived state of the individual (quality of affect or psychological well-being). The rehabilitation process usually begins with a person whose competence has been reduced by trauma or pathology: a physical illness, a deficit in sensory or motor function, cognitive impairment, or deficiencies in one or more activities of daily living (ADL) (Lawton & Brody, 1969). The base levels of many other more complex activities in the work, leisure, and social spheres are likely to be lowered by the pathology.

The environmental side is represented by the strength of the demand the environment makes on the person (called "press" by Murray [1938]). Competence and press are denoted schematically in Figure 9-1. In shorthand terms, Figure 9-1 suggests that regardless of level of personal competence there is a range of environmental demand within which the person can achieve a positive outcome in either behavior or affect (represented by the asymmetric central section of Figure 9-1 formed by the diagonals). This feature of the press–competence model thus portrays the person and the environment as alternative points of application of an intervention: in the one case, therapy; in the other, prosthesis. Bringing environmental demands within the range of favorable outome is what prosthetics does, whether in the form of a traditional body prosthesis or of an environmental intervention that alters sensory stimuli, rearranges furniture, redesigns the living area, or creates whole houses, buildings, or neighborhood systems.

Part of the rationale for focusing on the physical environment is stated in the form of what I have called "the environmental docility hypothesis." In this view, personal limitations such as deprivation or physical or psychological impairment render the person more susceptible to the influence of environmental demands. In its worst sense, vulnerable people are selectively sensitive to further decline if they are in noxious or incongruent environments. The positive side of the docility hypothesis, however, is that a given amount of favorable environmental change will selectively benefit the most impaired people. Thus,

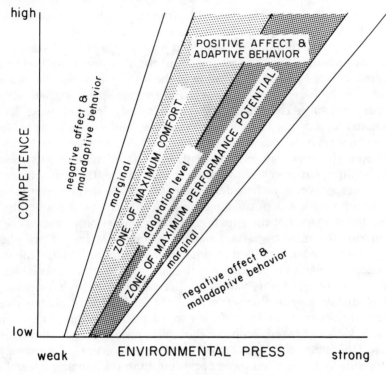

Figure 9-1 Environmental press.

if we can create a physical environment that facilitates competent behavior among a substantial number of users, the intervention may sometimes be more efficient than one-to-one intervention.

Body prostheses—for example, an artificial limb, hearing aid, or eyeglasses—need no further specification. There are many less familiar prostheses on such a microscale. Also not traditionally thought of as prostheses are arrangements of furniture, design of furniture and other decor, choices of interior and exterior materials, lighting, and arrangements of larger spaces, as in the structure of entire dwelling units, institutions or clusters of dwelling units, neighborhoods, transportation systems, and consumer or service resources. For our particular purpose here, the major contexts of application will be the institution and the dwelling unit.

The Institution

Arranging the physical environment of an institution to maximize the production of competent behavior may be easier when designing a new institution than when attempting to modify an existing one. The basic structure of a building should provide prosthetic functions. Beyond obvious signaling and life-maintaining technologies, support for basic ADL can be afforded if the design team keeps in mind such principles as providing visual feedback about the way one looks by means of mirrors placed with consideration of the stature and mobility characteristics of the user; access to closets and storage space, located within the personal space defined by the person's bed; clear pathways, with functional lighting, to bathroom, to corridor, and to seating area. Just as basic are physical characteristics that provide knowledge to the person about the everyday environment, such as orientation aids. Some basic building structures, through their asymmetry, their affordance of visual perspective, and their deliberate attempts to denote appropriate use through design or furnishings, may fortify the person's ability to assess the demands of the situation and respond appropriately.

Some of the most important deficits in impaired people are likely also to be the most neglected in rehabilitative efforts. Perhaps the major enemy of institutional quality is the lack of sensory and social stimulation. Providing sensory variety is often possible through furnishings and relatively easy-to-alter aspects of the environment. Often overlooked, however, is the opportunity to orient the building to enhance outside views, toward both aesthetically pleasing and stimulating views. The opportunity to watch other people in action—for example, a busy sidewalk—is often more appealing than unchanging natural or manmade views.

Watching activity inside the building or on its grounds serves several prosthetic functions, beginning with sheer stimulation, as described previously. Watching other people behave is also a potent way of maintaining or augmenting one's social skills. A link to normative ways of behaving is provided by places to sit where everyday functional activities occur. Another increment of prothesis occurs when the ongoing behavior provides a motivating force. For example, being able to watch others engaging in a game, in occupational therapy, or other enriching activities may be a stimulus for the watcher to join the activity. Finally, the simple presence of other people constitutes the strongest motivation to join them in social interaction.

The design conclusions of these observations, then, are to deliberately expand spots of natural activity to include informal seating space. Such space puts the person on the continuum of involvement that runs from passive sensory stimulation to active social integration.

The Dwelling Unit

By contrast with the design of an institution, ordinary home environments can be made more functional by attention to smaller details that are more easily accomplished and often less expensive than larger structural features would be. The same principles that enhance the ability to find and select one's own clothes, negotiate the pathway to the bathroom and use of the toilet, and perform the operations involved in bathing, grooming, and eating can be applied to the home. Enriching stimuli, including the all-important contact with external world afforded by radio, television, and telephone, can be provided. The view of entrance walk and sidewalk is one such important feature.

Within the limits of this chapter only illustrative examples are possible. The practice of behavioral design is capable, however, of addressing most disabilities in most environments, with the goal of minimizing the behavioral or psychological consequences of the disability. One can summarize yet another total presentation in the conclusion that sufficient use of an effective prosthesis makes possible an increment in competence, thus taking on the function of therapy.

The significance of the prosthetic environment for training in rehabilitation is very clear. It is usual for there to be little or no expertise in physical design in most service-giving settings. One important exception, of course, is occupational therapy (OT), which is often where prescriptions for prostheses and modifications of existing environments begin. The problem is that there is too little OT time to go around, especially in community-based in-home care agencies. There is thus a strong likelihood that any member of a rehabilitation team may be called on in a variety of situations to provide ideas about the design of the rehabilitation environment. It is suggested that the primary requirement for such intervention is sensitization to the possibilities for prosthetics in this larger sense. Such intervention can come during the planning, design, or furnishing stage of a new treatment setting or in the major remodeling or reuse planning stage of an existing facility, but it is especially relevant to the continuous functioning of a rehabilitation program in which the maximum use of the existing setting needs to be made with only minimum expenditure. Although there will always be a need for the expert in behavioral design, and the addition of OT time to every team is desirable, a small amount of in-service training regarding the uses of the environment across disciplines is likely to result in a major improvement in the total quality of care.

NOTES

1. This section was contributed by Elaine M. Brody.
2. This section was contributed by Avalie R. Saperstein.
3. The PGC Family Respite Care Program is supported by the John

A. Hartford Foundation, Inc., of New York and the Pew Charitable Trusts of Philadelphia.

4. This section was contributed by M. Powell Lawton.

REFERENCES

Blenkner, M. (1965). Social work and family relationships in later life with some thoughts on filial maturity. In E. Shanas & G. F. Streib (Eds.), *Social structure and the family: Generational relations*. Englewood Cliffs, NJ: Prentice-Hall.

Brody, E. M. (1990). *Women in the middle: Their parent care years*. New York: Springer Publishing Co.

Brody, E. M., Kleban, M. H., Johnson, P. T., Hoffman, C., & Schoonover, C. B. (1987). Work status and parent care: A Comparison of four groups of women. *Gerontologist, 27*, 201–208.

Brody, S. J. (1987). Strategic planning: The catastrophic approach. *Gerontologist, 27*, 131–138.

Brody, S. J., Poulshock, S. W., & Masciocchi, C. F. (1978). The family caring unit: A major consideration in the long-term support system. *Gerontologist, 18*, 556–561.

Brotman, H. B. (1980). Every ninth American. In U.S. Senate Special Committee on Aging (Eds.), *Development in aging: 1979* (Vol. 1). Washington, DC: U.S. Government Printing Office.

Crystal, S. (1982). *America's old age crisis: Public policy and the two worlds of aging*. New York: Basic Books.

Doty, P., Liu, K., & Weiner, J. (1985). An overview of long-term care. *Health Care Financing Review, 6*(3), 69–78.

Fulton, J. P., & Katz, S. (1986). Characteristics of the disabled elderly and implications for rehabilitation. In S. J. Brody & G. E. Ruff (Eds.), *Aging and rehabilitation: Advances in the state of the art* (pp. 36–46). New York: Springer Publishing Co.

Horowitz, A. (1985). Family caregiving to the frail elderly. In C. Eisdorfer, M. P. Lawton, & G. L. Maddox (Eds.), *Annual review of gerontology and geriatrics* (Vol. 5, pp. 194–246). New York: Springer Publishing Co.

Lawton, M. P., & Brody, E. M. (1969). Assessing older people: Self-maintaining and instrumental activities of daily living. *Gerontologist, 9*, 179–186.

Lawton, M. P., Brody, E. M., & Saperstein, A. R. (1989). A controlled study of respite service for caregivers of Alzheimer's patients. *Gerontologist, 29*(1), 8–16.

Lindsley, O. R. (1964). Geriatric behavioral prosthetics. In R. Kastenbaum (Ed.), *New thoughts on old age*. New York: Springer Publishing Co.

Lingg, B. A. (1975) Women Social Security beneficiaries aged 62 and older, 1960–1974. *Research and Statistics Notes, 13*

Murray, H. A. (1938). *Explorations in personality*. New York: Oxford University Press.

National Center for Health Statistics. (1985). *Advance report of final divorce statistics, 1983, 34*(9) (Suppl.). Washington, DC: U.S. Department of Health and Human Services, Public Health Service.

National Center for Health Statistics. (1986) *Advance report of final marriage statistics, 1983, 35*(1) (Suppl.). Washington, DC: U.S. Department of Health and Human Services, Public Health Service.

Shanas, E. (1961). *Family relationships of older people* (Health Information Foundation, Research Series 20). Chicago: University of Chicago.

Soldo, B. J. (1982). *Supply of informal care services: Variations and effects on services utilization patterns* (Contract No. HHS-100-80-0158, DHHS). Washington, DC: Georgetown University, Center for Population Research.

Stone, R., Cafferata, G. L., & Sangl, J. (1987). Caregivers of the frail elderly: A national profile. *Gerontologist, 27*, 616–626.

U.S. Department of Health and Human Services, Public Health Service. (1985). *Women's health: Report of the Public Health Service Task Force on Women's Health* (Vol. 2). Washington, DC: U.S. Government Printing Office.

U.S. Department of Labor, Bureau of Labor Statistics. (1986). *Employment in perspective: Women in the labor force* (Report No. 729). Washington, DC: U.S. Government Printing Office.

Weed, J. A. (1981). National estimates of marital dissolution and survivorship. *Vital and Health Statistics: Series 3. Analytic studies, No. 19* (DHHS Publication No. PHS 81-1403). Washington, DC: U.S. Government Printing Office.

10

Environmental Factors in Rehabilitation of Disabled Elderly People

Lorraine G. Hiatt

- A client comes to the office and the specialist answers the client's questions about condition and capacity without regard to living situation.
- Prostheses are prescribed without reference to where they will be used.
- Multiple impairments of the individual are not taken into account in initial assessment, conversation, or therapeutic regimen.

These are examples of practice lacking a concern for the environment, of rehabilitation that separates the individual from his or her context.

Rehabilitation has traditionally been conceptualized and taught as a transaction between clinician and client, sometimes one involving various tools, conversations, and actions or instructions. The complex role that environments play in the evaluation, the individual's well-being and capacity to implement changes in behavior and/or to achieve desired results, has all too often been overlooked or oversimplified. The environment is more constant than the most ambitious caregiver. The least we can do is marshall it effectively.

This chapter will show that understanding and incorporating the attributes of environmental design into professional practice will improve both the interactions and outcomes and that this contextual approach to rehabilitation is particularly relevant to older people. It will begin by clarifying the objectives of the contextual or environmental approach and the background information needed to implement that approach. Discussions of the major themes in environmental design, specific aspects of rehabilitation in the environmental context, and common obstacles to implementing the contextual approach follow. The chapter concludes with recommendations for ensuring the place of environmental considerations in the future of rehabilitation.

OBJECTIVES OF THE CONTEXTUAL MODEL OF REHABILITATION

- Actively assess the environment in conjunction with assessment of the individual.
- Utilize information on functional characteristics of older people and the interactive effects of physical, psychosocial, cultural, and emotional attributes when considering or prescribing activities, prostheses, or changes in behavior.
- Utilize the ambient qualities of environment: lighting levels, reduced noise, increased tactile stimulation, and aroma, as appropriate, to reinforce positive outcomes.
- Consider the image of devices in the setting as a whole: how can the person look acceptable and "normal" in his or her context?
- Utilize environmental design features to improve aspects of social interaction, such as comfortable seating and seating distances, supports for balance, alternatives to standing.

DEFINITIONS AND ROLES OF THE ENVIRONMENT

Four attributes of the environment are significant to rehabilitation (or habilitation, as the case may be) (Hiatt, 1985):

1. *The physical environment.* These are measurable features: spaces the person inhabits, their configuration and size, the features of those spaces, which include lighting, acoustics, texture, aroma, and air quality. The physical environment also includes the hand-held objects and tools—from toothbrush to steering wheel, from handrail to wheelchair.

2. *The social environment.* This refers to "people" issues: How many people does the individual regularly interact and live with? What are their roles and implications for rehabilitation?

3. *The psychological environment.* Psychological attributes of the environment range from mental images ("pictures in the head") to preferences. It is important that rehabilitation professionals extend beyond their own images of how people do or ought to live and begin to consider the context and imagery of the client.

Psychological attributes of the environment also refer to reactions to appearance, preferences, and ambience. Although generalizations regarding the preferred look, color, or feeling are not particularly valuable, it is often worthwhile to understand a particular client's assessment of the context and of the prosthesis in relation to the context.

By reaching for a better understanding of the client's preferences, it is often possible to get at difficult constructs such as motivation and likelihood of follow-up.

4. *The cultural environment.* Cultural attributes of environmental design refer to (a) traditions, (b) regulations and codes, (c) patterns, and (d) habituated practices. To make a difference, to make changes, it is important to consider the effects of these variables. One of the reasons environmental design suggestions go unheeded is that those who make them have insufficient experience in working the idea through the individual's culture. Whether prescribing a prosthesis or recommending furniture rearrangement, care must be taken to consider how the new recommendation will fit within the individual's cultural surroundings. This is particularly important for older people, who may require familiarity as a way of functioning and conserving energy.

THE IMPORTANCE OF A CLIENT'S SOCIAL HISTORY

Geriatric rehabilitation and medicine involves paying particular heed to the strengths and the needs of older people. While formal training may focus on biological theories and changes relevant to later life, geriatric education and training should also orient the specialist to the time and techniques necessary to obtain a meaningful social history and a greater understanding of the supports available for the individual to work with. Such information should include the following:

1. Global information on the macroenvironment: (a) the place one lives, (b) neighborhood supports and qualities, (c) access to transportation/assistance.
2. Specific information on the microenvironment: (a) the settings one occupies and (b) the physical, psychological, and social features of those settings.

3. The person's reaction to the cultural context: (a) the importance of tradition, regulations, patterns, etc.; (b) the acceptability and fit of recommended actions in this context.

MAJOR THEMES IN ENVIRONMENTAL DESIGN

What may distinguish some older people from the typically conceptualized client who presents for rehabilitation is a state of frailty. Frailty does not characterize all older people, but when it does, the environment is likely to be more significant.

Environmental design may have a particular role in the lives of frail older people. Furnishings and features of each room or place become increasingly significant when one has difficulty transferring weight, balancing, walking, standing, or generating the energy required to be mobile (Hiatt, 1988a, 1988b; Kaufman, 1987). When we are mobile, we can shift position or relocate; that becomes less likely with frailty. Features of the environment may contribute to the complications, burdens, or experiences of an impairment. For example, poor light may hasten the rate of retinal deterioration (Cullinan, 1986); background noise may impede speech intelligibility, especially for consonants (McCartney, 1979); and ineffective seating may contribute to problems in toileting, manual dexterity, and even in walking (Finlay, Bayles, Rosen, & Milling, 1983). By being alert to the environment, the practitioner may reduce the compression of symptoms, that is, prevent some of the untoward suffering that is inappropriately accepted as a consequence of normal aging but is more aptly a function of poorly designed environments (Fozard, 1981).

The environment may be thought of as having objects and tools of habilitation (Hiatt, 1987a, 1987b). For example, well-designed and well-placed landmarks may aid wayfinding, contributing to a concept of competency (Weisman, 1987); and textures and objects may be so visceral or available that they stimulate the alertness of cognitively impaired elderly, effectively helping to direct and concentrate flagging attention span (Cohen & Eisdorfer, 1979).

The offset handle, for example (referred to as the Bennett Biocurve™), may facilitate the use of pots, forks, knives, hammers, shovels, and all manner of formerly straight-handled objects (Faletti, 1984; "Some Old Ideas," 1983). The design of the handle helps compensate for difficulties in dexterity. Similarly, the built-up handles of knives and pens and the flanged handles of doors and faucets may also give the older person greater ability to use features of the environment with comfort and somewhat greater speed, and they may make a difference between independence and dependence.

SPECIFIC PROFESSIONAL INSIGHTS

As one who spends more than 200 days a year in institutions, planning and evaluating facilities and programs (for nearly 20 years), I have observed many ways in which specific professions within rehabilitation and geriatrics could be more vigilant about environmental design. There are, of course, exceptions; those exceptional cases have helped me understand the value of new experiences and approaches that do embrace environmental design considerations.

Physical Therapy

Too much rehabilitation of older people is focused on clinical procedures such as gait training using parallel bars and nontraditional floor surfaces in clinical facilities. In some 500 facilities, I have visited only a handful of physical therapy (PT) programs that extend services that consider the environments that older people actually occupy. Evergreen Manor in Oshkosh, Wisconsin,[1] for example, has developed a two-pronged PT program, with therapists working both in specialized clinical facilities and out on the unit. The advantages are that role models are provided, that nursing assistants and nursing staff learn better transfer techniques, and the team efforts that everyone speaks about really begin to occur. A similar program has been implemented at the Jewish Home of Worcester, Massachusetts, with an added feature. Therapists are involved in positioning and in prescribing better seating, much like the model established at the American Rehabilitation Foundation in Minneapolis[1] (formerly the Sister Kenny Institute). The Delaware state hospital system offers PT with floor surfaces to practice on that emulate home and community conditions.

PT facilities also need some attention. Mobility areas and gyms are seldom free of glare. Wet areas (areas designated for water therapy) seldom provide either adequate privacy or nonslip floors. Many areas are even covered with ceramic tiles, which are expensive to clean and more slippery when wet.

PT programs in general would benefit from using familiar objects and images to stimulate positive self-concepts, providing role models, markers of progress, and even nonclinical-looking materials and equipment. This is one place where a little color, some patterned sheets, and some imagery would be a gratifying change.

Occupational Therapy

The most important consideration for occupational therapy is that it be available. Too often, occupational therapy is either combined with activities programs or omitted all together. Manual dexterity is essential, as are maintenance of other fine motor skills. Learning to use actual implements is also extraordinarily important. Often occupational therapy is offered only to older people who will go to home environments, when there are environmental and product-use issues in other supportive environments as well. It is time to extend both occupational and physical therapy resources beyond the few who will go back home and be rehabilitated and to focus on reduction of compression of symptoms, on prevention, and on working with mentally impaired persons.

Both occupational and physical therapy services have been driven by reimbursement available (through Medicaid, Medicare, or similar third-party payment programs). Programs and facilities favor the person who has had a stroke and will regain gross and fine motor function. But the allied health professions have valuable insights to offer on positioning, ambulation, balance, transfer, and conduct of activities of daily living in the actual spaces provided—at home or in an institution.

Occupational therapy should include work with objects and textures to cue memory and improve attention span, much the same as therapists have used objects to help regain or maintain manual skills. They offer great promise for older people. At Peninsula United Methodist Home in Wilmington, Delaware, for example, an occupational therapist was instrumental in developing the program for cognitively impaired persons. At Evergreen Manor, occupational therapists have worked with other departments to encourage frail *and* mentally impaired persons to feed themselves more independently.

The field of occupational therapy will increase its effectiveness when the products used and promoted take on a more normal, familiar appearance, from plate guards to plates with beveled edges, and are used by all.

Vision Care Professionals

The potential for rehabilitation and training for people who are partially sighted or blind has been well documented (Genensky, 1980; Rosenbloom & Morgan, 1986) and effectively demonstrated at centers such as the Santa Monica Center for Partially Sighted, Carroll Center for the Blind, New York Lighthouse, and Detroit Society for the Blind, among others.[1] Vision care specialists began alerting their peers to the concept of "low vision" more than 20 years ago (Faye & Hood, 1976). This was a landmark in rehabilitation because it signified a new awareness on the part of medical and related professionals that, although total rehabilitation is certainly preferred, the capacity for people to work with the best correctable function is also a worthy medical and allied health effort. The concept of low-vision services embraces effective evaluation, medical correction as appropriate, and adaptive devices and environmental amenities such as lighting. Effective low-vision services extend beyond prescriptive devices and environments to include education in any skills necessary for independence: mobility, reading options, communication, identification, financial entitlements, and so on. Teaching the individual to optimize the lighting, ambience, and factors such as texture and contrast may be a key to effective visual care services. (For an example of a resource kit that focuses on using the environment to optimize vision, hearing, and memory and that draws on self-help and mutual aid skills of older people, see Hiatt, Brieff, Horwitz, & McQueen, 1982.)

One of the breakthroughs characterizing recent developments in low-vision services is the emphasis on ecologically valid assessments. For example, European researchers in vision care of the aging have argued that vision evaluations need to be made both in clinical settings and in the actual environment in which one operates or functions (Cullinan, 1986). That same philosophy could well be applied to hearing, speech intelligibility, memory, and overall mobility assessments related to the risk of falls.

Vision evaluations need to be an entitlement of people receiving long-term care, in part to rule out factors that are correctable but also because visual disorders may be masked as mental dysfunction (Snyder, Pyrek, & Smith, 1976).

Audiology and Speech and Hearing

These services need an approach similar to low vision, that is, a major promotional campaign to emphasize optimizing residual skills. At worst, audiology is confused with or becomes a conduit to sales of hearing aids without the essential ingredients of training, seeking alternatives, or environmental management. At best, training related to effective use of residual hearing may provide a bridge to coping with other late-life difficulties or changes in functional capacity. Rehabilitation for older people needs to embrace acoustical issues in the use of the environment. Both professionals and clients need to be oriented toward noise abatement as a means of improving speech intelligibility. By focusing only on the ear, ear wax, and hearing aids, we lose a great opportunity to minimize agitation (Ohta, Carlin, & Harmon, 1981) and to optimize the sense of hearing (Fozard, 1981; Hiatt Brieff, Horwitz, & McQueen, 1982).

Other Disciplines

There are roles for dentists in many aspects of habilitation. It is inappropriate for community-based nutrition programs and institutions to segregate people according to whether or not they spill at mealtime, when proper dental care, combined with effective occupational therapy training, might provide procedures and interventions that minimize unacceptable eating behavior. Selecting chairs that fit under tables and offering appropriate foods and implements are environmental techniques for extending therapy.

The podiatrist is a key to maintenance of mobility, to keeping the feet in both walking and standing order. One could envision a day when the gift shop of the hospital, retirement community, and senior center is reconceptualized as a "sensorium emporium," a place that provides specialists and specialty shoppers; where the podiatrist (or other specialist) makes an initial evaluation, and the consumers are able to find many options in style, price, and detail to suit their needs.

Even the role of pharmacist has evolved—a model that might well be emulated by audiology—from marketer or "rep" for the pharmaceutical companies to a recognized advocate of safe drug use and cautious evaluation of drug interaction, as well as an advocate for effective, low-cost generic products. In some cases professionals such as nursing home nurses would benefit from the same one-to-one contact provided by pharmacists to individuals regarding prescription and nonprescription products.

OBSTACLES TO ENVIRONMENTAL IMPROVEMENT

Most rehabilitation professionals would agree that environmental factors are important to clients' well-being. But there are a number of misconceptions that needlessly prevent or muddle efforts toward environmental design improvements.

Assumed Expertise and Incorrect Information

A degree in rehabilitation does not necessitate expertise in environmental design. We often encounter gerontologists, social workers, rehabilitation workers, and physicians who make global generalizations that are either unfounded or only partly correct, as in the following examples.

"Carpet creates problems for older people." There are advantages, even for some wheelchair users, to softer surfaces. The products used to make carpeting have changed. There are newer materials that look like carpet, clean like vinyl, and wear like rubber. The well-meaning rehabilitation individual needs to be very cautious regarding such generalizations (Pease, 1986).

"Older people need companionship and do not benefit from privacy. In fact, privacy yields isolation." The definitive research on this matter has not been done. But general data from environmental psychology suggest that the option to to choose visual and actual privacy may stimulate social behavior and that a certain amount of solitude may be invigorating even for cognitively impaired persons (Laufer & Wolfe, 1977; Pastalan, 1986).

"Bright colors are good. Older people need pastel colors." Would that it were as simple as using color to evoke some intended behavioral response. Despite the desire of many who decorate, color alone cannot be expected to elicit particular behavior. In part, this is because color perceptions are complex, a function of (a) light, (b) amount, (c) texture, (d) distance from viewer, (e) cultural familiarity and psychological associations, and, in regard to older people, (f) the degree of yellowing of the lens (Fozard, 1981).

Color may have individual meaning; a person may develop a preference for the idea of a certain color. But there is little evidence of normative effects of color on all people, other than those data suggesting that discrimination of blues from greens and identification of violets can be more difficult for some people. Often, color preference is compounded by culture and memory: we recall a lifelong preference for violet or green or blue even though the color we are presented with does not "read" as clearly as what we recall.

The resolution seems to be to (a) ask individuals to become involved in the selection; (b) use actual conditions of lighting, surfaces, and amount; and (c) consider the relationship between figure and ground— what you are attempting to emphasize versus what needs to recede. For this reason, we often avoid distinctive patterns on floors in the areas used for thoroughfares (they make the surface appear to have objects or contours, even steps). In design, we often urge those planning environments to go beyond color and the visual environment to obtain their effects, to look instead at the panoply of textures, touchable surfaces, methods of controlling background noise, and use of objects.

These are just three of many examples suggesting that when the rehabilitation specialist decides to work with design, the requirements include avid reading (of well-researched publications), continual exploration, and alertness to new product developments.

False Economic Barriers

A second reason environmental design information does not get put to work is that defeating attitudes toward cost preclude meaningful discussions about the options available. "We would like to do more, but it would cost too much." "Functional design costs more, right?"

In fact, in new construction, many of the attributes that make a building or space functional are not more expensive. A more productive way of thinking about costs is to consider life cycle rather first-time design costs. Design costs are experienced once. For most organizations, the greatest factor in operating costs is labor, and ineffective design is often inefficient, labor-intensive design:

- Poor light requires more time in transactions and may make people more vulnerable to falls and attendant liability.
- Poorly configured rooms such as toilet rooms may make disabled older people more staff-dependent and require more time for staff to provide assistance. The result is higher labor costs and poorer ratios of staff to older people, as well as greater dependency of the older people.
- Uncontrolled acoustics may contribute to higher agitation and stress, not only for older people but also for caregivers. This may contribute to higher rates of turnover, more errors of commission/ omission, and hence higher operating costs.
- Poorly selected seating may contribute to diminished mobility, falls, poor posture, and less independent transfer (e.g., standing to sitting positions, and reverse). Again, this is labor-intensive.

Not to even consider the possibilities of functional design is therefore usually a false economy.

Views of Frail Older Users as a Minority

"Very few of the clients are older people." Hospitals used to make that argument; now the data suggest that, with DRGs, the older clients are a substantial proportion of the patient-day care load. The features that benefit older people typically benefit most adults: better lighting, glare reduction, noise abatement, attention to balance and surface changes to reduce risk of falls—these are factors that do not preclude use by society at large.

Ill-Conceived Regulatory Barriers

"These are nice ideas, but the regulators would never allow them." Or "We meet codes. Why should we consider these things?" First, few regulations are based on research. Those that are, are seldom based on empirical research with a representative range of older people. This means that a building can meet the code without meeting the needs of older people.

The solution seems to be to bring research into the regulatory process. Where there is a valid reason for providing water closet–mounted grab rails rather than wall-mounted rails or for making rooms large enough for the person to wheel the wheelchair rather than allowing only space for the wheelchair to be passed (i.e., wheeled by someone else), this information needs to be brought to the attention of those who regulate. Similarly, professional organizations and schools need to work toward making the regulations responsive to older people, to research, to new technologies, and to innovation. Why should we build today's buildings to yesterday's knowledge base? Thus, a new role for rehabilitation professionals seems to be called for: as advocates of appropriate design, as speakers or protagonists before those who are charged with regulations and life safety.

Waiting for Perfection

"Just send us to some 'perfect' environments and we'll copy their facilities." Sadly, there are no perfect environments, just better environments. Rather than attempt to copy from facilities toured, it is important to put good information to work, to ask whom the design is used by, whether it works, how it works, what else might have been done, and so on.

The solution is to send more informed and questioning professionals into the field to make evaluations of environments and to be open to all ideas.

Deferred Involvement and Responsibility

"Somebody else will take care of it." The fact is that for years nobody has. Older people themselves have not been strong advocates of functional design, in part because there are so few "living, breathing" models of design that optimize what people can do. By finding groups of rehabilitation and geriatric professionals who will advocate for functional environments, we are more likely to see these models emerge. To avoid the topic is to invite certain risks:

- Architects and engineers who design without a full understanding of older people, of multiple impairments, of potentiality for environmental compensation.
- Interior design that focuses on "the look" rather than a terrific-looking *and* functional product.
- Environments that are safe but not particularly effective from a therapeutic standpoint.

- Low maintenance but possibly low function and low appeal.[2]
- Perpetual purchase, as by purchasing agencies, of geriatric wheelchairs and other devices that are not in the best interests of older people but are used because they are there.
- The disabled elderly do not get to use functional design.

THE FUTURE

Who will translate all of this, orchestrate it all, make it all happen? There are those who suggest that more effective rehabilitation/habilitation for older people needs the same concerted effort of professionals facing the more dramatic crises in health, such as polio, AIDS, measles, prenatal care. That is, no one professional will make it all happen. When we see the emergence of geriatric nurse practitioners, for example, in programs such as Rose Hospital in Denver, Colorado, the possibilities of better, more personalized care come alive. But even these well-trained professionals (who do go to the home and are engaged in environmental design concerns) cannot function without the assistance of a full range of peers.

Effective rehabilitation, meaningful habilitation, and the panoply of options available to the individual need to be both coordinated and yet diffuse.

1. All professionals, including physicians, need to understand habilitation and rehabilitation of older people; they need to see the use of noninvasive techniques for coping and be able to access these with the same alacrity with which they write prescriptions. This means the information must be part of basic medical education and of actual practice; it must be available to the practicing, degreed professional on an ongoing basis.

2. Much of geriatrics and gerontology may need to be adopted in some form of continuing education because (a) many professionals age with their practice and begin to relate to the needs of older people only as they gain clinical experience, and (b) geriatrics and gerontology continue to lose some of the competition for time in medical school and allied health training because they are often tied to chronic rather than acute health needs.

3. All of those practicing geriatric professionals need to be able to turn to indentifiable colleagues within their own discipline, as well as across disciplines, for factual, well-researched information.

4. We need a data base, federally available, of sources and evaluations of devices, environments, and model rehabilitation/habilitation

programs for older people (Hiatt, 1987b; LaBuda, 1986). We have data sources primarily for people with singular disabilities (Karp & Lucas, 1986), with some information on aging. We have a few catalog and related sources (Crawford, 1985; Hale, 1979; LaBuda, 1986). But to continue to separate the device from evaluation and context is to lose a great opportunity. With the skills older as well as younger people have demonstrated in appropriately designed computer training programs (Furlong & Kearsley, 1986), it would be intriguing if older people themselves operated such a data base.

5. Conferences are not a bad medium for introducing the concepts of gerontological habilitation/rehabilitation. They may even serve as a forum for alerting people to the fact that there is something about design worth considering. But conferences are seductive; to know the information is there is different from being able to implement it effectively. Consequently, we need media that grapple with "how to," and we need opportunities for people to obtain personalized advice, perhaps using telecommunications as well as consultancy where necessary. The telecommunications and consultancy models may help develop enough models of workable programs to stimulate people to obtain hands-on experience.

Utilizing environmental design information will require specializing training; it is not intuitive and not gleaned through casual reading. But a future that combines the knowledge of rehabilitation and habilitation skills with active environmental design recommendations will go a long way to offer new opportunities for the aging, including those who are both old and frail.

NOTES

1. Addresses of facilities mentioned:

American Foundation for the Blind, 15 West 16th Street, New York, NY, 10011 (publications, films, and conferences).
American Rehabilitation Foundation, Sister Kenny Institute, 1800 Chicago Avenue, Minneapolis, MN (publications, direct services, and educational workshops).
Carroll Center for the Blind, 770 Centre Street, Newton, MA, 02158 (publications and direct services).
Center for the Partially Sighted, 1250 Sixteenth Street, Santa Monica, CA.
Evergreen Manor, 1130 No. Westfield, Oshkosh, WI.

Greater Detroit Society for the Blind, 16625 Grand River, Detroit, MI 49227.

New York Association for the Blind, The Light House, 111 East 59th Street, New York, NY 10022 (publications, conferences, direct services, and research).

2. The worst example: shiny floors. Shiny floors may look terrific, but they are not low-maintenance. They require a two- to three-step process of cleaning and must be cordoned off during cleaning. This poses risks. A shiny floor can be dangerous to older people; glare makes attentiveness more difficult and provides false information on ground changes and contours. It may even be associated with greater risk of falls. Yet, culturally, we have come to accept shiny floors as appropriate for kitchens and bathrooms at home and for institutional or public building hallways. Nonglare materials would serve all people much more effectively.

REFERENCES

Cohen, D., & Eisdorfer, C. (1979). Cognitive theory and assessment of change in the elderly. In A. Raskin & L. Jarvik (eds.), *Psychiatric symptoms and cognitive loss in the elderly* (pp. 273–282). New York: Halsted.

Cullinan, T. (1986). *Visual disabilities in the elderly*. New York: PSG.

Crawford, I. (1985). *Aids to independence: A guide to products for the disabled and elderly*. Seattle: Self-Council Publishing.

Faye, E. E., & Hood, C. M. (1976). Visual rehabilitation in the geriatric population. In E. E. Faye & C. M. Hood (eds.), *Clinical low vision* (pp. 123–126). Boston: Little, Brown.

Finlay, O., Bayles, T., Rosen, C., & Milling, J. (1983). Effects of chair design, age, and cognitive status on mobility. *Age and Ageing, 12,* 323–335.

Fozard, J. (1981). Person-environment relationships in adulthood: Implications for human factors engineering. *Human Factors, 23*(1), 7–28.

Furlong, M., & Kearsley, G. (1986). Computer instruction for older adults. *Generations, 11*(1), 32–34.

Genensky, S. (1980). *A comprehensive community care system for the partially sighted older persons: Progress report* (Project Number 90-A-1600). Santa Monica, CA: Center for the Partially Sighted Older Persons.

Hale, B. (1979). *The source book for the disabled*. New York: Bantam.

Hiatt, L. G. (1985). Understanding the physical environment. *Pride Institute Journal of Long-Term Home Health Care, 4*(2), 12–22.

Hiatt, L. G. (1987a). Environmental design and mentally impaired older people. *Alzheimer's disease: Problems, prospects, and perspectives* (pp. 309–320). New York: Plenum.

Hiatt, L. G. (1987b). Supportive design for people with memory impairments. In A. Kalicki (ed.), *Confronting Alzheimer's disease* (pp. 138–163). Owings Mills, MD: National Health Publishing.

Hiatt, L. G. (1988a). Mobility and indepenence in long-term care: Implications for technology and environmental design. In G. Lesnoff-Caravaglia (ed.), *Aging in a technological society* (pp. 58–64). New York: Human Sciences Press.

Hiatt, L. G. (1988b). Technology and dreams of aging. Why not listen to the older consumer. *Perspectives on Aging, 17*(1).

Hiatt, L. G., Brieff, R., Horwitz, J., & McQueen, C. (1982). *What are friends for?* New York: American Foundation for the Blind.

Karp, F., & Lucas, M. (1986). Abledata. *Generations, 11*(1) :35.

Kaufman, T. (1987). Posture and age. *Topics in Geriatric Rehabilitation, 2*(4) :13–28.

LaBuda, D. (1985). *The gadget book.* Glen View, IL: AARP/Scott Foresman.

LaBuda, D. (1986). Bringing gerontologists and technologists together. *Generations, 11*(1) :8–11.

Laufer, R. S., & Wolfe, M. (1977). Privacy as a concept and a social issue: A multidimensional developmental theory. *The Journal of Social Issues, 33*(3): 22–42.

McCartney, J. (1979). Hearing problems: Speech and language problems associated with hearing loss and aural rehabilitation. In M. V. Jones (ed.), *Speech and language problems of the aging.* Springfield, IL: Charles C. Thomas.

Ohta, R. J., Carlin, M. F., & Harmon, B. M. (1981). Auditory acuity and performance on the mental status questionnaire in the elderly. *Journal of the American Geriatrics Society, 29*(10) :476–478.

Pastalan, L. (1986). Six principles for a caring environment. *Provider, 12*(4) :4–5.

Pease, J. (1986). Carpeting. *Generations, 11*(1) :41–44.

Rosenbloom, M. W., & Morgan, M. W. (eds.). (1986). *Vision and aging: General and clinical perspectives.* New York: Professional Capitals Cities.

Some old ideas with a new twist. (1983). *Newsweek, 101*:61.

Snyder, L., Pyrek, J. D., & Smith, K. C. (1976). Vision and mental function. *Gerontologist, 16*(3) :491–495.

Weisman, G. D. (1987). Improving way-finding and architectural legibility in housing for the elderly. In V. Regnier & J. Pynoos (eds.), *Housing the aged: Design directives and policy considerations* (pp. 441–464). New York: Elsevier.

11

Preventive and Therapeutic Nutrition

Ruth L. Weg

A long time ago (460–377 B.C.) Hippocrates included a particular combination of nutrients in any therapeutic regimen for his patients. Ho, a Chinese physician of the 6th century B.C., believed that food affected health by enhancing the yin (the female principle) and yang (the male principle) of the body. Later a Chinese physician of the 11th century had more definitive ideas—a proper diet could make a difference in the treatment of the disease. He said, "Experts at curing disease are inferior to those specialists who warn against disease. Experts in the use of medicines are inferior to those who recommend proper diet" (Tannahill, 1973, p. 178). Prophetically, this physician connected wellness, preventive medicine, and diet, suggesting that after-the-fact medical care, though necessary, could be inferior, and that attention to nutrition was more effective than drugs. It has taken almost 10 centuries for the allied health professions in research, academe, practice, and governmental agencies to recognize the significance of appropriate nutrition in the treatment and prevention of disease and the maintenance and promotion of health and vitality at any age, including the middle and later years.

And now, rehabilitation for elders, which had its early beginnings about 40 years ago in Great Britain, has come of age. Geriatric rehabilitation is increasingly perceived as multidisciplinary, holistic, and an integral part of geriatric medicine. Both geriatric medicine and rehabilitation are based on the use of multidimensional team efforts in the maintenance and restoration of functional capacities. At last the negative attitude that all capacities and functions of older persons decline, never to be restored to any degree, has begun to give way to a more optimistic appraisal of the nature of aging, impairment, functional disability, and rehabilitation.

The growth of positive attitudes in geriatrics is built on the beliefs and evidence that rehabilitation of elders is not only possible but successful; improving function rather than curing is viable as an objective; and some age-related changes and problems earlier thought to be inevitable are the result of misuse, disuse, and pathology and therefore subject to intervention. It is increasingly suggested that disease prevention and health promotion can delay and eliminate some of the aforementioned changes and/or disorders. Nutritional adequacy, although only one factor in health promotion and disease prevention programs, is particularly significant in its correlation with the major chronic disorders and in maintenance of normative physiology of aging. Among committed elders and allied health professionals, nutritional changes have proved to be among the more accessible health-promoting activities to maintain vitality and wellness (Harper, 1982).

Additional research on the details of nutritional adequacy, deficiencies, and excesses related to elders (rather than only young adults) needs to be completed before conclusions can be made and particular dietaries can be called definitive. However, secondary data suggest nutritional interventions in addition to other rehabilitative techniques for those elders with certain disorders and diseases. Nutrition manipulation has been demonstrated to potentiate other therapies and enhance recovery while providing the individual patient/client with energy and raw materials to maximize function.

NUTRITION AND HEALTH/WELLNESS

There are still insufficient useful data about elders and nutrition regarding assessment, nutrient requirements, health/disease, knowledge, food preferences, eating habits, results of nutrition education programs, and varied dietary intakes. What valid dietary knowledge is becoming available has been minimally applied up to this time. However, the current emphasis on nutrition by government and the allied health professions is being matched by the lay public's interest and slowly changing eating habits.

Much of what is in articles and books on elders and nutrition has been largely extrapolated from studies with younger adults. The last Recommended Dietary Allowances (RDA), 1980, identified people 51 years of age and over as a homogeneous group with identical nutritional requirements. Different recommendations were indicated only for energy requirements with time: energy allowances for the 41-to-74-year-old group were to be reduced to 90% of that required as younger adults and further reduced for those 75 and over. The range indicated for men from 23 to 76 + years was 3100 to 1650 kcal; for women, 2400 to 1200 kcal. To date, there has been no effort to reflect the differences in older persons resulting from the wide variation in mobility, activities, health status, community or institutional living, and so on. Therefore, although the RDAs continue to be reference values for group meal planning, caution must be exercised in their use for individuals.

Information about nutrition in ethnically, culturally, and regionally different groups of older persons is negligible. The heterogeneity among older persons also relates to those who are active, well, and independent and those who have become ill, homebound, impaired, bedridden, or institutionalized. There is increasing consensus that fulfilling nutritional requirements results in a sense of well-being, heightened awareness and motivation, and improved response to other therapies in use with the latter groups of elders. The limited and limiting environments in which they are bound to live—deprivation of sensory and personal stimulation, difficulties with purchase and preparation of food, diminished sense of self, and isolation from societal activities—all interact to lower appetite and actual food intake, initiating or exacerbating malnutrition. More research in breadth and depth is needed before health professionals, caretakers, and society can develop health and nutrition programs to fit needs and customs of the heterogeneous populations of older persons. Nutrition as an area of research, professional education, and practice is in a period of renaissance and is a variable receiving particular attention in health maintenance and treatment of disease for the middle and later years (Roe, 1987; Young, 1986).

Many controversies continue: assessment, nutrient requirements, dietary intakes, and suggested changes in nutritional patterns as prevention and therapy among elders. Whereas aging, nutrition, and their interactions were rarely addressed 10 years ago, except as afterthoughts, the past 5 years have witnessed an acceleration of interest, purposeful research, articles and books, and signs of improved practices. This trend continues, even though major gaps in essential nutritional, biochemical, and physiological normative data for groups of older persons remain (Smith & Gilligan, 1988).

The westernized diet of the last 65 to 70 years is now identified as harmful to the nation's health and particularly to the middle-aged and older population, among whom the chronic diseases show a greater incidence. This dietary pattern, with high intake of refined carbohydrates (sugars, white flour), dairy products, beef, pork, fats of animal origin, and excess salt, is deficient in complex carbohydrates, vitamins, minerals, whole-grain cereals, fresh fruits, and vegetables. Moreover, the westernized dietary habits are highly correlated with the incidence and severity of the killer chronic diseases. Dietary intakes of this kind have contributed to subclinical malnutrition, caries, obesity, lowered immune response, bowel dysfunction, atherosclerosis, hypertension, coronary heart disease, and cancer (Weg, 1980a, 1980b).

Epidemiological and experimental research indicates that a number of the chronic disorders (e.g., coronary heart disease, diabetes, atherosclerosis, and hypertension) are susceptible to dietary (and exercise) therapy. Dietary intake intervention in which low-fat, low-cholesterol diets were used for patients with coronary heart disease (CHD) slowed and even reversed the rate of pathogenesis in atherosclerosis (Thuesen, Henriksen, & Engby, 1986). Recovery of cognitive capacity as well as energy, overall immune response, and other physiological parameters have been reported following restoration of appropriate nutrition (Wurtman & Wurtman, 1986). Dietary intake does make a difference, and this fact suggests that rehabilitation related to cognition, immune capacity, osteoporosis, atherosclerosis, CHD, and hypertension requires nutritional adequacy to meet individual needs.

MALNUTRITION: A FACT OF LIFE IN THE LATER YEARS

Malnutrition has no single causative factor; it has a number of interactive variables that contribute to the loss of appetite and poor eating habits. The variety of stressors that some elderly face exacerbate diminishing reserves, subclinical malnutrition, and a problematic appetite. These lead to dietary intakes that do not meet individual nutrient requirements and/or situations that develop.

When older persons are admitted to the hospital or nursing home, they are often identified as already in protein–calorie malnutrition. Rehabilitation for persons who are poststroke, postfracture, or recuperating from other surgical or medical procedures can become more difficult if malnutrition is disregarded or only casually treated. Superimposed on preexisting mild malnutrition and the trauma of disease or fracture are the psychosocial problems that surface with the move to the hospital or nursing home. These affective, social, and psychological stressors, such as unfamiliar surroundings, eating alone, loss of autonomy and independence, diminished sense of self, decrease in functional capacity, and frequently full-blown depression, all impinge negatively on appetite and nutritional status. These stressors, singly or interacting, have been demonstrated to heighten nutrient needs (Mitchell & Lipshitz, 1982).

Although this chapter focuses on the physiological factors, it is clear that nutrition and physiology do not exist in a vacuum. There is ongoing modulation of both by inability to prepare food (disability, facilities, living arrangements); transportation, social isolation; apathy, depression, diminished self-image; poverty; westernized diet; ignorance regarding balanced, appropriate diet; poor dentition, digestive system dysfunction or disease; other major chronic diseases; alcoholism and other drug abuse; emotional, affective deprivation; and institutionalization.

ANATOMY AND PHYSIOLOGY OF THE DIGESTIVE SYSTEM

Changes in the digestive system, beginning in the mouth and ending at the anus, can exacerbate nutritional risk.

It has been estimated that, up to the 1980s, one half of Americans over the age of 65 had lost all of their teeth. Mastication is affected by problematic dentition resulting from neglected caries earlier in life and from periodontal deterioration and dentures. Nutritional intake becomes restricted to soft, highly refined carbohydrate food and low bulk, contributing to a deficient and poorly balanced diet. Missing teeth and/or poorly fitting dentures do more than diminish appetite; self-image and self-confidence are also at risk.

The assumed decrease with time in number and effectiveness of taste buds could be related to loss of appetite and possibly to anorexia. Atrophy of taste buds and nasal receptors diminishes the capacity for taste and smell, minimizes anticipatory gastric secretions, and reduces the consciousness of hunger and thirst. Both senses may be at increased risk with age but appear also to be influenced by a number of factors unrelated to age. The results of studies are equivocal: some suggest inevitably higher taste and smell thresholds; others find that, without pathology and among nonsmokers, taste and smell are well maintained into the later years. Most esophogeal dysfunctions and discomforts (e.g., dysphagia and hiatus hernia), although more prevalent with age, are disease-related and not inevitable with the years.

The gastric mucosa appears to show a number of age-related changes; some are significant and affect nutritional status. Various degrees of gastric atrophy occur in normative aging, characterized by a reduction of chief and parietal cells and reduced secretions. Hydrochloric acid, pepsin, and gastric mucus secretions all diminish, and if atrophy is extreme, malabsorption develops, as do the consequent deficiencies of vitamin B_{12} and iron.

As the primary site for nutrient absorption, the small intestine is central to nutritional status. Few studies have been undertaken to support precise evidence of age-related structural and consequent absorptive changes, but medical texts continue to describe alterations in the small bowel based on hospitalized elderly with disease. When these surface changes become extensive among persons who already have low dietary intake and/or malabsorption, malnutrition is intensified. Because of a decline in pancreatic lipase and possible delay in gastric emptying of fats, digestion and absorption of dietary fat are also less efficient. There is an increased requirement for fat-soluble vitamins and calcium (Ca). A habitual use of mineral oil may include the dissolution of fat-soluble vitamins in the oil, their lowered absorption, and therefore a potential deficiency of these critical micronutrients.

Ca and vitamin D absorption diminish with age. Low plasma concentrations of the active metabolite of vitamin D, instrumental in Ca absorption, are found among elders with an adequate dietary intake, so it is reasonable to suggest that the requirement for vitamin D rises with age. Substances that may decrease iron absorption include antacids that raise gastrointestinal pH levels, drugs that may form organic iron complexes (e.g., cholestyramine), and increased dietary fiber. An acid medium facilitates iron absorption, so reduction in the secretion of gastric juices and the presence of achlorhydria may also lower intestinal absorption. Nevertheless, iron deficiency anemia, the most common anemia in later years, is most often considered a function of gastrointestinal blood loss rather than decreased iron absorption. In summary, the specifics of significant changes in absorptive capacity among elders are not known. Nutrient deficiencies may be associated with borderline age-related decrease in intake and absorption or with pathology. Among elders, reduced intake can be a result of depression or lack of appetite as a result of taste and smell diminution, drugs, and disease.

The aging large bowel (colon) has been intensively researched and has received considerable attention in medical practice. A number of benign and pathological conditions have come under careful scrutiny. Only a few normative aging changes have been identified in Western societies: increased incidence of diverticula and decreases in motility, rectal wall elasticity, and sphincter tone. Dehydration among elders and lower stool sensitivity contribute to one of the more common complaints among elders, constipation. A prudent dietary intake (high in fiber), more regular exercise (e.g., walking), conscious increase in fluid intake, and making appropriate time for evacuation can minimize or avoid constipation without the use of drugs.

Despite widespread complaints, it is still apparent that normative aging finds relative anatomical and physiological integrity in the gastrointestinal tract. The most troublesome aspects of the "aging gut" are related primarily to pathology, diverticular disease, inflammatory bowel disease, neoplasia, polyps, and cancer. If damage is extensive (e.g., gastric bleeding and atrophy) and there is a loss of proteins and minerals, plus deficiencies of serum proteins, folic acid, vitamin B_{12}, iron, and potassium, then supplementation would be appropriate (Exton-Smith & Caird, 1980).

ELDERS: AT NUTRITIONAL RISK

There is growing acceptance that elders are at nutritional risk, particularly for nutrient deficiencies (Munro, 1980). Malnutrition—more specifically, undernutrition, identified as either biochemical or clinical deficiencies—has been called one of the most pervasive, potentially debilitating problems of elders in the United States. More than 50% of the older population has been estimated as borderline or deficient in nutritional status (Young, 1982a, 1982b). Not many persons over the age of 74 were part of the National Health and Nutrition Examination Surveys conducted by the U.S. Department of Agriculture in 1974 and 1982, so there are insufficient data on the extent of elder malnutrition.

However, until new information accumulates from the Health Promotion and Disease Prevention Supplement and the Supplement on Aging to the National Health Interview survey, the RDA values and expert research inquiries and observations on malnutrition among elders will continue to be the references for evaluation.

It is conceivable that long-term subclinical malnutrition that results from the typical westernized diet, lack of health professionals' attention to nutrient intake, mistaken information about foods, isolation, poverty, and pathology can further stress a physiology that may be functioning with low nutrient and tissue reserves and a slowly deteriorating homeostatic response. A variety of complaints heretofore assume to be inevitable with age (e.g., fatigue, headaches, lowered resistance to disease, insomnia, depression, and confusion) are correlated in part with inadequate, inappropriate nutrition, whether deficiencies or excesses (Weg, 1980b). Any subclinical or chemical nutrient deficiency would exacerbate a physiology already at risk.

Survey Studies

The Ten States Survey that covered a nonrandom sample of the population included people over 59, and the USDA Household Food Consumption Survey studied more than 550 people over 74 years of age (U.S. DHEW, 1972). Those surveys focused on food in the household without any biochemical measures of nutritional status (Butler, 1987). Nevertheless, even these methodologically flawed surveys indicate that elders below poverty level or in poor health have inadequate nutrition. Further, they demonstrated that low or deficient nutrient intakes in the older population were more widespread than generally assumed—especially Ca, iron, vitamins A, C, and B complex, and protein—coupled with low energy levels. Other micronutrients frequently suggested as deficient in the dietary intake of particular socioeconomic and ethnic groups were vitamins D, B_{12}, B_6, and folate.

Additional data on the dietary practices and nutritional status of older persons have been provided by investigations that were smaller, regional, and in different settings (e.g., communities, hospitals, or nursing homes). Although these studies cannot be extrapolated to all elders, the nutritional data add insight concerning how older persons eat, and they assist in the determination of priorities for additional research and policy changes. In community-based studies, total daily calories were generally below the RDA. Protein and niacin were below standard in more than one third of those studies, the micronutrients Ca, iron, and vitamins A, C, B_1, B_2, and B_3 were most frequently found to be inadequate (Butler, 1987).

These micronutrients are intimately involved in bone remodeling, blood cell formation, and countless processes (e.g., immune capacity) that are part of healing and rehabilitative regimens. Patients with inadequate nutrition in hospitals, nursing homes, or home recuperation will mend more slowly and probably decline further in nutritional status, a clinical barrier to recovery. There is also the potential for additional functional difficulties beyond the immediate dysfunction being treated.

Hospital Stays and Nutrient Adequacy

Hospitalization is another nutritional risk factor and is particulary significant to the older patient. Hospital stays may heighten malnutrition through low-calorie liquid intake in preparation for particular diagnostic procedures (Weinsier et al., 1979). In some patients there is measurable weight loss during patient workup before appropriate dietary intakes have been put in place (Mitchell & Lipschitz, 1982). Protein-calorie malnutrition has been correlated with immune dysfunction, cardiac and respiratory insufficiency, altered gastrointestinal function, and inadequate response to chemotherapy (Newmark, Sieblett, Black, & Geller, 1981).

In patients who experience acute or chronic medical and/or surgical illness, the importance of nutritional support is accepted and increasingly implemented. But there has been little study of nutritional assessment and support of patients admitted to a rehabilitation unit. Nutritional assessment for all rehabilitation patients is essential to the rehabilitation regimen. If the assessment indicates malnutrition, nutrient and metabolic support should be undertaken to restore protein levels and immune capacity (Newmark et al., 1981).

Studies document the increase of existing malnutrition (upon hospital admission) and the greater incidence of infection, anemia, and general morbidity and mortality in the malnourished geriatric patient. On admission, older patients are more frequently seen to be suffering from protein-calorie malnutrition than are those under 65, 61% as compared with 28% (Biena, Ratcliff, Barbour, & Kummer, 1982). More than two thirds of patients over 60 referred to a nutrition support team over an 18-month period also showed protein-calorie malnutrition (Mitchell & Lipschitz, 1982). There is little doubt that additional affective and psychological factors are involved in prolonged malnutrition among elders during a hospital stay or residence in nursing homes. Isolation, loneliness, feelings of nonpersonhood, dependence, and depression contribute to loss of appetite and minimal dietary intake.

Low-Calorie Diets—Obesity

The low-calorie diets that many elders are either persuaded to adopt or that result from a loss of appetite, illness, poverty, and/or isolation lead to malnutrition. Scientists and clinicians alike have assumed that energy needs diminish with the decreased physical activity of the later years. Nutrient requirements are dependent on many variables—not only on assumed lower energy expenditure and reduction in lean body mass but on the reduced efficiency of protein utilization with age, drug intake, and minimal exposure to sunlight (Roe, 1987). Specific nutrients may be required in larger concentrations among elders, particularly in rehabilitation, because there is a gradual but definitive decrease in tissue function over time. Normative nutritional values and nutrient requirements will change in the face of disease, drugs, and gradual decline of functional efficiency with time (e.g., homeostasis, enzyme induction). In view of these alterations and the individual differences among elders, low calorie intake cannot be advised unless a nutrient assessment has demonstrated that increased nutrient density is unnecessary. This is true for elders in the community and particularly signficant for those older persons who are in recovery and rehabilitation, both of which increase nutritional requirements for body function. More research is needed to establish norms from age-related data for nutrient requirements (protein and micronutrients) in different states of mental and physical health, in varied living situations, and with individual dietary and drug histories before noncontroversial recommendations can be made (Munro, 1980). Therefore, a reduced caloric intake without guidance and information becomes another risk factor (Weg, 1980a).

Overnutrition or excess dietary intake is also a form of malnutrition. Obesity and excess weight are among the risk factors for the major chronic diseases—atherogenesis, cardiovascular disease, glucose intolerance, diabetes, hypertension, osteoarthritis, renal and gall bladder disease—as well as for increased surgical morbidity/mortality. Serious risks also appear to be associated with extreme leanness: an elevated mortality was found at the lower end of of the leanness scale. (Andres, 1980). After a review of worldwide mortality statistics, Andres emphasizes that there is hazard with both extremes, overweight and underweight.

Immune Response

Immune function has been shown to be compromised in malnourished hospital patients, small-for-gestational-age infants, and the elderly. For centuries the association between malnutrition and increased morbidity and mortality related to infectious diseases has been recognized. Only recently has it been understood that immune system function is affected by nutritional deficiencies, excesses, and imbalances (Chandra, 1985). This suggested relationship is reasonable because proteins and micronutrients are essential in the synthesis of antibodies, hormones, and cell proliferation, all significant processes in the immune response. Reduced immunocompetence is reported to occur in genetically obese experimental animals and humans. Excessive intakes of fat, particularly polyunsaturated fatty acids (e.g., linoleic and arachidonic acids), zinc, iron, and vitamin E are immunosuppresive. An imbalance of single nutrients is relatively uncommon in humans, but investigations of specific vitamins, minerals, trace elements, and protein are carried out with experimental animals. In these animals deficiencies of protein, some amino acids, and vitamins A, E, and B_6, folate, and minerals such as zinc, iron, and copper are associated with reduced immunocompetence.

Suppression of efficiency in the immune response by malnutrition contributes to complications in hospitalized patients (Chandra, 1985). When adequacy of the dietary intake is restored, immune capacity and response are improved. This was demonstrated in a study of 21 elders (60 years and older) in whom 8 weeks of nutritional supplementation (i.e., 500 kcal/day plus vitamins, minerals, and trace elements) was provided, resulting in enhancement of both nutritional status and immune response (Chandra, 1982). Much remains to be elucidated, especially with respect to the effect of single nutrients on immunity in humans. But it is clear that rehabilitation requires as efficient an immune response as possible in order to minimize any new interfering disease and enable the available nutrients to be fully utilized for rehabilitative therapy.

Polypharmacy

Another important barrier to adequate nutrition and rehabilitation among elders relates to drug-induced overnutrition and deficiencies. Drug absorption, distribution, and metabolism are altered with age. Systemic changes in the gastrointestinal tract, liver, kidney, and body composition (an increasing proportion of body fat to lean body mass) are involved. Multiple drugs, malnutrition, and pathology all modify these processes, leading at times to drug toxicity and lack of effectiveness. Older persons probably use close to 30% of all prescription drugs and an undetermined amount of over-the-counter drugs as well. Medical practitioners share in the abuse or misuse of medications by elders because a large number of drugs are used in after-the-fact treatment or palliation of presenting symptoms (Roe, 1987). There are drugs that affect nutrient absorption: antacids, hypocholesterolemic agents, cimetidine (used in peptic ulcer management), anti-inflammatory medication for gout and rheumatoid arthritis, chemotherapuetic agents for cancer (e.g., methotextrate), laxatives (mineral oil), and antibiotics (Roe, 1987). Foods and drugs interact, and certain foods will modify particular drug absorption, bioavailability, and efficacy, often slowing down absorption, treatment, and rehabilitation.

In this "pill for every occasion" society the uses and purposes of drugs have not been sufficiently explored with older patients. Uninformed drug prescriptions and poor eating habits aggravate an already problematic nutrient status.

NUTRITION INTERVENTION: PREVENTION AND THERAPY AS REHABILITATION

Foods and their nutrients provide energy and intermediate substances used in syntheses: maintenance of structure by proteins of all kinds (e.g., antibodies, enzymes, hormones), wound healing, growth and repair, mobilization and replication of T and B lymphocytes, neurotransmitters, and the like. Without the appropriate quantity and quality of the major and micronutrients in the dietary intake, many cell processes are disrupted; cells become disorganized, dysfunctional, and die. Damage ensues at the level of tissues, organs, and organ systems.

Effective nutritional manipulation has been used throughout this century for earlier stages of life—fetal, infancy, childhood, young adulthood—with no information on "long range effects of this diet" (Hegstead, 1979, p. 1997). Such imperfect and incomplete knowledge has been the basis of dietary guidance to Americans from nutritionists, other health professionals, and government. Generally, this has not been the practice with and for elders.

There is no alternative to a commitment to improvement of the nutritional status of all persons, and particularly that of the middle-aged and elderly, who are at demonstrable risk. Coronary heart disease, hypertension, major cancers, diabetes, and osteoporosis have been repeatedly shown to be epidemiologically and experimentally associated with dietary excesses and deficiencies of the westernized diet (Weg, 1980a). This indictment suggests that the adoption of the prudent diet is a scientifically responsible decision in spite of incompletely validated data (Hegstead, 1979). The prudent diet fulfills human requirements and appears to offer some protection against the major killer diseases. It is also a measurable therapeutic tool in the management of these disorders—a primary step in rehabilitation. A few selected examples of dietary manipulation as a rehabilitative factor in restoration of function are illustrated by the diseases discussed below.

Atherogenesis, Coronary Heart Disease

Increased plaque development in the walls of the arterial blood vessels and narrowing of vessel diameter are central factors in coronary heart disease. Coronary heart disease, like many other chronic disorders, is multifactorial in basis: in any one individual the disease may be correlated with smoking, diet, atherosclerosis, hypertension, hypercholesterolemia, hyperlipidemia, sedentary life-style, family history, obesity, diabetes mellitus, or a combination of these factors. In preventive postinfarct therapy, an alteration of the dietary patterns has proved to lower the incidence of recurrence of myocardial infarction. Cardiac rehabilitation is part of patient management for individuals who have cardiac disease or those who appear to be at increased risk. The objectives are to help the patient return to usual activities and reach a comfortable state of wellness. Techniques include life-style changes that will delay the progression of the disease, prevent another cardiac accident, or prevent/delay disease onset for those at risk (Palmer & Sonnenberg, 1984).

Epidemiological studies indicate that countries and groups in which diets are low in saturated fat and cholesterol do not have high incidence of coronary heart disease (Turner, 1982). It has been shown that the concentration of low-density lipoprotein (LDL) cholesterol is correlated with atherogenesis, and high-density lipoprotein is negatively related to atherogenesis and coronary heart disease (Castelli et al., 1977). For 4 years, both the American Heart Association (AHA) and the National Institutes of Health have advised that the maximum blood cholesterol should be less than 200 mg; some suggest 180 mg. The data from a new cholesterol investigation, a follow-up on the Multiple Risk Factor Intervention Trial (MRFIT), indicate that heart disease risk increases as serum cholesterol increases. MRFIT participants (males) with cholesterol from 182 to 202 mg demonstrated a 31% higher risk for death from coronary disease than those with a more average blood level of 164 mg (Tufts University, 1987).

Dietary strategies for lowering serum cholesterol and fat intake are varied. More recently, studies have indicated that diets rich in fish oil (specifically the omega-3 fatty acid constituent) decrease blood triglyceride-rich lipoproteins and plasma cholesterol, biosynthesis of fatty acids, and very low density lipoproteins (VLDL) by the liver (Kronhout, Basschuter, & Coulander, 1985; Phillipson, Rothrock, Conner, Harris, & Illingworth, 1985). Fish oil has been shown to control hyperlipidemia and thrombosis. High consumption of fish by a group of Dutch men followed for 20 years was inversely correlated with death from heart disease (Kronhout et al., 1985). A diet of vegetable oils was less effective, so unsaturated acids in fish oil would appear to have a significant potential for management (rehabilitation) therapy and prevention. Further research is needed to confirm these data, but waiting to change to a prudent diet until critical studies have been completed would appear to be clinically unnecessary.

In an effort to assist those who are at risk for coronary heart disease, the AHA has proposed a more aggressive three-phase plan to lower blood cholesterol by modifying daily intake (from 300 to 200 mg, and finally to 150 mg/day) and to reduce the percentage of calories from fat (from 30% to 25% to 20%). Changing the diet to low-fat, low-choles-terol, high-fiber intake, rich in vegetables, fruits, and whole grains can lower both blood cholesterol and LDL (Tufts University, 1987).

Until the early work of Burkitt, Walker, and Painter (1974) in Africa with dietary fiber and diverticulosis, fiber was considered primarily for its laxative properties. Their emphasis on the relationship between di-etary fiber and disease triggered greater interest and research in a range of metabolic processes and fiber. Studies relevant to atherogen-esis and CHD involve the use of diets with high fiber concentrations in diabetes and hypercholesterolemia. The most recent approach to treat-ment of diabetes prescribes diets high in complex carbohydrates and fiber (HCF), a regimen that results in significant decreases in glycosuria and glycemia and a reduction in the requirement for insulin or other hyperglycemic agents (Kritchevsky, 1986). A recent study of three groups of Seventh-Day Adventists—vegetarians, lacto-ovo vegetarians, and nonvegetarians—and the general public investigated serum lipids and dietary components (Kritchevsky, Tepper, & Goodman, 1984). The fiber intake differences among the groups were in pectin and lignin. Vegetarians ate twice as much pectin as the other three groups—67% more than lacto-ovo vegetarians and 88% more than the other two groups. Total cholesterol level in vegetarians was 30.3% lower than the public; in nonvegetarians, only 10.3% lower. In lacto-ovo vegetarians cholesterol levels were 7.2% lower than in nonvegetarians. Many di-etary components are instrumental in cholesterol metabolism, and fiber intake is one of those factors. In rehabilitation, both cardiac and dia-betic, attention to the nature of carbohydrates and fiber in the diet is yet another variable over which control can be exercised and positive results can be anticipated.

Brain Function

There is increasing evidence that nutrition affects the composition and probably the function of the brain (Wurtman, 1982). Work with mon-keys (Connor & Connor, 1985) demonstrated that within a few weeks a diet high in omega-3 fatty acids changes the composition of the brain. Primates deprived of these acids during gestation or infancy suffered visual problems. With monkeys that had fatty acid deficiencies, a diet of 12% fish oil for 8 to 12 weeks proved to increase brain cell membrane content of omega-3 fatty acid from 3.9% to a normal 21.2% (determined by biopsy). Primate brain composition is therefore not fixed, as scien-tists had thought earlier, but is susceptible to dietary changes. Good-win, Goodwin, and Garry (1983) suggest that mild nutrient deficiencies may, over time, contribute to a deterioration in thinking ability in older

Americans. In a study examining the correlation between nutritional status and cognitive function in a group of 260 healthy men and women over 60, those with low dietary intake and low levels of riboflavin, folic acid, and vitamins B_{12} and C tended to perform most poorly in psychological tests. Those with low blood levels of riboflavin or folic acid scored lower on tests for abstract thinking and problem-solving ability, and those low in vitamin C or B_{12} had lower test scores on both memory and problem solving. These facts suggest that in the management of memory and problem-solving deficits, serious consideration should be given to nutritional assessment and restoration of nutrient deficiencies to effect some rehabilitation in capacity to function. Because some elders may be lifelong heavy drinkers or more recent alcoholics, the resulting lack of adequate levels of thiamin, folic acid, and vitamins B_6, B_{12}, or C should be restored as part of a rehabilitation plan.

Osteoporosis—Calcium

Several government surveys indicate that substantial segments of the U.S. population—in particular, females 12 years of age and older—have Ca intakes below the RDA for that mineral on any given day. The Ca deficit in many individuals may be greater than that indicated by these surveys because many nutritional experts consider the RDA for Ca to be low, at least for postmenopausal and elderly women.

Potential problems associated with prolonged inadequate Ca intake include accelerated bone loss (bone mass), which predisposes to osteoporosis; alveolar bone loss; potential oral problems such as periodontitis; and a rise in blood pressure, or hypertension. Twenty-five percent of Caucasian women 65 and over experience one or more osteoporosis-related fractures. The profile most frequently at risk is the small-boned, thin, Caucasian, relatively inactive female. Aging appears to be marked by a decrease in Ca absorption and may necessitate an adjustment, at times because of inadequate conversion (with less exposure to sunlight) of vitamin D to the active metabolite calcitriol, which is "the physiological stimulus to intestinal transport of Ca" (Roe, 1987, p. 69). Calcitriol also stimulates the release of Ca from the skeleton, a process requiring the simultaneous release of parathyroid hormone (Miller & Norman, 1984).

It has been determined that a lack of physical activity, as well as nutrient-drug and nutrient-nutrient interactions, affects the absorption and excretion of calcium. Dietary factors that are part of the Ca absorption, retention, and balance picture include magnesium, protein, vitamin D, phosphorus, lactose, and fiber.

Lactose increases intestinal absorption and retention of Ca, whereas excessive dietary fiber may impair intestinal absorption by forming insoluble Ca salts. Alcohol may decrease appetite (displacing Ca-containing food) and increase the loss of fat in feces, thereby lowering vitamin D absorption and reducing Ca absorption and retention (Heaney, 1986; Roe, 1987).

Elders who are hospitalized or in nusing homes are particularly at risk for Ca balance and maintenance of skeletal health. For those who experience prolonged bed rest for medical or surgical reasons (including fractures), the immobilization and lack of sunlight exacerbate Ca loss. Exercise, dietary intake with balanced nutrients involved in Ca metabolism and well-functioning circulation and execretion, muscle mass and tone maintenance, apparently essential in minimizing bone mass and fragility, are increasingly difficult to achieve. These situations add a series of barriers to rehabilitation and improvement in physical and mental status.

The amount of dietary Ca is no indication of how much is utilized, as only 30% of dietary Ca is absorbed, the remaining 70% being excreted in feces. Dairy foods provide the best nutritional source quantitatively and qualitatively, high bioavailability presumably due to presence of lactose, phosphopeptides, and vitamin D. Other foods, such as canned sardines, salmon with edible bones, tofu, and dark green leafy vegetables (collards, kale), are Ca-containing, although in much smaller quantities than milk and milk products. The choice of Ca supplements should be made in terms of bioavailability of elemental Ca. They rank in the following order: Ca carbonate (40% Ca), Ca lactate (13%), Ca gluconate (9%), bone meal (31%), and dolomite (22%). The last two may be contaminated with toxic metals (e.g., lead and cadmium) and should be avoided if possible.

Osteoporosis develops over a period of years. With time, if the disease progresses, there is a loss of height, poor posture, and backache. There are gender differences in severity and incidence; in women both are four times higher than in men. Although diminution of estrogen during and after menopause has been considered to accelerate bone loss, there is a lack of agreement on the benefit of estrogen therapy (Recker et al., 1977). There are differences of opinion regarding the most effective treatment and rehabilitative program for osteoporosis. Various therapies attempt to prevent, treat, and/or reverse osteoporosis; some are more successful than others with individual patients. Certain nutrients are of particular concern: high protein intake can lead to increased Ca excretion; both excess and very low fat intake impair Ca absorption. Epidemiologically, populations from fluoride-rich water areas have a lower incidence of osteoporosis. Recommended treatment regimens have included a variety of nutrient combinations: vitamin D or its active metabolite calcitriol, fluoride Ca supplementation (800–1500 mg/day), and estrogen or estrogen/progesterone therapy (especially for menopausal and postmenopausal women) (Jowsey, 1976). The genetics of bone—its porosity and size—presents a potential for the amount of compact bone available at maturity and into the later years. Life-style factors (exercise, diet, drugs, other disorders or diseases) can maximize or minimize that potential. Rehabilitation of the older osteoporotic patient must take into consideration the multifactorial bases involved.

Cancer

In persons with malignancy, protein-calorie malnutrition is frequent as a result of low dietary intake and tumor metabolic aberrations. Cachexia—an extreme state of protein-calorie malnutrition common in advanced cancer—is considered the major factor for increased morbidity and mortality and diminished capacity for aggressive cancer treatment (Nixon et al., 1980). The elderly are at greater risk for cancer-induced malnutrition. Therefore, nutritional management and support are necessary steps in protecting malnourished elders without frank disease and essential during cancer treatment for elders at risk for severe malnutrition or cachexia (Hardy et al., 1986).

CONCLUSION

Most of the examples of intervention are related to use of dietary modification in therapy. One of the significant issues, not discussed but a logical corollary, is that inadequate nutritional status of one or more nutrients can initiate a cascade of events that has serious consequences for relatively healthy elders as well as those already at risk nutritionally or systemically and those with frank disease. Fatigue, anemia, general malaise, depression, and confusion can be functions of nutrient deficiencies, and the so-called inevitable syndrome of "aging symptoms" is left unquestioned, untreated. Prevention of disease, rehabilitation, health promotion, a philosophy of living for all persons, and a person-oriented approach to health care can be satisfactorily translated only if optimal nutritional status is one of the important considerations. Rehabilitation at any level—respiratory, cardiac, cancer, fracture, stroke—cannot be undertaken with expectation of good to optimal results without an adequate nutritional status, the maximum possible for that individual patient.

There is no acceptable alternative to a relatively healthful later life—economically or in terms of human suffering. A portion of what was earlier perceived as inevitable deterioration and disease for all who reached "old" is now increasingly seen as responsive, in part, to interventions of one kind or another. Rehabilitation is an essential part of any medical management with the objective of maximizing whatever potentials exist that can enable a patient to return to purposeful, livable existence.

The evidence is persuasive: food and nutrients appear to be instrumental both in contributing to disorders and in reversing or staying the destructive progress of the major chronic diseases common among elders. Nutrition as prevention and in overall support of energy and systemic fucntion into the later years needs further carefully designed research to permit definitive conclusions. Epidemiological and descriptive studies point the way. The prudent diet continues to be worth the effort. Nutritional therapy has been demonstrated to work; rehabilitation to adequate function cannot take place effectively or be sustained without it. Surely, rehabilitation cannot rest only on optimizing the nutritional intake. Without adequate nutrients tailored to the need of the patient, attention to other significant health variables such as exercise, stress management, improved social and living arrangements, and economic support, the malnourished individual will still be functionally impaired.

It is fair to note that any rehabilitation undertaken will not succeed without consideration for nutrition. Nutrients and dietary patterns are the only sources of energy and substances for cellular and systemic functions and important areas of daily living. The time has passed when elders are "too old" to be rehabilitated and for rehabilitation to remain focused on the walker or Hydrocolator.

REFERENCES

Andres, R. (1980). Effect of obesity on total mortality. *International Journal of Obesity, 4*, 381–386.

Biena, R., Ratcliff, S., Barbour, G. L., & Kummer, M. (1982). Malnutrition in the hospitalized geriatric patient. *Journal of the American Geriatric Society, 30*(7), 433–436.

Burkitt, D. (1982). Disease of affluence. In J. Rose (Ed.), *Nutrition and killer diseases: The effects of dietary factors on fatal chronic diseases* (pp. 1–7). Park Ridge, NJ: Noyes.

Burkitt, D. P., Walker, A. R. P., & Painter, N. S. (1974). Dietary fiber and disease. *Journal of the American Medical Association, 229,* 1068–1074.

Butler, R. E. (1987). Nutrition in the elderly. *Generations, 12*(1), 45–49.

Castelli, W. P., Doyle, J. T., Gordon, T., Hames, C. G., Hjortland, M. C., Hulley, S. B., Kagan, A., & Zukel, W. (1977). HDL cholesterol and other lipids in coronary heart disease: The cooperative lipoprotein phenotyping study. *Circulation, 55,* 767–772.

Chandra, R. K. (1982). *Primary and secondary immunodeficiency disorders.* Edinburgh: Churchill Livingston.

Chandra, R. K. (1985). *Nutrition immunity and illness in the elderly.* New York: Pergamon Press.

Connor, W. E., & Connor, S. L. (1985). The dietary prevention and treatment of coronary disease. In W. E. Connor & J. D. Bristol (Eds.), *Coronary heart disease: Prevention complications and treatment* (pp. 43–64). Philadelphia: J.B. Lippincott.

Exton-Smith, A. N., & Caird, F. I. (Eds.). (1980). *Metabolic and nutritional disorders in elderly.* Bristol, UK: Wright & Sons.

Goodwin, J. S., Goodwin, J. M., & Garry, P. J. (1983). Association between nutritional status and cognitive functioning in a health population. *Journal of the American Medical Association, 249*(21), 2917–2931.

Hardy, C., Wallace, C., Khansur, T., Vance, R. B., Thigpen, J. T., & Balducci, L. (1986). Nutrition, cancer, and aging: An annotated review: 2. Cancer cachexia and aging. *Journal of the American Geriatrics Society, 34,* 219–228.

Harper, A. E. (1982). Nutrition, aging, and longevity. *American Journal of Clinical Nutrition, 36,* 737–749.

Heaney R. P. (1986). Calcium, bone health, and osteoporosis. In W. A. Peck (Ed.), *Bone and mineral research annual: Vol. 4. A yearly survey of developments in the field of bone and mineral metabolism* (pp. 225–301). Amsterdam: Elsevier.

Hegstead, D. M. (1979). Optimal nutrition. *Cancer, 43,* 1996–2003.

Jowsey, J. (1976). Prevention and treatment of osteoporosis. in M. Winick (Ed.), *Nutrition and aging Vol. 2* (pp. 131–144). New York: John Wiley & Sons.

Kritchevsky, D. (1986). Geriatric diabetes: Latest research on the role of dietary fiber. *Geriatrics, 41*(5), 117–122.

Kritchevsky, D., Tepper, S. A., & Goodman, G. (1984). Diet, nutrition intake, and metabolism in populations at high and low risk for colon cancer: Relationship of diet to serum lipids. *American Journal of Clinical Nurtition, 40,* 921–926.

Kronhout, D., Basschuter, E. G., & Coulander, C. (1985). The inverse relationship between fish consumption and 20 year morbidity from CHD. *New England Journal of Medicine, 13*(19), 1205–1209.

Miller, B. E., & Norman, A. W. (1984). Vitamin D. In L. J. Machlin (Ed.), *Handbook of vitamins: Nutritional biochemical and clinical aspects* (pp. 45–97). New York: Marcel Dekker.

Mitchell, C.O., & Lipschitz, D. A. (1982). Detection of protein calorie malnutrition in the elderly. *American Journal of Clinical Nutrition, 35,* 398–406.

Munro, H. N. (1980). Major gaps in nutrient allowances. *Journal of the American Dietetics Association, 76*(2), 137–144.

Newmark, S. R., Sieblett, D., Black, J., & Geller, R. (1981). Nutritional assessment in a rehabilitation unit. *Archives of Physical and Medical Rehabilitation, 62,* 279–282.

Nixon, D. W., Heymsfield, S. B., Cohen, A. E., Kutner, M. H., Ansley, J., Lawson, D. H., & Rudman, D. (1980). Protein calorie undernutrition in hospitalized cancer patients. *American Journal of Medicine, 68,* 683–690.

Palmer, S., & Sonnenberg, L. (1984). Cardiac rehabilitation: Role of the dietitian in a multidisciplinary team. *American Journal of Intravenous Therapy and Clinical Nutrition,* 9–18.

Phillipson, B., Rothrock, D. W., Conner, W. E., Harris, W. S., & Illingworth, P. R. (1985). Reduction of plasma lipids, lipoproteins and apoproteins by dietary fish oils in patients with hypertriglyceridema. *New England Journal of Medicine, 13*(19), 1210–1216.

Recker, R. R., et al. (1977). Effects of estrogens and calcium carbonate on bone loss in post-menopausal women. *Annals of Internal Medicine, 87*(6) 649–655.

Roe, D. A. (1987). *Geriatric nutrition* (2d ed.). Englewood Cliffs, NJ: Prentice-Hall.

Smith, E. L., & Gilligan, C. (1988). Diet, exercise and chronic disease: Patterns in older adults. *Nutrition Review, 46*(2), 45–51.

Tannahill, R. (1973). *Food in history.* New York: Stein & Day.

Thueson, L., Henriksen, L. B., & Engby, B. (1986). One year experience with a low fat, low cholesterol diet in patients with coronary heart disease. *American Journal of Clinical Nutrition, 44,* 212–219.

Tufts University. (1987). *Diet and Nutrition Letter, 5*(1), 2. Medford, MA: Author.

Turner, R. W. D. (1982). Diet and epidemic coronary heart disease. In J. Rose (Ed.), *Nutrition and killer diseases: The effects of dietary factors on fatal chronic diseases* (pp. 30–49). Park Ridge, NJ: Noyes.

U.S. Department of Health and Welfare, Consumer and Food Economics Research Division. (1972). *Food and nutrient intake of individuals in the United States: USDA household food consumption survey 1965–1966.* Washington, DC: U.S. Government Printing Office.

Weg, R. B. (1980a). Changing physiology of age: Changing nutrition. *U.S.C. Journal of Continuing Dental Education, 1*(1), 3–22.

Weg, R. B. (1980b). Prolonged mild nutritional deficiencies: Significance for health maintenance. *Journal of Nutrition for the Elderly, 1*(1), 3–22.

Weinsier, R. L., Hunker, E. M., Krumdieck, C. L., & Butterworth, Jr., C. E. (1979). Hospital malnutrition: A prospective evaluation of general medical patients during the course of hospitalization. *American Journal of Clinical Nutrition, 32,* 418–426.

Wurtman, R. J. (1982). Nutrients that modify brain function. *Scientific American, 246*(4), 50–60.

Wurtman, R. J., & Wurtman, J. J. (1986). *Nutrition and the brain: Vol. 7. Food constituents affecting normal and abnormal behaviors.* New York: Raven Press.

Young, E. A. (Ed.). (1986). *Nutrition, aging and health.* New York: Alan R. Liss.

Young, V. R. (1982a). Nutrition. In J. W. Rowe & R. W. Besdine (Eds.), *Health and disease in old age.* (pp. 317–333). Boston: Little, Brown.

Young, V. R. (1982b). Plasma amino acids and proteins. In *Assessing the nutritional status of the elderly: State of the art report of the Third Ross Roundtable on Medical Issues* (pp. 35–38). Columbus, OH: Ross Laboratories.

12

Rehabilitation in Ethnic Minority Elderly

F. M. Baker, Louis M. Kamikawa,
David S. Espino, and Spero Manson

The U.S. population is comprised of a multiplicity of ethnic subpopulations. The elderly are often discussed as a monolithic group, but this is an incomplete picture. Although the elderly population in various communities in the United States may be somewhat homogeneous, there are other communities whose populations are markedly diverse. These differences may be based on culture and/or ethnic heritage as well as on historical experiences. To facilitate an effective rehabilitative intervention with these varying populations, this chapter will present an overview of four major ethnic populations within the total U.S. population: Afro-Americans, American Indians, Asian-Americans and Pacific Islanders, and Hispanics. Each ethnic group will be discussed separately within an overarching format: demographic data, psychosocial history and unique concerns, and specific intervention techniques for effective engagement in the rehabilitative task(s). There are commonalities in experiences in the United States for these groups who have been identified as "visible minorities"; there are also very divergent experiences, as exemplified by the internment of Asian-Americans during World War II and the "trail of tears" relocation of American Indians. The ethnic elders of these populations were born in the early 1900s or earlier. If they were the first generation resident in the United States, issues of language and acculturation may remain significant concerns for these elders, now in their 70s and 80s, as they attempt to identify resources to aid with the multiple changes of aging. If resident in the United States for several generations, access to education, housing, and health care may have been restricted by legislation and/or by custom at both the state and federal levels. In addition, the cultural definition of illness, mechanisms of seeking care, definition of health care personnel, and the expectations of health care settings differ among these groups and sometimes differ markedly from the middle-class Northern European models of care that are viewed as the norm for health care in the United States. In truth, a significant portion of poor white Americans have a different definition of illness and seek care in alternative settings because of ineligibility to enter the health care system.

The concept of an explanatory model posits that each person, as a consequence of primary socialization processes and cultural member-ship, possesses a relatively coherent framework for organizing his or her experience, knowledge, manifestation, and expectations of illness. Explanatory models encompass the cultural idioms, labels, and meta-phors that people use to talk about illness. In addition, they character-ize beliefs about etiology, associated signs and symptoms, predispos-ing social situations, and perceived treatment alternatives. Lay referral networks—spouse, family, and friends—assist in defining which treat-ment alternative to apply in given circumstances. Physicians, nurses, and other allied health professionals possess their own distinct explan-atory models, typically embodied in the *International Classification of Disease*, 9th edition. This "medical" explanatory model is acquired through extensive training: another form of socialization. Conse-quently, health care encounters can be seen as the negotiation of ex-planatory models between patient and provider. Patient satisfaction, compliance with medical regimens, and even recovery time appear to be closely tied to the successful alignment of these conceptual frame-works.

Thus, the focus of this chapter is to facilitate knowledge of four eth-nic groups within the U.S. population: elders who generally differ in in physical appearance as well as in culture and customs from the white American elder. Although there are similarities in addressing the phys-ical and financial changes that accompany aging, there are other very different concerns for these populations that influence their involve-ment in rehabilitative therapies.

AFRO-AMERICANS

Demographics

Afro-Americans comprise 12% of the U.S. population, based on the 1980 U.S. Census. Eleven percent of the total Afro-American population are aged 60 years or older, some 2.4 million persons. The old-old are the fastest-growing segment of this older population (Gibson, 1986). Since 1900 it has been noted that Afro-Americans surviving to age 75 live longer than do white Americans of the same age (Gibson, 1986). An Afro-American woman aged 80 in 1978 had a life expectancy of 11.5 more years, in contrast to a life expectancy of 8.8 more years for an Afro-American man, 8.8 more years for a white woman, and 6.7 more years for a white man (Gibson, 1986). This increased survival for Afro-American elders has been termed the racial mortality "crossover" effect. Although long observed, it has not been systematically studied. Whereas 29.9% of the Afro-American population is below the poverty level, compared to 9.4% of white Americans, more Afro-American elders (31.7%) than white American elders (10.7%) are below the poverty level. The average number of persons per Afro-American family was 3.72, compared with 3.9 persons per white American family. Although a visible population, it is important to establish the specific ethnic heritage of the older Afro-American, which may be a mixture of cultures. The diversity of ethnic heritage is illustrated by the recent immigration of persons from the Caribbean (West Indians) and the mixture of Afro-Americans with American Indians and Northern Europeans.

Psychosocial History and Unique Concerns

Afro-Americans were forcibly removed from their agrarian or nomadic tribal communities that emphasized the value of family and the good of the community. With other ethnic groups, Africans were used as slave labor and then became the primary focus of the slave trade when they did not die from the environmental differences or the labor on the plantations in North and South America and the Caribbean (Baker, 1988a). Although chattel slavery in the United States disrupted family bonds and community ties, alternative extended families evolved. The Afro-American elder of 1989 has heard the oral history of the dark passage and Reconstruction and has personally experienced segregation, desegregation, and the black revolution. The Secretary's Task Force on Black and Minority Health (1985) documented the loss of Afro-Americans by homicide, suicide, and accidents in their early adult years in the 1920s and 1930s. Afro-Americans who survive to age 60 are at risk of death from cardiovascular disease caused by obesity and hypertension and have a higher prevalence of diabetes (particularly black women).

When compared to white Americans, Afro-Americans have a higher age-adjusted mortality rate for cancer of the breast (females under 40), cervical and uterine cancer, multiple myeloma, and esophageal, laryngeal, prostatic, and stomach cancer (Baquet, 1988). Visual problems, particularly glaucoma, are frequently found among Afro-Americans. Having reviewed the existing international data concerning the incidence and prevalence of dementing illness, Baker (1988b) suggested that multi-infarct dementia and alcoholic dementia may occur more frequently in Afro-American elders than clinically diagnosed Alzheimer's disease. The specific patterns of illness and alcohol use described in the few existing studies provide suggestive evidence for this hypothesis. The loss of the traditional support of the Afro-American network and the loss of the family by death, divorce, or relocation of adult children are factors that increase the risk of the Afro-American elder's becoming unable to cope with the stressors of aging. Many older Afro-Americans face the quadruple jeopardy of "being old, poor, black, and female."

In the 1980s the church (Taylor & Chatters, 1986) and the community remain important psychological and social resources for the Afro-American elder. The self-esteem of the Afro-American is enhanced in late adult life because the roles of mentor in the community and in the family and of senior elder in the church are new or existing roles that can be expanded when the role of worker is ended by retirement (Taylor, 1988). It is not unusual to find an Afro-American elder providing day-care supervision for a grandchild—biologic or adopted—a role reinforcing the elder's sense of continuing contribution and importance to the family.

The Afro-American elder of the 1990s was born in the first 20 years of this century. As part of the African heritage, the medicine man served the tribe with his knowledge of roots and leaves that had medicinal properties. The indigenous healer in the black community continues today in the person who "works roots" and "prescribes" specific teas for fever and diarrhea. Although many Afro-American elders no longer seek care from a "root doctor," they may consult with the nurse who lives next door, their pastor, or the pharmacist before seeking treatment in a formal health care setting. With the development of various means of communication (radio, television, print media) has come the definition of specific signs and symptoms as an illness, rather than an assignment of symptoms to "just getting older." The Afro-American elder remains stoic and is more likely to minimize pain. It is important to observe both verbal and nonverbal behavior of the Afro-American elder to make sure that a specific rehabilitative program is not exceeding the limits of tolerable discomfort, for example, to achieve the gain of increased endurance and improved range of motion and strength.

Rehabilitation Task: Specific Interventions

The Afro-American elder presenting as a patient requiring a specific rehabilitative task is more likely to have been born in the southern states and to have completed less than 12 years of formal education because of segregation and poverty during childhood and adolescent years. Unlike other ethnic groups, his or her primary language has, for the most part, been English. This elder is likely to be in weekly, if not daily, contact with adult children, surviving siblings, and long-standing friends as well as church members, regardless of geographical residence. If the elder in her 80s is the sole survivor of her family, her social network may consist of extended-family members, who can be an important resource to the rehabilitative therapist. These extended-family members may assist in range of motion exercises or speech therapy programs and may minimally provide transportation for the elder. If the elder has difficulty with written instructions, the extended-family member or church member may review the instructions and treatment regimens with the older patient. Although some may be without persons from their family of origin or family of procreation, other resources exist that can be mobilized to enable them to complete the program of rehabilitation.

The Afro-American elder has experienced the segregation of health care facilities. So the elder's expectations of the health care setting and the health care team may be somewhat skewed. A courteous, respectful approach to the Afro-American elder that acknowledges his or her personhood, together with respect for the wisdom of advanced years and the person's ability to survive hostile environments, will begin the evaluation for treatment on a positive basis.

Identifying and establishing relationships with the social support system of the Afro-American elder will facilitate compliance with treatment. In addition to monitoring the elder's completion of the rehabilitative program, the extended-family member or other significant person(s) in the elder's life can facilitate the completion of the therapeutic plan as well as participating in the ongoing treatment program.

It is important to remember the diversity and heterogeneity of people, particularly Afro-American elders. Thus, the initial assessment should establish the patient's level of education, work, and retirement resources, both financial and interpersonal. Afro-American elders include the retired heads of well-known Afro-American insurance companies and publication corporations as well as administrators of academic institutions. Although a small percentage of the Afro-American population in general and of the Afro-American elderly specifically, there is an Afro-American middle-class with the knowledge base and expectations that arise from education, experience, and resources.

Finally, the Afro-American extended family should be recognized as an important resource for the rehabilitation therapist. Although several miles or thousands of miles away from the Afro-American elder, the members of the extended family (Martin & Martin, 1978) can maintain weekly contact with the elder(s). Biologic family members and adopted family members can check with the Afro-American elder daily to monitor health status as well as to provide needed assistance with shopping and transportation. In the absence of extended family in the elder's community of residence, church members may fill this role. Identifying the members of this support network will provide important information regarding cognitive and functional status; this is also a resource for transportation to appointments. If the rehabilitative program requires specific activity by the elder (e.g., home exercises), an extended-family member can work with the elder to ensure that the program is implemented as prescribed. In instances where there is an increased risk for a major depressive episode during rehabilitation, the support network of the elder can provide important longitudinal information about his or her mood, attitude, and cognitive functioning.

AMERICAN INDIANS

Demographics

Recent estimates indicate at least a doubling of the number of American Indians 65 years of age and older by the year 2000. American Indian elders now comprise slightly more than 5% of the Indian population, which totals 1.5 million. More than 300 different tribes are recognized by the federal government. These tribes are distributed across 278 reservations and 209 villages. Although more than half of their members live in urban settings, the majority of elderly American Indians still tend to reside in rural reservation communities.

Older whites enjoy, on a per capita basis, 40% to 59% more income than that of older American Indians. Relatively speaking, older urban Indians fare much better than older rural Indians; rural Indian elders generate 70% or less of the income of urban Indian elders. About one eighth of whites 65 years and older are at or below the poverty line, compared to one third to one half of their Indian counterparts. Although there is essentially no difference between the two groups in labor force participation or employment, a greater proportion of older American Indians are below the poverty level.

Three-fourths of rural American Indians 65 to 74 years of age live with their families. Only 50% of all urban Indians of the same age live with their families, compared to 18% for all older white Americans. Although it would seem that American Indian elders living in rural areas have a greater potential for family support, over twice as many rural as urban Indian families with aged members fall below the poverty line. Thus, rural Indian families are significantly reduced in ability to provide needed care.

Advancing age increases the likelihood that a Native American elder will live alone or move into an institutional setting. At least one third of the population 75 years and older, Indian or white, rural or urban, lives alone. Yet there are dramatic urban/rural differences in the proportion of aged persons living in institutional environments. For example, older urban Indians occupy homes for the aged at twice the rate of older rural Indians despite the fact that a greater proportion of rural (5.8%) than urban (4.7%) Indians are 75 years of age or older. This pattern of utilization of institutional care by Indian elders may be an artifact of the availability of space as well as economic profitability.

Physical health problems play a large role in the lives of older American Indians. For example, 73% of the elderly Indian population is estimated to be mildly to totally impaired in their ability to cope with the basics of daily living. Forty percent of all adult Indians have some form of disability. Tuberculosis is five times more prevalent among Indians than among non-Indians. Liver and gallbladder disease, rheumatoid arthritis, and diabetes occur far more frequently within this special population than in any other. Other health problems include obesity, hypertension, pneumonia, poor vision, and dental decay. The impact of these diseases is reflected in the significantly higher rates of depression among elderly Indians compared to those of elderly non-Indian persons (National Indian Council on Aging, 1981). The physical as well as psychological consequences contribute substantially to the decreased longevity of this special population compared to that of whites (Manson & Callaway, 1988).

Psychosocial History and Unique Concerns

The attitudes of American Indian elders toward illness and health care have been relatively unexamined by past research. Most of the work to date has emphasized epidemiologic trends in morbidity and mortality with little regard for the ways that older Indians conceptualize the nature of their health problems and appropriate responses to them. Gradually, however, this situation is beginning to change, and some suggestive data are emerging.

In 1980 Manson and colleagues (Manson, Murray, & Cain, 1981) studied the daily problems faced by 231 older Indians (mean age, 62.1 years) living on two Pacific Northwest reservations and in a nearby city. Physical illness and resulting limitations on activities of daily living (ADL) were found to have occurred with alarming frequency among these individuals. These older American Indians resisted solutions by refusing to utilize social, economic, and psychological resources available to them. This decision resulted in high levels of persistent stress. American Indian elders would not actively seek help from either formal or informal sources of support, except in life-threatening circumstances. The vast majority of these older adults, especially those from the urban area, were unaware of potentially appropriate services, did not know how to seek information about needed care, and expressed concern about what people might think of them if they did seek such help.

More recently, Baron and colleagues (in press) annually interviewed 316 older members (mean age, 60.8 years) of four Pacific Northwest reservations about various aspects of their physical and mental health status. These individuals were selected originally because they had been seen for the first time in a local health clinic, during the 1984 calendar year, for one of three chronic physical health problems: rheumatoid arthritis, diabetes, and ischemic heart disease. The results show that access to medical care, specifically transportation, was a frequent problem. Most respondents were generally satisfied with the care received but wished more of it if possible. Significant percentages of these older Indians were treated by traditional healers in the local communities (41%) for their particular health problems and practiced their own cultural forms of "self-care" (63%). A measure of health locus of control revealed a slight trend toward externality, which increased with the amount of pain associated with a health problem and the problem's apparent progressiveness (typically worsening) over time. Many American Indian elders generally felt that the cause and course of their physical illnesses were beyond their immediate control. Religion, family, spouse, friends, and health care professionals were, in descending order of importance, cited as major strengths in enabling respondents to cope with the difficulties posed by their illnesses. Many of them reported the availability of a confidant (82.1%), which was strongly associated with the older person's degree of life satisfaction.

There have been few studies of American Indian explanatory models. One unique example can be found in the Manson, Shore, and Bloom (1985) study of depression among the Hopi. By eliciting and comparing local explanatory models to DSM-III diagnostic criteria for major depression, these investigators were able to demonstrate the manner in which Hopi categories of illness relate to this psychiatric disorder, yielding specific diagnostic and treatment recommendations. Diabetes, rheumatoid arthritis, hypertension, and other significant health problems common to older American Indians could be profitably examined in the same fashion.

Rehabilitative Task: Specific Interventions

When delivering health care to older American Indians, one frequently asks: How will these individuals react to the tasks that are intrinsic to good medical practice? How can such tasks be more appropriately and effectively introduced to them? There are no simple answers. Some answers can be developed from a careful elicitation of the explanatory models that patients present during actual encounters. It may be more productive, in the current absence of data, to consider the perspective of the providers and their assumptions about rehabilitative services for this special population.

Manson et al. (in press) recently surveyed Indian Health Service (IHS) personnel ($N = 208$) from 11 service units and 3 of 10 regional offices about long-term care principles and activities. The respondents included administrators, physicians, clinic nurses, community health nurses, pharmacists, nutritionists, optometrists, physical therapists, community health representatives, and social workers. They were a stable and experienced group. The respondents' definitions of long-term care almost invariably centered around institutionalization: 81% named the nursing home as the only or primary service setting. Only community health-oriented personnel (e.g., community health nurses, community health representatives, and social workers) mentioned a range of possible settings beyond the nursing home. The professional background of the respondent proved to be related consistently to differences in opinion about long-term care.

Older American Indians are no strangers to complicated human service systems. Through the IHS, the Bureau of Indian Affairs (BIA), and tribal and state programs, they come into regular contact with the full array of professionals and allied health personnel. Unfortunately, this contact tends to be fragmented and managed in a discontinuous fashion, resulting in increased miscommunication of treatment purpose and specific course of treatment. The multidisciplinary model that characterizes the state of the art in geriatric and rehabilitative medicine does not exist in the settings where most older American Indians receive their health care. Such basic elements as case management are typically absent. In this context, different disciplinary assumptions about health services continue unchecked, with potentially damaging consequences for older Native American patients. This is particularly true for Native American elders, who are not likely to seek care, who are unlikely to believe that they can influence their health status, and who do not conceptualize illness in the same manner as do those who treat them.

Training professionals to surmount these barriers is a serious challenge. Specifically, the practitioner needs to be able to (1) enter the delivery system with a clear understanding of his or her professional role and those of other service providers; (2) recognize his or her own assumptions about illness and elicit those of patients as well as co-workers; (3) encourage and actively promote interdisciplinary approaches to care; (4) "read" bureaucratic organizations, moving within and across them at minimal cost to oneself or colleagues; (5) determine the multiple constituencies (e.g., patient, family, co-workers, tribe, other agencies) that may lay claim to one's time, energy, and expertise; (6) collaborate either directly or through referral with native healers; and (7) initiate basic program planning that maximizes provider agency coordination and community involvement. Clearly, the successful provision of rehabilitative services to older Americans depends on much more than technical knowledge and skill. It involves discovering the cultural meanings of contexts for their appropriate application.

ASIAN AMERICANS AND PACIFIC ISLANDERS

The term Pacific/Asian American is a generic identifier that includes two broad ethnic minority groups: Asian Americans and the Pacific Islanders. The Pacific Island group includes Fijian, Guamanian, Hawaiian, Micronesian, Samoan, and Tongan; among the Asian Americans are the Burmese, Cambodians, Chinese, East Indians, Indonesians, Japanese, Koreans, Laotians, Malayans, Pilipinos,[1] Thais, and Vietnamese.

There are at least 18 Pacific Island and Asian American population groups, each with its own history, religion, language, and culture. Each group experienced immigration to the United States, accommodation to the dominant culture, and development as a community in various regions of the country. Also, there are differences within each of the Pacific/Asian population groups with respect to religion, dialect spoken, food preference, and customs. These groups are also differentiated by the time of immigration to the United States, the conditions under which they came, where they settled to form their communities, and by their aspirations and opportunities—or lack of opportunities— as noted by their achievements in education, occupational choices, income, and social mobility.

Unlike the immigrants from Western European countries, Pacific/ Asian immigrants experienced isolating governmental mechanisms: the denial of citizenship and of the right to own property, the threat of deportation, the lengthy incarceration in camps. Racially biased legislation[2] hampered the economic, social, and psychological well-being of the Pacific/Asian elderly who were affected most by these enactments. This legislation led to feelings of distrust, helplessness, powerlessness, and fear of government and alienated the Pacific/Asian elderly from society at large. As a result there was a reluctance or refusal on the part of many Pacific/Asian elderly to utilize public and social and health services, contrary to the perception that the Pacific/Asian Americans "take care of their own."

A study of New York City's Chinatown illustrates the reluctance of Asian-American elderly to utilize available services. Nearly 33% of the older, unattached males in the Community Service Society caseload had no prior contact with any agency, either public or voluntary. When one considers the multiple problems of single elderly men, the figure is striking. Many of these men are eligible for public welfare support "but refuse to apply or withdraw their applications when they discover the sort of personal information required" (Cattell, 1962).

Beyond the variation of racial discrimination and prejudice, the Pacific/Asian elderly are continually encountering obstacles to their full participation in American society. A research report for the Training Project for Asian Elderly (Chinn, 1973), funded by the Administration on Aging (AoA), concluded:

> "There is strong sentiment that the Asian elderly do not receive social services because of language, racial, and cultural barriers. Health and welfare agencies have few bilingual staff, haphazard provision for non-English-speaking clients, and very little publicity to the Asian community about their services.

Asian Americans often fail to seek and use existing services to which they are entitled because of language and cultural barriers and unfamiliarity with the social service bureaucracies. Consistent with these findings is the report of the White House Conference on Aging (1972) of a study that showed that 34% of the Pacific/Asian elderly who were interviewed had never had a medical or dental examination.

The diversity and complexity of the Pacific/Asian community has been broadened by the emergence of new immigrant groups made up of Cambodians, Guamanians, Laotians, Samoans, Thais, and Vietnamese. These recently formed communities have no socioeconomic base from which they can develop services for their elderly. The cultural shock experienced from their recent immigration is an additional stressor for the elderly of these communities. The combination of these factors makes this group of Pacific/Asian elderly an especially vulnerable high-risk population.

Demographic Profile

The population of Pacific/Asians in the United States increased by 128% between 1970 and 1980. In 1970 there were 1.5 million Pacific/ Asians, and a decade later that number had increased to 3.5 million. This represented a higher rate of growth than that of any other minority group in the nation. This trend is expected to continue into the next two decades, with the number of Asian elders increasing faster than younger cohorts.

The Pacific/Asians live predominantly in the western part of the United States, in urban areas, and they tend to cluster in geographically defined communities. However, there has been a significant shift in the population between 1970 and 1980. In 1970, 86% of the Pacific/ Asian population lived in the West; by 1980, only 70% lived in the West.

The median age of the Pacific/Asian population is 28.7 years, higher than that of the other three largest ethnic groups but lower than that of the white population (31.3 years). The mortality rate is 3.2 deaths per 1,000 population. Fifty-eight percent of Pacific/Asian women are in the workforce, a rate higher than that of the white population.

The median income level for Pacific/Asian families was $22,713, higher than that of any other group. However, the ratio of the number of working adults to the total number of adults in an Asian "family" is greater than in other groups. The number of working adults inflates the "family" income and masks the true extent of poverty among Pacific/Asians. Moreover, there are substantial differences in income among Asian subgroups: the Japanese represent the highest-income group; the Vietnamese, the lowest-income group ($12,840). The overall poverty rate for Pacific/Asians is 13.1%. This percentage is deceiving because of the wide variance within the Pacific/Asian subpopulations. The percentage of Japanese families below the poverty level is 7%, in contrast to 35% of Vietnamese families.

Specific data about Asian Americans and Pacific Islanders have been limited. Prior U.S. census surveys did not collect specific data on them, lumping them together under nonwhite groups.

The lack of formal research studies that focus on Pacific/Asians has serious consequences for the Pacific/Asian community. Little is known regarding utilization of services, illness patterns, and the preferences of the elderly that can be used in planning and providing health services. Accurate knowledge is particularly significant in providing services to people with little or no English facility or knowledge of the American culture.

Psychosocial History and Unique Concerns

Patterns of behaviors and attitudes regarding health care vary among the 18 subethnic groups of Pacific/Asians. It is important to stress that the generalizations made for the Pacific/Asian populations as a whole can be used only as a benchmark, a means of developing an infrastructure for designing health care curricula and programs. An optimum health care model that may be appropriate for one subset of Pacific/Asians may be quite alien to another.

Most of the current elderly Pacific/Asian population are first generation, immigrant, or second/third generation. This mixed population results in a variety of attitudes toward health. The attitudes of first-generation Pacific/Asian elders toward medicine and health care are reflective of the agrarian cultures in which they grew up. These elders have no frame of reference for a formal, institutionalized health care system. From the Pacific/Asian elders' perspective, health care is provided in an informal milieu, usually by the person to himself or herself or to a family member, by a tribal leader, or by a medicine man or woman.

The context of providing health care is based on long-standing community relationships. Consequently, a formalized health care program is not only unfamiliar but has no contextual framework for many older Pacific/Asians. Because health care providers are so enmeshed in the "system" and grew up using it, it is hard for them to appreciate that someone in the United States may neither understand nor have a working knowledge of the formal health care system existing in the United States. Although acupuncture has been used in China for centuries, only in the last 10 years has it been accepted by the U.S. medical community. Acceptance of an alternative health system requires time. It is well documented that older Chinese rely heavily on folk doctors and herbalists, the traditional healers of Chinese medicine.

Although varying from group to group, similar modes of health care provision can be found in each of the Pacific/Asian groups. An accredited physician may be sought by members of some groups; the preference is to see a "family" doctor. Pacific/Asian elders' knowledge of health care services continues to be limited and circumscribed. For instance, Pacific/Asian elders rarely use the services of an occupational therapist, physical therapist, nurse practitioner, or recrational therapist.

Ethnic foods and diets also have been a long-standing problem, and public debate has done little to resolve the issues. Traditionally, health professionals have not been willing to consider ethnic foodstuffs comparably with Western foods, stubbornly requiring Pacific/Asian elders to eat American food. Some of the resistance on the part of the professionals is based on their own lack of information and knowledge.

In some of the Pacific/Asian languages the word *illness* does not exist. Although there are descriptive terms for specific ailments, there are no generalized or encompassing terms. An acute change in health may be perceived as synonymous with death. Hospitals and other institutional settings are perceived with fear. Chinese in Boston consistently refused hospitalization, surgery, or diagnostic studies because of such fear (Li, Schlief, & Gaw, 1972). When folk medicine and Western medicine come into conflict, the Pacific/Asian elder will favor the more familiar folk practices over a physician's advice.

The ghettoizing of Pacific/Asians (such as Chinatowns), the consistent and continuing discriminating practices, and the lack of accessibility and availability of ethnic-appropriate services have been as significant in sustaining the old health practices as has the language barrier. Language has been used as the basis for explaining the underutilization of services by Pacific/Asians. Although a factor, it is not the only cause for the underutilization of services by Pacific/Asian elders. Further studies are necessary to identify the multiple contributing factors.

Rehabilitative Task: Specific Interventions

The recent rediscovery of home-based health care services was concurrent with the shift of emphasis from institutional to home care in the United States. The concept of home-based care parallels the traditional practices of developing services for older Pacific/Asians. In a 1980 study funded by the Administration on Aging, the only group preferring ethnic-specific programs was the Pacific/Asian elderly. Further, the Pacific/Asian respondents wanted those programs to be based in the community. The undergirding of such a system would be community-knowledgeable staff, bilingual/bicultural staff, and an integrated-service facility.

The multidisciplinary team can be effective only if it is perceived as being part of the community, particularly because the services provided by some of the professionals are not readily accepted. It is difficult for older Pacific/Asians to see a physician, but a "therapist" is unheard of in the "old country." The community setting provides the opportunity for nonprofessional contact, for example, a chance meeting on the street or when shopping. Although older Pacific/Asians prefer being treated by a person of the same or similar ethnic background, they are accepting of nonethnic persons who participate in their community. Entry into Pacific/Asian communities requires the establishment of a relationship with the community leaders. Efforts at outreach activity and educational/informational activities should be directed to Pacific/Asian community leaders, who will transmit the information to the community members. Informational materials must be translated into the appropriate languages. If the multidisciplinary team does not include any bilingual/bicultural members, it will be essential to hire an interpreter.

The introduction of an intermediary—the interpreter—further complicates communication. Developing an optimum working relationship between the rehabilitation therapist and the interpreter will be key in the success of service delivery. A partnership between the two specialists occurs when the therapist embodies technical expertise and the interpreter provides cultural and language expertise. Choosing a trained interpreter with background in medical terminology and experience with patient encounters is critical. Fluency in language does not imply fluency in medical terminology or skill in working with people seeking health care. Neither family members nor friends are recommended as interpreters. Both may be too close to the individual seeking care, which can influence the interpretation. The interpreter must be capable of translating cultural differences: often words are not translatable and concepts must be transmitted in culturally appropriate terms.

The relationships of culture and social structure as determinants of health problems are very rarely examined; in cases where they are explored, few studies address them comprehensively. Evolving social relationships and changing cultures are particularly important in any investigation of the Pacific/Asian elderly. The roles of the family and community support systems in all of the Pacific/Asian communities are essential in meeting the special needs and circumstances of their elderly. The informal indigenous components of a natural support network consists of the family and relatives, family associations, district associations, credit associations, mutual aid or benevolent societies, social/recreational clubs, and a variety of community caretakers and caregivers, such as religious leaders, village headmen, elders, herbalists, and practitioners of traditional folk medicine. This natural support network is turned to for guidance and counsel in times of personal or family crisis. However, under the influence of the dominant society and the corresponding socioeconomic changes, such support systems have changed, and the historical ability of the community to care for its elderly has correspondingly been modified. As a result, the Pacific/

Asian community looks increasingly to institutionalized secondary service systems.

Research data that deal with cultural differences in problem definitions and coping mechanisms are sorely needed to undergird any attempts at curriculum development. Ongoing social characteristics, such as morbidity rates, must be collected in the Pacific/Asian population. Educational institutions and academicians involved in research and the training of health professionals must begin to address the issues and problems of health care provision and utilization with culture and community environment as major determining variables.

HISPANICS

Hispanics constitute the fastest-growing ethnic group in the United States, with persons age 65 and older constituting the most rapidly increasing segment (Lacayo, 1984). Many of these elderly Hispanics suffer from diseases and functional disabilities that necessitate intensive rehabilitation services. Within this section we will review the Hispanic demographic imperative confronting the United States, discuss the disease and disability issues of the Hispanic elderly, and review the special problems encountered when interfacing with the Hispanic elderly. Recommendations will be made concerning the approach to rehabilitation in the Hispanic elderly.

Demographic Data

Large gaps exist in our understanding of the Hispanic elderly population, in part because of earlier research that placed all Hispanic subgroups under the category of "Hispanic." Gradually, there has been a realization that the Hispanics are indeed a mixture of specific diverse and divergent ethnic subgroups. According to Cubillos and Prieto (1987), the Hispanic elderly population in the United States is distributed as follows: 54.2% Mexican-American, 13.6% Cuban-American, 8.9% mainland Puerto Rican, 6.5% Central/South American origin, and 16.8% from other Latino backgrounds. Each of these populations has different cultural mores and backgrounds.

Lack of official documentation of Hispanic elders has hampered the collection of meaningful data on the various ethnic subgroups. When regional, socioeconomic, and acculturation differences are considered, the difficulty in formulating global conclusions regarding the Hispanic aged population become evident.

Despite these problems, some data have been gathered. The Hispanic elderly are more likely to live in the community and are less likely to be institutionalized than are their non-Hispanic white counterparts. Hispanic elders are more likely to live in multigenerational families. These families provide a supportive environment, with extended-family networks and their social supports (Markides, Boldt, & Ray, 1986). These supports are indispensable in the rehabilitation process.

The Hispanic elderly appear to be the least-educated group of the aged; the median number of school years attained is 7.4, compared to 12.1 for the non-Hispanic white subgroup. This fact has implications for the preparation of educational materials or for giving instructions regarding rehabilitation regimens or treatment plans.

The Hispanic elderly suffer to a large degree from low incomes and poverty. The median per capital income for Hispanic elderly in 1986 was $5,510, compared to $8,544 for non-Hispanic white elderly. Although Hispanics are less likely to have Social Security at all, in comparison to the general elder population, their income is primarily from Social Security. Hispanics are less likely to have any form of health insurance than are non-Hispanic whites. For these reasons, income and ability to pay rehabilitation costs must be a major factor when considering rehabilitation of the Hispanic elder. The Hispanic aged tend to underutilize many types of health care services.

It appears that the Hispanic elderly population suffers from a high rate of activity limitation resulting from chronic conditions. For example, 47.5% of Hispanics versus 44.3% of non-Hispanic whites reported some limitation of activities (National Center for Health Statistics, 1984). In addition, the Mexican-American/other Hispanic and Puerto Rican elderly are more likely, at 20% and 25%, respectively, to report limitations deriving from chronic disease.

In Hispanic institutionalized populations, the ethnic minority groups have higher rates of disability, as measured by activities of daily living (ADL), than do non-Hispanic white elders (Espino, Neufeld, & Mulvihill, 1988). Despite this higher level of ADL dysfunction, elderly Hispanics appear to consume lower levels of agency-provided community services (Greene & Monahan, 1984).

Mental diseases and dysfunctions remain a sigificant disabling factor among Hispanic elders. Depression and dysphoria associated with physical disability appears to be more prevalent in elderly Hispanics than in non-Hispanic white populations (Kemp, Stapes, & Lopez-Aqueres, 1987). The implications are an increasing need for medical and psychiatric services because of the projected growth of the Hispanic elder population, which deserves further study and attention.

Psychosocial Issues and Unique Concerns

The Hispanic elderly population suffers from specific problems that impede the access and delivery of rehabilitation services. It is important to be aware of these problems and to avoid labeling the Hispanic elder as noncompliant, with the negative stigma this term engenders.

The Hispanic elder suffers from a lack of formal education. Because formalized education imparted no particular advantage to persons in the settings in which many of these elders grew up, it was not emphasized. In agrarian settings it was important to apprentice with older farmers to acquire the practical knowledge necessary to assure success in the future. Therefore, the Hispanic elder may be knowledgeable in specific areas such as agriculture, but this knowledge base is either ignored or discounted by the health care providers delivering care to this special population. Written materials are given to the patient, albeit in Spanish, but in most cases no effort is made to determine whether the patient can indeed read the material presented. This can lead to difficulties in following treatment regimens, especially with the interactive participation required by the rehabilitation process.

The Hispanic elder also may suffer from a language barrier. In the communities where the majority of Hispanic elders live, Spanish is the dominant tongue and often the only language spoken. Although this is more than adequate for most of the elder patients' needs, they are often severely lacking in the verbal skills necessary to communicate problems and progress when the time comes to interact with the health care system. For example, one study showed that Hispanic elders received lower scores on a mental status questionnaire simply because they failed to understand the questions (Escobar et al., 1986). Solutions to this problem are expected to be further hampered by the "English Only" movement, which will place the monolingual Hispanic elder at an even greater distance from the rehabilitative care system. When the aged Hispanic does interface with the health care sector, problems may arise because of the need for a translator. Translators are often family members and are selected not because of their extensive background in languages but most often because they happen to be convenient. This can lead to problems in effective translation arising from translator-patient interactions, ethnocentric perceptions, self-perceptions on the part of the informal translator, and poor paraphrasing. These problems, as well as a history of prejudice or neglect on the part of the formalized health care system, has led Hispanic elders to rely more on informal health care systems. These systems have been dramatized in the lay press and literature as consisting primarily of "formalized" informal health care providers such as the *santero* in the mainland Puerto

Rican group or the *curandero* in the Mexican-American group. Although these informal health care systems are still utilized frequently, the urban Hispanic elder relies more on the "home remedy" system, which consists of various folk and herbal cures handed down by the elders to the next generation.

Rehabilitative Task: Specific Interventions

In many instances, key elders in the family are involved in decisions concerning health care for the individual members of the family. It is important not to discount this system. Many times the decisions concerning rehabilitation regimens or prescriptions are not made by the patient but by the dominant elder in the Hispanic household. It is important to try to identify this person or persons and involve them in the rehabilitation process.

Access to rehabilitation services may be hampered by an inability to access or pay for these services. The Hispanic elderly, like other groups of elders, take pride in always paying their debts. As a result, they may be reluctant to mention to their health care providers that the costs of certain rehabilitation modalities or prescriptions are a barrier to utilization. The elders may also be unaware of Medicare benefits or may equate them with "welfare" and consequently are reluctant to access the governmental programs to which they may be entitled. Hispanic elders may be unfamiliar with the rehabilitation services offered within the community. In one study, only 32% of Mexican-Americans were familiar with the rehabilitation services available in the county surveyed, compared with 79% of non-Hispanic white respondents (Omohundro, Schneider, Marr, & Grannemann, 1983). Finally, the Hispanic aged population may be unfamiliar with public transportation routes outside their neighborhoods, physically restricting their access to rehabilitative services.

Underutilization of formalized services is multifactorial. The extended family unit tends to take care of their own ill and disabled members, especially the elderly. Use of formalized services is sometimes viewed as failure on the part of the family or individuals in that family. In addition, the Hispanic elderly tend to view all health care facilities as highly impersonal, highly specialized places, where family support sysems and social networks are often excluded. Subsequently, utilization of specific services occurs only as a last resort. Underutilization of specific rehabilitation services, such as mental health services, may be caused by Hispanic culture-specific perceptions regarding mental illness and its treatment. These perceptions could be based on indigenous perceptions of the nature of mental illness, expecially within the Mexican-American community (Keefe, 1978). As a result of these attitudes, Hispanics may be resistant to using certain types of formalized rehabilitation services, including rehabilitative medical services. These special problems can cause difficulty in delivering rehabilitation services and may indirectly lead to increased rates of institutionalization for the Hispanic elderly.

In summary, the Hispanic elderly are a conglomeration of distinct ethnic subgroups. In the approach to rehabilitation, the specific factors influencing the subgroup being serviced must be taken into consideration. Barriers of language, income, and physical access must be addressed prior to the initiation of services. Rehabilitation programs must be tailored to the educational level of the patient. Further, services should be innovative by incorporating the patient's agrarian background into the rehabilitation process. More research is needed to identify each subgroup's needs in the area of rehabilitation, with special emphasis on gender differences. These approaches should allow for more involvement of Hispanic elders in the lengthy rehabilitation process.

CONCLUSION

The population of ethnic elders is growing at an increasing rate. The complexity of subpopulations within the Afro-American, American Indian, Asian-American and Pacific Islander, and Hispanic ethnic groups have been documented. The rehabilitation therapist is encouraged to recognize that alternative natural or traditional healers may be the first health resource selected by the ethnic elder and that ethnic elders may have their own explanatory models of illness differing from that of Western medicine. Finally, it is important to use a nonfamilial and unbiased translator to communicate effectively with the ethnic elder who is monolingual in a non-English language. Suggestions for engaging the ethnic elder in the rehabilitative task as well as gaining acceptance within the specific ethnic community have been presented. Knowledge of the history of and sensitivity to cultural definitions of illness and health care on the part of the therapist will facilitate the development of an effective therapeutic alliance with ethnic elders and their families.

NOTES

1. There is no *f* sound in the Pilipino language, and the Pilipino community generally prefers this spelling and pronunciation.

2. Chinese Foreign Miners Tax of 1850, the Chinese Exclusion Act of 1882, the Japanese Alien Land Law of 1913, the Filipino Exclusion Act of 1934, and the antimiscegenation statutes of 1935.

REFERENCES

Baker, F. M. (1988a). Afro-Americans. In L. Comas-Diaz & E. E. H. Griffith (Eds.), *Clinical guidelines in cross-cultural mental health* (pp. 151–181). New York: John Wiley & Sons.

Baker, F. M. (1988b). Dementing illness and black Americans. In J. S. Jackson (Ed.), *The black American elderly: Research on physical and psychosocial health* (pp. 215–233). New York: Springer Publishing Co.

Baquet, C. R. (1988). Cancer prevention and control in the black population: Epidemiology and aging implications. In J. S. Jackson (Ed.), *The black American elderly: Research on physical and psychosocial health* (pp. 50–68). New York: Springer Publishing Company.

Baron, A. E., Manson, S. M., & Ackerson L. M. (in press). Depressive symptomatology in older American Indians with chronic disease. In C. Attkisson & J. Zitch (Eds.), *Screening for depression in primary care.* New York: Routledge.

Cattell, S. H. (1962). *Health, welfare, and social organization in Chinatown, New York City.* New York: Community Service Society of New York.

Chinn, G. (1973). *On the feasibility of training Asians to work with the Asian elderly: A preliminary assessment of needs and resources available to Asian elderly in Seattle.* Seattle: Demonstration Project for Asian Americans.

Cubillos, H. L., & Prieto, M. M. (1987). *The Hispanic elderly: A demographic profile.* Washington, DC: National Council of La Raza.

Escobar, J. I., Burnam, P., Karno, M., Forsythe, A., Landsverk, J., & Golding, J. M. (1986). Use of mini-mental state examination in a community population of mixed ethnicity. *Journal of Nervous and Mental Disorders, 174,* 602–614.

Espino, D. V., Neufeld, R. R., & Mulvihill, M. K. (1988). Hispanic and non-Hispanic elderly on admission to the nursing home: A pilot study. *Gerontologist, 28,* 821–824.

Gibson, R. C. (1986). *Blacks in an aging society.* New York: Carnegie Corporation.

Greene, V. L., Monahan, D. J. (1984). Comparative utilization of community based long-term care services by Hispanic and Anglo elderly in a case management system. *Journal of Gerontology, 39,* 730–735.

Keefe, S. E. (1978). Why Mexican Americans underutilize mental health clinics: Fact and fallacy. Spanish Speaking Mental Health Research Center monograph series, Vol. 7, 91–108.

Kemp, B. S., Stapes, F., & Lopez-Aqueres, W. (1987). Epidemiology of depression and dysphoria in an elderly Hispanic population. *Journal of the American Geriatrics Society, 35,* 920–926.

Lacayo, C. G. (1984). Hispanics. In E. B. Palmore (Ed.), *Handbook on the aged in the United States*. Westport, CT: Greenwood Press.

Li, F., Schlief, Y., & Gaw, A. C. (1972). Health care for the Chinese community in Boston. *American Journal of Public Health, 62*, 536–539.

Manson, S. M., & Callaway, D. (1988). Health and aging among American Indians: Issues and challenges for the biobehavioral sciences. In S. M. Manson & N. Dinges (Eds.), *Health and behavior: A research agenda for American Indians*. (pp. 160–210). Denver, CO: University of Colorado Health Sciences Center.

Manson, S. M., Murray, C. M., & Cain, L. D. (1981). Ethnicity, aging, and support networks: An evolving methodological strategy. *Journal of Minority Aging, 6*(2), 11–37.

Manson, S. M., Shore, J. H., & Bloom, J. D. (1985). The depressive experience in American Indian communities: A challenge for psychiatric theory and diagnosis. In A. Kleinman & B. Good (Eds.), *Culture and depression* (pp. 331–368). Berkeley, CA: University of California Press.

Markides, K. S., Boldt, J. S., & Ray, L. A. (1986). Sources of helping and intergenerational solidarity: A three generations study of Mexican Americans. *Journal of Gerontology, 41*, 506–511.

Martin, E. P., & Martin, J. M. (1978). *The black extended family*. Chicago: University of Chicago Press.

National Center for Health Statistics. (1984). *Health indicators for Hispanic, black, and white Americans* (Series 10, No. 148). Washington, DC: U.S. Department of Health and Human Services, National Health Survey.

National Indian Council on Aging. (1981). *American Indian elderly: A national profile*. Albuquerque, NM: National Indian Council on Aging.

Omohundro, J., Schneider, M. J., Marr, J. N., & Grannemann, B. D. (1983). A four-country needs assessment of rural disabled people. *Journal of Rehabilitation, 4*, 19–24.

Task Force on Black and Minority Health. (1985). *Task force report on black and minority health: Vol. 1. Executive summary*. Washington, DC: Department of Health and Human Services.

Taylor, R. J. (1988). Aging and supportive relationships among black Americans. In J. S. Jackson (Ed.), *The black American elderly research on physical and psychosocial health* (pp. 259–281). New York: Springer Publishing.

Taylor, R. J., & Chatters, L. H. (1986). Church-based informal support among elderly blacks. *Gerontologist, 36*, 637–642.

U.S. Bureau of the Census. (1980). Demographic aspects of aging and older populations in the United States. *Current Population Reports: Special Studies*. Washington, DC: U.S. Government Printing Office.

White House Conference on Aging, 1971. (1972). *Special concerns sessions reports: The Asian American elderly*. Washington, DC: U.S. Government Printing Office.

Part V

The Practice Model: Continence

13

Maintaining and Restoring Continence

Neil M. Resnick and Thelma J. Wells

Urinary incontinence is a significant clinical problem affecting 15% to 30% of community-dwelling elderly (Herzog, Diokno, & Fultz, 1989; Resnick, Wetle, Scherr, Branck, & Taylor, 1986), one third of older individuals in acute-care settings (Resnick & Paillard, 1984; Sier, Ouslander, & Orzeck, 1987), and approximately half of institutionalized elderly (Ouslander, Kane, & Abrass, 1982). Medically, individuals are predisposed to perineal rashes, pressure sores, urinary tract infections, urosepsis, falls, fractures, and recurrent lower limb cellulitis associated with urine-soaked shoes in individuals with impaired peripheral sensation. Incontinent individuals are frequently embarrassed, isolated, stigmatized, depressed, and regressed; they are also predisposed to institutionalization, although the extent remains undefined (Herzog, Diokno, & Fultz, 1989; Ory, Wyman & Yu, 1986). In America, over $8 billion was devoted to incontinence in 1984 (Hu, 1986), exceeding the annual combined cost of dialysis and coronary artery bypass surgery (Resnick & Yalla, 1985).

Given the significance of this problem, it is remarkable to find it largely neglected. The major barrier to appropriate evaluation and treatment in urinary incontinence is attitude: attitudes about loss of urine control, attitudes about aging, and attitudes about rehabilitation of the aged. These can merge to create sometimes subtle, other times obvious obstacles to both rudimentary and quality care. Both older people and their health care providers may falsely believe that urinary incontinence is an inevitable consequence of aging and that there are no efficacious treatments for the elderly. Mitteness (1987), in an anthro-pological study of 30 community-living incontinent individuals (mean age, 74 years), found that the most frequently held belief about the cause of incontinence was that normal body processes weakened with age, that is, urine control ability just wore out. This belief, combined with embarrassment and/or shame, may explain the common finding that incontinent elders do not always tell their physicians about this problem. In one study of noninstitutionalized persons 60 years of age or older, 38% of incontinent men and 49% of women had not told a doctor about their involuntary urine loss (Diokno, Brock, Brown, & Herzog, 1986).

In Mitteness's (1987) research, two thirds of the incontinent subjects had told a physician about wetting symptoms, but half of them recalled that their symptoms were ignored or dismissed. Another 10% were given an explanation but no treatment or advice. Almost one third did recall a physician recommendation for either further evaluation or treatment with surgery or medication. Interestingly, half of those given such recommendations refused treatment, most often rejecting sur-gery. Another 14% were given behavioral suggestions, such as restrict-ing night fluids, but the instructions were often limited or unclear. The findings from this small study based on incontinent individuals' recall and perceptions suggest that many physicians have limited enthusiasm and knowledge about evaluating and treating this common clinical problem.

As a guide to confronting and changing negative attitudes and non-responsive behavior, it may be useful to consider specific terminology and cultural generalities. The term *incontinent* is problematic. It carries mixed or unclear meaning for most older individuals. Some well-read elders may recall the word from 19th-century novels, in which it com-monly meant "not restricting the passions or appetites, particularly the sensual" (*Webster's New Twentieth Century Dictionary*, 1978). Thus, ask-ing someone if he or she is incontinent may either be bewildering or especially offensive. It is much more useful to ask, "Do you have any uncontrolled urine loss?" or "Does urine come away when you don't want it to and you get wet?" or simply, "Do you have a urine wetting problem?" Giving examples of different kinds of urine loss (e.g., when one coughs or sneezes) is helpful. Using clearly descriptive phrases in a sensitive manner should enhance communication and provide per-mission to talk about this very personal and often hidden problem.

It is especially important also to ask about toileting frequency be-cause some individuals may never wet themselves but toilet so often that they are virtual slaves to their bladder. Questioning about both day and night toileting patterns will determine if there is dysfunctional voiding, a serious energy drain for older people. In the prevalence study previously noted, 5% of continent men and women voided 11 or more times in a 24-hour period (Diokno et al., 1986).

Culture refers to learned ways of acting and thinking that are transmitted from generation to generation. Within Western culture, loss of urine control beyond childhood is a taboo, a social prohibition. Children are taught that "big girls/boys don't wet their pants," and infractions from childhood may be traumatically remembered in adulthood. Culture prescribes different gender rules for urine control behavior, which may create differences in how men and women respond to involuntary urine loss. These cultural prescriptions may invade the examining room, with considerable discomfort mutually perceived if the dyad is male/female rather than the same gender. Written symptom questionnaires filled out in advance while in the waiting room may reduce discomfort and serve as a communication vehicle. Embarrassment on the part of the incontinent person should be expected; verbal acknowledgment and acceptance of this feeling is usually helpful.

Incontinent individuals in either acute- or long-term-care institutions may have wetting behavior accepted as a norm for old age or because it has a low priority among more interesting conditions. Depression, associated with illness and institutionalization, may worsen with incontinence. The environment, including staff behavior, equipment, and space utilization, impacts on urine control to a great extent in such settings. It is essential to seek specific information about patient toileting and staff routines. Neither adequate evaluation nor most treatment/management programs will work without staff understanding and cooperation.

This chapter will review the basics of urine control in the elderly. This will entail a brief review of relevant anatomy and physiology, a consideration of the impact of normal aging, a theoretical explanation of what can go wrong, and a review of what does go wrong, with information for diagnosis and treatment. Attention will also be paid to environmental factors and products for wetting management.

LOWER URINARY TRACT ANATOMY AND PHYSIOLOGY

The lower urinary tract includes the urine outlet (urethra) and the muscular storage and contractile bladder (detrusor) portion. A sphincter (internal urethral) is located in the region of the bladder neck; predominantly smooth muscle, it is autonomically innervated. A few centimeters distal to this is the external sphincter, composed of striated muscle and under voluntary control via the pudendal nerve.

The innervation of the lower urinary tract is derived from three sources: the parasympathetic (S2–S4), the sympathetic (T10–L2), and the somatic (voluntary) nervous systems (S2–S4). The parasympathetic nervous system innervates the bladder; increased cholinergic activity increases the force and frequency of bladder contraction, whereas reduced activity has the opposite effect. The sympathetic nervous system innervates both the bladder and the urethra, its effect determined by local receptors. Beta receptors predominate in the bladder body; their stimulation relaxes the bladder. Alpha receptors are at the bladder base and in the proximal urethra; their stimulation contracts the internal sphincter. Thus, activation of the sympathetic nervous system facilitates storage of urine in a coordinated manner. The somatic nervous system innervates the urogenital diaphragm and the external sphincter; the external sphincter probably receives other innervation as well (Torrens & Morrison, 1987). The central nervous system integrates control of the urinary tract, the pontine micturition center mediating synchronous sphincter relaxation and detruser contraction and centers in the frontal lobe, basal ganglia, and cerebellum (among others) exerting inhibitory and facilitative effects.

Storage of urine is mediated by bladder relaxation and closure of the sphincters. It is accomplished by central nervous system inhibition of parasympathetic tone, whereas sphincter closure is mediated by a reflex increase in alpha-adrenergic and somatic activity. Voiding occurs when bladder contraction, mediated by the parasympathetic nervous system, is coordinated with sphincter relaxation. Normally, most adults have the first sensation of the need to void when the bladder holds about 150 ml, with maximum capacity ranging on average from 350 to 500 ml.

THE IMPACT OF AGE ON CONTINENCE

Normal aging affects the lower urinary tract in a variety of ways but does not cause incontinence. Cross-sectional studies suggest that bladder capacity, the ability to postpone voiding, bladder compliance, and urinary flow rate probably decline in both sexes, whereas maximum urethral closure pressure and urethral length probably decline in women. The prevalence of uninhibited contractions probably increases with age. Postvoiding residual volume may increase but probably to no more than 25 to 50 ml. The individual's excretion pattern may alter, with many healthy elderly excreting the bulk of their urine during the night rather than before bedtime as in younger individuals. This is true even for those without peripheral venous insufficiency, renal disease, heart failure, or prostatism. Thus, one to two episodes of nocturia per night may be normal, especially if the pattern is long-standing and unchanged and other conditions have been excluded. Finally, virtually all men experience an age-related increase in prostatic size. This gland, located at the base of the bladder, may impede urine outflow as it enlarges.

These age-related changes predispose to incontinence. Coupled with the increased likelihood that an older person will be subjected to an additional pathologic, physiologic, or pharmacologic insult, incontinence in an older person is often caused by a precipitant outside the lower urinary tract that is amenable to medical intervention. Treatment of the precipitant alone may be sufficient to restore continence. Thus, causes of incontinence in the elderly can be categorized as transient or established (Resnick, 1988).

CAUSES OF INCONTINENCE

Transient Incontinence

Transient incontinence is common in the elderly, affecting up to one-third of community-dwelling incontinent individuals and up to one half of hospitalized incontinent patients (Torrens & Morrison, 1987). The causes can be recalled easily using the mnemonic "DIAPPERS" (misspelled with an extra *P*; Resnick, 1984) (see Table 13-1).

In *delirium*, incontinence is an associated symptom that will abate once the underlying cause of confusion is identified and treated. Symptomatic *urinary tract infection* causes transient incontinence with dysuria and urgency defeating the older person's ability to reach the toilet.

Table 13-1 Causes of Transient Incontinence[a]

*D*elirium/confusional state
*I*nfection—urinary (symptomatic)
*A*trophic urethritis/vaginitis
*P*harmaceuticals
*P*sychological, especially depression
*E*ndocrine (hypercalcemia, hyperglycemia)
*R*estricted mobility
*S*tool impaction

[a]Adapted from Resnick (1984).

Asymptomatic infection, more common in the elderly, is usually not a cause of incontinence (Boscia et al., 1986; Resnick, 1988).

Atrophic vaginitis only occasionally causes transient incontinence, but it commonly contributes (Robinson, 1984). It can be present as urethral "scalding," dyrusia, dyspareunia, urinary urgency, or urge or stress urinary incontinence. In demented individuals, vaginitis may present as agitation. The symptoms are readily responsive to treatment with a low dose of estrogen, administered either orally (conjugated estrogen 0.3 mg/day) or topically. Symptoms respond in a few days to 6 weeks, although the intracellular biochemical response may take much longer (Semmens, Tsai, Semmens, & Loadholt, 1985). Although duration of therapy has not been well established, a low dose of estrogen on a daily basis for 1 to 2 months, with tapering to 2 to 4 times per month, is helpful. After 6 months, estrogen can be discontinued entirely in some patients, although recrudescence is common. Because the estrogen dose is low and given briefly, its carcinogenic effect is likely slight if present at all. The only adverse effect observed is mild and irregular vaginal bleeding in a small percentage of patients.

Pharmaceuticals are one of the most common causes of voiding dysfunction. Long-acting sedative/hypnotics, such as diazepam and flurazepam, have longer half-lives in the elderly and thus may accumulate, inducing confusion and secondary incontinence (Resnick, 1988). Alcohol both induces a diuresis and clouds the sensorium. "Loop" diuretics induce a brisk diuresis, which may overwhelm bladder capacity and result in incontinence. Vincristine can cause a partially reversible neuropathy associated with urinary retention (Wheeler, Siroky, Bell, & Babayan, 1983).

Three quarters of the elderly use nonprescription agents (Goldsmith, 1985) for conditions such as insomnia. Because many do not consider them as "medicines" worth mentioning to their physicians, it is necessary to inquire about such drugs directly. If the agents have anticholinergic effects, urinary retention and overflow incontinence may result. If the drug contains alpha agonists (such as decongestants), acute retention can occur in the male with otherwise asymptomatic prostatic enlargement. Medications with alpha antagonists may precipitate stress incontinence in the older female (Mathew, McEwen, & Rohan, 1988). Calcium channel blockers reduce smooth muscle contractility throughout the body, and the bladder is no exception; they frequently induce urinary retention that is occasionally significant (Resnick, 1988).

Psychological causes of incontinence have not been well studied in the elderly but are probably uncommon; intervention is properly directed at the psychological disturbance, usually depression or lifelong neurosis. Persistent incontinence warrants further evaluation. *Endocrine* causes of incontinence include those conditions that both cloud the sensorium and induce a diuresis, primarily hypercalcemia and hyperglycemia.

Restricted mobility commonly contributes to incontinence in the elderly. It can result from arthritis, hip deformity, poor eyesight, inability to ambulate, fear of falling, a stroke (Brocklehurst, Andrews, Richards, & Laycock, 1985), or simply being restrained in a bed or a chair. A careful search will often identify correctable causes.

Stool impaction has been implicated as a cause of urinary incontinence in up to 10% of patients referred to incontinence clinics (Resnick, 1988); the mechanism may involve stimulation of opioid receptors (Hellstron & Sjoqvist, 1988). Patients usually present with either urge or overflow incontinence and typically have associated fecal incontinence as well. Disimpaction restores continence.

These eight reversible causes of incontinence should be assiduously sought in every elderly patient. In one series of hospitalized patients, when these causes were identified, continence was regained by most of those who became incontinent in the context of acute illness (Resnick & Paillard, 1984). Regardless of their frequency, however, their identification is important in all settings because they are easily treatable.

Established Incontinence

Lower Urinary Tract Causes

If leakage persists after transient causes of incontinence have been addressed, the lower urinary tract causes of established incontinence must be considered. These are caused by dysfunction of the bladder, the outlet, or both. The lower urinary tract can malfunction in only four ways. Two involve the bladder and two involve the outlet: The bladder either contracts when it should not (detrusor underactivity) or fails to contract when or as well as it should (detrusor underactivity); alternatively, outlet resistance is high when it should be low (obstruction) or low when it should be high (outlet incompetence).

1. *Detrusor overactivity*, the most common cause of geriatric incontinence (Resnick, 1988; Resnick, Yalla, & Laurino, 1989) is a condition in which the bladder contracts precipitantly, usually emptying itself completely. It exists as two physiologic subsets, one in which contractile function is preserved and one in which it is impaired. The latter condition has been termed detrusor hyperactivity with impaired contractility (DHIC) (Resnick & Yalla, 1987). Urodynamic evaluation with fluo-

roscopic monitoring and micturitional urethal profilometry identifies this disorder, which presents clinically as the great mimic, often as stress incontinence or outlet obstruction.

Detrusor overactivity usually presents clinically as urge incontinence. It may result from damage to the CNS inhibitory centers due to a stroke, Alzheimer's disease, or Parkinson's disease. Alternatively, the etiology may be in the urinary tract itself, where a source of irritation— such as cystitis (interstitial or radiation- or chemotherapy-induced) or a stone—overwhelms the brain's ability to inhibit bladder contraction. Two other important local causes are outlet obstruction and outlet incompetence, both of which may lead to secondary detrusor overactivity (Abrams, 1985; McGuire & Savastano, 1985). Given the commonality of detrusor overactivity and findings from a recent study of no definite association between it and cognitive status, it is no longer tenable to ascribe incontinence in demented individuals a priori to detrusor overactivity (Resnick, 1988; Resnick, Yalla, & Laurino, 1989).

2. *Detrusor underactivity*, the least common cause of geriatric incontinence, may result from mechanical injury to the nerves supplying the bladder (e.g., disk compression) or to autonomic neuropathy (e.g., diabetes). Alternatively, the detrusor may be replaced by fibrosis and connective tissue, as occurs in men with chronic outlet obstruction or occasionally in women for unknown reasons. In these cases, when the obstruction is removed, the bladder fails to empty normally.

3. *Outlet incompetence* is the second most common cause of incontinence in older women (Resnick, 1988; Resnick, Yalla, & Laurino, 1989) and is caused most often by pelvic floor laxity. Urethral hypermobility allows the proximal urethra and bladder neck to herniate through the urogenital diaphragm when abdominal pressure increases. This results in greater pressure being transmitted to the bladder than to the urethra and results in stress incontinence. A less common cause is sphincter incompetence, in which the sphincter is so weak that merely the hydrostatic weight of a full bladder overcomes outlet resistance. Known as Type 3 stress incontinence (McGuire, Lytton, Pepe, & Kohorn, 1976), in the elderly it generally results from repeated operative trauma or diabetes; occasionally, no precipitant is identified.

4. *Outlet obstruction* is the final lower urinary tract cause of incontinence and the second most common cause in older men (Resnick, 1988; Resnick, Yalla, & Laurino, 1989). If caused by neurologic disease, it is invariably associated with a spinal cord lesion (detrusor sphincter dysergia). Alternatively, and much more commonly, obstruction results from prostatic enlargement, carcinoma, or urethral stricture in men; anatomic obstruction is uncommon in women in the absence of a large cystocele, which can prolapse and kink the urethra if the patient strains to void.

Clinically, it is useful to rearrange these four basic pathophysiologic mechanisms into two categories: disorders of storage (detrusor overactivity or outlet incompetence), in which the bladder empties at inappropriate times; and disorders of evacuation (detrusor underactivity or outlet obstruction), in which the bladder empties incompletely, leading to progressive urine accumulation and overflow. In the first category, the bladder is normal in size; in the second, it is distended.

Functional Incontinence

Incontinence in the presence of normal bladder and urethral function is often called functional and may be caused by a variety of situational factors such as environmental limitations, mentation, mobility, manual dexterity, or motivation. Attention to these factors can significantly improve urine control. Coupled with behavioral training programs, functional attention can significantly reduce institutional incontinence (Wells, 1988).

THE DIAGNOSTIC APPROACH

The diagnostic approach has three purposes: to determine the cause of the incontinence, to detect related urinary tract pathology, and to evaluate comprehensively the patient, the environment, and the available resources. The practitioner should keep in mind that not all detected conditions can be cured (e.g., invasive bladder carcinoma); optimal diagnostic and treatment strategies remain to be determined. Simple interventions may be effective even in the absence of a diagnosis (Resnick, 1990a; Wells, 1988), and for many elderly persons, diagnostic tests are themselves often interventions. Nonetheless, the approach outlined here is relatively noninvasive, accurate, and easily tolerated.

History

Characterize the voiding pattern, determining if symptoms of abnormal voiding are present, such as straining or a sense of incomplete emptying. Obtain detailed description of the incontinence: onset, frequency, severity, pattern, precipitants, palliating features, associated symptoms and conditions, and any night leakage.

Voiding Record

A voiding record kept by the patient or caregiver for a 48–72-hour period is critically important. Volume voided provides an index of functional bladder capacity and, together with the pattern of voiding and leakage, can be quite helpful in pointing to the cause of the leakage.

The history and voiding record permit symptomatic characterization of the incontinence as *urge*, precipitant leakage of a large volume preceded by a brief warning of seconds to minutes; *reflex*, precipitant leakage not preceded by a warning; *stress*, leakage occurring coincident with and only in association with increases in abdominal pressure; *flow*, continual dribbling; and *mixed*, usually a combination of urge and stress (Hald, Bates, & Bradley, 1984).

Targeted Physical Examination

Check for signs of neurologic disease—dementia, stroke, cord compression, neuropathy (autonomic or peripheral)—as well as for functional impairment and general medical illness. Also check for spinal column deformities or dimples suggestive of dysraphism, for bladder distention (pointing to an evacuation disorder), and stress leakage. For the latter ask the patient to stand with a full bladder, relax, spread her legs, and cough. If leakage occurs, note whether it is coincident with the stress maneuver or delayed for more than 5 to 10 seconds. If delayed, detrusor overactivity (triggered by coughing) rather than outlet incompetence is suggested.

Check the rectum for fecal impaction and masses. Prostate size is less important to assess because, as determined by palpation, it correlates poorly with the presence or absence of outlet obstruction (Meyhoff, Ingemann, Nordling, & Hald, 1981; Resnick, 1984). Assess motor innervation by checking volitional contraction and relaxation of anal sphincter, testing for anal wink (S4–S5), bulbocavernosus reflexes (S2–4), and perineal sensation. In an older person, the absence of sacral cord reflexes is not necessarily pathologic, nor does their presence exclude an underactive detrusor (resulting from a diabetic neuropathy, for example).

In women, check for pelvic muscle laxity (cystocele, rectocele, enterocele, uterine prolapse). Removing one blade of the vaginal speculum, sequentially apply the remaining blade to the anterior and posterior vaginal walls and ask the patient to cough. However, the presence or absence of pelvic floor laxity reveals little about the cause of an individual's leakage. Detrusor overactivity may exist in addition to a cystocele, and stress incontinence may exist in the absence of a cystocele.

Atrophic vaginitis is characterized by mucosal friability, petechiae, telangiectasia, and vaginal erosions (Robinson, 1984); loss of rugal folds and the presence of a thin, shiny-appearing mucosa are signs of vaginal atrophy rather than atrophic vaginitis. The bimanual exam excludes pelvic masses.

The examination concludes when the patient voids and is catheterized for a postvoiding residual volume (PVR). Adding the PVR to the voided volume provides an estimate of total bladder capacity and a crude assessment of bladder proprioception.

Laboratory Investigation

In addition to a urinalysis and urine culture it is useful to measure BUN and serum creatinine. In any patient with sterile hematuria or one at high risk for bladder carcinoma (e.g., a male smoker), a urine cytology should be obtained. In a man whose residual urine is greater than 150 ml, renal sonography should be obtained to exclude hydronephrosis.

Urodynamic Testing

Urodynamic testing is probably warranted when diagnostic uncertainty may affect therapy, when empiric therapy has failed and other approaches would be tried, when surgical intervention is planned, and to exclude obstruction that would be corrected in the patient with overflow incontinence (Ory, Wyman & Yu, 1986; Resnick, Yalla, & Laurino, 1989).

A variety of possible diagnostic tests is available. Although these are individually determined, they commonly include the following: cystometry to evaluate bladder proprioception, compliance, capacity, and stability; urethral profilometry (during filling and voiding) to evaluate urethral anatomic length, functional length, maximum urethral pressure, maximum urethral closure pressure, and the length and height of the prostatic area in males; uroflowmetry as an aid to screening for obstruction in men; electromyography to evaluate the distal urethral sphincter, determining the integrity of its innervation, testing its response to reflex stimuli, and characterizing its behavior during voiding; and radiographic evaluation. Optimally, the radiographic and urodynamic evaluation are performed simultaneously, allowing correlation of visual and manometric information. If this is not feasible, substantial information can be gleaned from cystography.

The precise role of urodynamic evaluation of the incontinent elderly individual remains to be determined. Although it pinpoints pathologic abnormalities, unless it is performed by a trained urodynamicist and incorporated into the overall clinical evaluation, it may not identify which of the abnormalities actually causes the patient's incontinence (Resnick, Yalla, & Laurino, 1989). However, urodynamic evaluation of elderly patients is reproducible, safe, and feasible to perform, even in frail and debilitated individuals. A more detailed discussion of urodynamic techniques is available elsewhere (Resnick, 1990b)

THERAPY

Treatment must be individualized because factors outside the lower urinary tract are also important. This section will suggest several treatments for each condition and provide some guidance for use. It assumes that serious underlying conditions and transient causes of incontinence have already been excluded.

Detrusor Overactivity

Detrusor overactivity is characterized by frequent periodic voiding with dryness in between. Leakage volume is moderate to large, with nocturnal frequency and incontinence common. Sacral sensation and reflexes are preserved; voluntary control of the anal sphincter is intact; and the PVR is generally less than 50 ml. Obstruction or stress incontinence may cause *secondary* detrusor overactivity that will remit with correction of the outlet abnormality (Abrams, 1985; McGuire & Savastano, 1985).

Pharmacologic intervention is usually helpful (Resnick, 1988). Anticholinergic agents, such as propantheline (15–120 mg/day) or oxbutynin (5–20 mg/day)—which combines both smooth muscle relaxant and anticholinergic properties—are frequently successful. Imipramine (50–150 mg/day), with a more complex mechanism of action; muscle relaxants such as flavoxate (300–800 mg/day); and calcium channel blockers have also been used. These drugs should be given in divided doses, starting with the lowest dose and building to maximum only if necessary and tolerated.

Bladder exercise, either alone or in combination with drug therapy, has been found to be helpful for those able to follow and comply with the routine (Wells, 1988). This involves drinking adequate fluid, keeping a diary of fluid intake and urine output, and progressively increasing the intervoidal interval. For those unable to follow such a regimen, prompted voiding techniques are often helpful (Schnelle, 1990). If not amenable to either drug or exercise therapy, treatment must be symptomatic. Attention to toilet substitutes, other behavioral programs, or product management may help.

Stress Incontinence

Characterized by daytime urine loss of small to moderate amounts, infrequent nocturnal incontinence, and low PVR in the absence of urine pooling in a large cystocele, stress incontinence is common in older women. The key to diagnosis is leakage that, in the absence of bladder distention, occurs coincident with the stress maneuver. The usual cause is urethral hypermobility resulting from pelvic floor laxity, but other conditions such as intrinsic sphincter incompetence (Type 3 stress incontinence), stress-induced detrusor overactivity, and urethral instability should be considered (Blaivas & Olsson, 1988; McGuire, 1978; Mcguire et al., 1976; McGuire & Savastano, 1985). This condition is uncommon in men unless the sphincter has been damaged by surgery.

Weight loss for those who are obese, therapy for precipitating conditions such as coughing or atrophic vaginitis, and sometimes insertion of a pessary can improve stress incontinence (Bhatia, Bergman, & Gunning, 1983). Pelvic muscle exercises are time-honored and frequently effective (Hadley, 1986; Resnick, 1988; Wells, in press). As a beginning technique, the patient is instructed to sit on the toilet and begin voiding. When voiding has started, she is asked to interrupt the stream by contracting the urinary sphincter for as long as possible. Initially, most elderly women are able to do so for no more than a second or two, but after a few weeks, many can prolong the duration of the contraction. Once the muscle to contract is recognized, a building program of exercise needs to be fit into daily routines. Although there is no agreed optimal technique or regimen, the exercise is usually considered a 10-second contraction followed by a 10-second relaxation, with about 100 of these units distributed in sets throughout the day (Wells, 1988).

If not contraindicated by other medical conditions, treatment with an alpha-adrenergic agonist such as phenylpropanolamine (50–100 mg/day in divided doses) may be used alone or added to a pelvic muscle program and is often beneficial for women. Imipramine, with beneficial effects on the bladder and the outlet, is a reasonable alternative for patients with evidence of both stress and urge incontinence if postural hypotension has been excluded.

If these methods fail, after further evaluation, surgical correction may be performed for urethral hypermobility; it is successful in the majority of selected elderly patients (Resnick, 1988). If sphincter incompetence is diagnosed, it may require a different surgical approach. Morbidity is higher, and precipitation of chronic urinary retention is more likely than with correction of urethral hypermobility (McGuire, 1978; Resnick, 1988). Other treatments for sphincter incompetence include periurethral injection of Teflon or collagen and insertion of an artificial sphincter, all of which are effective in selected cases (Resnick, 1988).

Outlet Obstruction

Outlet obstruction causes incontinence in up to 5% of elderly women (Resnick, 1988; Resnick, Yalla, & Laurino, 1989). The etiology is usually a large cystocele that distorts or kinks the urethra during voiding. Other causes include bladder stones, bladder neck obstruction, and distal urethral stenosis. If a large cystocele is the problem, surgical correction is usually required; it should include an outlet suspension if urethral hypermobility is also present. Bladder neck obstruction is also corrected easily, using local anesthesia, and is thus feasible for even the frailest elderly patient. Distal urethral stenosis can be dilated and treated with estrogen.

In men the cause of obstruction is usually a stricture, carcinoma, or prostatic enlargement. Although transurethral resection prostatectomy (TURP) or even suprapubic retropubic prostatectomy is optimal and feasible for the elderly, newer approaches (e.g., bladder neck incision with bilateral prostatotomy) (Mebust, Holtgrewe, Cockett, Peters, & Writing Committee, 1989; Orandi, 1985; Resnick, 1988) have made surgical decompression feasible for even the frailest individuals.

Administration of alpha-adrenergic antagonists, as a symptomatic treatment until more definite therapy is necessary and feasible, is also an option (Caine, 1986). Phenoxybenzamine in adequate doses (5 to 20 mg/day) is probably superior to prazosin (1 to 2 mg four times a day), but concern about its carcinogenic potential in mice has mitigated against its use.

Underactive Detrusor

Incontinence caused by an underactive detrusor is associated with a large residual urine and overflow incontinence. Leakage of small amounts of urine occurs frequently throughout the day and night. The patient may also note hesitancy, diminished and interrupted flow, a need to strain to void, and a sense of incomplete emptying. If the problem is neurologically mediated, perineal sensation, sacral reflexes, and control of the anal sphincter are frequently impaired. Before detrusor weakness can be diagnosed, however, outlet obstruction must first be excluded.

Management of detrusor underactivity is directed as reducing the residual volume, eliminating hydroenphrosis (if present), and preventing urosepsis. Indwelling or intermittent catheterization to decompress the bladder for up to a month (at least 7–14 days), while reversing potential contributors to impaired detrusor function (fecal impaction and medications), is a first step. Augmented voiding techniques (such as double voiding and implementation of the Crede and Valsalva maneuver) may help if the patient is able to initiate a detrusor contraction and is not distressed. An alpha-blocker such as prazosin may further facilitate emptying by reducing outlet resistance. Bethanechol (40—200 mg/day in divided doses) is occasionally useful in the patient whose bladder contracts poorly because of treatment with anticholinergic agents that cannot be discontinued (e.g., neuroleptic agents).

If, after decompression, the detrusor is acontractile, the patient should be started on intermittent catheterization or an indwelling urethral catheter. Intermittent self-catheterization is preferable and requires only clean, rather than sterile, catheter insertion. This technique is painless, safe, inexpensive, and effective, and it allows individuals to carry on with their usual daily activities.

ENVIRONMENT

The environment includes toilets or toilet substitutes and access to them to maintain urine control, as well as behavioral treatment programs that focus on caregiver practices. In general there is a serious lack of accessible public toilets. This may be a reason some elderly people limit or cease activity outside the home. Certainly, senior centers and other high-density elder areas should have multiple toilets, clearly marked and equipped with mobility aides. In private homes, toilet access problems may include stairs, raised thresholds, poor lighting, and, in some rural situations, lack of indoor plumbing. Institutional settings may not always provide within-room or connecting toilets but even when so provided, access may be difficult for wheelchairs and walking frames (Brink & Wells, 1988; Snow, 1988; Wells & Brink, 1988).

Toilet substitutes are commodes, bedpans, and urinals. There is a great variety in these products, including many options for improved use and comfort. Toilet substitutes should be selected on an individual basis, with both the patient and caregiver in mind. Consultation with occupational therapists or other knowledgeable professionals is most useful (Brink & Wells, 1988; Snow, 1988; Wells & Brink, 1988).

Behavioral treatment programs have been used primarily for individuals with functional incontinence—that is, the cause of wetting is due to something other than a transient or established incontinence etiology. Commonly those with impaired cognition benefit most. Although terminology is not standardized for these treatments, they can be considered: routine toilet use, habit retraining, and behavior modification (Wells, 1988). The goal of routine toilet use is to keep the bladder relatively empty, thereby reducing the degree of interval wetting. Individuals are toileted every 2 to 4 hours on a fixed schedule and fluid intake may be limited in quantity or time taken. Habit retraining is more individualized and has a goal the regaining of the bladder sensation stimulus—toilet use response pattern. This involves adequate fluid intake, observation of the voiding pattern, and adjustment of prompted voiding to the observed schedule. Last, behavior modification is more comprehensive, with specific positive reinforcers for appropriate toilet use or dry garments identified with immediate and consistent application. That is, correct behavior is rewarded; negative behavior results in reward withholding. The goal of behavior modification is appropriate toilet use or dryness. All of these behavioral treatments have had some clinical testing and report promising to excellent results.

PRODUCTS FOR WETTING MANAGEMENT

Many elderly people cope with urine wetting by using household materials for clothing protection, such as pieces of toweling, tissue pads, or washcloths. Women also commonly buy menstrual products for use in urinary incontinence. However, recent product development and mass marketing have made available a wide variety of garment-type products especially for management of wetting. These, plus bed pads, external occluding devices, external collecting devices, and indwelling catheters, will be briefly discussed (Snow, 1988; Wells & Brink, 1988).

Wetting management with products is palliative. It is best considered a temporary step while adequate evaluation or initial treatment is underway. Sometimes products provide a valued adjunct to a limited treatment program. And sometimes a wetting management product is the best or only aid available.

Protective garments include both disposable and washable diapers and undergarments as well as washable pant/disposable pad systems. The most descriptive and comprehensive list of such products is available from Help for Incontinent People, P.O. Box 544, Union, SC 29739 (*The Guide of Continence Products and Services*, $3.00). Selection involves consideration of user ability and activity, such as cognition and mobility, wetting volume and frequency, fecal continence or incontinence, storage, disposal, cost, and fit. In regard to fit, leakage occurs most often at the sides of the crotch area often because of poor leg-top fit or limited absorption against the urine flow rate. Consumers and practitioners suffer from limited knowledge and experience with new products, often dismissing ones that have not been properly fitted or appropriately used. Increasingly, video teaching tapes, written materials, and convention or workshop product displays provide valuable education about product use. In addition, consumers are being offered free samples, low-cost start-up trials, and discount coupons for good products.

Bedpans can also be washable or disposable, although the least expensive disposable pad is most commonly used. Often these minimally absorbent, too small pads turn out to be costly because many are used at one time. Of special note among newer products is a washable bed draw sheet suitable for home or institutional use. Used over a plastic draw sheet, it has a soft top layer that passes urine into the lower holding layer, leaving skin dry. It is one of the few products to have had numerous supportive clinical trials.

External occluding devices are available in this country only for men. The penile clamp compresses the urethra to occlude flow. Its use requires mental competency and manual dexterity, and it should not be used for patients with detrusor overactivity. External collecting systems are available for both men and women. Most common is male condom drainage. Here false economy often prevails, with selection of the least expensive but most fragile, poorly attaching product. At a minimum, condom drainage should have a formed base to prevent twisting. Reusable penile sheath collecting systems are available and need careful fitting. Women currently have a choice of two commercial external collecting systems, and it is likely that others will follow. Women with senile vaginitis must be watched closely for skin irritation. In general, both men and women on external collecting systems need careful skin care and constant monitoring.

Indwelling catheters are essential for urinary retention, sacral pressure sores, and sometimes for quality-of-life considerations such as comfort for those with significant immobility and pain. Unfortunately, catheters may be defended as a quality-of-life decision when adequate evaluation and/or other treatment programs have not been tried. Teflon-coated latex-rubber catheters are thought to create less urethritis and outflow blockage than other catheters. Size should be 16–18 French with a 5-cc balloon, minimally inflated. Catheter leakage, apart from twisted tubing, is most often the result of a bladder spasm and is not solved by replacement with a larger catheter. In fact, such a response usually increases spasms, with consequent leakage. If not medically contraindicated, a mild anticholinergic medication—for example, oxybutynin chloride (Ditropan®) 2.5 to 5 mg—may eliminate the bladder spasms and leakage.

SUMMARY

Urinary incontinence is a common problem in the elderly. It is also commonly neglected because of a variety of negative attitudes and lack of knowledge. There are many possible causes for uncontrolled urine loss, and each has one or more treatment strategies available. In addition, attention to the environment and wetting management with selected products may prove helpful.

REFERENCES

Abrams, P. (1985). Detrusor instability and bladder outlet obstruction. *Neurology Urodynamics 4*, 317–328.

Bhatia, N. N., Bergman, A., & Gunning, J. E. (1983). Urodynamic effects of a vaginal pessary in women with stress urinary incontinence. *American Journal of Obstetrics and Gynecology, 147*, 876–884.

Blaivas, J. G., & Olsson, C. A. (1988). Stress incontinence: Classification and surgical approach. *Journal of Urology, 139*, 727–731.

Boscia, J. A., Kobasa, W. D., Abrutyn, E., Levinson, M. E., Kaplan, A. M., & Kaye, D. (1986). Lack of association between bacteriuria and symptoms in the elderly. *American Journal of Medicine, 81*, 979–982.

Brink, C. A., & Wells, T. J. (1988). Environmental support for geriatric incontinence. In J. Ouslander (Ed.), *Clinics in geriatric medicine* (pp. 829–840). Philadelphia: W. B. Saunders.

Brocklehurst, J. C., Andrews, K., Richards, B., & Laycock, P. J. (1985). Incidence and correlates of incontinence in stroke patients. *Journal of the American Geriatrics Society, 33*, 540–542.

Caine, M. (1986). The present role of alpha-adrenergic blockers in the treatment of benign prostatic hypertrophy. *Journal of Urology, 136*, 1–4.

Diokno, A. C., Brock, B. M., Brown, M. B. & Herzog, A. R. (1986). Prevalence of urinary incontinence and other urological symptoms in the noninstitutional elderly. *Journal of Urology, 136*, 1022–1025.

Goldsmith, M. F. (1985). Research on aging burgeons as more Americans grow older. *Journal of the American Medical Association, 253*, 1369–1405.

Hadley, E. (1986). Bladder training and related therapies for urinary incontinence in elderly people. *Journal of the American Medical Association, 256*, 372–379.

Hald, T., Bates, P., & Bradley, W. E. (1984). *The standardisation of terminology of lower urinary tract function.* Glasgow: International Continence Society.

Hellstron, P. M., & Sjoqvist, A. (1988). Involvement of opioid and nicotinic receptors in rectal and anal reflex inhibition of urinary motility in cats. *Acta Physiologica Scandinavica, 133*, 559–562.

Herzog, A. R., Diokno, A. C., Fultz, N. H. (1989). Urinary incontinence: Medical and psychological aspects. *Annual Review of Geriatrics and Gerontology, 9*.

Hu, T. (1986). The economic impact of urinary incontinence. *Clinics in Geriatric Medicine, 2*(4), 673–687.

Mathew, T. H., McEwen, J., & Rohan, A. (1988). Urinary incontinence secondary to prazosin. *Medical Journal of Australia, 148,* 305–306.

McGuire, E. J. (1978). Reflex urethral instability. *British Journal of Urology, 50,* 200–204.

McGuire, E. J., Lytton, B., Pepe, V., & Kohorn, E. I. (1976). Stress urinary incontinence. *Obstetrics and Gynecology, 47,* 255–264.

McGuire, E. J., & Savastano, J. A. (1985). Stress incontinence and detrusor instability/urge incontinence. *Neurology Urodynamics 4,* 313–316.

Mebust, W. K., Holtgrewe, H. L., Cockett, A. T. K., Peters, P. C., and Writing Committee. (1989). Transurethral prostatectomy: Immediate and postoperative complications. A cooperative study of 13 participating institutions evaluation 3,885 patients. *Journal of Urology, 141,* 243–247.

Meyhoff, H. H., Ingemann, L., Nordling, J., & Hald, T. (1981). Accuracy in preoperative estimation of prostatic size. *Scandinavian Journal of Urology and Nephrology, 15,* 45–51.

Mitteness, L. S. (1987). So what do you expect when you're 85?: Urinary incontinence in late life. *Social Health Care, 6,* 177–219.

Orandi, A. (1985). Transurethral incision of prostate (TUIP): 646 cases in 15 years—a chronological appraisal. *British Journal of Urology, 57,* 703–707.

Ory, M. G., Wyman, J. F., & Yu, L. (1986). Psychosocial factors in urinary incontinence. *Clinical Geriatric Medicine, 2*(4), 657–671.

Ouslander, J. G., Kane, R. L., & Abrass, I. B. (1982). Urinary incontinence in elderly nursing home patients. *Journal of the American Medical Association, 248,* 1194–1198.

Resnick, N. M. (1984). Urinary incontinence in the elderly. *Medical Grand Rounds, 3,* 281–290.

Resnick, N. M. (1988). Voiding dysfunction in the elderly. In S. V. Yalla, E. J. McGuire, A. Elbadawi, & J. G. Blaivas (Eds.), *Neurology and urodynamics: Principles and practice* (pp. 303–330). New York: Macmillan.

Resnick, N. M. (1990a). The initial approach to the incontinent patient. *Journal of the American Geriatrics Society.*

Resnick, N. M. (1990b). Voiding dysfunction and urinary incontinence. In C. R. Castle & D. Riesenberg (Eds.), *Geriatric medicine* (2d ed.). New York: Springer-Verlag.

Resnick, N. M., & Paillard, M. (1984). Natural history of nosocomial incontinence. In *Proceedings of the 14th Annual Meeting, International Continence Society* (pp. 471–472).

Resnick, N. M., Wetle, T. T., Scherr, P., Branck L., & Taylor, J. (1986). Urinary incontinence in community-dwelling elderly: Prevalence and correlates. In *Proceedings of the 16th Annual Meeting, International Continence Society* (pp. 76–78).

Resnick, N. M., & Yalla, S. V. (1985). Management of urinary incontinence in the elderly. *New England Journal of Medicine, 313,* 800–805.

Resnick, N. M., & Yalla, S. V. (1987). Detrusor hyperactivity with impaired contractile function. An unrecognized but common cause of incontinence in elderly patients. *Journal of the American Medical Association, 257*, 3076–3081.

Resnick, N. M., Yalla, S. V., & Laurino, E. (1989). The pathophysiology and clinical correlates of established urinary incontinence in frail elderly. *New England Journal of Medicine, 320*, 1–7.

Robinson, J. M. (1984). Evaluation of methods for assessment of bladder and urethral function. In J. C. Brocklehurst (Ed.), *Urology in the elderly* (pp. 19–54). New York: Churchill Livingstone.

Schnelle, J. F. (1990). Treatment of urinary incontinence in nursing home residents by prompted voiding. *Journal of the American Geriatrics Association*.

Semmens, J. P., Tsai, C. C., Semmens, E. C., & Loadholt, C. B. (1985). Effects of estrogen therapy on vaginal physiology during menopause. *Obstetrics and Gynecology, 66*, 15–18.

Sier, H., Ouslander, J., & Orzeck, S. (1987). Urinary incontinence among geriatric patients in an acute-care hospital. *Journal of the American Medical Association, 257*, 1767–1771.

Snow, T. L. (1988). Equipment for prevention, treatment, and management of urinary incontinence. *Topics in Geriatric Rehabilitation, 3*, 58–77.

Torrens, M., & Morrison, J. F. B. (Eds.). (1987). *The physiology of the lower urinary tract*. New York: Springer-Verlag.

Webster's New Twentieth Century Dictionary. 2d ed. (1978). New York: Collins World.

Wells, T. J. (1988). Additional treatments for urinary incontinence. *Topics in Geriatric Rehabilitation, 3*, 48–57.

Wells, T. J. (1990). Pelvic floor exercises. *Journal of the American Geriatrics Society*.

Wells, T. J., & Brink, C. A. (1988). Elimination: Urinary. In I. Burnside (Ed.), *Nursing and the aged* (3d ed., pp. 484–520). New York: McGraw-Hill.

Wheeler, J. S., Siroky, M. B., Bell, R., & Babayan, R. K. (1983). Vincristine-induced bladder neuropathy. *Journal of Urology, 130*, 342–343.

Part VI

The Practice Model: Mental Health

14

Mental Health Issues in the Disabled Elderly

May L. Wykle and Lorraine C. Mion

When my cousin Nellie turned 100 years old, she decided not to walk anymore. She simply stated, "I've walked for 100 years, and that's long enough." This decision dismayed her 78-year-old daughter who was herself physically unable to care for someone who was immobile. Up to her 100th birthday, and in spite of a crippling arthritis condition, cousin Nellie was functionally independent in most of her activities of daily living (ADL) and required very little assistance from her daughter. But with Nellie's refusal to walk she became increasingly dependent to the point that her daughter could no longer care for her and had to place her in a nursing home.

In the nursing home, the staff did little to encourage activity or to explore her emotional state. At first, the staff would get her up into a chair for most of the day, but even this activity ceased when cousin Nellie sustained a leg fracture. At the time of this writing, cousin Nellie is completely bedfast, her arthritis has progressed, and she is dependent on the staff for all of her care.

She is depressed, not eating well, losing weight, and is angry with her daughter. Periodically she cries she is ready to die. On the other hand, she is cognitively intact and is glad she is in her "right mind." She enjoys and looks forward to visits from her family, and relishes her daughter's homemade soup. Cousin Nellie is a prime example of the complex interactive effects of the psychological and physical components that not only accompany but contribute to functional disability in the elderly and impede the rehabilitation process. It is not enough to focus our attentions and interventions on the biophysical aspects of a disability when the emotional component plays a critical role in motivating the elderly individual to achieve his or her maximal functional level.

—May Wykle

233

Perhaps one of the greatest fears of growing old is the loss of health and functional ability. Disability refers to aberrations in the functional performance of the individual and encompasses the physical, social, emotional, and cognitive domains (Jette & Branck, 1985). Excess disability is a reversible deficit that exists when the magnitude of the disability in function is greater than might be accounted for by the basic physical illness or initial physiology (Brody, Kleban, Lawton, & Silverman, 1971).

The prevalence rate of disability in the United States has increased significantly in the past two decades. Between 1966 and 1979 the prevalence rate rose from 213 per 10,000 to 365 per 10,000 people, an increase of 71.4% (Galvin, 1988). This increase is mainly a result of two major trends in our society. First, with an aging population there is an increased prevalence of chronic health problems. A summary estimate by the National Center for Health Statistics showed that disabling chronic conditions rose sharply with increasing age (Feller, 1983). Among those 18 to 44 years of age, 0.8% had a major limitation in an activity of daily living, whereas those 65 to 74, 75 to 84, and 85 + years of age had respective proportions of disability of 6.9%, 16.0%, and 43.6%. Second, the medical technological advances in our society have saved lives but often with concomitant disabilities. Additionally, those disabled at a younger age are now living into old age.

This high prevalence of disability in old age is likely to have a profound effect on life satisfaction. The elderly disabled person often suffers from the stigma attached to a disabling illness and may experience a loss of self-esteem along with fears of decline and impending death. A functional disability is a threat to the self-concept, especially when independence is valued. This is true of those elderly who believed in self-sufficiency and independence as a way of life. Because aging is often seen as a gradual loss of functioning, a functional disability may intensify dependent feelings in aged persons as the disability interacts with the aging process.

Self-esteem, or the view of oneself, is fundamental to a person's mental health and is greatly influenced by one's perceived achievements, roles, and activities. The advent of a disabling illness can result in role loss. Thus, the loss of health, physical function, and independence can negatively influence one's appraisal of self-capability and worthiness. Moreover, admission to the hospital setting usually entails a significant loss of control and independence for elderly patients, making the elderly vulnerable to powerlessness.

Postive mental health is closely associated with a person's physical state and living environment. Therefore, to effectively treat mental health problems of the aged, the physical state and functional status need to be addressed, as well as the social-psychological environment.

Mental health initiatives have remained in the background in health care policies affecting the elderly. Furthermore, the mental health issues of the elderly disabled are just beginning to emerge. These issues encompass a wide range of concerns. They include the psychological impact following the onset of a physical disability; the importance of health workers' attitudes toward the elderly disabled; family and caregiver attitudes, the attitudes of the elderly disabled toward themselves, and the impact of these attitudes on outcomes; the family and caregiver needs in caring for the elderly disabled; autonomy and decision making in the elderly disabled; the unique needs of the cognitively impaired, the elderly mentally retarded, and the elderly with chronic mental illness; therapeutic approaches, education, and research needs.

PSYCHOLOGICAL IMPACT OF DISABILITY ON THE ELDERLY

Not only does functional disability have a profound psychological impact on aged persons, but the psychosocial stress arising from functional problems can accentuate physical symptoms. Because of the interactive effects of psychological and physical distress, it is helpful for health professionals to have a working knowledge of behavioral responses to a disability condition.

The disability stimulates specific behaviors that are influenced by the person's previous adjustment patterns, the degree of functional impairment, the abruptness of the disability onset, the prognosis, and the meaning of the affected body part for the person. Any disability is a threat to the self and thus always evokes some anxiety with a concomitant need for adaptation. Moreover, a disabling illness can also create crisis situations for the patient in which anxiety is escalated. Therefore, a necessary part of comprehensive care is to support the aged person's adaptive behaviors in order to prevent decompensation.

With support from families and professionals, many aged persons are able to maintain behavior within an adaptive healthy range when subjected to the stress of a functional disability. The health professional frequently assesses the patient's coping mechanisms and dependency needs in order to provide ongoing support and to assist the patient to achieve balance. By reinforcing existing coping mechanisms that are appropriate for the reduction of anxiety and supporting the patient's problem-solving skills, health professionals draw on the inherent strengths of disabled elderly patients.

The use of defense mechanisms is the ego's attempt to deal with the anxiety that stems from a functional disability. In spite of the defense mechanisms, however, a certain amount of anxiety becomes manifested through behaviors. The energy discharged through behavior is necessary to restore the individual's equilibrium.

A person's defense mechanisms in response to a disability can be broadly categorized into two different modes: flight into health or flight into illness. A defense mechanism is effective when it eases psychological stress and allows the individual to expend energy on the recovery process. If the person's defense mechanisms fail, a pathologic process can evolve, with resultant intense psychiatric symptoms. Two defense mechanisms, denial and regression, are frequently manifested by the disabled elderly. They are discussed below in greater detail.

Denial

Denial occurs during the early stages of recovery after the initial stressful onset of the disability. Through denial the patients deal with increased tension and anxiety by protecting themselves from reality. Intolerable thoughts are disowned during this process. Although the ego rids itself of unpleasent facts (such as the disability), it retains its ability to test reality. Patients manifest denial by disclaiming any physical or functional changes. They may even deny the severity of the disability.

Denial works well for the elderly person who has been independent and views sickness as a sign of weakness. Denial of the disability can be partial or complete and may include a "splitting" of thoughts, feelings, and behaviors.

Intervention for denial is essential when patients either compromise their recovery process or fail to participate in the rehabilitation program. In the past, therapy was aimed at confronting the denial. Direct attack, however, usually makes patients more defensive. They will relinquish their need to deny once they feel more secure. It must be remembered that denial can be quite useful for patients when they are suddenly faced by the realization of a disability. The health professional provides reasons for the patient's participation in the rehabilitation program but does not at this stage dwell on the patient's dependency or fearfulness.

Limits are firmly but gently set when the denial behavior interferes with the rehabilitation program. Care is provided in a manner that emphasizes the patient's worth even though the individual may be in a dependent state. Elderly patients experiencing denial need to exert control over activities and routines whenever feasible. They also need reassurance that it is acceptable to request assistance from the caregiver.

Regression

Regression is a defense mechanism that facilitates acceptance of a reduced ability to function and is often seen in those who are faced with a disability. The patient reverts to the behavior pattern of an earlier stage of development, thus enhancing the occurrence of dependency. The disabled elderly who use regression place themselves in the hands of competent others. They often become self-centered and concerned only with their immediate needs and interests during this time. The patients also focus on the caregiver's acceptance or rejection of them. Regression can be helpful to patients in the early phase of their disability, in that it conserves energy. If prolonged, however, regression blocks rehabilitative efforts. The interdisciplinary team needs to consider this mechanism when the patient seems to be more functionally dependent than can be accounted for by the physical disability.

ANXIETY IN THE REHABILITATION SETTING

The disabled elderly often experience fluctuating levels of anxiety that can range from mild to severe. The level of anxiety engendered depends on the patient's maturity, use of coping mechanisms, support resources, level of self-esteem, and need tension.

Signs of anxiety can be observed in the patient's appearance, behavior, and conversation. Several observable signs of anxiety are usually necessary to designate the patient behavior as anxious. With mild anxiety the signs are fewer and less prominent, and thus it is important to validate the impression with the patient. Mild levels of anxiety can be beneficial, in that mental facilities are heightened. As the level of anxiety increases, however, mental capacities are overworked and can be paralyzed or decompensate. Signs of anxiety become more pronounced as the level of anxiety increases.

It is imperative that members of the rehabilitation team take steps to lower their own anxiety level as well as the patient's because anxiety can be felt empathically and is easily communicated to others. If the anxiety is not reduced, other patients and staff are caught up in the tension, and a spiraling effect can ensue.

The types of interventions used by the health professional depend on the level of the patient's anxiety. These include explanations, exploration of feelings, and interventions for severe anxiety. The capacity to tolerate stress varies among individuals, and the primary purpose of any intervention is to support the patient's coping mechanisms to prevent further escalation of the anxiety.

A large part of the health professional's work is to encourage disabled elderly patients to express their concerns and anxieties about their functional capability, to help them realize the universality of fear in their situations, to help them seek outlets for their tensions, and to allay negative feelings whenever possible. Major underlying problems should be handled by professionals trained in psychotherapy. The rehabilitation professional needs to be able to recognize normal anxiety reactions and to report exaggerated reactions that may indicate the need for psychiatric referral.

Crisis may occur in the elderly disabled person at any time during the rehabilitative process. A crisis ensues whenever the person is met with overwhelming anxiety created by biologic, physiologic, or social-psychological threats to the self. It can occur when a person is unable to effectively use customary methods of coping. The individual requires active assistance because he or she is not able to cope successfully with the sudden disorganization. Intensive support is the essential element of crisis intervention to help maintain the individual's integrity and ability to use coping mechanisms. Crisis, according to Caplan (1964), is self-limiting. The outcome of a crisis is governed by the type of interaction that takes place between the individual and key figures in the environment during the time of the crisis.

Shontz (1975) describes several phases or stages that occur during a crisis that are similar to the stages of dying as described by Kubler-Ross (1969). These stages are initial impact, realization, defensive retreat, acknowledgment, and adaptation. The model is useful in explaining what an elderly person experiences when faced with a functional disability, even though individual reactions to a disability vary. All elderly persons are not equally vulnerable to all categories of stress, but there is thought to be some commonality in the reactions. Knowledge of these commonalities can facilitate plans for rehabilitation activities.

ADAPTIVE BEHAVIORS

The following six behaviors are all adaptive behaviors that are common reactions of aged persons to a functional disability.

Aggression is another method of handling stress-induced anxiety and allows the patient to feel less helpless and more powerful in response to the functional disability. Elderly persons are often angry at the loss of health and question their treatment. They may project anger onto others and become irritable, uncooperative, and demanding. It is important that health care professionals accept the patient's hostility and make a conscious effort not to react negatively. Methods of dealing with aggressive behavior include anticipating and acting on the patient's demands. Expression of anger in socially acceptable ways prevents anger from being turned inward, perhaps leading to depression. A sense of autonomy and personal control over the environment and the opportunity to participate in the planning and implementation of the rehabilitation plan of care are necessary to alleviate the patient's sense of powerlessness.

Dependency, a common behavior of the disabled individual, is a reaction that may follow the stage of accepting an illness or functional disability. Although dependency is a form of regression, it is also a part of learning to trust. These elderly patients may not want to do much for themselves and passively accept total care. Supportive care is indicated in the early stages, with gradual advancement from doing *for* the patients to doing *with* the patients, and finally facilitating self-care. In this way patients are able to return gradually to helping themselves as they learn more about their functional disability.

Overdependency is a form of excess disability. It exists when patients show physical readiness to progress but prefer to remain physically dependent. Limits are set on those activities that further promote dependency. Appropriate interventions at this time include the use of saturation (anticipating and meeting patients' needs before the patients mention them) and encouragement to do more for themselves. Assurance is given these patients that they will not be abandoned by the members of the interdisciplinary team.

Withdrawn patients are apt to be labeled as "good" patients as they do not pose problems for the staff. Because withdrawn patients demand little from others, they may be overlooked. These patients also regress more readily to earlier levels of behavior at which they can accept their disability. Withdrawn patients need gentle encouragement to talk, to express feelings, and to relate to the staff. Even if the time is spent in silence, just sitting with the patients increases their sense of self-worth.

Suspicious individuals have difficulty with trust and may have had previous experiences in which they learned to distrust caregivers. Suspiciousness in elderly patients is not uncommon; misinterpretation of the environment may be the result of aging sensory deficits. They are often suspicious of the health care team, the routines, the medicines, and the procedures. They need to talk about their concerns but should not be forced to do so. It is imperative that staff members keep any promises that are made, in order to build a trusting relationship. Explanations of procedures of the rehabilitation plan and the establishment of expected routines allay fears and suspicions.

Somatic behavior is a flight into illness reaction to anxiety. Anxiety is expressed as a variety of physical complaints, preoccupations with bodily functions, or feelings of pain. Elderly disabled patients legitimize their need for attention through these complaints. Staff members may become angry or frustrated with elderly persons who use somatic behavior because symptomatic complaints, such as backache, headache, or fatigue, are often vague. Yet there is always the possibility that these symptoms are truly connected with an illness. This situation places the staff in a dilemma. All complaints, particularly in the elderly, need to be accepted and investigated prior to diagnosing somatic behavior. Somatic behavior is lessened through time spent with patients listening to complaints and the use of saturation.

Depressed behavior is not an uncommon response to disability. In making an assessment of the person who is depressed, the health professional needs to be aware of the following signs of depression: (1) decreased interaction with others, (2) lack of interest in activities or environment, (3) voiced concern about the disability and amount of required care, (4) expressed wish for or concerns about dying, (5) dependent behavior, (6) decreased activity, and (7) complaints of weakness or fatigue. If the depressive behavior becomes prolonged or intensified, a clinical depression is likely to result.

CLINICAL DEPRESSION

Of all of the functional psychiatric disorders affecting the elderly, depression is the most prevalent. It has been estimated that 5% to 10% of the elderly residing in the community have a clinically significant depressive episode. Rates as high as 24% to 64% have been reported in elderly hospitalized patients and 80% in the nursing home population (Blazer, 1982; Borson, Liptzin, Nininger, & Rabins, 1987). The importance of diagnosing depression in this age group is reflected in the frequency of suicides. Indeed, suicide rates in the United States are highest for those 65 years and older (Blazer, Bachar, & Manton, 1986). Despite the prevalence of depression and its severity, it is frequently overlooked or misdiagnosed in elderly individuals (German et al., 1987; Harris, Mion, Patterson, & Frengley, 1988) and particularly in the disabled. A variety of explanations account for this anomaly.

Depression in the elderly can frequently be masked or present with atypical symptomatology (Blazer, 1982; Gurland, 1976). For example, once considered the hallmark of a major depressive illness, dysphoria is no longer considered a necessary prerequisite in the DSM-III-R (APA, 1987) taxonomy, a change of criteria that takes into account the absence of dysphoria in many depressed elderly individuals. Instead, loss of pleasure can be substituted as an expression of a depressed mood.

Usual age-related changes, such as altered sleep patterns, may be mistaken for signs of depression. Conversely, the same symptoms or complaints as a result of depression may be attributed to usual age-related changes. Moreover, some age-related changes may actually increase the likelihood of depression, such as alterations in norepinephrine and serotonin levels.

Many symptoms of depression, such as fatigue, weakness, and pain, are common in other disease states. The task of separating multiple physical illnesses and conditions that occur in the elderly from that of depression can be formidable (Steuer, Bank, Olsen, & Jarvik, 1980). Additionally, specific physical disease states have been shown to be accompanied by depression in a high percentage of patients, such as in thyroid disease. Not only the physical diseases but the concomitant drug therapies used to treat the illnesses can have a depressive effect on the elderly. The most notorious of these are the antihypertensives, especially reserpine (Lippmann, 1983).

Besides the interaction between physiological and biochemical factors, various external events and the psychodynamics of an individual's response to losses also play a role in the development of depression in later life. External events or sociological factors include enforced retirement, role loss, loneliness, and isolation. Loss of physical function secondary to poor health or a major physical illness has been found to be highly associated with depression (Gurland, Golden, Lantigua, & Dean, 1986; Harris et al., 1988). In the elderly disabled, loss of functional ability is often a precipient of depressive symptomatology. Such a reaction is not uncommon but could lead to more serious clinical depression.

One of the difficulties in the hospital or nursing home setting is to differentiate the symptoms of grief following loss of health and function from that of depression. Grief in disabled persons is the pain that results from the loss of self, whether loss of physical function, loss of mental function, changed appearance, loss of expectations, or loss of relationships with significant others. As a consequence, disabled persons suffer a diminishment in their sense of self-worth. The emotional sequelae to loss of health are similar to those that occur with the loss of a loved one and usually follow a relatively predictable course.

Symptoms of grief include preoccupation with the loss, somatic distress, inappropriate behavior, and hostility. Feelings of despair, helplessness, protest, and sadness are also normal reactions to loss. Health care workers can misinterpret these symptoms. In a prospective study of 100 consecutive psychiatric consultations in a rehabilitation setting, Gans (1981) found that only 28 of these patients were clinically depressed but that team members believed 44 were depressed. It is interesting to note that of the 28 depressed patients almost one third suffered from a pathological grief reaction. Gans also found that the elderly patients frequently manifested depression as somatic preoccupation and/or paranoid thinking and could be overlooked as suffering from depression.

Recognition of the grieving process is paramount in disabled individuals, especially soon after the disabling event. Severity of the disability and recent onset are positively associated with the degree of psychiatric distress (Cassileth et al., 1984). Complications of grief include major depression and pathological grief manifested as persistent compulsive overactivity without a sense of loss (Stewart & Shields, 1985).

In the rehabilitation setting it is not uncommon for elderly patients to exhibit a range of symptomatology from demoralization, grief, and minor depression to that of a major clinical depression. Because of the combination of age-associated biochemical and physical changes, multiple drug therapies and interactions, loss of physical function, and possible presence of pain, it comes as no surprise that a high proportion of elderly disabled persons may suffer from depressive symptomatology.

It behooves health professionals to be sensitive to the complex myriad of conditions contributing to depression. Depressed elderly individuals respond favorably to a variety of psychotherapeutic interventions. If left undetected and untreated, the depression will impede the rehabilitation process in the elderly disabled.

RESTORING COMPETENCE AND CONFIDENCE TO THE FUNCTIONALLY DISABLED OLDER PERSON

Various studies have been done in the area of personal control and autonomy and the effects on elderly individuals when autonomy is enhanced or restricted (Averill, 1973; Langer & Rodin, 1976). In general, these studies have demonstrated that enhancement of autonomy and personal control positively correlates with physical and psychological health and that restriction of autonomy has negative effects on health.

Abramson and Seligman (1978) reviewed the debilitating consequences of uncontrollable events that can lead to learned helplessness.

Learned helplessness occurs when a person continues to behave as if unable to control his or her environment or events because of past aversive stimuli that were uncontrollable. Continuing expectations of helplessness, in turn, can be sufficient conditions for depression. In the institutional setting, the potential for powerlessness is high, and the passive behavior often encountered in elderly nursing home patients may be accounted for by their loss of control (Fuller, 1978). Similarly, this can be applied to the elderly disabled. Exaggerated helplessness is said to occur when individuals utilize their disability as a means of relating to others and maintaining close contact. The following case example illustrates the phenomenon of exaggerated helplessness in an elderly woman.

> Mrs. G. is an 80-year old lady who was recently widowed and lives alone. Mrs. G.'s daughter comes to her home after work to prepare the evening meal for her. The daughter does this out of the belief that her mother is too weak and physically unable to perform this task, a belief that Mrs. G. does little to dispel. Yet Mrs. G. bakes desserts to serve her friends and guests. In this instance Mrs. G. uses an exaggerated helplessness around cooking as a means to maintain daily contact with her daughter.

Interventions that overly assist or help the elderly individual can have detrimental effects. Avorn and Langer (1982), in a controlled trial involving elderly intermediate-care residents of a nursing home, demonstrated that the group that was overly helped in completing a puzzle had greater deficits in several measured area. When compared to the nonintervention group and the "encouraged only" group, those who were actively assisted had poorer completion of the task, decreased speed of performance, greater perception of task difficulty, and decreased self-confidence. The authors warn that "the expectation of disability becomes disabling itself" (p. 400).

These findings have important implications around the issues of motivation, attitudes, and behaviors toward the elderly disabled, as well as the attitudes and behaviors of the elderly disabled themselves.

Attitudes

Negative feelings or attitudes about the elderly persist in our society and among various health professionals (Barta Kvitek, Shaver, Blood, & Shepard, 1986; Benedict & Ganikos, 1981; Ray, Raciti, & Ford, 1985). Several studies have demonstrated the influence that negative attitudes can have on the day-to-day care of elderly patients. The efficacy of rehabilitation programs for the elderly disabled has been demonstrated within the past decade in what was once considered an area for primarily a younger population (Gregor, McCarthy, Chwirchak, Meluch, & Mion, 1986; Lefton, Bonstelle, & Frengley, 1983; Rubenstein et al., 1988). In spite of these recent advances in addressing physical disability in the elderly, the elderly remain underserved in many rehabilitation centers. The existence of an age bias in physical therapists was shown to result in less aggressive or lower goals for the elderly patient (Barta Kvitek et al., 1986). Indeed, Cohen (1988) has postulated that it is the elderly disabled who are "the victims of low goal formulation and underestimated potentials for self-realization" (p. 24).

In exhibiting negative attitudes toward the elderly disabled, health professionals perpetuate the belief that the elderly disabled are not worthy of rehabilitative efforts. Similarly, the mental health needs of the elderly, particularly those of the elderly disabled, have been ignored. Historically, the aged have seldom been chosen for treatment by mental health professionals. Moreover, most students in the health professions have not been required to work with elderly persons as part of their supervised training experience. Consequently, most mental health professionals are reluctant to work with the elderly (Wykle, 1986).

Additionally, a pessimism or skepticism can prevail regarding the efficacy of therapy for the elderly disabled individual. The elderly disabled cannot but be aware of the overt and covert negative messages sent by professionals and family alike. Unfortunately, if these beliefs are internalized, the elderly disabled person will believe that these low goal formulations are the best that could be achieved. Sullivan (1953) discusses reflected self-appraisals and their effect on one's self-esteem. In this theory self-esteem is defined by others' appraisals of one's functional ability. Consequently, negative attitudes toward the elderly disabled will discourage rehabilitation. Moreover, some contend that ageism exists within the elderly disabled themselves (Butler, 1975). In effect, a self-fulfilling prophecy occurs that can intensify mental health problems. The consequences of these attitudes are reflected in the barriers raised to rehabilitation and to a return to as full a social life as is possible (DeJong & Lifchez, 1983).

Family

The family can have a significant positive influence in maintaining and promoting the elderly disabled person's physical and mental well-being. It has been substantially documented that families provide considerable physical, emotional, social, and economic support to their chronically ill relatives (Brody, 1981). Moreover, patients who are emotionally supported by their families respond more favorably in the hospital and in the home settings (Dzau & Boehme, 1978). Thus, it is important to consider the patient's entire family during the rehabilitation process. Families need to be actively involved from the commencement of therapy. The progression of rehabilitation therapy is such that the transfer of major responsibility of caregiving proceeds from the health care professionals to the disabled individual. Often, however, family members assume the major responsibility of care for the elderly disabled relatives until such time they are able to assume responsibility for themselves. The goal, then, is to assist the elderly individual in a therapeutic program within the context of the family unit (cf., Chapter 9, E. Brody, this volume).

The amount of involvement and the role that the family plays in caring for the disabled aged relative will vary depending on the family structure, the quality of the relationships, the economic resources, and the competing demands on the family's time and energy. A careful assessment of the family will identify potential problems as well as strengths that can affect the elder's care.

The assessment begins on admission to the rehabilitation program by eliciting the family's perceptions of the major problems and the possible solutions as well as the role of the rehabilitation program in the elderly individual's health care process. It is not uncommon for the elderly patient and family members to have unrealistic expectations and lack of knowledge regarding the extent and consequences of the disease. A frequent comment by families is "They [referring source] told us that you'd teach Mom to walk again." Conversely, there are those families who set too low expectations and do not want their elderly relative encouraged in an active rehabilitation program. An attitude of "she deserves to rest" prevails. Not knowing the family's perceptions and expectations at the outset can lead to difficulties in communication, goal setting, and obtaining the optimal level of functioning.

The rehabilitation team obtains information pertaining to the tangible support and economic resources that the family is able to provide, such as food, housing, and transportation. Recent events that may significantly affect the functioning of the family unit, such as a change in income, a death, or another serious illness, are also assessed. Stresses on the individual members among the different generations are identified because family conflicts that may or may not involve the patient can surface at this time.

A thorough assessment of the family provides information on the various roles of the family members, their patterns of interactions, and their psychosocial needs. In this way, the family's ability to function as a support system is realistically explored. Although it is true that family members provide significant support to the elderly disabled, it is not without cost to them: physically, mentally, emotionally, and economically. Family counseling, therefore, is often appropriate and of primary importance.

Interventions with family are directed toward increasing the functioning of the elderly disabled while maintaining or promoting the mental health stability of the family unit. First and foremost is teaching the family about the patient's usual aging changes as well as the impairment in capabilities from the specific disease conditions. It is important for the family to understand the functional limitations imposed by the illness, the behavioral changes and cognitive impairment, and what they can expect from the older disabled person in day-to-day situations. The purpose of this is to avoid under- and overhelping the elderly relative. Those functions that elderly persons are capable of doing for themselves are accentuated and encouraged.

Second, the family's ability to perform skills that the elderly disabled individual is unable to perform must be explained and taught early in the rehabilitation program. There are times when the elderly disabled cannot physically perform certain tasks. The willingness as well as the ability of the family to perform these tasks should be ascertained. Even very caring families may find it physically or emotionally difficult to help the elderly disabled individual. Indeed, a significant number of the caregivers are themselves aging or in poor health. Techniques of caring for the elderly disabled should be explained and demonstrated to the family. As the family performs these skills under the guidance of the health care professionals both in hospital and, if possible, at home, anxieties and fears of both the patients and families are allayed. This also allows the health care professionals to examine the physical and emotional capabilities of the family members and make adjustments in the plan of care as needed. In a 4-year follow-up study of stroke patients, Brocklehurst, Morris, Andrew, Richards, and Laycock (1981) found that the number of primary caregivers reporting poor health tripled within the year following the stroke. It needs to be emphasized to family members that maintaining their own physical and emotional well-being is essential in providing long-term care to the elderly disabled.

Third, the patient and the family are informed about community resources. The health professionals can access and coordinate resources that will assist the patient and family with the demands of the disability. This includes day care and respite activities.

Lastly, family members need to work through their own feelings regarding the elderly relative's disability. Individual as well as group therapies for relatives can be helpful in assisting families to work together collaboratively. Groups can provide opportunities for education, support, and ventilation.

THE MENTALLY RETARDED, CHRONICALLY MENTALLY ILL, AND THE COGNITIVELY IMPAIRED

Several subgroups of the elderly disabled have special mental health issues and needs. There are the elderly mentally retarded, the elderly chronically mentally ill, and the cognitively impaired elderly.

Mentally Retarded

A subgroup of the elderly disabled are the mentally retarded (MR). Because of the advances in health care in this century, the MR are surviving longer into old age. There is no age definition for a "geriatric" MR individual, and it appears that the MR begin the aging process at an earlier age than the rest of the population. Even if the chronological age of 65 years is used as a marker of old age, there are approximately 196,000 MR individuals over the age of 65 in the U.S. (Walz, Harper, & Wilson, 1986).

The aging of this group has serious implications for the health care system that will need to be addressed. Medical management becomes increasingly difficult with the emergence of chronic illnesses and functional disabilities. For the MR individual cared for at home, the caregiver situation is likely to change. The caregiver may die or no longer be able to physically care for the MR individual. At present, both nursing homes and residential homes for the MR are reluctant to care for this aging population because of the complex medical and behavioral management problems.

It is not unlikely that aged individuals who are MR and have a physically disabling condition would benefit from a course of rehabilitation. Bearing in mind the cognitive limitation, the standard rehabilitation program can be adapted to meet realistic goals.

Chronically Mentally Ill

Rehabilitation professionals will encounter the chronically mentally ill as this population ages and develops physical illnesses and functional disabilities. The aging of the chronically mentally ill population requires an approach that addresses the usual age-related changes as well as the effects of long-term somatic therapies and perhaps institutionalization. The improved therapies for schizophrenia and manic-depressive illness, for example, have allowed individuals suffering from these diseases to remain functional. Consultation with the psychiatric liaison will best assist the interdisciplinary rehabilitation team in providing a comprehensive plan of care and management of psychotropic drugs.

Cognitively Impaired

The cognitive impairment that accompanies a variety of pathological brain conditions, such as dementia and stroke, can have an impact on the rehabilitative process and outcome. Various areas of cognition are affected, including judgment, memory, and attention span. Successful rehabilitation, however, can be accomplished for those elderly disabled who have mild to moderate cognitive impairments. Careful assessment of the elderly person's memory, concentration, and ability to imitate is essential in setting realistic goals. Most elderly patients with mild to moderate degrees of cognitive impairments are able to learn concrete activities that aid in motor skills and activities of daily living (ADL). Opportunities are provided for repetitive action-oriented activities that promote functional abilities to the highest possible level. When working with cognitively impaired individuals, it is helpful to diminish or control other stimuli in the environment. Competing noises, such as from the television and radio, can easily distract the patient. Difficult motor tasks can be broken down to simpler one- or two-step processes. Use of similar routines or movements can stimulate the learning of a new motor skill. Maintenance of a predictable routine with primary team members decreases unnecessary exposure to confusing stimuli (cf., Gottlieb, Chapter 15 for fuller discussion).

MENTAL HEALTH INTERVENTIONS

Effective mental health interventions for the emotional component of a functional disability in the elderly are those that reinforce their positive coping mechanisms. The rehabilitation team cannot underestimate the support needed by the older person to participate in a rehabilitation plan. For example, a 76-year-old man who suffered from a stroke was able to have a knee brace removed 2 weeks earlier than anticipated. He attributed this progress to the encouragement of the physical therapy assistant who worked with him weekly and constantly reminded him, "I know that you can do more." He was thus challenged by the positive support. In addition to socioemotional encouragement, good medical management is extremely important, particularly in the earlier stages of the disability. Careful medical management treats the bio-physical needs to enhance the patient's maximal physical domain and prevents the occurrence of disease and treatment complications. In this way the medical and physical management provides stability and reas-surance for the disabled individuals and thus strengthens self-esteem. As patients accept their disability and work toward rehabilitation goals, one is likely to see more compliance and positive behavior changes. The health care professionals must remember, however, that during the course of rehabilitation the individual may regress. Facing the day-to-day stress of expected compliance to therapy routines and medica-tions may be exhausting and lead to feelings of demoralization, depres-sion, or anxiety. Anxiety fluctuates during the course of a disabling illness and may escalate to a crisis situation. Health professionals need to know how to assess and intervene in a crisis at any point during rehabilitation.

Research has demonstrated that elderly persons do benefit from psy-chotherapies (Borson et al., 1987). Mental health treatment in the el-derly has been neglected in the past, but attitudes toward psychiatric treatment in aged persons are changing. Positive outcomes have erased the interference and negative stereotypes that picture elderly disabled persons as unable to benefit from aggressive therapy.

Individual counseling may be warranted for the functionally disabled elderly person. As patients come to grips with their disability and learn to confront self-esteem issues, counseling provides support for positive coping and sound decision making. Counseling also helps motivation as the individual gains strength from the interpersonal relationship. More intense psychotherapy may be needed if there are signs of clini-cal depression, high levels of anxiety, or frequent crisis events. It is useful to discuss with patients in detail the grief that accompanies the loss of functional independence. Compliance issues, overdependency, and excessive use of alcohol and drugs are often better dealt with in individual therapy. Restoration of dignity and worth to the older per-son through counseling will ease the loss of self-sustaining activities that threaten the quality of life.

Working with the disabled elderly in groups has been successful in pro-moting mental health (Burnside, 1983). Group participants profit from peer support, the sharing of concerns, and group problem solving. In-teraction with the group members is in itself therapeutic if the group has skilled leadership. Cognitive therapy, group psychotherapy, and guided imagery can be used with the elderly during rehabilitation. Ex-ercise groups also strengthen the emotional health of disabled persons. An example of an activity that can be used by the frail elderly is "Easy

Does It Yoga" (Wykle, 1984), an exercise routine that combines meditation and physical movement.

Family therapy is useful when family members have problems with communication or lack understanding of the elderly person's functional disability. Counseling older couples has also been extremely helpful in understanding their roles in the rehabilitation program. For example, a tearful 72-year-old woman with progressive arthritis was seen in an elderly assessment clinic because of severe depression. She had been on a number of medications for depression, none of which was effective. Her husband was 86 years old and could not understand the limitations of her illness and why she was not content to enjoy their retirement or fulfill her role as a housewife. The husband and wife were unable to communicate and agree on their role activities. A counselor was instrumental in improving their communication and relationship. Subsequently, the woman's depression improved.

Educating family members about the elderly person's functional disability helps them determine their ability to care for the individual in the home. Caregivers can obtain respite counseling, knowledge of resources, and formal and informal support through family counseling. The disabled elderly individual directly benefits from the psychological support of the family.

EDUCATIONAL AND TRAINING NEEDS

Education in the mental health issues of the elderly disabled is of major importance because of the psychological impact on attaining, maintaining, and regaining physical health. In the fields of geriatrics and gerontology, mental health in the elderly has not been a part of the health care educational mainstream, and deficiencies in this area exist in most of the current health professional programs. A critical goal is to infuse these programs with the current knowledge of aging and care of the elderly. The programs need to incorporate a strong clinical component whereby students gain the necessary skills and techniques to intervene effectively and successfully with the disabled elderly. To accomplish this, it is necessary to have well-prepared faculty to serve as role models and stimulate enthusiasm in both didactic and clinical activities. There are few professionals, however, who specialized in geriatric mental health. Subsequently, there is a need for graduate and postgraduate programs to educate or prepare professionals in the area of geriatric mental health and in particular the psychological needs of the disabled elderly.

Psychogeriatric care can be very demanding; it requires the resources of multiple disciplines. A multidisciplinary educational approach that encompasses a wide variety of information is helpful for students to understand and appreciate the complex set of interactions that occur among staff, patients, and families. A variety of settings can be used for the geriatric mental health clinical experience in the educational program and may include acute-care hospitals, rehabilitation units, nursing homes, ambulatory care facilities, psychiatric facilities, and home care.

The rehabilitation setting offers several advantages for basic student education in the care of the disabled elderly. A strong focus on functional performance, utilization of interdisciplinary teams skilled in multidimensional assessment, and an emphasis on chronic conditions rather than acute processes are available for the clinical experience. The rehabilitation setting also allows students to follow patients who usually make substantial improvements in ADL and instrumental activities of daily living (IADL). This experience is especially important in promoting positive attitudes and enthusiasm toward health care of the elderly. Most professional caregivers were not introduced, as students, to aged persons as a necessary part of their supervised clinical experience. They lacked opportunities, therefore, to develop the sensitivity, competence, and satisfaction that come from providing educative and corrective experiences for elderly persons.

Students of all disciplines working with the elderly need to learn the epidemiology of aging; differentiate between normal aging and disease processes; develop a sensitivity to the aging process; enhance communication and interpersonal skills in order to work effectively with individual patients, families, groups, and a variety of health professionals; experience working with families and with other disciplines in care planning; and gain knowledge of the community resources. Contact with both healthy and psychologically ill elderly is necessary to develop comprehensive geriatric mental health skills and to understand and differentiate the psychiatric illnesses from the normal aging process. Understanding the social, economic, ethical, cultural, and community influences on the mental health of the elderly is another key component of the core curriculum. A focus on specific psychiatric syndromes and treatment regimens, such as pharmacokinetics and phamacodynamics, that may be required for the elderly is also a necessary requirement in the educational programs.

RESEARCH NEEDS

As with the educational and training programs, multidisciplinary research approaches in geriatric mental health are essential because no one profession or discipline is capable of adequately meeting the multiple complex needs, including that of excess disability, of the elderly disabled. Because of the relatively recent phenomenon of an increased life span, little is known about the growth and development tasks for this age group. More longitudinal studies are required to better understand the normal aging process.

Research questions concerning the mental health needs of the elderly disabled involve several areas. Questions concerning the common behavioral problems in the elderly include assaultive and agitated behavior, wandering, depression, somatic behavior, hallucinations and delusions, and acute and chronic confusional states. With the alarming rise in the incidence of behavioral problems in the elderly there is a need to understand and manage these disorders.

Another area for elderly mental health research is the effect of psychological stress on physical health in terms of onset and course of physical disorders. Conversely, there is a need to understand the effect of a physical disorder on the elderly patient's psychological health. Moreover, the interactive effects of coexisting physical and psychological disorders require further study to comprehend the interrelationship of physical and mental health conditions. This knowledge would enable health care professionals to develop more effective interventions for the disabled elderly. Well-designed experimental studies on the effectiveness of various mental health interventions and programs include pharmacological studies and studies of various therapies, such as group, family, and cognitive therapies.

Research results of geriatric mental health studies should be widely publicized and disseminated so that they can be used by practitioners and taught by educators. Research in the area of mental health and excess disability for the functionally disabled elderly commands high priority because the knowledge generated can improve their quality of life.

REFERENCES

Abramson, L. Y., & Seligman, M. E. (1978). Learned helplessness in humans: Critique and reformulation. *Journal of Abnormal Psychology, 87*, 49–74.

American Psychiatric Association. (1987). *Diagnostic and statistical manual of mental disorders* (3rd ed., rev.). Washington, DC: Author.

Averill, J. R. (1973). Personal control over aversive stimuli and its relationship to stress. *Psychological Bulletin, 80*, 286–303.

Avorn, J., & Langer, E. (1982). Induced disability in nursing home patients: A controlled trial. *Journal of the American Geriatrics Society, 30*, 397–400.

Barta Kvitek, S. D., Shaver, B. J., Blood, H., & Shepard, K. F. (1986). Age bias: Physical therapists and older patients. *Journal of Gerontology, 41* (6), 706–709.

Benedict, R. C., Ganikos, M. L. (1981). Coming to terms with ageism in rehabilitation. *Journal of Rehabilitation, 47,* 10–17.

Blazer, D. (1982). The epidemiology of late life depression. *Journal of the American Geriatrics Society, 30*(9), 587–592.

Blazer, D. G., Bachar, J. R., & Manton, K. G. (1986). Suicide in late life: Review and commentary. *Journal of the American Geriatrics Society, 34*(7), 519–525.

Borson, S., Liptzin, B., Nininger, J., & Rabins, P. (1987). Psychiatry and the nursing home. *American Journal of Psychiatry, 144,* 1412–1418.

Brocklehurst, J. C., Morris, P., Andrew, K., Richards, B., & Laycock, P. (1981). Social effects of stroke. *Social Science and Medicine, 15A,* 35–39.

Brody, E. M. (1981). "Women in the middle" and family help to older people. *Gerontologist, 21,* 471–480.

Brody, E. M., Kleban, M. H., Lawton, M. P., & Silverman, H. A. (1971). Excess disabilities of mentally impaired aged: Impact of individualized treatment. *Gerontologist, 11,* 124–133.

Burnside, I. (1983). *Working with the elderly: Group processes and techniques* (2nd ed.). North Scituate, MA: Dunbury Press.

Butler, R. N. (1975). *Why survive? Being old in America.* New York: Harper and Row.

Caplan, G. (1964). *Principles of preventive psychiatry.* New York: Basic Books.

Cassileth, B. R., Lusk, E. J., Strouse, T.B., Miller, D. S., Brown, L. L., Cross, P. A., & Tenaglia, A. N. (1984). Psychosocial status in chronic illness: A comparative analysis of six diagnostic groups. *New England Journal of Medicine, 311*(8), 506–511.

Cohen, E. S. (1988). The elderly mystique: Constraints on the autonomy of the elderly with disabilities. *Gerontologist, 28,* 24–31.

DeJong, G., & Lifchez, R. (1983). Physical disability and public policy. *Scientific American, 248,* 41–49.

Dzau, R. E., & Boehme, A. R. (1978). Stroke rehabilitation: A family-team education program. *Archives of Physical Medicine and Rehabilitation, 59,* 236–239.

Feller, B. A. (1983). *Americans needing help to function at home: Advancedata 92* (DHHS Publication PSH-83–1571). Hyattsville, MD: National Center for Health Statistics.

Fuller, S. (1978). Inhibiting helplessness in elderly people. *Journal of Gerontological Nursing, 4,* 18–21.

Galvin, D. E. (1988). Employers discover value of rehabilitation. *Rehabilitation Report, 4,* 1–3.

Gans, J. S. (1981). Depression diagnosis in a rehabilitation hospital. *Archives of Physical Medicine and Rehabilitation, 62,* 386–389.

German, P. S., Shapiro, S., Skinner, E. A., Von Korff, M., Klein, L. E., Turner, R. W., Teitelbaum, M. L., Burke, J., & Burns, B. J. (1987). Detection and management of mental health problems of older patients by primary care providers. *Journal of the American Medical Association, 257*(4), 489–493.

Gregor, S., McCarthy, K., Chwirchak, D., Meluch, M., & Mion, L. C. (1986). Characteristics and functional outcomes of elderly rehabilitation patients. *Rehabilitation Nursing, 11,* 10–14.

Gurland, B. J. (1976). The comparative frequency of depression in various adult age groups. *Journal of Gerontology, 31*(3), 283–292.

Gurland, B. J., Golden, R., Lantigua, R., & Dean, L. (1986). The overlap between physical conditions and depression in the elderly: A key to improvement in service delivery. In D. Nayer (Ed.), *The patient and those who care: The mental health aspect of long-term physical illness* (pp. 23–36). Nantucket, MA: Watson Publishers International.

Harris, R. E., Mion, L. C., Patterson, M. B., & Frengley, J. D. (1988). Severe illness in older patients: The association between depressive disorders and functional dependency during the recovery phase. *Journal of the American Geriatrics Society, 36,* 890–896.

Jette, A. M., & Branck, L. G. (1985). Impairment and disability in the aged. *Journal of Chronic Disease, 38,* 59–65.

Kubler-Ross, E. (1969). *On death and dying.* New York: Macmillian.

Langer, E. J., & Rodin, J. (1976). The effects of choice and enhanced personal responsibility for the aged: A field experiment in an institutional setting. *Journal of Personality and Social Psychology, 34,* 191–198.

Lefton, E., Bonstelle, S., & Frengley, J. D. (1983). Success with an inpatient geriatric unit. *Journal of the American Geriatrics Society, 31,* 149–155.

Lippmann, S. L. (1983). Durg therapy for depression in the elderly. *Postgraduate Medicine, 73,* 159–173.

Ray, D. C., Raciti, M. A., & Ford, C. V. (1985). Ageism in psychiatrists: Association with gender, certification, and theoretical orientation. *Gerontologist, 25*(5), 496–500.

Rubenstein, L. Z., Wieland, G. D., Josephson, K. R., Rosbrook, B., Sayre, J., & Kane, R. L. (1988). Improved survival for frail elderly inpatients on a geriatric evaluation unit (GEU): Who benefits? *Mental Health Issues, 41*(5), 441–449.

Shontz, F. C. (1975). *The psychological aspects of physical illness and disability.* New York: Macmillan.

Steuer, J., Bank, L., Olsen, E. J., & Jarvik, L. F. (1980). Depression, physical health and somatic complaints in the elderly: A study of the Zung Self-Rating Depression Scale. *Journal of Gerontology, 35*(5), 683–688.

Stewart, T., & Shields, R. (1985). Grief in chronic illness: Assessment and management. *Archives of Physical Medicine and Rehabilitation, 66,* 447–450.

Sullivan, H. S. (1953). *The interpersonal theory of psychiatry.* New York: W. W. Norton.

Walz, T., Harper, D., & Wilson, J. (1986). The aging developmentally disabled person: A review. *Gerontologist, 26,* 622–629.

Wykle, M. (1984). Exercise and depression among the elderly. *Teaching Nursing Home Newsletter, 4,* 1.

Wykle, M. H. (1986). Mental health nursing: Research in nursing homes. In M. S. Harper & B. D. Lebowitz (Eds.), *Mental illness in nursing homes: Agenda for research* (pp. 221–234). Rockville, MD: National Institute of Mental Health.

15

Rehabilitation and Dementia of the Alzheimer's Type

Gary L. Gottlieb

Dementia of the Alzheimer's type (DAT) is now recognized widely as an important illness affecting function and quality of life, especially in the elderly (Reisberg, 1983). In its severe form, dementia affects more than 5% of people over 65 years of age. Additionally, mild to moderate dementia probably afflicts an additional 10% to 15% of this population (Schneck, Reisberg, & Ferris, 1982). Between 50% and 70% of all dementias are thought to be caused by DAT. This illness is characterized by an irreversible and progressive decline in cognitive and functional abilities. All aspects of DAT must be understood in functional terms. Therefore, this disorder must be considered a condition in the domain of rehabilitation. However, rehabilitation efforts must be tertiary in nature: retained assets must be optimized, excess disability must be palliated, and family and systems issues must be addressed proactively.

Until recently the clinical characteristics of this illness had not received adequate attention. Therefore, rational rehabilitation strategies for patients with DAT and for their caregivers have not been developed.

DAT has now been studied systematically, and a descriptive phenomenology of this disorder has emerged. These data provide a framework for long-term management of afflicted individuals. This chapter will synthesize existing knowledge of the course of DAT and its effects on cognition, function, and behavior to derive a treatment strategy in the tradition of rehabilitation. Experimental attempts to enhance cognition with behavioral and cognitive psychological approaches will not be addressed. Similarly, research efforts assessing the effects of chemical agents on the neurodegenerative process will not be discussed.

THE CLINICAL PRESENTATION—DIAGNOSTIC ISSUES

A standard description of the clinical presentation of DAT is provided by the American Psychiatric Association (1980, 1987) *Diagnostic and Statistical Manual* (DSM-III) and its recent revision (DSM-III-R):

> The essential feature is the presence of dementia of insidious onset and gradual progressive course for which all other specific causes have been excluded by the history, physical examination, and laboratory tests. The dementia involves a multifaceted loss of intellectual abilities such as memory, judgment, abstract thought, and other higher cortical functions, and changes in personality and behavior.

DSM-III-R describes the course of the disease:

> The onset is insidious, and the course is one of uniform, gradual progression. In the early stages, memory impairment may be the only apparent cognitive deficit. There may also be subtle personality changes, such as the development of apathy, lack of spontaneity, and a quiet withdrawal from social interactions. Individuals usually remain neat and well groomed and, aside from an occasional irritable outburst, are cooperative and behave in a socially appropriate way.

> With progression to the middle stage of the disease, various cognitive disturbances become quite apparent, and behavior and personality are more obviously affected. By the late state, the individual may be completely mute and inattentive. At this point he or she is totally incapable of caring for himself or herself. This stage leads inevitably to death. With senile onset, the average duration of symptoms, from onset to death, is about five years. (American Psychiatric Association, 1980, 1987, p. 103)

This definition and subsequent descriptions of DAT (McKhann et al., 1984) are accurate but limited in scope and clinical applicability. They do not adequately describe the trajectory of disability imposed by this disorder. Details of the functional decline associated with DAT are essential to the development of a true rehabilitative effort. Additionally, several key clinical issues are not addressed:

1. The DSM-III-R definition of dementia is so broad that clinicians could legitimately consider a large proportion of the older adult popu-

lation to be a victim of this disorder. The clinician's judgment regarding "a multifaceted loss of intellectual abilities" needs to be supplemented by objective criteria. This will allow homogeneous client populations to be identified.

The need to enhance the clinical criteria for dementia with objective assessments was recognized by the National Institute of Neurological and Communication Disorders and Stroke (NINCDS-ADRDA) Work Group (McKhann et al., 1984). Their report suggests a number of criteria that could be used to define dementia. However, specific operational criteria are not recommended for mental status, functional ability, or other clinical assessments. The NINCDS-ADRDA Work Group suggests that

> a score (on psychometric assessments) falling in the lowest fifth percentile of an individual's normal control group (matched for age, sex, and local education), may be designated as "abnormal." One or more abnormal scores will identify an individual for research purposes who is highly likely to be cognitively impaired. Progressive worsening can be established by comparison with the patient's previous performance on these tests.

More distinct definitions of dementia are required for the purpose of planning treatment strategies for afflicted individuals and their families. Useful parameters are necessary for newly evaluated individuals for whom precise longitudinal data on particular psychometric tests over several years may not be available. Additionally, more specific descriptions of the functional concomitants of dementia and the associated trajectory of disability are necessary.

2. DSM-III-R provides no precise information that the clinician can use to distinguish normal aged persons from clients with DAT. The NINCDS-ADRDA criteria begin to clarify this issue. They suggest areas of impairment, including "deficits in two or more areas of cognition" and "impaired activities of daily living and altered patterns of behavior." However, more detailed descriptions of the nature of functional impairment are required for rehabilitation purposes.

3. Although DSM-III-R describes the progression of symptoms through early, middle, and late stages, clearer descriptions of the phenomenology of disease severity are necessary to establish expected individual functional and decision-making abilities.

4. Although DSM-III-R estimates the "average duration of symptoms, from onset to death," more precise data regarding the expected duration of illness and the course of progressive decline are necessary for ongoing evaluation of functional capacity and for family and support network planning.

5. DSM-III-R regards the diagnosis of DAT as dependent on exclusion of other etiologies of dementia. This is not satisfactory. This disorder can be defined with inclusion criteria derived from the known nature of the illness process. Exclusion criteria can then be applied systematically. In this way, illnesses that are similar to DAT can be ruled out for the purposes of consistent functional assessment and exploitation of retained assets.

The NINCDS-ADRDA report made important progress in this regard. It provides criteria for possible, probable, and definite DAT. Exclusionary criteria are detailed, and general inclusionary criteria are suggested. However, to optimize autonomous function and to limit caregiver stress, more definitive criteria are necessary.

Recent intensive study of DAT and its progressive course permits clinicians to approach cognitive impairment more rationally. Greater understanding of the longitudinal progression of intellectual decline and its behavioral concomitants allows health care providers to anticipate changes in function. This insight can support the enhancement of retained assets and the prevention of some morbid outcomes.

A summary of current knowledge regarding the definition of dementia, the staging of DAT, the stage-specific prognosis of the disorder, and inclusion criteria will be employed to describe the trajectory of the disability caused by DAT. Accepted functional and cognitive descriptive phenomenology will be used as a framework for rehabilitative approaches.

NORMAL AGING, ALZHEIMER'S DISEASE, AND A FRAMEWORK FOR REHABILITATION

Reisberg and his colleagues (1985, 1986) studied longitudinally a large sample of older adults and clients who met NINCDS/ADRDA criteria for probable DAT. They followed 106 community-residing subjects (mean age, 70.6 years; range, 60–83 years) over a mean 3.6-year interval (range, 2.8–5.1 years). Subjects were assessed functionally, neuropsychologically, and behaviorally at regular intervals over the course of the study. These data and the clinical aspects of function during normal aging and in progressive DAT provide substantial evidence for defining disease boundaries, for prognostic purposes, and for rehabilitative initiatives. Employing this continuum, Reisberg and associates (Reisberg, Ferris, DeLeon, & Crook, 1982) identify seven distinguishable stages:

No Cognitive Decline

Clients are normal clinically; they have no complaints of cognitive difficulties. A clinical interview does not demonstrate evidence of memory deficit. Adaptation to the physical and developmental challenges of aging should be nurtured by health care providers, by family, and by employers. Addressing the losses and stressors associated with the normal aging process may be useful in prevention of dysphoria, social isolation, and inappropriate withdrawal from challenging activities.

Very Mild Cognitive Decline (Forgetfulness Phase)

Clients complain of difficulties with memory. Often they report forgetting where they have placed familiar objects and forgetting well-known names. Clinical examination does not reveal evidence of memory impairment. No objective deficits in employment or in social situations are manifested. Rigorous functional assessment generally fails to demonstrate a decline in competence.

All 40 subjects at this stage who were followed longitudinally in the study described were alive and community-residing at follow-up. Ninety-five percent of these individuals were not notably worsened in their clinical and cognitive abilities (notable change was defined by movement of two stages within this scale) (Reisberg et al., 1985, 1986). Subjective forgetfulness of this severity appears to be consistent with the normal aging process (Bergmann, 1985; Mortimer, 1983; Mortimer, Schuman, & French, 1981).

Individuals at this phase display appropriate concern about their symptoms. Even minor changes in cognitive function may trigger considerable anxiety and self-doubt. Highly skilled workers may question their abilities in performing complex tasks even when no diminution in function is evident. "Self-testing" and frequent quizzing by a concerned spouse provoke further uncertainty. Anxiety may impair concentration, thereby "confirming" the fear.

Individualized assessment requires a detailed understanding of the functional requirements of everyday life. Strategies for minimizing the stress and the dependence on memory function for specific tasks may improve confidence and productivity. Educational interventions should reinforce the normative nature of early forgetfulness and the futility of constant testing behaviors. Psychotherapeutic interventions may be useful in reducing anxiety and in diminishing fears and exaggerated preoccupation with potentially catastrophic outcomes. For example, cognitive behavior therapy (Beck, Rush, Shaw, & Emery, 1979) may improve affective responses to dysfunctional "automatic thinking" stimulated by a perceived decline in cognitive ability. Similarly, educational and supportive interactions with spouses, companions, and colleagues can reduce constant scrutiny of cognitive function when it is unnecessary and potentially destructive. These interventions focus on alleviation of excess disability: that component of dysfunction not attributable to limitations in functional capacity.

Mild Cognitive Decline (Early Confusional Phase)

At this stage objective evidence of memory impairment is demonstrated only through an intensive interview. This evaluation should include a structured mental status examination (Kahn, Goldfarb, Pallack, & Peck, 1960; Jacobs, Bernhard, Delgado, & Strain, 1977; Pfeiffer, 1975; Folstein, Folstein, & McHugh, 1975), a functional assessment, and other formal clinical cognitive assessments (Cole, Dastoor, & Koszyck, 1983; Reisberg, Schneck, Ferris, Schwartz, & DeLeon, 1983). Concentration deficits may also be evident on clinical testing. Occasionally, clients may have difficulty in remembering the names of people whom they have just met.

Decreased performance becomes apparent in demanding employment and social situations. Difficulties in finding words and in remembering names may compound these frustrations. Important objects are often lost or misplaced. Clients may get seriously lost when traveling to unfamiliar places. However, the ability to travel to well-known locations is preserved.

Of 32 individuals with this level of impairment who were followed prospectively by Reisberg and his colleagues (1985, 1986), one was deceased, one was institutionalized, and three were notably worse at follow-up. However, more than 85% of these individuals were *not* notably worse at follow-up, and more than half performed as well or better in several domains of function. Therefore, Reisberg et al. suggest that this stage may represent a border area consistent with the earliest manifestations of DAT in some cases. However, clinicians cannot make any diagnosis with great confidence at this phase.

A comprehensive assessment of function is necessary to determine the extent of retained assets. Highly challenging tasks at work and at home may become impossible or dangerous. Whenever possible, these functions should be evaluated directly. Overlearned skills are generally preserved, and they should be exploited. However, structuring of responsibilities and clear definition of expectations are necessary to reduce uncertainty. For example, a former accountant or bookkeeper will likely retain the ability to perform arithmetic calculations at this stage. Bill paying may reinforce self-esteem and autonomy for these individuals. However, for the first time, checklists, a limit in the number of bills to be paid at a given time, and review by a spouse may be necessary to ensure success. Similarly, a daily calendar, list making, written directions, and a medication distribution system may be useful.

Mild to moderate anxiety frequently accompanies the decline in cognition and in function. Anxiety may worsen if clients are forced to cope with employment and social demands that they had previously found to be challenging but that they are no longer capable of negotiating. In particular, individuals who rely heavily on cognitive skills to function socially and vocationally may become disabled by anxiety. Anxiety is more prevalent and more severe at this stage than it is during the forgetfulness phase. Additionally, this degree of anxiety may impair cognitive function to a greater extent. Psychotherapeutic interventions may palliate some of the behaviors that contribute to uncertainty, self-doubt, and agitation. However, very anxious cognitively impaired people may not be accessible to traditional therapeutic modalities unless adjuvant pharmacotherapy is employed.

Pharmacotherapeutic interventions for treatment of anxiety in even mildly cognitively impaired individuals requires ongoing assessment of risk and benefit. Benzodiazepine anxiolytics are central nervous system (CNS) depressants. Lucki & Rickels (1988) have demonstrated that these agents cause cognitive impairment acutely in young unimpaired anxious subjects. Additionally, some impaired individuals may become disinhibited behaviorally in response to CNS depression (Salzman, 1984). Metabolic changes associated with aging may increase the elimination half-life of benzodiazepines and increase the accumulation of active metabolites long after administration (Stoudemire & Fogel, 1987). Therefore, considerable caution is required when these drugs are employed in mildly cognitively impaired elderly patients. However, when anxiety is disabling and it clearly interferes with function and cognition, pharmacologic symptom reduction may be useful. Prior to initiation of a course of benzodiazepines, sensitive measures of observed function and behavior should be obtained. Short-acting agents (e.g., lorazepam, oxazepam, alprazolam) that are easily metabolized and have *no* active metabolites are preferable. Minuscule doses should be employed only intermittently, on an as needed (prn) basis. Functional and behavioral instruments should be readministered at regular intervals. This protocol will allow ongoing assessment of the utility of drug treatment and of potential adverse consequences.

Buspirone, a non-benzodiazepine anxiolytic was introduced recently. Although this agent does not affect cognition acutely in young healthy subjects (Lucki & Rickels, 1988), its CNS effects on cognitively impaired older adults have not been assessed. Buspirone requires chronic administration, and anxiolytic effects are attained only after 2 to 6 weeks of administration. Cautious use of this drug may be a worthwhile alternative in very anxious individuals at this stage of impairment.

Moderate Cognitive Decline (Late Confusional Phase)

At this stage, impairment is manifested in numerous functional and cognitive domains: clients exhibit diminished ability to recall recent events in their lives and current events in society. In contrast to conventional wisdom, clients also display a deficit in the ability to recall personal history accurately. Concentration impairment is evident on direct testing. Traveling alone may become frustrating and dangerous. Difficulties in management of personal finances may endanger personal and family welfare.

At this stage, clients cannot perform complex tasks accurately and efficiently. However, certain important abilities are usually preserved. Clients remain well oriented to time and person. Familiar persons and faces can be distinguished readily from strangers. There is generally no deficit in the ability to travel to familiar locations.

Reisberg et al. (1985, 1986) followed 22 clients in this late confusional phase longitudinally. Six of these individuals had died, six others were institutionalized, and four DAT victims followed from this stage were community-residing but notably worse on follow-up. Only six individuals seen initially at this phase had not declined notably at follow-up. None of the clients who were at this level of impairment at baseline demonstrated clinically notable cognitive or functional improvement at follow-up.

These observations suggest an operational definition of the boundaries between the normal aging process and DAT. More than two thirds of the individuals who were followed at the fourth stage had progressed substantially at follow-up. In contrast, 90% of those people who were staged initially in the two milder phases of impairment did not progress significantly. Therefore, for rehabilitative and prognostic purposes, this fourth stage is the earliest phase in which DAT may be diagnosed with *relative* uncertainty (N.B.: only a tissue diagnosis, obtained most humanely postmortem, can "confirm" this diagnosis!)

Caregiver support and appropriate planning must be intensified at this stage. Independent living situations must be evaluated for their appropriateness. If they are available, family members must be mobilized to plan and to share the potential burden of care. Legal and financial issues must be addressed so that autonomy, personal liberty, and retained functional assets can be preserved and protected. Some caregiver respite may be necessary. However, family and caregiver denial may prevent initiation of some of these interventions. For example, Reisberg, Gordon, and McCarthy (1985) found that caregiver denial often parallels patient denial in the relatively early stages of the dementing process. Considering the overwhelming loss faced by individuals and their loved ones, some denial may be an adaptive response. Therefore, supportive and directive psychotherapeutic interventions for the family and a potential system of care may be necessary to initiate a comprehensive treatment plan.

Although denial may protect the affected individual from fully conscious recognition and acceptance of the nature of the loss associated with this disorder, depression may complicate the presentation. At this phase in particular, depressive symptoms can affect quality of life adversely and contribute substantial potentially treatable excess disability. Additionally, despair among caregivers may diminish the viability of a network of support. This may affect individual function adversely.

Several studies have examined the prevalence of depression and depressive symptoms in patients with DAT and other dementias: Miller (1980) found that a majority of ambulatory elderly patients with "senile dementias" of various etiologies were mildly to moderately depressed. In two separate studies, Reifler et al. (Reifler, Larson, & Hanley, 1982; 1986) found prevalence rates of 19% and 31% of major depressive disorder in geriatric outpatients with cognitive impairment. Lazarus, Newton, Cohler, Lesser, and Schweon (1987) and Merriam, Aronson, Gaston, Wey, and Katz (1988) studied large samples of well-diagnosed ambulatory patients with probable DAT. Data provided by caregivers in those studies suggest prevalence rates for depression in DAT of 40% and 86%, respectively. Other studies have reported clinically significant depression in 15% to 57% of DAT patients (Kral, 1983).

Depressive symptoms may be difficult to distinguish from a full-blown major depression in dementia victims. People with major depressive disorder, DAT, or both disorders simultaneously, may experience psychomotor retardation, difficulties with sleep, appetite disturbance, social withdrawal, apathy, and constricted affect (Miller, 1980). Although the studies cited support the importance of depressive symptoms in clients with DAT, diagnostic difficulties may underlie the range of prevalence estimates. For some clients, depressive symptoms may be part of the process of deterioration in DAT. For others, episodes of major depression may be superimposed on the degenerative process. Dysphoria is an integral part of some syndromes of dementia. It has been suggested that mood disturbance may be a direct consequence of brain damage (Meyers & Alexopoulos, 1988); Reifler et al., 1982, 1986). This effect has been demonstrated in depressive syndromes following stroke (Robinson, Lipsey, & Price, 1985; Robinson, Starr, & Kubos, 1983).

Depression has been shown to cause difficulties with motivation in the physical rehabilitation process (Kemp, 1986). This may be complicated by reluctance of third-party payers to reimburse rehabilitation services for "poorly motivated" clients. These clients may become stranded at a suboptimal level of function.

The literature regarding treatment of depression in dementia is growing rapidly. Although it is premature to draw conclusions from the small number of available clinical trials, there is some evidence that affective symptoms may improve with antidepressant treatment of depression in DAT (Reifler et al., 1986). Additionally, family satisfaction and patient well-being and motivation improve with diminution of depressive symptoms. Unquestionably, the disability imposed by DAT affects an entire family or system of care. Reduction of depressive symptoms in the afflicted individual will improve system function. Similarly, control of anxiety and dysphoria in the caregiver(s) may allow the system to thrive and preserve life quality for all involved.

Moderately Severe Cognitive Decline (Early Dementia Phase)

At this stage clients cannot survive without substantial assistance. During interviews they are unable to recall an important aspect of their current lives. They may have difficulty recalling their address or telephone number, the names of some members of their family, or the names of the schools they attended. Frequently, these individuals are somewhat disoriented to time or to place.

Clients at this stage retain knowledge of many key facts regarding themselves and significant others. They generally know their own names and they usually know their spouse's and children's names. They usually require no assistance with toileting or eating, but they may have some difficulty in choosing proper clothing.

Caregiver stress may impose the most important limitations on overall family function at this stage. Spouse caregivers begin to grieve the loss of intimacy, interdependency, and companionship inherent in the cognitive decline of a loved one. Preservation of caregiver health and life quality is essential to optimization of the function of the entire system. As many as 55% of spouse caregivers of patients with DAT suffer significant depressive symptoms over the course of the disease (Cohen & Eisdorfer, 1988).

Respite may reduce perceived caregiver stress. Additionally, structured day programs can provide a predictable, well-structured and nurturant environment for the affected client. Although there are no scientific data available demonstrating improved functional outcomes in day care or respite treatment programs, subjective observations suggest that apathy and withdrawal may diminish with participation. Additionally, Masciocchi, Brody, and Poulshock (1978) demonstrated that day-care programs may improve measures of satisfaction in caregivers.

Environmental consistency is particularly important at this stage. Unfamiliar circumstances may exacerbate agitation and temporarily worsen cognitive function. Reinforcement of overlearned activities and the use of overlearned cues may be useful. Predictable circumstances allow clients to perceive a greater sense of control.

Severe Cognitive Decline (Middementia Phase)

At this stage, clients are generally unable to describe virtually any recent events and experiences in their lives. They may occasionally forget the name of their spouse. However, they retain limited knowledge of their past lives. Clients appear to be oblivious to their surroundings, the year, or the season. They may have difficulty counting or spelling simple words.

At this stage clients require substantial assistance with the activities of daily living. For example, they may become incontinent. Also, they require assistance in traveling. Sometimes they retain the ability to travel to familiar places. Clients almost always recall their own names. Often they continue also to be able to distinguish familiar from unfamiliar persons in their environment.

Behavioral changes occur frequently at this stage. These symptoms vary from individual to individual. Common worrisome behaviors include hallucinations, delusions, combativeness, agitation, negativism, and wandering. These comprise the most common noncognitive excess disability at this stage.

Merriam et al. (1988) found that caregivers of community-residing DAT victims reported significant agitation in 61% of the individuals whom they cared for. They found that perceptual disorders (auditory and visual hallucinations, misinterpretations, and misrecognition of stimuli) were highly correlated with severity of cognitive dysfunction. In a study of a group of outpatients with dementias of various etiologies, Swearer, Drachman, O'Donnell, and Mitchell found "a significant relationship between the severity of dementia and the presence and severity of behavioral disturbances" (p. 786). This finding was confirmed by Rovner, Kafonek, Filipp, Lucas, and Folstein (1986). In their study of community nursing home residents, they found that hallucinations and delusions correlated significantly with severity of dementia and with behavioral disturbance. Controlling for severity of dementia, they also found that residents with delusions and hallucinations were significantly more disordered behaviorally than were individuals without these disturbances. Rovner et al. concluded that psychotic symptoms may be more important determinants of behavioral problems than severity of cognitive impairment. Additionally, at least one study has demonstrated an association between severity of psychosis in clients with DAT and functional deterioration (Mayeux, Stern, & Sano, 1985). These studies support the potential utility of specific psychiatric rehabilitative interventions in reducing morbidity and in improving function for these clients.

Neuroleptic medications are used commonly for remediation of behavioral symptoms in clients with DAT. Comprehensive literature reviews (Devanand, Sackeim, & Mayeux, 1988; Helms, 1985; Risse & Barnes, 1986) suggest that there is little scientific support for the widespread use of these agents: few controlled clinical trials have been performed; diagnostically homogeneous patient samples have been not used; the effects of neuroleptics on cognition and function have not been assessed; and most studies have been performed in institutional settings. A synthesis of existing literature demonstrates that although effects are modest, neoroleptics are superior to placebo in controlling anxiety, suspiciousness, uncooperativeness and hallucinatory behaviors (Devanand et al., 1988; Barnes, Veith, Okimoto, Raskind, & Gumbrecht, 1982; Petrie et al., 1982). However, neuroleptics affect poor self-care, social withdrawal, wandering and cognition minimally (Barnes et al., 1982).

Neuroleptics are most valuable for the management of behavioral disorders associated with dementia, particularly when specific psychiatric symptoms are present. Appropriately prescribed neuroleptics may reduce caregiver stress, delay the need for institutional management, and improve adaptation to new environments. However, extrapyramidal side effects, tardive dyskinesia, sedation, and anticholinergic effects may limit potential functional improvements. Therefore, tiny doses should be employed for short periods of time in the *most* necessary circumstances.

Certain behaviors common to demented clients may be remediable by environmental manipulation. For example, wandering is a symptom that is difficult to manage at home and in institutional settings. Wandering does not appear to respond to pharmacotherapies. In fact, neuroleptics may aggravate this problem by causing akathisia, an extrapyramidal side effect manifested by motor restlessness. Therefore, nonpharmacologic strategies may be more valuable.

From their evaluation of institutionalized clients, Dawson and Reid (1987) found that wanderers were more active physically premorbidly than were nonwanderers. They concluded that wandering may represent an adaptive effort to reduce a specific distressing symptom. They suggested that interventions that addressed the "source" of the wandering may reduce the frequency and the severity of the symptom. Additionally, Dawson and Reid found that wanderer clients had greater difficulty with speech, reading, and orientation. They recommend special activity programs that can be mastered, providing "room to roam," and attempting to optimize cognitive function.

Rader and her colleagues (Rader, 1987; Rader, Doan, & Schwab, 1985) have developed a rehabilitative approach to the management of agitation and wandering. They characterize wandering as an "agenda behavior," and they emphasize an empathic approach tailored to the individual. They maintain that these behaviors are not merely the manifestations of neurological deterioration. They believe that these symptoms represent attempts by clients to recapitulate aspects of their premorbid lives. In an effort to test this hypothesis, Rader et al. constructed a long-term care unit with a high staff-to-client ratio. Staff members were sensitized to the time and attention required to identify and address specific client needs. The investigators placed subtle identification badges on the residents, they allowed substantial freedom of movement, and they developed an emergency procedure to find residents if they got lost. They found that this approach resulted in a diminution of combative episodes by clients and a reduction in injuries to staff over a 3-year period. Wandering individuals were located quickly, and no client injuries were attributable to wandering. This approach is intuitively appealing, and it should be evaluated with a controlled clinical trial. Outcomes should include client function and morbidity as well as the costs and benefits of increased staff time and changes in levels of staff stress.

In another innovative rehabilitation approach, Cleary et al. (1988) developed a "reduced stimulation" unit for DAT victims. Their 16-bed closed unit has a neutral color scheme and has no televisions, radios, or telephones. This milieu provides freedom for walking, eating, and resting wherever the client desires. Consistent daily rest periods and defined small-group activities are employed to structure time. Staff and families are trained to speak slowly and quietly and to provide choices rather than confrontation. Clients, their families, and staff were assessed before the unit opened and 3 months later. Clients sustained a significant improvement in the ability to perform ADL. Although overall behavioral ratings were unchanged, evidence of improved nutritional status and a reduction in the use of restraints and tranquilizing medications were demonstrated. Additionally, family satisfaction improved significantly.

This innovative model addresses patient, family, and staff issues in a tertiary rehabilitation effort for dementia clients. Although it is too small to generalize, pilot data are adequately encouraging to suggest the need for a controlled clinical trial.

These innovative initiatives are exciting contributions to the rehabilitation of clients with dementia. Larger demonstration projects to assess the generalizability of these models and their outcomes should be pursued.

Very Severe Cognitive Decline (Late Dementia Phase)

At this stage clients progressively lose overlearned language skills. As the disease progresses, all speech ability is lost and, ultimately, autonomous ambulation is lost. In those patients who survive, skills required to sit up, smile, and hold up one's head deteriorate (Reisberg, 1986; Reisberg, Ferris, & Franssen, 1985). Medical comorbidities and complications of DAT frequently cause death prior to this stage (Reisberg, 1983). However, even at this terminal phase, rehabilitation efforts, focused on family adaptation and the grieving process, are necessary.

SUMMARY

At present, the progressive course of decline caused by DAT is inevitable. Although remarkable advances in understanding the pathophysiology of this disorder have been made, the primary degenerative process remains untreatable. However, descriptive phenomenology and longitudinal study have provided a framework for rehabilitation: illness boundaries are now definable and stage-specific excess disability can be anticipated. This information allows active treatment to optimize function throughout the trajectory of disability. These data also reaffirm this deteriorating process as fertile turf for rehabilitation. Rational rehabilitation strategies may prolong preservation of retained assets and improve short-term functional outcomes. These considerations are essential in the development of appropriate care plans for individuals and of appropriate health policy for the aging population.

REFERENCES

American Psychiatric Association. (1980). *Diagnostic and statistical manual of mental disorders* (3d. ed.). Washington, DC: Author.
American Psychiatric Association. (1987). *Diagnostic and statistical manual of mental disorders* (3d ed., rev.). Washington, DC: Author.

Barnes, R. Veith, R., Okimoto, J., Raskind, M., & Gumbrecht, G. (1982). Efficacy of antipsychotic medications in behaviorally disturbed dementia patients. *American Journal of Psychiatry, 139,* 1170–1174.

Beck, A. T., Rush, A. J., Shaw, B. F., & Emery, G. (1979). *Cognitive therapy of depression.* New York: Guilford Press.

Bergmann, K. (1985). Epidemiological aspects of dementia and considerations in planning services. *Danish Medical Bulletin, 32*(Suppl. 1), 84–91.

Cleary, T. A., Clamon, C., Price, M., et al. (1988). A reduced stimulation unit: Effects on patients with Alzheimer's disease and related disorders. *Gerontologist, 28,* 511–514.

Cohen D., & Eisdorfer, C. (1988). Depression in family members caring for a relative with Alzheimer's disease. *Journal of the American Geriatrics Society, 36,* 885–889.

Cole, M. G., Dastoor, D. P., & Koszyck, D. (1983). The Hierarchic Dementia Scale. *Journal of Clinical and Experimental Gerontology, 5,* 219–234.

Dawson, P., & Reid, D. W. (1987). Behavioral dimensions of patients at risk of wandering. *Gerontologist, 27,* 104–107.

Devanand, D. P., Sackeim, H. A., & Mayeux, R. (1988). Psychosis, behavioral disturbance, and the use of neuroleptics in dementia. *Comprehensive Psychiatry, 29,* 387–401.

Folstein, M. F., Folstein, S. E., & McHugh, P. R. (1975). Mini-Mental-State: A practical method for grading the cognitive stage of patients for the clinician. *Journal of Psychiatric Research, 12,* 189–198.

Helms, P. M. (1985). Efficacy of antipsychotics in the treatment of the behavioral complications of dementia: A review of the literature. *Journal of the American Geriatrics Society, 33,* 206–209.

Jacobs, J. W., Bernhard, M. R., Delgado, A., & Strain, J. F. (1977). Screening for organic mental syndromes in the mentally ill. *Annals of Internal Medicine, 80,* 40–46.

Kahn, R. L., Goldfarb, A. I., Pollack, M., & Peck, A. (1960). Brief objective measures for the determination of mental status in the aged. *American Journal of Psychiatry, 117,* 326–328.

Kemp, B. (1986). Psychosocial and mental health issues in rehabilitation of older persons. In S. J. Brody & G. E. Ruff (Eds.), *Aging and rehabilitation: Advances in the state of the art.* New York: Springer Publishing Co.

Kral, V. A. (1983). The relationship between senile dementia (Alzheimer type) and depression. *Canadian Journal of Psychiatry, 28,* 304–306.

Lazarus, L. W., Newton, N., Cohler, B., Lesser, J., & Schweon, C. (1987). Frequency and presentation of depressive symptoms in patients with primary degenerative dementia. *American Journal of Psychiatry, 144,* 41–45.

Lucki, I. & Rickels, K. (1988). The effect of anxiolytic drugs on memory in anxious subjects. *Psychopharmacology Ser., 6,* 128–139.

Masciocchi, C., Brody, S. J., & Poulshock, S. W. (1978, November). *Assessment of geriatric day hospital clients compared to normative criterion groups.* Paper presented at the 31st Annual Scientific Meeting of the Gerontological Society, Dallas, TX. [Abstract, *Gerontologist, 18*(5, Part 2).]

Mayeux, R., Stern, Y., & Sano, M. (1985). Heterogeneity and prognosis in dementia of the Alzheimer type. *Bulletin of Clinical Neuroscience, 50,* 7–10.

McKhann, G., Drachman, D., Folstein, M., Katzman, R., Price, D., & Stadlar, E. M. (1984). Clinical diagnosis of Alzheimer's disease: Report of the NINCDS-ADRDA Work Group under the auspices of Department of Health and Human Service Task Force on Alzheimer's Disease. *Neurology* (Cleveland), *34*, 939–944.

Merriam, A. E., Aronson, M. K., Gaston, P., Wey, S., & Katz, I. (1988). The psychiatric symptoms of Alzheimer's disease. *Journal of the American Geriatrics Society, 36*, 7–12.

Meyers, B. S., & Alexopoulos, G. (1988). Age of onset and studies of late-life depression. *International Journal of Geriatric Psychiatry, 3*, 219–228.

Miller, N. E. (1980). The measurement of mood in senile brain disease: Examiner ratings and self reports. In J. O. Cole & J. E. Barrett (Eds.), *Psychopathology in the aged.* New York: Raven Press.

Mortimer, J. A. (1983). Alzheimer's disease and senile dementia: Prevalence and incidence. In B. Reisberg (Ed.), *Alzheimer's disease: The standard reference* (pp. 141–148). New York: Free Press/Macmillan.

Mortimer, J. A., Schuman, L. M., & French, L. R. (1981). Epidemiology of dementing illness. In J. A. Mortimer & L. M. Schuman (Eds.), *Epidemiology of dementia* (pp. 3–23). New York: Oxford University Press.

Petrie, W. M., Ban, T. A., Berney, S., et al. (1982). Loxapine in psychogeriatrics: A placebo- and standard-controlled clinical investigation. *Journal of Clinical Psychopharmacology, 2*, 122–126.

Pfeiffer, E. A. (1975). Short Portable Mental Status Questionnaire for the assessment of organic brain dysfunction in the elderly. *Journal of the American Geriatrics Society, 23*, 433–441.

Rader, J. (1987). A comprehensive staff approach to problem wandering. *Gerontologist, 27*, 756–760.

Rader, J., Doan, J., & Schwab, M. (1985). How to decrease wandering, a form of agenda behavior. *Geriatric Nursing, 6*, 196–199.

Reifler, B. V., Larson, E., & Hanley, R. (1982). Coexistence of cognitive impairment and depression in geriatric outpatients. *American Journal of Psychiatry, 139*, 623–626.

Reifler, B. V., Larson, E., Teri, L., & Poulsen, M. (1986). Dementia of the Alzheimer's type and depression. *Journal of the American Geriatrics Society, 34*, 855–859.

Reisberg, B. (1983). *Alzheimer's disease: The standard reference.* New York: Free Press/Macmillan.

Reisberg, B. (1986). A systematic approach to identifying reversible causes. *Geriatrics, 41*, 30–46.

Reisberg, B., Ferris, S. H., DeLeon, M. J., & Crook, T. (1982). The Global Deterioration Scale for assessment of primary degenerative dementia. *American Journal of Psychiatry, 139*, 1136–1139.

Reisberg, B., Ferris, S. H., DeLeon, M. J., & Crook, T. (1985). Age-associated cognitive decline and Alzheimer's disease: Implications for assessment and treatment. In M. Bergener, M. Ermini, & H. B. Stahelin (Eds.), *Thresholds in aging* (pp. 255–292). London: Academic Press.

Reisberg, B., Ferris, S. H., & Franssen, E. (1985). An ordinal functional assessment tool for Alzheimer's type dementia. (1985). *Hospital and Community Psychiatry, 36*, 593–595.

Reisberg, B., Ferris, S. H., Shulman, E., Sternberg, G., Buttinger, L., Sinaik, E., Borenstein, J., DeLeon, M. J., & Cohen, J. (1986). Longitudinal course of normal aging and progressive dementia of the Alzheimer's type: A prospective study of 106 subjects over a 3.6 year mean interval. *Progress in Neuro-Psychopharmacology and Biological Psychiatry, 10*, 571–578.

Reisberg, B., Gordon, B., & McCarthy, M. (1985). Insight and denial accompanying progressive cognitive decline in normal aging and Alzheimer's disease. In B. Stanley (Ed.), *Geriatric psychiatry: Ethical and legal issues.* Washington, DC: APA Press.

Reisberg, B., Schneck, M. K., Ferris, S. H., Schwartz, G. E., & DeLeon, M. J. (1983). The Brief Cognitive Rating Scale (BCRS): Findings in primary degenerative dementia (PDD). *Psychopharmacology Bulletin, 19*, 47–50.

Risse, S. C., & Barnes, R. (1986). Pharmacologic treatment of agitation associated with dementia. *Journal of the American Geriatrics Society, 34*, 368–376.

Robinson, R. G., Lipsey, J. R., & Price, T. R. (1985). Diagnosis and clinical management of post-stroke depression. *Psychosomatics, 26*, 769–778.

Robinson, R. G., Starr, L. B., & Kubos, K. L. (1983). A two-year longitudinal study of post-stroke mood disorders: Findings during the initial evaluation. *Stroke, 14*, 736–741.

Rovner, B. W., Kafonek, S., Filipp, L., Lucas, M. J., & Folstein, M. F. (1986). Prevalence of mental illness in a community nursing home. *American Journal of Psychiatry, 143*, 1446–1449.

Salzman, C. (1984). Treatment of anxiety. In C. Salzman (Ed.), *Clinical geriatric psychopharmacology.* New York: McGraw-Hill.

Schneck, M. K., Reisberg, B., & Ferris, S. H. (1982). An overview of current concepts of Alzheimer's disease. *American Journal of Psychiatry, 139*, 165–173.

Stoudemire, A., & Fogel, B. S. (1987). Psychopharmacology in the medically ill. In A. Stoudemire & B. S. Fogel (Eds.), *Principles of medical psychiatry.* Orlando, FL: Grune and Stratton.

Swearer, J. M., Drachman, D. A., O'Donnell, B. F., & Mitchell, A. L., (1988). Troublesome and disruptive behaviors in dementia: Relationships to diagnosis and disease severity. *Journal of the American Geriatrics Society, 36*, 784–790.

16

Management of Pain: A Necessary Adjunct to Enhancing Mobility

Mathew H. M. Lee and Masayoshi Itoh

The interrelationship of pain and mobility, as one grows older, presents a complex problem that heretofore has not been examined in the literature as critically as it should have been. Each problem has its own set of approaches for management and enhancement of therapeutic results. When compounded with the physiological changes of aging, the immobilization syndrome, multiple medical diagnoses, and drug interactions to achieve maximum pain reduction and to maintain maximum mobility require careful analysis and planning (Itoh, Lee, Eason, Herring, & Rybsteen-Blinchik, 1984).

This chapter will discuss the epidemiology of pain; its classification, measurement, and treatment approaches; and basic geriatric rehabilitation principles to enhance maximum functioning in activities of daily living (ADL).

PAIN

As we approach the end of the 20th century, the mass media is inundated with reports of drug abuse, crime, homelessness, hunger, and war all over the world. However, it is recognized that, even in a utopian society, humans cannot avoid death and pain. Although death can be viewed as a final resolution and rest, pain is the hallmark of human suffering, requiring an enormous financial input to cure, control, and prevent.

Pain, an extremely complex phenomenon experienced by almost all human beings at one time or another, is still very difficult to define. The English language contains an assortment of words to define pain: ache, smart, twinge, twitch, throe, throb, and so on, each having a somewhat different connotation. Quantitatively, an even wider variety of words can be employed to describe pain's characteristics: excruciating, sharp, dull, throbbing, annoying, and so on.

Webster's New World Dictionary defines pain as a "sensation of feeling when hurt, mentally or physically, especially distress, suffering, great anxiety, anguish, grief" or "a sensation of hurting, or strong discomfort, in some part of the body caused by an injury, disease, or functional disorder and transmitted through the nervous system." *Dorland's Medical Dictionary* defines pain as "a more or less localized sensation of discomfort, distress, or agony, resulting from the stimulation of specialized nerve endings." Benjamin Crue et al. (1979) defines pain as anything that the patient says it is, illustrating the great difficulty involved in managing certain types of pain in a clinical setting.

Although, traditionally, pain has been considered a sensation originating from a sensory nerve ending, a variety of clinical presentations that do not originate from the periphery have been identified, creating disparity among the experts. Two schools of thought have emerged: peripheralist and centralist. For our purposes, we will define pain as the "host's perception or recognition of a noxious sensation," thus differentiating it from "nociperception," which is the system's perception of injurious or traumatic stimuli. One may argue that a noxious sensation need not be limited to pain but may refer to a certain odor, loud noise, extreme temperature, and the like. With an emphasis on perception or recognition rather than a noxious sensation, we have a working definition for the epidemiology of pain.

Epidemiology of Pain

As the term suggests, epidemiology originally dealt with infectious diseases in terms of their cause, propagation, and final outcome. However, decades of experience have proved that the same investigatory method can be applied to all types of disease conditions. Thus, the modern concept of epidemiology is a study of the distribution of a disease or condition in a population and of the factors that influence this distribution.

In epidemiology it is widely recognized that the causation of an illness or condition requires the simultaneous interaction of three causative factors: host, agent, and environment. Although enkephalin and endorphin studies indicate that invertebrates may experience pain, our discussion will confine itself to the human as host.

Host characteristics that may have a direct or an indirect effect on the formation of pain are indicated in Table 16-1.

Many variables are involved in determining the host factors. Although studies have shown that a person's pain threshold rises with age, there is no agreement on the pain threshold in women as opposed to men. Furthermore, in certain cultures the free expression of pain is not regarded as appropriate behavior; therefore, pain tolerance or susceptibility is not accurately represented by self-expression. The expression of pain may sometimes be a tool for gaining attention.

With reference to the epidemiology of pain, the agent is sometimes referred to as the noxious stimulus. Although the primary agent is external and is responsible for acute pain, the secondary agent is responsible for the recovery stage of acute pain and perhaps chronic pain. Regardless of the nature of the agent (Table 16-2), the host perceives pain without distinction.

Quantity/dose, duration, and frequency are applicable to both the primary and secondary agent and determine whether the noxious stimulus will pass the pain threshold.

If pain is the host's reaction to the primary or secondary agent, then perhaps the previously stated causation-of-illness theory cannot be applied to pain. It may be perceived that the interaction between the host and the agent can produce pain, and thus the third factor, environment, has no place in the epidemiological triad. Therefore, the following example is offered. At the moment a bullet penetrates a soldier's body, the soldier should feel extreme pain. However, often pain is not felt until the blood from the wound is seen. In a case such as this, the soldier is in a very special environment—the battlefield—and thus the

Table 16-1 Host Factors of Pain[a]

Physical	Psychological
Visual acuity	Memory
Coordination	Judgment
Pain tolerance	Experience
Body constitution, genetic	Educational, cultural
Age	Dependency
Sex	Anxiety
	Expectation
	Ego strength, coping ability

[a]Itoh et al. (1984).

Table 16-2   Agent Factors of Pain[a]

Primary agent	Secondary agent
Mechanical	Pathophysiological
Chemical	Psychogenic
Electrical	Quantity/dose
Thermal	Duration
Radiation	Frequency
Infectious	
Inflammatory	
Oncogenic	

[a] Itoh et al. (1984).

simple interaction between the host and the agent does not produce pain. The environmental factors of pain are listed in Table 16-3.

Although the physical environment is usually more directly related to the primary agent, or acute pain, than to the secondary agent, chronic pain, it is often recognized that humidity and/or climate have an effect on the latter.

Classification of Pain

Clinically, pain is usually classified as acute, chronic, or malignant (e.g., pain from a malignant tumor). It should be emphasized that this classification is strictly clinical, not epidemiological. A clinical approach

Table 16-3   Environmental Factors of Pain[a]

Physical
Meteorological (climate, temperature, humidity, etc.)
Visibility (darkness, light, etc.)
Condition of ground or floor
Noise level
Psychological
Relationship with family and/or friends
Social norm
Political (judicial)
Mechanization
Economic and occupational
Disability and compensation
Job market
Enforcement of occupational safety

[a] Itoh et al. (1984).

to acute, chronic, and malignant pain is quite distinct from that of an epidemiological approach.

Epidemiologically, the terms *acute* and *chronic* are used in relation to the time period involved. Acute pain is usually characterized by sudden onset and short duration, whereas chronic pain usually refers to a condition lasting for an indefinite period. With approriate treatment, the duration of acute pain, with its sudden onset and frequently great severity, is empirically predictable.

The course of chronic pain, on the other hand, may vary; its severity may fluctuate and its duration is not predictable. The most common type of chronic pain is the acute-chronic type: an individual initially experiences an episode of acute pain, but the pain persists far beyond the empirically predictable period. However, the severity of the pain usually diminishes from that experienced during the acute phase.

The second type of chronic pain is the chronic recurrent model: mild to moderate pain begins gradually, without an acute pain episode and with or without a clinically identifiable cause, and subsides with or without treatment. At a later date a similar pain sensation manifests in the same manner as the previous one, with such episodes repeated thereafter.

In acute pain the agent factor is usually identifiable, whereas the agent factor in chronic pain may or may not be identifiable.

In the clinical classification of pain, acute and chronic pain are quite similar to the epidemiological classification. However, malignant pain does not fit either model, as its agent factor is known; its onset is not sudden but more often gradual. The pain is usually very severe and its duration is indefinite. Clinical management of this type of pain is shown in Table 16-4.

State of Aponia

Aponia is a Greek word meaning "freedom from pain." A state of *aponia* is a condition under which one does not perceive pain in spite of the

Table 16-4   Management of Pain

Clinical Management	Acute	Chronic	Malignant
Surgery	As indicated	Often no	No
Narcotics	Limited use	No	Unlimited use
Mild analgesics	As indicated	Very useful	No effect
Physical therapy	Sometimes	Often indicated	Very limited usefulness

presence of painful stimuli or the simultaneous interaction of the three causative factors of pain. This condition can be created artifically by means of general or local anesthesia.

In the illustration of environmental factors, a wounded soldier in the battlefield has already been described. A question such as "Is such human behavior limited to a battlefield?" or "Is the environment alone responsible for such behavior?" must be answered.

Similar episodes occur in civilian life. In 1977 three similar cases, all involving females, were reported in the newspapers. Two women who were involved in separate train accidents and one in an automobile accident had one or more extremities severed and later restored by microsurgery. The most striking feature in the newspaper accounts was that these women did not complain of any pain. One responded, "My hand." The second said, "Let me get up, I will be all right." The third woman was reported to have had a smile on her face. Newspaper accounts of these events conspicuously mentioned an apparent lack of pain (Itoh & Lee, 1979).

When a powerful agent interacts with the other factors, there are two clinically recognizable outcomes: (1) loss of consciousness, similar to general anesthesia or (2) total *aponia* without loss of consciousness, the equivalent of local anesthesia. Those who lost consciousness remembered experiencing an excruciating noxious sensation and then fainting, possibly from loss of blood.

On the other hand, there are those who, experiencing *aponia*, turned out to be poor historians with regard to the accident, claiming a total absence of pain and often some euphoric or intoxicated feeling. It is reasonable to speculate that both loss of consciousness and *aponia* constitute a host reaction caused by a still unknown neurochemical process to preserve the integrity of the entire neurotransmission system for survival.

Measurement and Assessment of Chronic Pain

Although pain is a very complicated symptom, the assessment of acute pain is far less troublesome than the assessment of chronic pain. Theoretically, the degree of pain perception corresponds to the degree of the agents' interaction. Because a tooth is innervated by only the sensory nerve, our group experimented with electrical stimulation to the dental pulp and obtained reproducible results (Dworkin, Lee, Zaretsky, & Berkeley, 1977). A group in Israel measured cerebral evoked potentials utilizing laser irradiation to the forearm as the agent (Carmon & Lee, 1978).

The assessment of chronic pain (Table 16-5) in a clinical setting is far

Table 16-5   Assessment of Chronic Pain

History of present illness including previous medical findings and treatment
History of previous illness and traumatic conditions
Occupational history
Physical examination
Neurological examination
Radiological examination
Clinical laboratory tests
Electrocardiogram
Electromyogram
Conduction velocity study
Thermogram
Electroencephalogram
CAT scan
MRI
Measurement of active and passive range of motion
Muscle strength testing
Splinting by a patient as protective mechanism during a specific activity
Muscle atrophy
Muscle spasm
Spasticity
Rigidity
Gross functional deficiency
Sensitivity to light touch or pressure by palpation
Deficiency in activities of daily living
Coordination or incoordination

more difficult than in experimental models. Direct or indirect information on the quality and/or quantity of chronic pain can be provided by physical examination.

Recently, infrared thermography has been increasingly utilized in the assessment of pain, particularly chronic pain (Lee & Ernst, 1989). Although it is often mistakenly believed that thermography shows pain, the thermogram actually shows only the symmetry or asymmetry of the thermal pattern on the dermal surface of a body. In general, the area where acute pain exists would show a higher temperature, and a lower temperature would usually correspond with chronic pain. There are cases, however, in which an abnormal thermogram does not indicate the presence of pain. The thermogram can, at best, confirm or deny a patient's claim.

Although pain is a symptom, one must recognize that it is the most subjective symptom, more so than any other symptom that a medical practitioner will encounter. It is so subjective that it is dependent on one's perception rather than sensation. Because perception is more a part of the psychological arena than a somatic phenomenon, the assessment of pain requires inquiries into the psychosocial functioning of the individual.

It has been said that individuals belonging to certain ethnic and/or cultural groups, such as those of Northern or Western European extraction or of Oriental extraction, exhibit less emotion and complain of pain less than members of Southern European or Latin groups. This conception may hold true to a certain extent under certain circumstances, but such labeling or generalization is very dangerous in the assessment of pain.

Another approach to the assessment of pain is to consider it as learned behavior. Although a child learns from the beginning to avoid and be afraid of pain, in his or her environment the child may learn that pain brings affection, sympathy, and a variety of gains. This learning process may cause the child to manipulate that environment through the expression of pain. Although this is relatively common in childhood, if such a learned-behavior pattern continues to develop into adulthood, the management of pain in such an individual becomes very difficult.

The value of history taking is that it describes the current situation and predicts the prognosis. This is true in an individual's medical as well as social history. As an evaluation tool for chronic pain, the social history reflects the feeling tone, ego function, and coping skills, the last being significant to ego functioning and to personality structure. The history also gives an indication of how an individual might be able to manage chronic pain and perhaps even the level of pain tolerance.

To gain insight into personality structure and functioning, the Minnesota Multiphasic Personality Inventory (MMPI) is often used for those with chronic pain. There is no need to go through a detailed assessment if the pain is a somatic symptom. It is very clear that the most careful assessment is fundamental to the rational and effective management of chronic pain (Figure 16-1).

DISABILITY

Disability is classified into two categories: (1) primary, the direct result of a disease or traumatic condition; and (2) secondary, a disability that did not exist at the onset of a disease or traumatic condition but subsequently develops. Paraplegia, quadriplegia following spinal cord injury, hemiplegia and/or aphasia associated with cerebrovascular accident, or inability to ambulate after the fracture of a hip would be

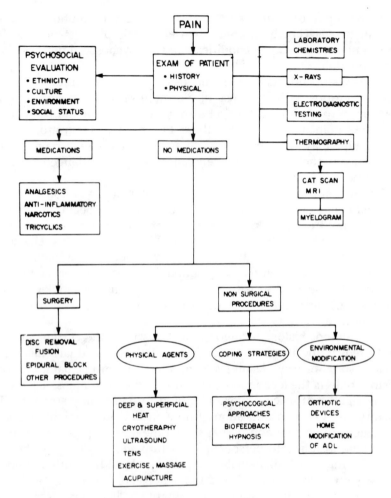

Figure 16-1   Algorithm for pain management.

considered examples of primary disabilities. Decubitus ulcer in paraplegia and quadriplegia, flexion contracture of the joints in the extremities of those with hemiplegia or rheumatoid arthritis, or muscle atrophy in paralyzed body segments would be considered examples of
secondary disabilities.

Primary disability is characterized by its sudden onset and the fact
that it is very disease-specific and not preventable. A secondary disability has an insidious onset; it is not disease-specific and is preventable.
A secondary disability can often be even more disabling than a primary

disability, as in the case of decubitus ulcer, which can be fatal unless treated promptly and appropriately (Lee & Itoh, 1984).

The primary mission of the rehabilitation team is to restore a patient's lost functions to their fullest capacity—physically, emotionally, socially, and vocationally (Lee, 1971). A major portion of the team's activities is devoted to the prevention of secondary disabilities, for example, bed and wheelchair positioning to prevent decubitus ulcers, range of motion exercises, or application of a sling or splint or muscle exercises for the prevention of disuse muscle atrophy. Even in a simple above-knee amputation, a great deal of effort is expended to prevent a flexion contracture of the hip joint.

IMMOBILIZATION

A component of ancient as well as modern medical treatment, the most rudimentary curative method for any disease has always been bed rest. For many years, a patient with acute myocardial ischemia (MI) was confined to bed rest for weeks, until it was found that prolonged bed rest during the recuperation period is not only unnecessary but harmful. Thus, today, many post-MI patients are instructed to be out of bed within a few days after an acute episode.

Previously, a plaster of Paris cast from the waist to the toes had been applied to an elderly patient with a hip fracture, making months of bed rest necessary. While the patient was in bed, it was common for a decubitus ulcer to develop, as well as hypostatic pneumonia, causing a very high mortality from hip fracture. Today death following hip fracture is practically nonexistent as a result of such procedures as open reduction and internal fixation, which make early ambulation possible and prolonged bed rest unnecessary.

According to the U.S. Public Health Service, disability resulting from immobilization was listed as one of the 10 leading preventable health problems in 1960. It is a well-known fact the immobilization causes osteoporosis. Various human experiments, including one involving the astronauts on the 14-day *Gemini* 7 voyage, proved that lack of stress to the bony structure increases calcium excretion and, in turn, a marked decrease in bony density develops.

Every pathophysiological change begins its development at the onset of immobilization. For example, the cardiac rate increases approximately 0.5 beats per minute for each day of immobilization, and the loss of muscle tone resulting from complete disuse is estimated to be 10% to 15% of total strength per week. After a few days of immobilization, an increase in blood flow was detected by means of radioactive strontium, possibly setting up the conditions for bony atrophy. Within 6 to 10 days of immobilization, the nitrogen balance of a healthy male subject reverses to a negative balance. The ill effects of immobilization become the secondary disability.

Iatrogenically imposed immobilization, with its deleterious effects, caused the above changes in young, healthy subjects. In an elderly person, osteoporosis as part of the gerontological process compounded with immobilization produces a disastrous outcome.

In addition, because of decreased social and economic responsibilities, the life-style of the elderly population tends to be much more sedentary. Furthermore, because society expects elderly people to lead very quiet and inactive lives, if one is very physically active, he or she might be viewed in one of two ways: either with praise and admiration or with criticism for "not acting his or her age." An elderly person needs a great deal of support, and if it is not given, he or she might resort to a physically inactive role. It should be noted that an elderly person may tend to experience situational depression (to be described later), and if in such a state of mind there is the smallest physical discomfort, that individual may begin self-imposed immobilization.

CHRONIC PAIN AND THE GERIATRIC PATIENT

Many groups in our society are deprived, socially, economically, and politically, on the basis of sex, race, ethnicity, or religion. The aged population also experiences discrimination; the difference being that the aged grew into their category, whereas the others were born into theirs. The deprived status of the elderly makes geriatric care even more delicate, complex, and challenging.

Knowledge of the physiological changes that occur with senescence is essential in evaluating all elderly persons. Impairment of many functions begins at about 30 years of age. Although functional decrements at the cellular level may not exceed 15%, total organic performance may depreciate by 40% to 60%. These declines are part of the gerontological process and are not caused by the various illnesses that are highly prevalent in the elderly population. When these conditions are compounded with the chronic diseases commonly found among this population, maintaining and/or restoring physical function among the elderly presents unique problems (Rusk & Lee, 1971).

Establishing the medical or surgical diagnosis of an ailment in the elderly patient is no more difficult than in the younger generation.

During the course of a diagnostic procedure, many incidental findings may be noted, additional diagnoses made, and an appropriate treatment plan for each clinical diagnosis developed. Because such additional conditions may be totally asymptomatic and not life-threatening, is it a clinician's duty to treat all diagnoses in the elderly patient?

It is important at this juncture to consider each diagnosis in light of the individual's functional ability in normal life. Anatomical or physiological correction is not always beneficial to the elderly patient as long as the individual is functioning normally according to age. "Treat the patient but not the diagnosis" is an old saying that is more appropriate when treating an older person.

The characteristics of chronic pain have already been discussed. When a young person experiences vague and mild pain or aching, they commonly say, "I must be getting old," implying that elderly people always have such pain or aching and that aging is associated with pain—a myth more than a fallacy.

It is quite probable that an older person may have pain in the neck, shoulders, fingers, and low back as a result of osteoarthritis, radiculopathy, osteoporosis, shortening of the tendons and muscles, overuse of muscles, or simple headache. All of these aches and pains are examples of chronic recurrent pain and may never be excruciating. Recurrence is such that in a 24-hour period there is usually a painful time (e.g., in the morning or during the night) and a painless time (as in midday). This does not mean that every old person has such pain; some are lucky enough to have no pain at all.

The assessment of chronic pain in general is a very difficult task. The physical information should definitely be obtained, but expensive and time-consuming examinations need not be performed unless such examinations are vital to the establishment of a clinical diagnosis. Instead, time should be spent in ascertaining the psychosocial history of the patient, which may provide more information than a physical examination because tests and examinations can only detect the probable cause of pain. Even if the diagnosis is established, there may not be many ways to cure the pain.

When a patient makes a statement such as "I have gotten used to this pain," it should not be taken at face value. No living creature on earth can get used to pain—it is fresh every time one feels it. Instead, such a statement should be interpreted as a sign of resignation and depression, which must be attributed to either a host characteristic or to the pain itself. If pain is the cause of depression, every effort should be made to alleviate it. If depression is among the host factors, psychosocial intervention would be appropriate.

The goals involved in the treatment or alleviation of pain may vary. Although developing a pain-free state may be ideal, it may not be the most realistic goal. It would be of more benefit to the patient to decrease the pain so that he or she would be able to function in all ADL without too much discomfort.

TREATMENT APPROACH FOR THE ELDERLY

The treatment of elderly patients is a very complex task (Itoh & Lee, 1979). It has been observed that elderly patients with or without organic mental syndrome (OMS) can exhibit acute OMS or an increase in the severity of their condition after general anesthesia. Many times it requires several days or weeks to recover. It is not clear whether acute OMS is caused by general anesthesia or by fluid imbalance during the postoperative period; time and again, a similar condition has been observed after an episode of dehydration lasting for a 24- to 48-hour period. Therefore, when a surgical procedure requiring general anesthesia must be performed for the restoration of function or for any other reason, utmost caution and meticulous care for an elderly patient is absolutely mandatory. It is most desirable to use local anesthesia whenever possible.

Because surgery presents a disadvantage, conservative treatment would be preferable. However, drug therapy for an elderly patient is not trouble-free. A sluggish metabolism combined with renal dysfunction, might, in some cases, cause an elevation of the drug in the patient's blood level. Although the patient may not admit it, he or she may be experiencing forgetfulness, poor vision, and/or incoordination, and thus compliance with the medication regime becomes questionable. Under- or overmedicating, whether by prescription or with over-the-counter drugs, is common among the elderly in the community. It is dangerous for a practitioner to tell a patient to "just take aspirin" because high doses of salicylates may cause severe gastrointestinal bleeding. It is therefore very important for the clinician to take time to explain the effect of the drug, the importance of compliance, and the possible side effects in layman's terms. Furthermore, it may be helpful for the patient to have a device such as a "dose pack" that will serve as a reminder of medication quantity and time. Large print on the prescription labels for elderly customers may also be useful.

The various heat therapy modalities are very useful, conservative approaches to the control of chronic pain, and when applied by a physical therapist, they are safe and effective. However, when such treatments are self-administered by a patient at home, they are not always safe, as forgetfulness, poor vision, incoordination, diminished skin sensation, and the like may cause a burn.

After the fifth and sixth decades of life, many men and women begin a somewhat lonely existence, some becoming widows or widowers, their children having grown up and left home, involved with raising their own families. Retirement, economic restrictions, and declining physical stamina (i.e., having a "good day" or a "bad day") contribute to the development of depression. In a hospital, rehabilitation center, or outpatient clinic, nurses who are in their grandchildren's age bracket call the elderly patients by their first names and often use baby talk when speaking to them. Younger health care providers must be sensitive to the feelings of elderly patients—simple words of gentleness, kindness, encouragement, understanding, and empathy are more therapeutic than any medication or physical modality.

MOBILITY

Rusk defines rehabilitation as the "ultimate restoration of a disabled person to his maximum capacity—physical, emotional and vocational." This definition implies that the maximum achievement of the rehabilitation process is the attainment of premorbid function or ability, a goal befitting geriatric rehabilitation rather than the rehabilitation of children or young adults, as the latter group is in need of further education and vocational training in order to become productive citizens.

The theoretically achievable goal (TAG) (Lee & Itoh, 1988) is the ultimate attainment in rehabilitation that a disabled person can reach under the most ideal physical, intellectual, mental, psychological, social, economic, and environmental conditions. For example, even if all other conditions are ideal, a person who lacks motivation because of a dependent personality cannot achieve his or her TAG. TAG is a weighted score assigned to certain essential activities or physical functions (see Figure 16-2 and Table 16-6).

The grading of the TAG ranges from the most fundamental body function to high physical and/or intellectual attainment. In geriatric rehabilitation, the highest TAG score is 75.

The TAG system is devised to fit all age groups, with a disproportionately high score assigned to ADL and a low score designated to mobility. Mobility in the TAG system refers to locomotion, a two-dimensional activity. To meet the needs of the elderly population, it is proposed in this chapter that mobility be defined as a three-dimensional activity involving movement of all body segments, encompassing ADL and locomotion.

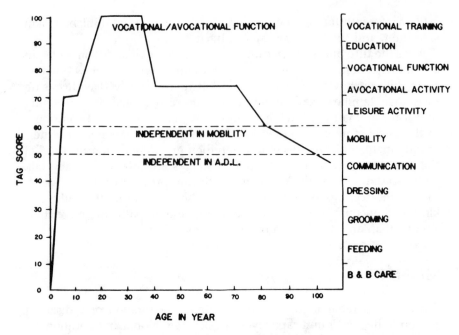

Figure 16-2   Theoretically achievable goal (TA6) score.

Table 16-6   Tag Score

Activities/functions	Points
Activities of daily living (maximum 50 points)	
Independent in bowel and bladder care	10
Independent in feeding	10
Independent in grooming	10
Independent in dressing	10
Independent in communication	10
Mobility (maximum 10 points)	
Independent in ambulation	10
Independent in mobility without ambulation	10
Independent in transfer activity	10
Educational, vocational, and avocational activity (maximum 40 points)	
Regain all or most of premorbid vocational and/or avocational functions	10
Completion of formal or higher education	10
Completion of vocational training or retraining	10

SHRINKING SPHERE

The "sphere" is composed of three-dimensional circles, each individual having his or her own sphere. The sphere can be viewed in terms of physical, educational, intellectual, emotional, psychological, social, economic, political, or geographic factors. Each individual has total control over the definition of the size of his or her own sphere. In childhood, the physical and educational sphere is on the increase, during young adulthood, the intellectual sphere is enlarging; by the time of retirement, the individual's sphere expands to its maximum in every aspect.

Retirement changes a person's sphere drastically. The social and geographical sphere contracts—contact with fewer people daily and no travel to the office or work place daily. When this theory of one's sphere is applied to the physical area, changes become more dramatic. Fatigue may mean confinement to one's own home; there also may be decreased range of joint motion caused by osteoarthritis, weakened muscle power as a result of disuse, diminished visual acuity, incoordination. These, *compounded with chronic pain, drastically restrict ADL functions* at home. Decreasing social contact may lead to depression. Thus, a variety of vicious cycles develop, and as a result, an elderly person is living in an ever shrinking sphere (Itoh, Lee, & Shapiro, 1984). On the other hand, some elderly do increase their sphere after retirement of their spouse and when their children have left home.

Doctors treating elderly people face the dilemmas of disuse atrophy, disability, depression, drugs, and dependency—the D's—the causes and results of the shrinking sphere to which pain further contributes.

CONCEPT OF UTOPIAN HEALTH

All health professionals who provide care must be acutely aware of the unique vulnerability and needs of the elderly patient. An older person must be kept as active, physically and mentally, as possible to prevent disuse atrophy of the muscles as well as mental atrophy. Although the prevention of a primary disability is in the province of preventive medicine, prevention of a secondary disability rests on all of the rehabilitation team members. Preventing depression by expanding the support system requires imagination, creativity, and dedication. Drugs to control the many diseases associated with aging must be used as necessary but in the smallest doses possible. Chronic pain must be controlled in order for a person to enjoy full mobility. If all of the above ingredients are provided, one can anticipate minimizing dependency.

The ideal style of living for the elderly is one in which the most expanded sphere possible can be maintained for as long as one lives. Although such an idea may be utopian, it is indeed possible to prevent shrinkage of the sphere.

CONCLUSION

Pain management of the geriatric patient will become more complex as increasing years are added to the elderly life span. The shrinking sphere and reduced ADL add insult to the problem. The health professional must commence clinical studies to help delineate appropriate care and must utilize aggressive and innovative teaching methods to present our current knowledge in order to affect the quality of life, the ultimate goal of health care.

REFERENCES

Carmon, A., & Lee, M. H. M. (1978). *Cerebral evoked potential, laser stimulation and treatment.* Paper presented at the Second International Symposium on Pain, Montreal.

Crue, B. L., Felsööry, A., Agnew, D., Kamdar, M. D., Randle, W., Griffith, S., Sherman, R., Menard P., & Pinsky, J. J. (1979). The team concept in the management of pain in patients with cancer. *Bulletin of the Los Angeles Neurological Societies* (special ed.), 44(1–4), 70–83.

Dworkin, B. R., Lee, M. H. M., Zaretsky, H. H., & Berkeley, H. A. (1977). Instrumentation and techniques: A precision tooth-pulp stimulation technique for the assessment of pain threshold. *Behavior Research Methods and Instrumentation, 9,* 463–465.

Itoh, M., & Lee, M. (1979). Epidemiology of pain. *Bulletin of the Los Angeles Neurological Societies, 44*(1–4), 14–31.

Itoh, M., Lee, M., Eason, A., Herring, G. M., & Rybsteen-Blinchik, E. (1984). Management of pain. In A. P. Ruskin (Ed.), *Current therapy in physiatry* (pp. 150–160). Philadelphia: W. B. Saunders.

Itoh, M., Lee, M., & Shapiro, J. (1984). Self-help devices for the elderly population living in the community. In T. F. Williams (Ed.), *Rehabilitation in the aged* (pp. 345–358). New York: Raven Press.

Lee, M. H. M. (1971). Geriatric rehabilitation. In H. A. Rusk (Ed.), *Rehabilitation medicine* (rev. ed., pp. 659–670). Philadelphia: W. B. Saunders.

Lee, M. H. M., & Ernst, M. (1989). Clinical and research observations on acupuncture analgesia and thermography. In B. Pomerantz & G. Stux (Eds.), *Scientific bases of acupuncture* (pp. 157–175). Berlin: Springer-Verlag.

Lee, M. H. M., & Itoh, M. (1984). Rehabilitation of the elderly stroke patient. *Mediguide to Aging, 1*(3), 1–5.

Lee, M., & Itoh, M. (1988). Geriatric rehabilitation management. In J. Goodgold (Ed.), *Rehabilitation medicine* (pp. 393–406). St. Louis: C. V. Mosby.
Rusk, H. A., & Lee, M. H. M. (1971). Rehabilitation of the aging: Introduction
to Old Age (symposium). *Bulletin of the New York Academy of Medicine, 47,*
1383–1388.

17

Rehabilitation and Geriatric Education: Mental Health Perspectives

Barry D. Lebowitz

The mental health perspective brings five issues to bear on the topic of geriatric rehabilitation: the quality of the science base, the characterization of the population, the accessibility of services, the requirements for personnel, and the funding for treatment.

THE QUALITY OF THE SCIENCE BASE

The broad topic of mental health research extends to almost all areas of contemporary research in the biological, clinical, behavioral, and psychosocial areas. Yet within this vast domain there is an excitement and a burst of scientific creativity never before experienced in these areas.

The past decade has seen mental health issues brought to the forefront of gerontological and geriatric discussion and, conversely, has seen aging issues being examined by those in the mental health field. These developments are made all the more striking when viewed in the context of the tremendous gains in a number of areas of basic science such as fundamental neuroscience, mechanisms of cognitive and intellectual function, and social network theory.

At the same time, important developments in methodology have provided the impetus for creative and sophisticated theory building. These developments have made it possible to examine increasingly complex models of more and more precise characterizations of the phenomena of interest in this field. In doing so, the artificial distinctions between disciplines have been pushed aside, and the mutual reinforcement of biological, clinical, behavioral, and psychosocial factors in mental health and mental illness has become the methodology of choice in complex, multidisciplinary studies.

There are many elegant and compelling examples of important advances in the science base of our field. Using the best of contemporary approaches in molecular genetics, St. George-Hyslop and colleagues (1987) have identified an area on chromosome 21 that may hold the genetic key to the familial form of Alzheimer's disease. Using monoclonal antibody approaches, Davies and associates (Wolozin, Pruchniki, Dickson, & Davies, 1986) have succeeded in identifying an antigen that seems to be a highly specific marker for the cellular pathology of Alzheimer's disease, a finding that could prove to be of considerable value in enhancing the early diagnosis of this disease. Although the treatment for the core cognitive symptoms of Alzheimer's disease remains elusive, many investigators have turned their attention to management of associated symptoms of depression (Reifler, Teri, & Rashkind, 1989), agitation (Salzman, 1988), and psychosis (Devanand, Sackeim, & Mayeux, in press) in the demented patient. Such studies may result in strategies for patient management that could well improve the community and institutional care of Alzheimer's disease patients. A significant aspect of this care is the stress that it places on the family responsible for providing support to the patient. E. Brody (1989) has highlighted the guilt, demoralization, and depression associated with the great burden of care of an Alzheimer's patient, and Kiecolt-Glaser and Glaser (1989) have demonstrated that caregivers of Alzheimer's disease patients have suppressed immune function on a variety of dimensions (e.g., percentages of total T lymphocytes and helper T cells).

In other areas of research, age of onset has been shown to be a significant concern in schizophrenia (Jeste et al., 1988) and in depressive disorder (Meyers & Alexopoulos, 1988), with investigation now explicating the impact of a variable age of onset on clinical presentation, the course of disease, and the outcome of treatment.

Research on acute treatment of depression in older patients has shown that treatment response to medications (Georgotas et al., 1986) and psychotherapy (Gallagher & Thompson, 1983) is substantial, though naturalistic follow-up has shown high rates of relapse and recurrence (Murphy, 1983). Research to establish protocols for continuation and maintenance treatment is now underway.

In sum, developments in basic science and clinical investigation are providing a firm base for treatment and prevention as well as for educational programs and for further research. Investigators are using the best of contemporary approaches to address questions on the onset, course, and outcome of disease, on the interaction of disease with normal age-associated changes in adult development, on the impact of comorbidity of acute or chronic conditions, and on the significance of age of onset of disorder. This rich body of science has developed a significant momentum with an ever accelerating pace of achievement and the development of therapeutic optimism to replace the nihilistic view of treatment for the mentally ill aged.

THE NATURE OF THE POPULATION

The key concept to be applied in achieving a perspective on the population of disabled older persons is that of heterogeneity (Brody & Ruff, 1986). There are three major contributions to the heterogeneity of the population: diagnosis, age of onset, and functional abilities.

Diagnosis constitutes one major source of heterogeneity. Clearly, all the highly prevalent chronic conditions contribute to disability. In a paper published in 1980, Morton Kramer pointed out that the prevalence of mental disorders is rising at an "alarming rate" and furthermore that the prevalence of the chronic illnesses is likely to increase in the years ahead. Two reasons account for this trend. One is the relatively large increases in the number of persons in age groups at high risk for developing mental disorders and chronic diseases. The second is the increase in the average duration of chronic diseases; this increase is a function of our capacity to arrest the fatal complications of such diseases and to prolong the lives of affected individuals. This perspective has been presented by others as well (Rice & Feldman, 1983), though this view is not held uniformly by those in the field (Fries, 1980).

Age of onset is a second dimension of differentiation in the population of disabled older persons. Those with late-onset disorder, such as the dementias that emerge after a lifetime of relatively good health, are clearly different from those born with Down's syndrome or those who develop schizophrenia in the third decade of their lives (Frazier, Lebowitz, & Silver, 1986).

The important contribution of geriatric rehabilitation is to replace diagnosis and age of onset with a metric of *function*, namely, the ability to accomplish various activites of daily living (ADL); a number of well-validated instruments for functional assessment have been developed and effectively used in both individual treatment planning and in overall health policy and planning (Kane & Kane, 1981). For example, ADL have been used as the basis for eligibility in a number of state and federal proposals for legislation in the area of long-term care. At the same time, however, both age and the diagnostic pathway by which a patient reaches a certain level of ADL function can determine not only treatment setting and modality but also eligibility and exclusion. In the area of mental retardation and developmental disabilities, for example, many patients and their families have confronted the situation in which continued participation in community programs has been denied because the individual has grown too old for continued eligibility. More recently, portions of the nursing home reforms in the 1987 Omnibus Budget Reconciliation Act (Public Law 100-203) exclude from admission patients who otherwise meet ADL criteria for nursing homes if the source of their disability is a major mental disorder.

The implications of these disparities in different areas of policy development are yet to be fully determined, but they do represent a clear signal that age and diagnosis, and not strictly ADL, are the important determinants of disability and treatment availability in at least that group of patients with mental disorder.

MENTAL HEALTH SERVICES FOR OLDER PERSONS

The availability and accessibility of community-based mental health services for the elderly have been issues of major concern for over a decade (Lebowitz, 1988). The disparity between the need for service and the small caseload of elderly patients generally documented in community mental health centers (CMHCs) has become even more notable as research in geriatrics has expanded, the broad range of serious disorders and mental health problems experienced by older persons has been identified, and additional therapeutic procedures have been described.

In the most general sense, a combination of factors is thought to account for the low utilization of CMHC services by elderly patients:

- Reimbursement for treatment of mental disorder under Medicare is substantially different from and less complete than reimbursement for physical disorder.
- The recognition of mental disorder in nursing homes is restricted by regulations that limit the number of residents with a primary psychiatric diagnosis, thereby limiting a potentially important site for development of CMHC services.
- Few mental health professionals have been trained to work with older persons.

- CMHC programs are not widely accessible and, even where available, tend to be isolated from the mainstream of community health and social services to the elderly.
- Mental health service programs have typically not engaged in aggressive outreach and case finding but instead have been content to rely on referrals and self-identification of potential patients or clients.
- Older persons have been seen as noncompliant, uninteresting, and generally inappropriate for treatment by many mental health professionals, who would rather deal with younger persons, who are considered attractive, verbal, intelligent, and sophisticated.
- Unfamiliarity with state-of-the-art research and practice has led many clinicians to conclude that no effective treatments or preventive interventions are available for use with older persons.
- Mental illness or the need for mental health treatment is not accurately or appropriately recognized (or is denied) by patients, members of their families, and even the primary care physicians who provide most of the care to the elderly.
- The stigma of mental illness is especially strong in the current cohort of elderly people, who tend to associate mental disorder with personal failure, spiritual deficiency, or some other stereotypic view.

Despite these formidable obstacles, it is becoming clear that some CMHCs have developed services for the elderly that have had higher utilization than is the norm of CMHCs in general. The success of these programs is very strongly related to two factors: (1) the existence of an aging services unit within the CMHC staffed by professionals with specialized training in geriatrics and (2) coordinated relationships between the CMHC and its local community counterpart for aging services, usually known as the Area Agency on Aging (Lebowitz, Light, & Bailey, 1987; Light, Lebowitz, & Bailey, 1986).

As the availability of a full range of community-based services has become broader and the so-called continuum of care has become more highly elaborated, a paradox has also become apparent. This paradox, stated at its simplest, is that as the range of community-based services has grown, the need for long-term institutional care has also expanded. Community services have not substituted for institutional care, and in fact, it has become apparent that community services do not serve as alternatives for institutional care (Callahan, 1989). There has been a clear displacement of services (e.g., nursing homes, not psychiatric hospitals, have emerged as the most frequent site for care of the elderly mentally ill), but there has been no reduction in the demand for institutional care.

REQUIREMENTS FOR PERSONNEL

Opportunities for education in gerontology and geriatrics are increasing at a sigificant rate. In medicine, geriatric subspecialization has been gaining acceptance; added qualifications through fellowship training or examination have been adopted for internal medicine and family practice and are soon to be implemented for psychiatry. Significant curriculum development efforts have been carried out in all mental health disciplines, and the number of texts, monographs, and specialized journals in gerontology and geriatrics has multiplied significantly. Psychology internships may be expanded and restructured to strengthen clinical specialization in particular areas, such as work with the elderly.

The number of postgraduate specialty training programs focused on services for the elderly has increased substantially in the past decade in all of the mental health disciplines; there are now more than 30 such programs. It is clear that these programs have had a substantial impact on the availability and accessibility of mental health services to older persons.

Estimates of numbers of personnel needed for the mental health disciplines are based on the following perspectives: Almost all clinicians in practice can provide service to geriatric patients; some of these clinicians will choose to concentrate their practice in the area of geriatrics; and a small group of academic geriatric specialists will assume leadership positions in education and research at universities, schools of medicine, and major teaching hospitals.

Projections of need for trained specialists in geriatric mental health have been developed by the Committee on Personnel for Health Needs of the Elderly (1988). Using estimates of need for treatment as revealed in epidemiology studies and medical care utilization surveys, the committee determined the need for academic geriatric psychiatrists to provide leadership in education, training, and research at 400 to 500. Similar estimates were made by the committee for many other health professions. Of particular interest are the estimates for the other "core" disciplines in the mental health field: psychology (900 academic), social work (800 academic), and psychiatric nursing (500 academic).

In the light of these estimates, the committee identified three types of training needs: (1) geriatrics should be part of the training of all clinicians, with appropriate didactic and clinical experience in the undergraduate professional curriculum as well as in postgraduate training and as part of continuing education; (2) increased educational experiences for special competency should be available; and (3) advanced training, through special postgraduate fellowships, should be available for those seeking academic careers.

In spite of these gains and record of success, however, the prospects for long-range stability in funding are highly uncertain in light of regularly declining appropriations and the absence of clear statutory mandates through targeted legislation development. Consequently, the personnel question remains a critical one for policy development and action.

FINANCING AND REIMBURSEMENT

Tied directly to the personnel question are issues of the financing of mental health care, particularly through Medicare and private health insurance. Since the inception of Medicare in 1965, treatment for mental illness has been subject to specific limitations—lifetime and spell-of-illness limitations for inpatient service in particular. Reimbursement for outpatient physician care is subject to an annual ceiling and a coinsurance rate of 50%, and services provided by other mental health professionals must be "incident to" physician services in order to be covered. Such differentials do not exist in treatment for nonmental illness, and these are generally thought to limit access and use of mental health professionals by the elderly.

Though this situation generally reflected the practice of private insurers at the time of the introduction of Medicare, the past two decades have seen substantial improvement in private sector coverage. The availability of new and effective treatments, changes in the delivery system, and the significant health care savings and productivity benefits produced by appropriate mental health treatments have now put the Medicare approach out of balance with private approaches. Thus, in the present situation, those dependent on Medicare coverage are significantly disadvantaged relative to the remainder of the population.

Recognition of this disparity and of the resultant financial barrier to the provision of appropriate care has been growing in recent years. In particular, recently enacted changes have raised the annual ceiling and provided reimbursement for specific pharmacological treatment approaches involving medication monitoring and management. This is a positive development and represents an important new perspective treatment for mental disorders.

SUMMARY

Research, education, service design, and financing for a remarkably heterogeneous population constitute the main areas of contribution of mental health to geriatric rehabilitation. Each is a piece of the overall picture, and even a brief overview shows the interlocking nature of the concerns. Over the past decade there has been substantial development in each of these areas. At the same time, the concerns and need for improvement have become equally apparent. Fulfillment of the promise in these areas will require the sustained efforts of many individual investigators, educators, and clinicians, whose work already demonstrates the potential that policy development can try to capture and formalize so that new levels in the state of the art can be achieved. These achievements, in turn, can be realized only if shaped by the leadership of forward-looking and innovative policymakers at all levels of government and in nongovernmental bodies. The challenge is enormous, but the rewards in development of successful approaches to the needs of sick old people and those who care for and about them are well worth the efforts of all of us.

REFERENCES

Brody, E. M. (1989). The family at risk. In E. Light & B. D. Lebowitz (Eds.), *Alzheimer's disease treatment and family stress: Directions for research*. Washington, DC: U.S. Government Printing Office.

Brody, S. J., & G. E. Ruff (Eds.). (1986). *Aging and rehabilitation: Advances in the state of the art*. New York: Springer Publishing Co.

Callahan, J. J. (1989). Play it again Sam—there is no impact. *Gerontologist, 29*, 5–6.

Committee on Personnel for Health Needs of the Elderly Through the Year 2020. (1988). *Report*. Washington, DC: U.S. Government Printing Office.

Devanand, D. P., Sackeim, H. A., Mayeux, R. (in press). Psychosis, behavioral disturbance, and the use of neuroleptics in dementia. *Comprehensive Psychiatry*.

Frazier, S. H., Lebowitz, B. D., & Silver, L. B. (1986). Aging, mental health, and rehabilitation. In S. J. Brody & G. E. Ruff (Eds.), *Aging and rehabilitation: Advances in the state of the art*. New York: Springer Publishing Co.

Fries, J. (1980). Aging, natural death, and the compression of morbidity. *New England Journal of Medicine, 303*, 130–135.

Gallagher, D., & Thompson, L. W. (1983). Cognitive therapy for depression in the elderly. In L. D. Breslau & M. R. Haug (Eds.), *Depression and aging*. New York: Springer Publishing Co.

Georgotas, A., McCue, R. E., Hapworth, W., Friedman, E., Kim, O. N., Welkowitz, J., Chung, I., & Cooper, T. B. (1986). Comparative efficacy and safety of MAOI's versus TCA's in treating depressed elderly. *Biol. Psych, 21*, 1155–1166.

Jeste, D., Harris, M. J., Pearlson, G. D., et al. (1988). Late onset schizophrenia: studying clinical validity. *Psychiatric clinics of North America, 11*, 1–13.

Kane, R. H., & Kane, R. L. (1981). *Assessing the elderly: A practical guide to measurement*. Lexington, MA: D.C. Heath.

Kiecolt-Glaser, J., & Glaser, R. (1989). Caregiving, mental health, and immune functioning. In E. Light & B. D. Lebowitz (Eds.), *Alzheimer's disease treatment and family stress: Directions for research.* Washington, DC: U.S. Government Printing Office.

Kramer, M. (1980). The rising pandemic of mental disorders and associated chronic diseases and disabilities. *Acta psychiatrica scandinavica, 62*(Suppl. 285), 382–397.

Lebowitz, B. D. (1988). Mental health services. In G. L. Maddox (Ed.), *Encyclopedia of Aging.* New York: Springer Publishing Co.

Lebowitz, B. D., Light, E., & Bailey, F. (1987). Mental health center services for the elderly: The impact of coordination with area agencies on aging. *Gerontologist, 27,* 699–702.

Light, E., Lebowitz, B. D., & Bailey, F. (1986). CMHCs and elderly services: An analysis of direct and indirect services and service delivery sites. *Community Mental Health Journal, 22,* 294–302.

Meyers, B. S., & Alexopoulos, G. S. (1988). Age of onset and geriatric depression. *International Journal of Geriatric Pschiatry, 3,* 219–228.

Murphy, E. (1983). The prognosis of depression in old age. *British Journal of Psychiatry, 142,* 111–119.

Reifler, B. V., Teri, L., Raskind, M., et al. (1989). Double-blind trial of imipramine in Alzheimer's disease patients with and without depression. *American Journal of Psychiatry, 146,* 45–49.

Rice, D., & Feldman, J. (1983). Living longer in the United States: Demographic changes and health needs of the elderly. *Milbank Memorial Fund Quarterly, 61,* 362–396.

St. George-Hyslop, P. H., Tanzi, R. E., Polinsky, R. J., et al. (1987). The genetic defect causing familial Alzheimer's disease maps on chromosome 21. *Science, 235,* 885–890.

Salzman, C. (1988). Treatment of agitation, anxiety, and depression in dementia. *Psychopharmacology Bulletin, 24* 39–42.

Wolozin, B. L., Pruchnicki, A., Dickson, D. W., & Davies, P. (1986). A neuronal antigen in the brains of patients with Alzheimer's disease. *Science, 232,* 648–650.

Part VII

The Practice Model: Assessment

18

Targeting Geriatric Assessment

Robert L. Kane

In contemporary discussions of geriatric care, two concepts rise to the surface: assessment and case management. They seem to be universal cures for whatever ails the system. Both are therefore worthy of closer examination. Like any potentially therapeutic intervention, each has to be used properly, in the correct amount, for the indicated problem. Not all assessments are the same, nor should they be. Assessments are done under different circumstances to achieve different ends. However, one fact remains common: assessment per se does not help anyone. Just as no patient is cured by a diagnosis, assessments derive their major benefit from their ability to lead to meaningful actions. This observation becomes more critical when the caregiver is faced with real constraints. Given a limited amount of time, how does one weigh the value of assessment against the value of action?

This issue of efficiency is not easily dismissed because the cousin of comprehensive assessment is interdisciplinary team care. In a field as wide-ranging as geriatrics, the first impulse is to convene a team. Interdisciplinary teams can be very useful in representing different perspectives and for assuring that the various aspects of a client's problems are not overlooked, but there is some question of how well they achieve their potential benefit (Schmitt, Farrell, & Heinemann, 1988). Moreover, they are very expensive. A 1-hour team meeting of four persons represents half of a person-day. One has to consider how many such meetings a program or society can afford. Sequential assessment by each member of a multidisciplinary team inevitably leads to redundant information collection and inefficiency.

There is little point in arguing too vehemently that an organized approach to collecting a comprehensive body of information is preferable to a haphazard, hit-or-miss approach, although some might rightfully note that comprehensive assessments are expensive and should be used sparingly in an era of cost-consciousness. The goal then is to trim the assessment to the point where the fat is gone but the muscle remains intact. Different amounts of muscle power may be needed for different tasks. In many cases it may suffice to assure that the insights of various disciplines have been tapped to develop the questions or items that constitute the assessment, but it may not require that each discipline be present to ask the questions. The important input may best come at the point of developing the format and providing a framework for translating the responses into a problem list and then into a care plan.

WHOM TO ASSESS

Because assessment is an expensive business, it should be employed with care. To paraphrase Gilbert and Sullivan, the object is to match the right assessment strategy to the appropriate client.

Some older persons need a comprehensive geriatric assessment. Such an investment is best directed at those persons who represent the classic geriatric paradigm: multiple, simultaneous, interactive problems. In some cases these persons present because of their problems; at other times they present because of their problems' sequelae, most often a need for long-term care (LTC). Certainly, before any momentous decision of the magnitude of a life sentence to long-term care is made, a thorough study to ask "is this trip necessary" is warranted on both clinical and fiscal grounds. If we are urging second opinions before surgery, surely we want a similar careful consideration of options before LTC.

Perhaps the largest single group of persons in need of comprehensive assessment are those suffering from dementia. In that instance much of the attention is focused on how to cope with the problem, especially how to support the family in their informal caregiving role. But assessment is also critical for those with more rehabilitative potential. In the most logical system, assessment is the precursor of a care plan. It is thus an essential ingredient in any LTC enterprise and is, in fact, mandated under the new nursing home regulations. Comprehensive assessments are also indicated for any clients who present as management problems, either because they have developed regimens that appear overly complex (and often internally inconsistent) or because they do not seem to be doing well under routine care.

The different reasons that precipitate an assessment imply different components to the assessment. No single model will suffice for all clients. The emphasis of the assessment should be shaped to meet the needs of the person being addressed. Thus, some general components will likely apply to virtually all situations even though the emphasis given to a particular aspect will vary with the circumstances.

The question of whom to assess can be approached in another way as well. In addition to questions of the different classes of geriatric clients, it is important to remember that many assessments must address the informal caregivers as well as the clients. In most cases, where there is a family, it is assessed along with the client. Past as well as, and perhaps even more than, current and anticipated caregiving needs to be explored and special attention paid to the burdens such care has and will extract.

WHAT TO ASSESS

The common language of geriatrics is function. However, our zeal to carry this message may have caused some to misinterpret it. The following equation serves as a reminder of the several components of function that geriatrics seeks to improve:

$$\text{FUNCTION} = \frac{\text{Health care} \times \text{Motivation}}{\text{Social and physical environment}}$$

The first crucial step in improving function is appropriate diagnosis and treatment. Concerns about function begin with a commitment to remediating the remediable. That is a necessary first step, but it is not sufficient. Function is also a product of the client's environment, both physical and psychological. The former is easy to understand but is nonetheless too often overlooked. The psychological dimension refers largely to our tendency to risk aversion, spurred by both a concern for safety and a fear of litigation.

A second negative environmental influence comes from a false sense of efficiency. Especially under the current pressures to shorten hospital stays and cut unit costs, there is a tendency to believe that quicker is cheaper. In the case of caring for dependent older persons, this too often translates into doing things for people rather than helping them (or encouraging them) to do things for themselves. The latter is often more time-consuming but is the essence of what we mean by rehabilitation.

Motivation plays an important role in determining a client's function. Even when testing performance directly, the person's willingness to put out the extra effort is a critical factor. When it comes to such areas as decisions about choices of care, much can be traced to the expectations that all players have about the outcomes of care. There are several prominent players. They include the formal care providers (who may not necessarily agree among themselves), the client, and the family. Each has concerns and beliefs about what will happen. Surfacing these is an important part of an assessment. The ultimate satisfaction with the outcome of a decision will be greatly influenced by the expectations of what is the natural course and can be achieved. Unvoiced, differing expectations can lead to different strategies and ultimately to dissatisfaction. Often the most important question asked in a geriatric assessment is "What do you expect will happen and what do you expect as a result of this assessment?"

The clinician has much to gain from pessimism. A cautious prognosis means that either the outcome is relatively positive or the prognosis is keenly accurate. Added to a general tendency toward ageism, this subtle incentive to underestimate the potential for improvement may create an unfortunate self-fulfilling prophecy. This is especially tragic in light of growing evidence of the potential for improving function even among seriously impaired (Manton, 1988).

To the extent that assessment leads to decisions, it is important to ascertain the preferences of the major participants in the decision making. These preferences are most commonly expressed in terms of specific modalities of care to be avoided or pursued. Indeed, one of the major impediments to good decision making is the tendency to define questions in terms of answers. Careful effort is required to ascertain the preferences for various outcome states, to examine the willingness to trade safety for autonomy. Couched in these terms instead of those of specific services, there is much greater opportunity for developing a flexible care plan. When the preferences of the different parties to the decision are disparate, it is important to recognize these differences and to reconcile them if there is to be any hope of achieving a satisfactory decision.

Similarly, a realistic care plan must take into account the resources available. Because most of the care given in LTC is family care, a careful weighing of the family's willingness and capacity to deal with the problems identified is critical. Unfortunately, theoretical care is not the same as real care. It is difficult for families to imagine the burdens imposed if they have not already undertaken them. The assessor/therapist is caught in an awkward dilemma about how vividly to paint the problems, in the need to trade accurate portrayal against inevitable discouragement. On the other hand, it is foolish to build a care plan on a foundation of enthusiasm alone.

EVIDENCE OF ASSESSMENT'S EFFECTIVENESS

Several reviews of the randomized clinical trials (RCTs) of geriatric evaluation units (GEUs) and similar efforts are available (Epstein et al., 1987; Kane, 1988; Rubenstein, 1987). Although they agree in the choice of the studies to be reviewed and the findings reported, they vary somewhat in the optimism they derive from the patterns of effects found. These studies suggest that geriatric evaluation usually does lead to at least some positive outcomes, but it is worthwhile considering the overall pattern in light of differences in the type of intervention provided and the persons for whom it is used. Table 18-1 summarizes some of the salient features of the RCTs reviewed by most authors.

The pattern of the findings as summarized in Table 18-1 suggests like correlation between input and outcome, except in the case of the Rubenstein study, which remains the most positive evidence of the efficacy of assessment. In fact, there is a wide variation in the nature of the interventions and the subjects treated. Rubenstein focused a comprehensive effort on patients destined for nursing homes. Williams (Williams, Williams, Zimmer, Jackson, & Podgorski, 1987) used an ambulatory program to address the same group. Hendricksen (Hendricksen, Lund, & Stromgard, 1984) and Vetter (Vetter, Jones, & Victor, 1979) each studied programs that employed home visitors to community living elderly. The former used a social worker and the latter a public health nurse. Becker (Becker, McVey, Saltz, Feussner, &

Table 18-1 Summary of GEU RCTs

Studies	Rubenstein (1984)	Hendricksen et al. (1984)	Vetter (1984)	Williams et al. (1987)	Becker (1986, 1987, 1988)[a]	Hogan et al. (1987)
Targeted on nursing home candidates	+ +	−	−	+ +	+	+ +
Extent of intervention benefits	+ + +	+	+	+ +	+ +	+ +
Reduced mortality	+ +	+ +	+	−	−	+
Improved function	+ +	−	−	−	−	−
Reduced utilization	+	+	−	+	−	−

Note. The signs in the table reflect the direction and intensity of the variable. For a more complete description of the studies, see Kane (1988).

[a] Allen et al., (1986), Becker et al. (1987), Saltz, McVey, Becker, Feussner, & Cohen (1988).

Cohen, 1987) and Hogan (Hogan, Fox, Bradley, & Mann, 1987) employed hospital geriatric consultation teams, but Hogan's subjects were more carefully screened in advance.

How then can we explain the effects of geriatric consultation? At least part of the answer may lie with the third leg of the functional stool. As noted earlier, improving function has at least three critical components. In addition to remediating the remediable and improving the environment, it is important to motivate the patient. A pessimistic provider is unlikely to encourage the patient. One of the things all of these studies seem to have in common is a person (or persons) who believe that improvement is possible. Addressing the patient's problems as manageable units and conveying a sense of optimism about the potential for improvement may be as important as what specific tasks are performed as a part of the assessment.

Moreover, the situation in geriatrics is more disparate. There is strong psychological evidence to suggest that people adopt negative, hostile feelings toward those they feel impotent to help. This phenomenon, labeled the Innocent Victim Syndrome, has direct implications for geriatrics and assessment. To the extent that clinicians are frustrated by the geriatric paradigm of multiple, simultaneous, interactive problems, they may not only be incapable of responding but may become hostile toward the very people who most need help. An answer lies in providing them with a structured approach to teasing apart the complex dilemma into manageable units, hence assessment.

WHEN TO ASSESS

There are multiple uses for geriatric assessment. Each of these uses suggests a somewhat different emphasis to the assessment. Indeed, one of the difficulties plaguing assessments has been the tendency to use a measure in a clinical context because it has worked well in a research setting. Assessments designed to identify problems are different from those used to determine eligibility for programs or benefits. Especially in the context of current legislation, there is a tendency to use functional deficiencies as the criteria for eligibility for programs. But there is a major difference in using such dysfunction as a threshold measure, by which any lesser disability qualifies for no assistance, or a as continuous measure, whereby the extent of assistance is titrated to the level of disability. Likewise, the assessment performed to develop a care plan will differ from that used to monitor progress. The latter will generally be shorter and more focused on problems already identified.

Probably the most critical time for an assessment is when an individual is contemplating a major change in life-style, such as entering a nursing home or a retirement community. Frequently, this decision is made during the hospital discharge process. At least two thirds of nursing home admissions come from acute hospitals. On such occasions it seems very fitting and worthwhile to invest the effort needed to make a good decision. The current DRG-attributed pressure to discharge patients as quickly as possible must give way to a recognition that the time and effort invested in a careful assessment can pay great dividends in terms of savings in unnecessary LTC or forms of such care that are contrary to the patients' desires or best interests. Unfortunately, our current system of fractured funding, with different primary payers for acute and LTC, creates few incentives for more careful consideration of posthospital events. To the contrary, the present measure of discharge planning success is the speed of launch rather than the destination.

MEASUREMENT ISSUES

There are some specific issues around measurement in assessment that bear more careful scrutiny.[1] These are not of the order of nitpicking about which instrument to use, but rather they explore the implications of different measurement strategies on major policy-related actions.

The problem is exacerbated when the activities of daily living (ADL) dependencies are used as threshold criteria of eligibility rather than as a continuous measure against which care can be titrated. Many of the current legislative proposals for LTC coverage use the threshold approach. In contrast, the Canadian system uses ADL as a basis for determining the intensity of services needed but does not struggle so hard with the question of a floor (Kane & Kane, 1985). They seem to feel that in many cases it takes more resources to worry about eligibility than to simply give the applicant a modest amount of care to meet the emergency. They are more trusting and work in a more cooperative mode than would be tolerable in our more entrepreneurial American society.

There is special cause for concern that the metric for any ADL measure may not be sensitive to the needs of dementia patients. There are two basic issues to consider. First, the number of dependencies depends on the denominator. It is not enough to talk about a single score (e.g., 5 of 7); it depends on which 7. Especially when you move to looking at smaller numbers, it is important to consider which ADL are the most relevant. Some, like bathing, are situationally determined. Some, like grooming, are hard to define and depend on your level of tolerance.

The second and more important point has to do with how you measure the ADL. Here the major distinction is between the usual measures based on ability to perform the task and the metric that uses human assistance. The latter is more relevant in calculating the cost of assistance and the amount of human time required. Ironically, supervising or cuing an activity can take more time (and hence cost more) than doing the task for a person. Because dementia patients are more likely to require supervision than task performance, they may fail the eligibility screen or be underassessed for assistance needs.

This distinction is also relevant when using ADL as the basis for calculating case mix. Such a formula is expected to reflect the effort required to care for different types of patients. But when disability is confused with the need for human assistance, there is an underrepresentation of needed effort. Because supervision and cuing may take more time than simple assistance, the care of dementia patients is generally rated very low on case-mix formulas like RUGS; many would argue inappropriately low.

DESIRED ATTRIBUTES

Ideally, one would like to see a measurement approach that

- can cover the spectrum of performance
- is easy and rapid to administer
- is sensitive to meaningful change in performance
- is stable within the same client over time
- performs consistently in different hands
- cannot be manipulated to meet the needs of either the provider or the client

The solution to this challenge is to create an assessment approach that incorporates the features designed to maximize these elements. To cover the broad spectrum sought and still be relatively quickly administered, an instrument should have multiple branch points. These permit the user to focus on the area along the continuum where the client is most likely to function and to expand that part of the scale to measure meaningful levels of performance. Branching can also ensure that the assessment is comprehensive but not burdensome. By using key questions to screen an area, the interviewer can ascertain whether there is a point in obtaining more detailed information in each relevant domain. Where the initial response is negative, they can go on to the next branch point.

Reliability is more likely to be achieved when the items are expressed in a standardized fashion tied closely to explicit behaviors. Whenever possible, performance is preferred over reports of behavior. One cannot expect to avoid totally the gaming of an assessment. If the client knows that poor performance is needed to ensure eligibility, he or she may be motivated to achieve the requisite low level. One can use some test of respondent bias, such as measures of social desirability, but they will not prevent gaming the system or detect all cheating.

Redundancy can be dramatically reduced by using computerized technology. Properly mobilized, computers can provide the structure needed to assure a comprehensive assessment with no duplication of effort. Because they are interactive, they can carry out much of the desired branching and can even use simple algorithms to clarify areas of ambiguity and retest areas where some unreliability is suspected. Similar algorithms can look for inconsistency as at least a screen for cheating.

FUTURE SCENARIOS

One of the perceived barriers to better assessment is the failure to pay for it. Some advocate a direct fee. Others look hopefully to a total reformation of the physician payment system, such as the RVS (Hsiao, Braun, Yntema, & Becker, 1988). Still others rely on using different types of caregivers, such as geriatric nurse practitioners (Kane et al., 1988). No single solution will carry the day or answer all of the needs. Direct payment will strongly induce behavior change, but it will also raise new issues about what is an assessment and how should such activities be organized. How thorough need such a procedure be to qualify for special reimbursement? Do we really want to spawn a new industry of Medicare-financed assessment centers? How closely should assessment be linked to primary care?

The key to LTC will lie with better information systems. Assessment will be a major part of such information systems. With computer support it will be possible to link assessments. Ideally, the assessments should be done by those who will use the information. The computer can provide the structure to guide what is assessed. It can provide both a checklist and a set of algorithms to direct the information-gathering process, drawing on the input of multiple disciplines but requiring less skilled persons to actually administer the questions. It can similarly transform the problems identified into care plans that are functionally derived. The same information base can be then used to monitor care, to feed back information on client progress to the caregivers on the firing line, and to provide a more reasonable basis for those who need to assess the care provided, especially in terms of the outcomes achieved.

As we think about assessments, we need to think not only about how to collect requisite information but how to display it to maximize the chances of its being used. Here again computers can play a vital role. The ability to transform data into graphs is a potent tool in providing the sought-after feedback to caregivers. Simply graphing change over time can convey some of the dynamism of LTC usually absent from single snapshots. Comparing actual course against expected can provide an even better measure of the real accomplishments of giving good care.

NOTE

1. There are several useful compendia of assessment approaches and pitfalls:

Kane, R. A., & Kane, R. L. (1981). *Assessing the elderly: A practical guide to measurement.* Lexington, MA: D. C. Heath.

McDowell, I., & Newell, C. (1987). *Measuring health: A guide to rating scales and questionnaires.* New York: Oxford University Press.

Israel, L., Kozerevic, D., & Sartorius, N. (1984). In A. Gilmore (Ed.), *Source book of geriatric assessment* (English ed.). Basel and New York: Karger.

REFERENCES

Allen, C. M., Becker, P. M., McVey, L. J., Saltz, C. Feussner, J. R., & Cohen, H. J. (1986). A randomized controlled clinical trial of a geriatric consultation team: Compliance with recommendations. *Journal of the American Medical Association, 255,* 2617–2621.

Becker, P. M., McVey, L. J., Saltz, C. C., Feussner, J. R., & Cohen, H. J. (1987). Hospital-acquired complications in a randomized controlled clinical trial of a geriatric consultation team. *Journal of the American Medical Association, 257,* 2313–2317.

Epstein, A. M., Hall, J. A., Besdine, R., Cumella, B., Feldstein, M., McNeil, B. J., & Rowe, J. W. (1987). The emergence of geriatric assessment units. *Annals of Internal Medicine, 106,* 299–303.

Hendricksen, C., Lund, E., & Stromgard, E. (1984). Consequences of assessment and intervention among elderly people: Three-year randomized controlled trial. *British Medical Journal, 289,* 1522–1524.

Hogan, D. B., Fox, R. A., Bradley, B. W. D., & Mann, O. E. (1987). Effect of a geriatric consultation service on management of patients in an acute care hospital. *Canadian Medical Association Journal, 136,* 713–717.

Hsaio, W. C., Braun, P., Yntema, D., & Becker, E. R. (1988). Estimating physicians' work for a resource-based relative-value scale. *New England Journal of Medicine, 319,* 835–841.

Kane, R. A., Kane, R. L., Arnold, S., Garrard, J., McDermott, S., & Kepferle, L. (1988). Geriatric nurse practitioners as nursing home employees: Implementing the role. *Gerontologist, 28,* 469–477.

Kane, R. L. (1988). Beyond caring: The challenge to geriatrics. *Journal of the American Geriatrics Society, 36,* 467–472.

Kane, R. L., & Kane, R. A. (1985). *A will and a way: What Americans can learn about long-term care from Canada.* New York: Columbia University Press.

Manton, K. G. (1988). A longitudinal study of functional change and mortality in the United States [Special issue: Social sciences]. *Journal of Gerontology, 43,* S153–161.

Rubenstein, L. Z. (1987). Geriatric assessment: An overview of its impacts. In L. Z. Rubenstein, L. J. Campbell, & R. L. Kane (Eds.), *Clinics in geriatric medicine* (pp. 1–15). Philadelphia: W. B. Saunders.

Saltz, C. C., McVey, L. J., Becker, P. M., Feussner, J. R., & Cohen, H. J. (1988). Impact of a geriatric consultation team of discharge placement and repeat hospitalization. *Gerontologist, 28,* 344–350.

Schmitt, M. H., Farrell, M. P., & Heinemann, G. D. (1988). Conceptual and methodological problems in studying the effects of interdisciplinary geriatric teams. *Gerontologist, 28,* 753–764.

Vetter, N. J., Jones, D. A., & Victor, C. R. (1979). Effects of health visitors working with elderly patients in general practice. *J R Coll Gen Pract 29,* 733–742.

Williams, M. E., Williams, T. F., Zimmer, J. G., Jackson, H. W., & Podgorski, C. A. (1987). How does the team approach to outpatient geriatric evaluation compare with traditional care: A report of a randomized controlled trial. *Journal of the American Geriatrics Society, 35,* 1071–1078.

Part VIII

The Practice Model: Ethical and Value Issues

19

Allocation of Resources to Rehabilitation: Intellectual and Political Challenges

Robert H. Binstock

The presentations in this volume, through their consistent therapeutic optimism, make it clear that much can be done to enhance present efforts at rehabilitation of older persons quantitatively and qualitatively. But a central question that implicitly underlies this optimism is, How can additional financial resources be allocated for geriatric rehabilitation?

In discussing this question I will deal only with the issue of how greater *public* resources might be allocated for this purpose and set aside issues of more effective marketing to patients who can pay for rehabilitation out of pocket (or through private insurance) and administration of existing Medicare provisions for reimbursing rehabilitation. The challenges of exercising political power to advance the cause of rehabilitation and aging are difficult enough in themselves. Indeed, before treating them, it will be helpful to place them briefly in historical context.

THE TRADITIONAL STATUS OF REHABILITATION AND AGING

For as long as most of us can remember, rehabilitation, in general, has been a comparatively drab backwater in the overall scene of American health care. Rehabilitation has been eclipsed by the prestige and glamour of medical care that has the inherent drama of dealing with acute episodes of illnesses and trauma and the relatively frequent "high tech" and "quick fix" dimensions of diagnosis and intervention.

Rehabilitation of older persons has been a particularly neglected aspect of health care (Kemp, 1985) for a variety of reasons. Perhaps the most fundamental reason for this is that the central axis of rehabilitative philosophy in this nation for more than half a century has been vocational (Baumann, Anderson, & Morrison, 1986; Brody, 1986). Consequently, an implicit—and sometimes explicit (see Avorn, 1984—societal attitude has been that it is "not worth it" economically to rehabilitate older persons who in most cases will spend few additional years at work.

Predominant societal values regarding rehabilitation have been mirrored, for the most part, in the outlooks and behavior of health care professionals. The comparatively low status of rehabilitation within the health care arena has not only reflected economic forces but values in the medical profession as well (Starr, 1983). It has been manifested in prestige hierarchies and organizational arrangements among health care professionals.

The relatively low priority that rehabilitation has received in the health care arena generally has been mirrored in the negligible attention that rehabilitation has received among professionals in the field of aging. Gerontologists and geriatricians have been increasingly and appropriately preoccupied throughout the last decade with issues of long-term care, the formidable challenges of providing care and societal supports for chronically ill and disabled older persons. But only a few (e.g., Brody, 1984–1985; Williams, 1984) have given much attention to rehabilitation as a dimension of care and treatment for the chronically disabled elderly. Not even the modest rehabilitative goal of actively working to maintain the existing functional capacities of elderly patients has received much focus, let alone the more ambitious goals of restoring or compensating for the loss of functional capacities.

In effect, until recently, long-term care for the elderly has been viewed by most professionals in the field in terms of the economic, institutional, service delivery, and familial burdens of giving care—without rehabilitation—to elderly, residual human entities as their functional capacities gradually erode or precipitously decline before death. Even among gerontologists and geriatricians, rehabilitation appears to have been regarded as a domain or set of activities relevant to the younger disabled population, even though 40% of the disabled persons in the United States are 65 years of age or older (Henriksen, 1978).

THE EMERGENCE OF THERAPEUTIC OPTIMISM

Within the past several years this traditional picture has begun to change. Rehabilitation of older persons has begun to attract increasing attention, within and beyond the arena of physiatrists and other rehabilitative professionals. In some measure this change has resulted from the initiatives of a handful of professional reformers. It also seems to be a result of the economic incentives generated by the fevered milieu of health care cost-containment efforts in this country, as spearheaded by the establishment of the Prospective Payment Systems (PPS) for reimbursing health providers for care of patients enrolled in Medicare.

Initiatives of Professional Reformers

In late 1984 the first national conference on Aging and Rehabilitation was convened in Washington, DC, under the auspices of some 20 federal agencies, led by the National Institute on Aging, the National Institute of Handicapped Research, and the National Institute of Mental Health, and coordinated by the Rehabilitation Research and Training Center in Aging at the University of Pennsylvania (see Brody & Ruff, 1986). Since then there have been a great many indications that rehabilitation is finally beginning to take its place on the agenda of care of older persons and that aging is becoming more relevant to the field of rehabilitation. The worlds of aging and rehabilitation appear to be discovering each other.

Consider just two symbolic examples. On the one hand, in the summer of 1985, *Aging*, a bimonthly magazine disseminated by the U.S. Administration on Aging, devoted a special issue to rehabilitation (U.S. DHHS, 1985). This was the 350th issue of a magazine that is circulated nationwide under the auspices of the federal agency charged with promoting and monitoring the overall well-being of older Americans. Yet it was the first time that rehabilitation of older persons was featured as a central concern. On the other hand, as a symbol of recognition flowing in the other direction, the American Academy of Physical Medicine and Rehabilitation unprecedently designated "Rehabilitation in an Aging America" as the theme for its 1986 annual meeting.

Incentives of Health Care Cost-Containment Efforts

More important perhaps than such symbols and the professional reform initiatives that they may reflect have been the economic incentives generated by the new Medicare payment systems that are bringing rehabilitation of the elderly more attention in the broader health care arena. Of particular importance has been the impact of Diagnosis Related Groups (DRGs), the current mechanism through which Medicare reimburses hospitals prospectively for patient care on the basis of the primary diagnosis assigned to the patient. Operating in the context of this payment mechanism, hospitals have a strong economic incentive to discharge Medicare patients from acute-care beds as soon as it is feasible to do so. Medicare's reimbursement for a patient's care is the same whether that patient occupies an acute-care bed for 5 or 15 days.

Under the pressures of DRGs, hospitals throughout the country have been "verticalizing" into—that is, developing, establishing, buying, and arranging working partnerships for—a variety of nonacute "step-down services" (Brody & Persily, 1984). Acute-care hospitals are now establishing their own inpatient rehabilitation units if they have not had them up to now, or expanding existing units; undertaking partnerships with or acquiring freestanding rehabilitation hospitals and skilled nursing facilities that include rehabilitation services as well as convalescent care; opening up outpatient rehabilitation services; and developing their own home health services that provide many elements of supportive care, including rehabilitation, in a community setting. Such services may well be perceived and used as an opportunity to improve a patient's functional capacities and quality of life. But they also enable hospitals to accelerate the movement—or step-down—of Medicare patients from acute-care beds in a responsible fashion when family supports are unavailable or insufficient to provide an adequate supportive environment for a discharged patient.

This verticalization by hospitals into what Brody (1987) has termed "short-term long-term care" appears to have come about largely as an economic strategy by hospitals as they have responded to the pressures of DRGs and other hospital cost-containment measures. By owning and/or operating these various step-down services that lie outside the DRG mechanism of reimbursement, hospitals are providing themselves opportunities for additional sources of revenue from Medicare and other health care payers. A focus on rehabilitation for older persons is central to this economic strategy because medically authorized rehabilitation is an important and at present a comparatively open-ended source of available revenue under Medicare reimbursement.

In effect, as a largely unintended consequence of hospital cost-containment policies under Medicare, rehabilitation of older persons is becoming a much more important concern in the health care arena than it has been in the past. From Medicare's inception in 1965, ironically, it provided reimbursement for posthospital extended-care services. But until the past few years, when cost-containment pressures have mounted, relatively few hospitals have given much attention to rehabilitation.

INTELLECTUAL CHALLENGES

Newly heightened interest in rehabilitation and aging, however, will not necessarily be automatically accompanied by significant, concomitant increases in the allocation of financial resources for this purpose. In our contemporary political economy, efforts to "contain health care costs" and "reduce the deficit" appear to be the overriding imperatives. In this context rehabilitation efforts will now be subject to greater analytical and critical scrutiny than ever before, as well as to likely changes in public policies that affect them. And because of the relatively poor state of knowledge about the extent and nature of rehabilitation efforts among older persons, their efficacy, and their costs (see Binstock, 1987), those of us who would be therapeutic optimists need to confront intellectual challenges as well as a political challenges.

As the few bits of data on the efficacy and costs of rehabilitation among older persons are subjected to increasingly critical examination, the onus will be on leaders in the field of rehabilitation and aging to undertake highly sophisticated, complex research efforts. Consider just three related examples.

One challenge will involve the arduous tasks of subdividing into relatively discrete categories the many diverse types of potential candidates for rehabilitation so that issues of efficacy and cost can be traced thoroughly in a highly differentiated fashion. This will require far greater efforts than those to date in distinguishing among patients, for example, not only with respect to type and severity of diseases and disabilities but also with respect to the presence of multiple disabilities and diseases, psychological profiles, and economic, social, and familial situations. We will need to focus on the patient, rather than on the disease or disability, as the unit of analysis. Or, to put it another way, the challenge is to translate the units of analysis in "best practice" into units of analysis for "best research."

A related challenge will be to match such relatively discrete distinctions with various kinds of rehabilitation. Empirical analyses of rehabilitative efficacy for each major category of patient will need to be conducted with an eye to differences among various kinds of rehabilitation settings and any significant variations in the substantive content of professional efforts made within each type of setting.

Still another challenge, following from these, will be the need to develop a genuine conceptual merging of rehabilitation and long-term care as parts of the same set of activities and as a unit of analysis for documenting the cost-effectiveness of rehabilitation. A true picture of the economic benefits that may be achieved through an investment in successful rehabilitation of a particular type of patient cannot be established without the larger and longer-term picture of the costs saved, if any, in the long-term supportive care that might have been subsequently required in the absence of rehabilitation.

The net savings shown from an analysis conceptualized and implemented in such a fashion could be substantial. For example, even to the extent that a type of rehabilitative effort is successful only 10% of the time, it might render unnecessary what would have been required in long-term care expenditures for those patients. Thus, the amount of unneeded long-term care expenditures on those successfully rehabilitated patients could more than offset the investment in the 90% of similar types of rehabilitative efforts that failed. But we will never find out if such net savings exist until we conceptually and analytically approach the activities involved in rehabilitation and long-term care as a merged unit of analysis for such research purposes.

With these few examples I am simply trying to suggest, of course, that there is great room for increased sophistication in our research and that such an improvement will be highly important for favorably waging a battle for public resources in the years immediately ahead. But successfully meeting the research and intellectual challenges will not in itself be likely to have a substantial impact in allocating greater resources to rehabilitation of older persons.

THE POLITICAL CHALLENGE

A far greater challenge is presented by the emergent political ethos regarding the categorical status of older persons within American health care. Even as this book reflects a marvelous growth in knowledge and practical guidelines for how to improve daily functional outcomes for older patients, the larger arena of public discourse in the United States has become replete with proposals to officially and categorically deny life-extending health care to older persons. And these are not proposals aimed just at patients sustained by feeding tubes or ventilators. At issue seems to be whether it is worth, in general, *saving the lives* of older people, let alone enhancing or maintaining their functional capacities through rehabilitation.

The Emergence of the Aged as Scapegoat

Contemporary proposals to deny health care to older persons appear to be part of a larger backlash in American society against an artificially stereotyped group termed "the aged." Prior to the late 1970s the predominant stereotypes of older Americans were compassionate; they were seen as poor, frail, and deserving. Since 1978, however, these compassionate stereotypes have virtually reversed (see Binstock, 1983). The immediate precipitating factor seems to have been a so-called crisis in the cash flow of the Social Security system, within the larger context of a depressed economy during President Carter's administration. But regardless of the specific cause, the reversal of stereotypes has continued unabated since then to the point where we now find—in the media, political speeches, public policy studies, and the writings of scholars—a new set of axioms:

- The aged are relatively well-off—not poor but in great shape.
- The aged are a potent political force because there are so many of them, and they all vote in their self-interest; this "senior power" explains why more than one quarter of the annual federal budget is spent on benefits to the aged.
- Because of demographic changes the aged are becoming more numerous and politically powerful and will claim even more benefits and substantially larger proportions of the federal budget. They are already costing too much and in the future will pose an unsustainable burden on the American economy.

These new stereotypes, devoid of compassion, can be readily observed in popular culture. Typical of contemporary depictions of older persons is a recent cover story in *Time* entitled "Grays on the Go" (Gibbs, 1988). It is filled with pictures of senior surfers, senior swingers, and senior softball players. Older persons are portrayed as America's new elite—healthy, wealthy, powerful, and "staging history's biggest retirement party."

A dominant theme in such accounts of older persons is that their selfishness is ruining the nation. The *New Republic* highlighted this selfishness theme early in 1988 with a cover displaying "Greedy Geezers." The table of contents "teaser" for the story that followed (Fairlie, 1988) announced that "the real me generation isn't the yuppies, it's America's growing ranks of prosperous elderly."

In serious forums of public discourse these new stereotypes of the prosperous, hedonistic, and selfish elderly have laid a foundation on which the aged have emerged as a scapegoat for an impressive list of American problems. As social psychologist Gordon Allport (1959) observed in his classic work on the *ABCs of Scapegoating*, "An issue seems nicely simplified if we blame a group or class of people rather than the complex course of social and historical forces" (pp. 13–14).

Demographers (e.g., Preston, 1984) and advocates for children have blamed the political power of the elderly for the plight of youngsters who have inadequate nutrition, health care, education, and supportive family environments. Former Secretary of Commerce Peter Peterson (1987) has proposed that a prerequisite for the United States to regain its stature as a first-class power in the world economy is a sharp reduction in programs benefiting older Americans. From the late 1970s until a few months ago there were many complaints that Social Security's Old Age and Survivors Insurance trust fund would be continually on the verge of going broke, thereby posing an intolerable tax burden to American workers and their employers. Now that projections show substantial trust fund surpluses for the decades ahead, economists have begun analyzing and debating whether such surpluses will adversely affect the performance of the American economy (Kilborn, 1988; Munnell & Blais, 1988).

Old-Age-based Health Care Rationing

Perhaps the most serious scapegoating of the aged—in terms of vulnerability for older persons and maybe vulnerability for all persons in our society—has been with respect to health care. A widespread concern about high rates of inflation in health care costs has somehow been refocused from the health care providers, suppliers, administrators, and insurers—the parties that are responsible for those costs—to the elderly patients that they charge for care.

Older persons curently account for one third of our annual health care expenditures (U.S. Senate Special Committee on Aging, 1988). Because the elderly population is growing, health care costs for older persons have been depicted as an unsustainable burden, or as some have put it, "a great fiscal black hole" (Callahan, 1987, p. 16) that will absorb an unlimited amount of our national resources.

This particular theme of scapegoating the aged has developed to the point that proposals have been put forward to deny life-extending health care to older persons. The substantial attention that such proposals have received in serious public forums may be the clearest signal that American public policy toward health care of the aging is approaching an important crossroads.

Health care in the United States has always been rationed informally on the basis of availability of resources and the individual conditions and characteristics of patients. But proposals for official policies that would deny care categorically, on the basis of membership in a demographically identified group, are a substantial departure from existing practices.

The suggestion that health care should be rationed on the basis of old age began to develop, through implication, in 1983. In a speech to the Health Insurance Association of America, economist Alan Greenspan, now chairman of the Federal Reserve Board, stated that 30% of Medicare is annually expended on 5% to 6% of Medicare eligibles who die within the year. He pointedly asked whether it is worth it (Schulte, 1983).

In 1984 the then governor of Colorado, Richard Lamm, was widely quoted as stating that older persons "have a duty to die and get out of the way" (Slater, 1984). Although Lamm subsequently retracted this specific statement, he has been traveling throughout the nation since leaving office, delivering this same message in a somewhat more delicately worded fashion (e.g., Lamm, 1987).

During the past few years this issue has spread to a number of forums. Philosophers have been generating principles of equity to undergird "justice between age groups" in the provision of health care (Daniels, 1988). Conferences and books have explicitly addressed the issue of "Should Health Care be Rationed by Age?" (Smeeding et al., 1987).

Late in 1987 this theme reached new heights of legitimacy with the publication of a widely reviewed book by Daniel Callahan, a well-known medical ethicist. The book, entitled *Setting Limits: Medical Goals in an Aging Society*, is a proposal that older persons should be denied life-extending health care if they are in their "late 70s or early 80s" and/or have "achieved a natural life span."

The significance of this book lies in the extraordinary attention it has received. It has been prominently reviewed in national magazines, *The New York Times, The Washington Post, The Wall Street Journal,* and just about every relevant professional and scholarly journal and newsletter. It is apparent that proposals for national policies to ration health care of older persons are an acceptable topic for public discussion in contemporary America.

Callahan (1987) views older Americans as "a new social threat" and a "demographic, economic, and medical avalanche . . . that could ultimately (and perhaps already) do great harm" (p. 20). His remedy for this threat is to use "age as a specific criterion for the allocation and limitation of health care" (p. 23). He justifies his proposal by emphasiz-

ing the burdensome costs of health care for older persons and by arguing that "the meaning and significance of life for the elderly themselves
is best founded on a sense of limits to health care" (p. 116).

Older persons, in addition to being numerous and requiring large
amounts of health care, are regarded by Callahan as selfish. He blames
their selfishness on "mainline" advocates for the aged who have
stressed for over two decades the rights and entitlements of the elderly
and have brainwashed older persons to believe that the process of
aging is utterly diverse, that the aged are varied (like any other age
group), and that old age is a time of renewed vigor, growth, self-dis-
covery, and contributions to the community.

Although Callahan (1987) presents his case for rationing in a judicious style, with a veneer of scholarly balance, his arguments are seriously flawed because they are often incomplete, imbalanced, illogical,
and internally contradictory (see Binstock & Kahana, 1988). Two flaws,
in particular, should be highlighted because of their very serious moral
implications in our society and for therapeutic optimism with respect to
the elderly.

One flaw is that Callahan does not even attempt to convey how
much money would be saved if his proposal were implemented. If the
costs of health care for older persons are an unsustainable burden for
our society, to what extent would that burden be relieved by old-age-
based rationing? Previous calculations have suggested that even if all of
the funds that are spent on very high cost Medicare patients who die
within a year were not expended, the savings would be negligible
(Rowe & Binstock, 1987).

In 1987 we spent more than $500 billion on health care in the United
States and $170 billion of that was on persons aged 65 and older. If
Callahan's proposal had been implemented, would the aggregate savings have been $1 billion, $5 billion, $25 billion? Assuming that any
amount of money could justify his proposal, shouldn't he provide
some basis for judging whether it is worth it? Otherwise, we are left
with what amounts to a naked attack on the lives of older persons.

The other major flaw is Callahan's total neglect of the moral implications of singling out any group of Americans as not worthy of life-
extending care. What impact would such a policy have on the moral
fabric of American society? What group might be singled out next as
undesirable, burdensome, and costly? If the aged can become vulnerable through scapegoating, who among us is next in line? Are the economic burdens of health care costs greater than the moral burdens of
officially denying health care to a demographically defined category of
citizens?

Despite such flaws, the very fact that a proposal such as Callahan's might be put forward and treated seriously in the mainstream of American public discourse is an indicator of a new vulnerability for the aged in American public opinion. This proposal and the attention it has received may not represent the climax of the process through which the aged have become a scapegoat in the 1980s. In addition to a continuing flow of media stereotypes of the old, the activities of a new organization, established to propound issues of "intergenerational equity"—Americans for Generational Equity (AGE)—appear to have solid political and financial backing (Quadagno, 1988). And as exemplified by the title of AGE's most recent conference, "Children at Risk: Who Will Support Our Aging Society?", this organization will likely persist in adding to the rhetoric that pits the young and the middle-aged against the old.

THE POLITICAL POWER OF THE AGING: A POTENTIAL RESOURCE?

The contemporary context in which the aged have emerged as scapegoat and old-age-based health care rationing has become an acceptable proposition for public discourse in America poses a substantial political challenge to those of us who would like to see greater resources allocated to rehabilitation of older persons. The political challenge now appears to involve two stages. The first is to combat successfully the notion that the relative worth of older persons is such that they might be denied life-extending care categorically, rather than on a case-by-case basis. Unless that notion is countered successfully, the second challenge—obtaining greater resources for rehabilitation and aging—is, in my view, hopeless.

Four years ago, at the first national Aging and Rehabilitation conference, Phyllis Rubenfeld (1986), as president of the American Coalition of Citizens with Disabilities, expressed the hope that a coalition of the organized constituencies of older persons and the disabled might become a powerful force in American politics. However, there has been no sign of such a movement since then. Indeed, the evidence and analysis in a case study of the politics involved in enactment of a recent long-term care bill in California (Torres-Gil & Pynoos, 1986) suggests that organized groups of the aged and disabled are more likely to compete with each other than to form an effective coalition.

Independent of whether such a coalition might ever be effectively forged, can the political power of the aged be drawn upon as a resource for allocating greater resources to rehabilitation and aging? After all, it is conventional wisdom in the media (e.g., Chakravarty & Weisman, 1988), as well as among those who would make the aged scape-goat, that older persons are one of the most powerful constituencies in American politics. As a brief examination of the aging in American politics will indicate, however, this bit of conventional wisdom—as is the case with much conventional wisdom—is very oversimplified.

The Voting Behavior of Older Persons

Persons aged 65 and older do constitute a large bloc of participating voters. They have comprised from 16.7% to 21% of those who have actually voted in national elections during the 1980s (U.S. Senate Special Committee on Aging, 1988). And this percentage is likely to increase in the next four decades because of projected increases in the proportion of older persons. But older persons do not vote in a monolithic bloc, and any more than middle-aged persons or younger persons do. Consequently, the aged do not wield power as a single-issue voting constituency.

Exit polls from presidential and congressional elections have shown repeatedly that the votes of older persons distribute among candidates in about the same proportions as the votes of other age groupings of citizens (see, e.g., *The New York Times/CBS News Poll*, 1988). This should not be surprising because there is no sound reason to expect that a cohort of persons would suddenly become homogenized in its political behavior when it reaches the "old age" category (see Simon, 1985). Diversity among older persons is as least as great with respect to political attitudes and behavior as it is in relation to economic, social, and other characteristics (Hudson & Strate, 1985).

But don't politicians behave as if older persons vote as a bloc in response to issues? Aren't they terrorized by so-called senior power? The answer is not so clear (Reimer & Binstock, 1978).

It is certainly evident that no politician goes out of his or her way to offend the aged. On the other hand, there have been numerous cases in recent years, enumerated below, when Congress has enacted legislation that has adversely affected the presumed interests of the aged.

AGE-BASED INTEREST GROUPS

Only limited power is available to "the gray lobby" (Pratt, 1976), the aging-based mass membership interest groups such as the American Association of Retired Persons (AARP), the National Council of Senior Citizens (NCSC), and dozens of other aging-based professional and business organizations "representing" older persons. As implied by the preceding discussion of electoral behavior, such organizations have not been able to cohere or even to shift marginally the votes of older persons. Although AARP claims more than 28 million members, for example, it does not control or demonstrably influence the votes of those members.

Experience in other modern democratic states, such as Great Britain and Sweden, has been comparable. When attempts have been made to organize the votes of older persons to affect the fate of a particular candidate, party, or proposition, they have not been notably successful (Heclo, 1974).

Organized demands of older persons have had little to do with the enactment and amendment of the major old-age policies such as Social Security and Medicare. Rather, such actions have been largely attributable to the initiatives of public officials in the White House, Congress, and the bureaucracy, who have focused on their own agendas for social and economic policy (Cohen, 1985a, 1985b; Derthick, 1979; Iglehart, 1989; Light, 1985).

Some forms of power, however, are available to old-age interest groups. First, in the classic pattern of American interest group politics, public officials find it both useful and incumbent upon them to invite such organizations to participate in policy activities. In this way public officials are provided with a ready means of having been "in touch" symbolically with millions of constituents, thereby legitimizing subsequent policy actions and inactions. A brief meeting with the leaders of these organizations can enable an official to claim that he or she has duly obtained the represented views of a mass constituency. This informal access to public officials provides some measure of opportunity, even if it is not decisive.

Second, their symbolic legitimacy enables them to obtain public platforms in the national media, congressional hearings, and national conferences and commissions dealing with old age, health, and a variety of subjects relevant to policies affecting aging. From these platforms the old-age organizations can exercise power by initiating and framing issues for public debate and responding to issues raised by others.

A third form of power available to old-age interest groups might be termed "the electoral bluff." Although these organizations have not demonstrated a capacity to swing a decisive bloc of older voters, no politician wants to offend "the aged" or any other latent mass constituency if it is possible to avoid doing so. In fact, the image of senior power is frequently invoked by politicians when, for one reason or another, they desire an excuse for doing nothing or for not differentiating themselves from their colleagues and electoral opponents.

These limited forms of old-age interest group power, as indicated above, have not played an influential role in shaping Medicare, Social Security, and other major programs as they have evolved into the present. The impacts of these organizations have been largely confined to the creation and maintenance of relatively minor policies that have distributed benefits primarily to researchers, educators, clinicians, and other practitioners in the field of aging, rather than directly to older persons, themselves (Binstock, 1972; Estes, 1979; Lockett, 1983).

In recent years the old-age organizations have been attempting to defend existing policies that benefit older persons, becoming one of what Heclo (1984) has termed "antiredistributive veto forces" in American politics. Yet a number of public policy decisions that are conventionally perceived as adverse to the self-interest of older persons have proved to be politically feasible in the 1980s through changes in Medicare, Social Security, and other programs. Medicare deductibles, copayments, and Part B premiums have increased continuously. Old Age Insurance (OAI) benefits have been made subject to taxation. The legislated formula for cost-of-living adjustments (COLAs) to OAI benefits has been rendered less generous. The redistributive mechanism of "minimum benefits" under Social Security was eliminated for new OAI eligibles at the outset of this decade (under the Omnibus Reconciliation Act of 1981). The Tax Reform Act of 1986 eliminated the extra personal exemption that all persons 65 years of age and older have been receiving in filing their federal income tax returns. And the progressive tax levied by Congress to finance the Medicare Catastrophic Coverage Act of 1988 evoked outcries of protest from middle- and upper-income elderly (see Tolchin, 1988).

These changes are relatively minor, of course, in comparison to drastic changes in old age programs—such as totally dismantling Social Security—proposed by some politicians and discussed by policy analysts in recent years. And efforts of old-age interest groups, through the limited forms of power available to them, may have had some impact in "containing the damage." But the relatively minor character of these changes is just as likely attributable to ways in which the underlying American penchants for political incrementalism and pragmatism are being expressed in response to the policy challenges of an aging society (see Heclo, 1988).

POLITICAL RESOURCES FOR ENHANCING REHABILITATION

It should be evident from this brief review of the politics of aging that the symbolic political legitimacy available to organized groups of older persons is their primary source of power and that the usefulness of this symbolic legitimacy is limited to only certain types of contexts. In recent years it has been applied primarily in defensive efforts to prevent public resources now available to older persons from being taken away, to avoid Draconian changes.

How can this power be applied for enhancing the resources available for rehabilitation?

The primary avenue available is through the politics of issue framing or, as it has been termed by political scientists, "agenda building" (Elder & Cobb, 1984). This political resource played a significant role in the early 1970s in establishing the National Institute on Aging (Lockett, 1983) and has been used effectively by AGE in shaping current policy alternatives regarding programs in aging (Quadagno, 1988).

Although professionals and reformers interested in rehabilitation and aging could, in principle, set a public agenda by themselves, their chances of success would be greatly enhanced if they could harness the symbolic legitimacy of AARP and other old-age-based interest groups. Meeting the intellectual challenge of documenting the efficacy and cost-effectiveness of rehabilitating older persons would only qualify proponents as respectable participants in public discourse on the issue but not necessarily gain them major public platforms.

The essential goal is to get the issue of geriatric rehabilitation on the public policy agenda so that politicians feel compelled to deal with it. As the legislative saga of the 1988 Medicare Catastrophic Coverage Act illustrates (see Iglehart, 1989), Congress can find any number of ways to finance programs once it feels that it must enact some policy to deal with a social problem that has been placed firmly on its agenda.

Those of us who would like to establish geriatric rehabilitation as a prominent goal on the policy agenda of the United States would greatly enhance our chances for success by working with the old-age interest groups. Mobilizing these groups, however, is not a simple challenge. To date, organized old-age interests have not even confronted, head on, contemporary proposals that would deny life-extending care to older persons categorically. In the hierarchy of health care issues, geriatric rehabilitation is substantially lower.

In sum, the challenges to those of us who would like to see greater allocation of resources to rehabilitation and aging are substantial and many. First, we need to document the efficacy and cost-effectiveness of rehabilitation in numerous specific, differentiated contexts. Second, we need to ally ourselves with the aging-based interest groups. Third, in such an alliance, we must cleanse the broader political atmosphere that denigrates the value of health care for older persons by publicly and effectively confronting proposals for denying life-extending care to older persons. And finally, and only then, will we be in a position to place firmly on the agenda of American politics the notion that rehabilitation of older persons is as an essential ingredient of health care as any other for which we allocate resources.

REFERENCES

Allport, G. W. (1959). *ABCs of scapegoating.* New York: Anti-Defamation League of B'nai B'rith.

Avorn, J. (1984). Benefit and cost analysis in geriatric care. *New England Journal of Medicine, 310,* 1294–1301.

Baumann, N. J., Anderson, J. C., & Morrison, M. H. (1986). Employment of the older disabled person: Current environment, outlook, and research needs. In S. J. Brody & G. E. Ruff (Eds.), *Aging and rehabilitation: Advances in the state of the art* (pp. 329–342). New York: Springer Publishing Co.

Binstock, R. H. (1972). Interest-group liberalism and the politics of aging. *Gerontologist, 12,* 265–280.

Binstock, R. H. (1983). The aged as scapegoat. *Gerontologist, 23,* 136–143.

Binstock, R. H. (1987). Rehabilitation and the elderly: Economic and political issues. In R. E. Dunkle & J. W. Schmidley (Eds.), *Stroke in the elderly.* New York: Springer Publishing Co.

Binstock, R. H., & Kahana, J. (1988). An essay on "Setting limits: Medical goals in an aging society, by Daniel Callahan." *Gerontologist, 28,* 424–426.

Brody, S. J. (1984–1985). Merging rehabilitation and aging policies and programs: Past, present, and future. *Rehabilitation World, 8*(4), 6–8, 42–44.

Brody, S. J. (1986). Impact of the formal support system on rehabilitation of the elderly. In S. J. Brody & G. E. Ruff (Eds.), *Aging and rehabilitation: Advances in the state of the art* (pp. 62–86). New York: Springer Publishing Co.

Brody, S. J. (1987). Continuity of care: The new-old health requirement. In B. C. Vladeck & G. Alfano (Eds.), *Medicare and extended care: Issues, problems, and prospects* (pp. 25–36. Owings Mills, MD: Rynd Communications.

Brody, S. J., & Persily, N. A. (Eds.). (1984). *Hospitals and the aged: The new old market.* Rockville, MD: Aspen Systems.

Brody, S. J., & Ruff, G. E. (Eds.). (1986). *Aging and rehabilitation: Advances in the state of the art.* New York: Springer Publishing Co.

Callahan, D. (1987). *Setting limits: Medical goals for an aging society.* New York: Simon and Schuster.

Chakravarty, S. N., & Weisman, K. (1988, November 14). Consuming our children? *Forbes,* pp. 222–232.

Cohen, W. J. (1985a). Reflections on the enactment of Medicare and Medicaid. *Health Care Financing Review, (Suppl.* 11).

Cohen, W. J. (1985b). Securing social security. *New Leader, 66,* 5–8.

Daniels, N. (1988). *Am I my parents' keeper? An essay on justice between the young and the old.* New York: Oxford University Press.

Derthick, M. (1979). *Policymaking for social security.* Washington, DC: Brookings Institute.

Elder, C. D., & Cobb, R. W. (1984). Agenda building and the politics of aging. *Policy Studies Journal, 13,* 115–130.

Estes, C. L. (1979). *The aging enterprise.* San Francisco: Jossey Bass.

Fairlie, H. (1988). Talkin' 'bout my generation. *The New Republic, 198*(13), 19–22.

Gibbs, N. R. (1988). Grays on the go. *Time, 131*(8), 66–75.

Heclo, H. (1974). *Modern social politics in Britain and Sweden: From relief to income maintenance.* New Haven, CT: Yale University Press.

Heclo, H. (1984). The political foundation of anti-poverty policy. In *IRP Conference papers on poverty and policy: Retrospect and prospects* (pp. 6–8). Madison, WI: Institute for Research on Poverty.

Heclo, H. (1988). Generational politics. In J. L. Palmer, T. Smeeding, & B. B. Torrey (Eds.), *The vulnerable* (pp. 381–442). Washington, DC: Urban Institute Press.

Henriksen, J. D. (1978). Problems in rehabilitation after age sixty-five. *Journal of the American Geriatrics Society, 26,* 510–512.

Hudson, R. H., & Strate, J. (1985). Aging and political systems. In R. H. Binstock & E. Shanas (Eds.), *Handbook of aging and the social sciences* (2nd ed., pp. 554–585). New York: Van Nostrand Reinhold.

Iglehart, J. K. (1989). Medicare's new benefits: "Catastrohic" health insurance. *New England Journal of Medicine, 320,* 329–336.

Kemp, B. (1985). Rehabilitation and the older adult. In J. E. Birren & K. W. Schaie (Eds.), *Handbook of the psychology of aging* (2nd ed., pp. 647–663). New York: Van Nostrand Reinhold.

Kilborn, P. T. (1988, April 2). New issue on budget horizon: What to do about surpluses. *The New York Times,* p. 1.

Lamm, R. D. (1987). A debate: Medicare in 2020. In *Medicare reform and the baby boom generation* (pp. 77–88). Washington, DC: Americans for Generational Equity.

Light, P. (1985). *Artful work: The politics of Social Security reform.* New York: Random House.

Lockett, B. A. (1983). *Aging, politics, and research: Setting the federal agenda for research on aging.* New York: Springer Publishing Co.

Munnell, A. H., & Blais, L. E. (1988). Do we want large Social Security surpluses? *The Generational Journal, 1*(1), 21–36.

The New York Times/CBS News Poll. (1988, November 10). *The New York Times.*

Peterson, P. (1987). The morning after. *Atlantic, 260*(4), 43–69.

Pratt, H. J. (1976). *The gray lobby.* Chicago: University of Chicago Press.

Preston, S. H. (1984). Children and the elderly in the U.S. *Scientific American, 251*(6), 44–49.

Quadagno, J. (1988). *Generational equity and the politics of class.* Paper presented at the annual meeting of the American Sociological Association, Atlanta.

Reimer, Y., & Binstock, R. H. (1978). Campaigning for the "senior vote": A case study of Carter's 1976 campaign. *Gerontologist, 18,* 517–524.

Rowe, J. W., & Binstock, R. H. (1987). Aging reconsidered: Emerging research and policy issues. In E. Ginzberg (Ed.), *Medicine and society: Clinical decisions and societal values* (pp. 96–113). Boulder, CO: Westview Press.

Rubenfeld, P. (1986). Ageism and disabilityism: Double jeopardy. In S. J. Brody & G. E. Ruff (Eds.), *Aging and rehabilitation: Advances in the state of the art* (pp. 323–328). New York: Springer Publishing Co.

Schulte, J. (1983, April 26). Terminal patients deplete Medicare, Greenspan says. *Dallas Morning News*, p. 1.

Simon, H. A. (1985). Human nature in politics: The dialogue of psychology with political science. *American Political Science Review, 79*, 293–304.

Slater, W. (1984, March 29). Latest Lamm remark angers the elderly. *Arizona Daily Star*, p. 1.

Smeeding, T. M., Battin, M. P., Francis, L. P. & Landesman, B. M. (Eds.). (1987). *Should medical care be rationed by age?* Totowa, NJ: Rowman and Littlefield.

Starr, P. (1983). *The social transformation of American medicine*. New York: Basic Books.

Tolchin, M. (1988, November 2). New health insurance plan provokes outcry over costs. *The New York Times*, p. 1.

Torres-Gil, F., & Pynoos, J. (1986). Long-term care policy and interest groups struggles. *Gerontologist, 26*, 488–495.

U.S. Department of Health and Human Services. (1985). *Aging* [Special issue on rehabilitation], *350*. Washington, DC: Administration on Aging, Office of Human Development Services.

U.S. Senate Special Committee on Aging. (1988). *Developments in aging: 1987* (Vol. 1). Washington, DC: U.S. Government Printing Office.

Williams, T. F. (Ed.). (1984). *Rehabilitation in the aging*. New York: Raven Press.

Index

Merriam, A., 263
Metabolism, 82–83, 284
Meyers, B., 263, 291
Meyhoff, H., 220
Milgram, S., 62
Miller, B. E., 179
Miller, N., 263
Milling, J., 153
Mineral oil, 170
Mion, L., 233–252
Mitchell, A., 265
Mitchell, C., 169, 173
Mitteness, L., 212
Mobility, 285–286
  aging process and, 78–84
  arthritis and, 86
  cervical spondylosis and, 88
  drug side effects and, 84–86
  foot problems and, 95–109
  frailty and, 153
  hip fractures and, 113–128
  illness markers and, 84
  incontinence and, 217
  interdisciplinary perspective on, 77–92
  myopathy and, 86–87
  neuropathy and, 87
  normal pressure hydrocephalus and, 88–89
  nutrition and, 167
  pain management and, 272–288
  Parkinson's Syndrome and, 87
  podiatrist and, 157
  rehabilitation and, 89–92
Model Spinal Cord Injury (SCI) Systems, 51
Moore, J. T., 112
Morgan, M. W., 155
Moritini, T., 80
Morrison, J., 214
Morrison, M., 316
Mortimer, J., 259
Moskowitz, R. W., 12
Motivation, 116, 285, 304
Motor neuron disease, 112
Mulvihill, M. K., 202
Munnell, A., 322

Munro, H. N., 171, 174
Murphy, E., 291
Murray, C. M., 192
Murray, H. A., 144
Murray, P. K., 128
Muscle atrophy, 281
Muscle imbalances, 86–87
Muscle mass, 81
Muscle relaxants, 222
Muscle strength, 80, 87, 91, 125
Musculoskeletal changes, 81–82
  disuse and, 90
  foot problems and, 102–103
Myocardial infarction, 121
Myocardial ischemia, 281
Myopathy, mobility and, 86–87

Nails, 101–102, 122
National Center for Health Statistics, 12
National Health Interview Survey, 12
National Nursing Home Survey, 12
National Institutes of Health Consensus Development Conference, 4
Nelson, C., 65
Nerve conduction velocity, 80
Nerve palsy, 87
Neufeld, R. R., 202
Neuroleptics, dementia and, 266
Neurologic exam, 121
Neuromuscular changes, 79–81
Neuropathy, mobility and, 87
Newmark, S., 173
Newport, M. L., 113
Newton, N., 263
Nixon, D. W., 181
Nocturia, 215
Non-dependency-creating services, 57, 60–61, 65–66
Nordling, J., 220
Normal pressure hydrocephalus, mobility and, 88–89
Norman, A. W., 179
Nurse practitioners, 161